AMERICAN INEQUALITY
A Macroeconomic History

JEFFREY G. WILLIAMSON
Department of Economics and
Institute for Research on Poverty
University of Wisconsin—Madison

PETER H. LINDERT
Department of Economics
University of California—Davis

ACADEMIC PRESS
A Subsidiary of Harcourt Brace Jovanovich, Publishers
New York   London   Toronto   Sydney   San   Francisco

339.2
W73a

This book is one of a series sponsored by the Institute for Research on Poverty of the University of Wisconsin pursuant to the provisions of the Economic Opportunity Act of 1964.

ACADEMIC PRESS, INC.
111 Fifth Avenue, New York, New York 10003

United Kingdom Edition published by
ACADEMIC PRESS, INC. (LONDON) LTD.
24/28 Oval Road, London NW1 7DX

Library of Congress Cataloging in Publication Data

Williamson, Jeffrey G.   Date
    American inequality.

    (Institute for Research on Poverty monograph
series)
    Bibliography: p.
    Includes index.
    1. Income distribution--United States--History.
2. Wealth--United States--History. 3. Cost and
standard of living--United States--History.
I. Lindert, Peter H. , joint author. II.   Title.
III.   Series: Wisconsin. University--Madison.
Institute for Research on Poverty. Monograph series.
HC110.I5W53   339.2'2'0973   80--23140
ISBN 0--12--757160--4

PRINTED IN THE UNITED STATES OF AMERICA

80 81 82 83   9 8 7 6 5 4 3 2 1

The Institute for Research on Poverty is a national center for research established at the University of Wisconsin in 1966 by a grant from the Office of Economic Opportunity. Its primary objective is to foster basic, multidisciplinary research into the nature and causes of poverty and means to combat it.

In addition to increasing the basic knowledge from which policies aimed at the elimination of poverty can be shaped, the Institute strives to carry analysis beyond the formulation and testing of fundamental generalizations to the development and assessment of relevant policy alternatives.

The Institute endeavors to bring together scholars of the highest caliber whose primary research efforts are focused on the problem of poverty, the distribution of income, and the analysis and evaluation of social policy, offering staff members wide opportunity for interchange of ideas, maximum freedom for research into basic questions about poverty and social policy, and dissemination of their findings.

CONTENTS

LIST OF TABLES   xiii
LIST OF FIGURES   xvii
PREFACE   xix

One
ISSUES AND EVIDENCE

1

THE ISSUES

The Inequality Facts   3
Searching for Explanations   5
The Equality–Growth Trade-off Debate   7

2

IN THE BEGINNING: THE DISTRIBUTION
OF WEALTH IN COLONIAL AMERICA

The American Dream and the Revisionists   9
Wealth Inequality in the Colonies   11
The Fallacy of Composition and the Trending Inequality Bias   21
Northern Quiescence and Southern Darkness   30

3

TRENDS IN WEALTH INEQUALITY SINCE 1774

Introduction   33
Wealth Concentration in the First Century of Independence   36

The Uneven High Plateau: Civil War to Great Depression   46
Twentieth-Century Leveling   53
Overview   62

4

TRENDS IN INCOME
AND EARNINGS INEQUALITY
SINCE 1816

Measuring Income Inequality   65
Wages, Earnings, and Income Inequality, 1816–1880   67
The Uneven Plateau: Civil War to Great Depression   75
Twentieth-Century Leveling   82
Distributional Stability since World War II   92
The Long View, Backward   94

5

PRICES, INEQUALITY, AND
ABSOLUTE LIVING STANDARDS

Forging a Link between Incomes and Prices   97
American Prices and Urban Inequality   98
Meanwhile, Back on the Farm   119
Prices, Living Costs, and Regional Incomes   127
Prices, Poverty, and Living Standards   130

Two
POTENTIAL EXPLANATIONS

6

COMPETING HYPOTHESES

Monocausality and History's Complex Stage   135
The Minor Actors and Supporting Roles   136
The Leading Actors   143
The Agenda   152

7

UNBALANCED GROWTH AND LABOR SAVING

Aggregate Labor Saving   155
Unbalanced Output Growth and Labor Saving   160
Unbalanced Productivity Growth   168

8

THE FACTOR INTENSITY ISSUE: WHO BUYS THE SERVICES OF AMERICA'S WORKING POOR?

Commodity Demand, Derived Factor Demand, and Distribution   179
The Unskilled-Labor Content of Commodities   180
Who Buys the Services of America's Working Poor?   183
Parameter Stability, Historical Laws, and
Nineteenth-Century Inferences   193
Alternative Measures of the Unskilled-Labor Content
of Commodities   198

9

LABOR SUPPLY GROWTH

The Correlation   203
The Growth of Skills in the Nineteenth Century   206
The Growth of Skills in the Twentieth Century   212

Three
QUANTITATIVE ACCOUNTING

10

EXPLAINING THE RISE IN EARNINGS INEQUALITY BEFORE WORLD WAR I

The Task   217
The Model   219
Explaining Trends in Wage Gaps before 1910   227

11

EXPLAINING TWENTIETH-CENTURY DISTRIBUTION TRENDS

The Task	239
New Parameters	241
Explaining Twentieth-Century Trends in Pay Ratios	244
Recent Experience and Prospects	251

12

INEQUALITY AND ACCUMULATION: A NINETEENTH-CENTURY GROWTH–EQUITY CONFLICT?

The Problem	255
The Relative Price of Capital Goods and Unbalanced Total Factor Productivity Growth	258
Modeling Nineteenth-Century Accumulation	263
Why Nineteenth-Century Net Investment Rates Rose: The Long View	269
Why Nineteenth-Century Net Investment Rates Rose: Shorter-Run Episodic Phases	274
The Gordian Knot Untied	279

13

THE SOURCES OF INEQUALITY

Three Centuries of American Inequality	281
The Sources of Inequality	285
Growth, Accumulation, and Equality	290

APPENDICES

A	TRENDS IN COLONIAL WEALTH INEQUALITY	295
B	UNDERLYING DATA FOR ANALYSIS OF COLONIAL WEALTH DECOMPOSITION	301

C   TOP WEALTH-HOLDER SHARES IN THE
    NORTHEAST, 1760–1891   303

D   OCCUPATIONAL PAY RATIOS IN THE NONFARM
    UNITED STATES SINCE COLONIAL TIMES,
    1771–1972   305

E   NOMINAL WAGE GAPS, URBAN VS. FARM, NEW
    ENGLAND, 1751–1900   313

F   TIME SERIES ON INCOME INEQUALITY IN THE
    UNITED STATES   315

G   THE PRICE OF "RAW" LABOR: WAGES OF
    EMPLOYED URBAN UNSKILLED WORKERS,
    1820–1948   319

H   FARM PRICES (USDA) RELATIVE TO URBAN PRICES
    (BLS) OF FIVE COMMODITIES, 1914–1948   321

I   "KOFFSKY-ADJUSTED" REGIONAL
    COST-OF-LIVING RELATIVES, 1840–1970   323

J   TWO MEASURES OF SKILLS   327

K   RETURN TO UNSKILLED LABOR FROM INDUSTRIES,
    1919 AND 1939   331

REFERENCES   335

INDEX   350

LIST OF TABLES

2.1	Colonial Population Trends	23
2.2	Age and Wealth in the Colonies, 1658–1774	26
3.1	Selected Measures of Wealth Inequality in the United States, 1774, 1860, 1870, and 1962	38
3.2	Unequal Slaveholding in the South, 1790–1860	44
3.3	Top Decile Shares of Total Wealth among Adult U.S. Males, 1860 and 1870	47
3.4	Holmes's Estimated Wealth Distribution for American Families in 1890	47
3.5	The Distribution of Wealth from FTC Sampled Estates, 1912 and 1923	50
3.6	Wealth Inequality Statistics, 1912 and 1923	50
3.7	Wealth Shares Held by the Top 1% and 10% of Decedents and the Living, Four Nations, 1907–1913	52
3.8	Share of U.S. Personal Wealth Held by Top Wealth Holders, 1922–1972	54
3.9	Top Percentile Shares of Estimated Net Worth among Households, 1922–1972	56
3.10	The Composition of Wealth, 1896–1973	60
4.1	Intrasectoral Wage Differentials, Nominal Daily Earnings, Urban Common Labor Relative to Farm Labor, 1850	73
4.2	Measures of Regional Income Inequality in the North, 1840–1900	74
4.3	The Underreporting of Personal Income by Type, 1946	88

5.1   Expenditure Elasticities: American Urban
       Workers, 1875–1950   99
5.2   Cost of Living in Eastern Cities, 1844–1860, by
       Socioeconomic Class   101
5.3   Cost-of-Living Incidence by Class and Its
       Components, Cities, 1844–1948   104
5.4   Cost of Living by Socioeconomic Class, Cities, 1890–1914   106
5.5   Cost of Living by Socioeconomic Class, Middle
       Atlantic Cities, 1855–1880   107
5.6   Cost of Living by Socioeconomic Class, Cities, 1914–1929   111
5.7   Deflation of Relative Income Shares, Nonfarm, 1917–1948   112
5.8   Prices and Urban Inequality: The 1914–1920
       Egalitarian Episode   114
5.9   Prices and Urban Inequality, 1929–1948   116
5.10   Prices and Urban Inequality, 1967–1975   117
5.11   Sensitivity Analysis for U.S. Urban Families:
       "Strategic" Commodities, Inflation, and Inequality   118
5.12   Farm Cost of Living, Absolute and Relative, 1890–1948   122
5.13   Ratio Farm to Nonfarm Wages, Nominal and
       Real: Douglas, 1890–1914   125
5.14   Ratio Annual Earnings (Full-Time Employees)
       Farm to Nonfarm, Nominal and Real: Lebergott,
       1910–1929   126
5.15   "Koffsky-Adjusted" Regional Cost-of-Living
       Indices, 1840–1970   128
5.16   Urban Cost-of-Living Indices, by Region and
       Commodity Group, 1851–1935   128
5.17   Cost-of-Living Impact: Coefficient of Variation in
       State Income per Worker, Nominal and Real,
       1840–1970   129
5.18   Cost-of-Living Impact: Changing Coefficient of
       Variation in State Income per Worker, Nominal
       and Real, 1840–1970   129
5.19   Trends in Real Wages and Earnings: The Urban
       Working Poor, 1820–1948   131
5.20   The Incidence of Poverty, 1870–1914, 1929–1944,
       1947–1955   132
7.1   Unbalanced Rates of Nineteenth-Century Output
       Growth, 1879 Prices   162
7.2   The Impact of Changing Output Mix on Unskilled
       Labor's Share, 1839–1899   164
7.3   The Impact of Changing Final Demand Mix on
       Unskilled Labor's Share, 1882/1886–1902/1906   166

7.4   The Impact of Changes in Output Mix on
      Unskilled Labor's Share, 1909–1975   167
7.5   Total Factor Productivity Growth in Agriculture,
      1800–1860   170
7.6   Total Factor Productivity Growth in Cotton
      Textiles, 1815–1859   170
7.7   Total Factor Productivity Growth in
      Transportation, 1815–1859   171
7.8   Total Factor Productivity Growth in Major
      Sectors, 1839–1973   172
7.9   Factor-Augmenting Biases Implied by Estimates
      of Sectoral Total Factor Productivity Growth
      Rates, 1839–1973   175
8.1   Payments Impact on Unskilled Labor, Direct and
      Indirect, of $1 Purchase of Output from Industry
      j, Compared with Direct Value-Added Shares,
      1963   184
8.2   Payments Impact on Unskilled Labor, Direct and
      Indirect, of $1 Expenditure on Final Demand,
      1963   187
8.3   Payments Impact on Unskilled Labor, Direct and
      Indirect, of $1 Consumption Expenditure by
      Region and Income Class, 1961–1963   191
8.4   Payments Impact on Unskilled Labor, Direct and
      Indirect, of $1 Expenditure on Final Demand,
      1919, 1939, and 1963   194
8.5   Payments Impact on Unskilled Labor, Direct and
      Indirect, of $1 Consumption Expenditure (A) by
      Region and Income Class, 1935–1936; (B) by
      Urban Workers, 1919   195
8.6   Late Nineteenth-Century Payments Impact on
      Unskilled Labor, Direct and Indirect, by Industry
      and on Final Demand   197
8.7   Alternative Measures of Payments Impact on
      Unskilled Labor, Direct and Indirect, of $1
      Purchase of Output from Industry j, 1963   200
9.1   Comparing the Rates of Change in the Wage
      Premium for Skilled Labor with Rates of Labor
      Force Growth, 1820–1973   206
9.2   Rates of Growth in School Enrollment and
      Attendance, 1850–1970   208
9.3   Growth Rates in Labor Force "Quality,"
      1839–1973   211

9.4   Growth Rates in Labor Force "Quality" and
      Schooling, Selected Periods, 1909–1972   213
10.1 Comparing Rates of Change in the Nonfarm
      Skilled-Labor Wage Ratio with Rates of Growth
      in Skilled and Unskilled Labor, 1839–1909   218
10.2 Factor Proportions in Three Sectors of the U.S.
      Economy, 1850 and 1900   228
10.3 Accounting for Changes in the Skilled-Labor
      Wage Premium $(\overset{*}{q} - \overset{*}{w})$, 1839–1909, Using 1850
      Factor and Sector Shares   231
10.4 Accounting for Changes in the Skilled-Labor
      Wage Premium $(\overset{*}{q} - \overset{*}{w})$, 1839–1909, Using 1900
      Factor and Sector Shares   234
11.1 Comparing Rates of Change in the Nonfarm
      Skilled-Labor Wage Ratio with Rates of Growth
      in Skilled and Unskilled Labor, 1909–1973   240
11.2 Factor Proportions in Three Sectors of the U.S.
      Economy, 1929, 1963, and 1976   242
11.3 Accounting for Changes in the Skilled-Labor
      Wage Premium $(\overset{*}{q} - \overset{*}{w})$, 1909–1973, Using 1929
      Factor and Sector Shares   245
11.4 Accounting for Changes in the Skilled-Labor
      Wage Premium $(\overset{*}{q} - \overset{*}{w})$, 1909–1973, Using 1963
      Factor and Sector Shares   248
11.5 Accounting for Changes in the Skilled-Labor
      Wage Premium $(\overset{*}{q} - \overset{*}{w})$, 1909–1973, Using 1976
      Factor and Sector Shares   252
12.1 Wealth per Capita and Capital per Worker
      Growth Rates, 1685–1966   256
12.2 Gross and Net Real Investment Shares,
      1817–1897   257
12.3 Estimating the Sources of Rising
      Nineteenth-Century Net Investment Rates: The
      Long View   273
12.4 Implied Net Rates of Return on Reproducible
      Capital Stock, c. 1817–c. 1897   275
12.5 Estimating the Sources of Rising
      Nineteenth-Century Net Investment Rates:
      Shorter-Run Episodic Phases   276

LIST OF FIGURES

2.1 Trends in colonial wealth inequality: Connecticut 15

2.2 Trends in colonial wealth inequality: Boston and Suffolk County 16

2.3 Trends in colonial wealth inequality: rural Massachusetts 17

2.4 Trends in colonial wealth inequality: the middle colonies 18

2.5 Age and relative wealth in the colonies, 1658–1753 27

2.6 Age and relative wealth in the colonies, 1774 28

3.1 Dating the rise of antebellum wealth concentration: Northeast 45

4.1 Occupational nonfarm pay ratios, 1771–1870 69

4.2 New England "wage gaps," 1761–1889 72

4.3 Selected measures of income inequality in the United States since 1913 and in seven earlier years 76

4.4 Occupational pay ratios in nonfarm United States since 1830 78

7.1 The Morishima–Saito index of U.S. labor saving, 1902–1955 158

7.2 An example of biased estimation of factor saving and the elasticity of factor substitution 160

7.3 Changes in wage premium for skilled labor compared with the relative "skills bias" implied by the imbalance in sectoral productivity growth, 1839–1973 176

9.1 Comparing the rates of change in the wage premium for skilled labor with rates of growth of the labor force, 1820–1973 205

9.2 The size and economic status of immigration flows
      into the United States, 1820–1920   209
10.1 The general-equilibrium model in rate-of-change
      form   224
10.2 Predicted and actual changes in the wage premium
      for skilled labor, 1839–1909   235
11.1 Actual and predicted changes in the wage premium
      for skilled labor since 1839   246
12.1 Some effects of improved supply of capital goods   261
12.2 Nineteenth-century shifts in investment and saving
      behavior   264

PREFACE

This book, like the transcontinental railway, began at both ends and met in the middle. Late one summer we were thinking independently about the same puzzle from two quite different perspectives. The puzzle was to explain why American earnings, income, and wealth seemed to be more unequal in some epochs than in others. Why did a substantial stream of empirical work starting with Simon Kuznets's classic seem to show equalization between the 1920s and the 1950s, with no clear trends just before or since? Economic intuition relating to depression, war, inflation, and the rise of government didn't seem to work. Adding to the puzzle were hints that some time in the nineteenth century distributions may have become more unequal.

Each of us simultaneously offered to give an economic history seminar at Wisconsin sketching out an explanation of these inequality trends. Like most experimental scientists, each of us had a prior hunch about what a detailed study would show. For Lindert, it was natural to explore the link between demographic movements, which was his previous research focus, and the inequality trends. Surely there was some link between the rise and fall of inequality and the dramatic swings in American fertility and immigration. For Williamson, the inequality movements bore a striking resemblance to patterns of unbalanced growth that had turned up in his research on developing economies of the Third World. Surely the inequality movements sprang partly from changes in the nature of technological change and partly from changes in capital accumulation rates. In two successive weeks, Wisconsin seminar participants were thus treated to two differing interpretations of the same proffered facts about inequality trends. The subsequent debate created the project that led to this book.

Having joined forces to attack a common puzzle, we found ourselves pushing in two directions: back into the historical data and forward into more refined explanations. We hope that our exploration of the data in Part One will induce other scholars to dig further, especially into the historical data antedating World War I. Deeper sampling of the probate and other wealth data and better nineteenth-century estimates of the occupational wage structure should help in interpreting the trends reported here. Others may be goaded by Parts Two and Three to devise further tests of competing hypotheses to explain long-run movements in aggregate inequality.

The authors would like to thank the Economic History Association, the American Economic Association, Princeton University Press, the University of Chicago Press, and the National Bureau of Economic Research for permission to reproduce here some of the authors' work that has appeared in the following publications: Jeffrey G. Williamson, "American Prices and Urban Inequality Since 1820," *Journal of Economic History*, 36 (June 1976), 303–333; "Strategic Wage Goods, Prices and Inequality," *American Economic Review*, 67 (March 1977), 29–41; "Inequality, Accumulation and Technological Imbalance: A Growth-Equity Conflict in American History?" *Economic Development and Cultural Change*, 27 (January 1979), 231–254, Tables 1–5, Figures 2 and 3; Jeffrey G. Williamson and Peter H. Lindert, "Long Term Trends in American Wealth Inequality," in James D. Smith (ed.), *Modelling the Distribution and Intergenerational Transmission of Wealth*, forthcoming, National Bureau of Economic Research; Peter H. Lindert, *Fertility and Scarcity in America*, Princeton, N.J.: Princeton University Press, 1978, Tables 7.1 and 7.2, Figure 7-5.

Partial financial support came at crucial times from the Institute for Research on Poverty at the University of Wisconsin–Madison. In addition, the project benefited from earlier funding for related projects by the National Science Foundation, the Rockefeller Foundation, the Population Council, and the University of Wisconsin Graduate School Research Committee. Helpful comments and criticisms were offered by colleagues at the Poverty Institute and the National Bureau of Economic Research (West), as well as by seminar participants at the following universities: British Columbia, California–Berkeley, California–Davis, California–Los Angeles, Duke, Essex, Stanford, Washington, Western Ontario, and Wisconsin–Madison. We gratefully acknowledge the able research of David Feeny, David Ortmeyer, and James Roseberry, as well as the computer assistance of James Oeppen and Nancy Williamson.

Part One
ISSUES AND EVIDENCE

THE ISSUES

The Inequality Facts

A great deal of information on trends in the inequality of American income and wealth has been gathered since World War II. The seminal contribution was *Shares of Upper Income Groups in Income and Savings* (1953), in which Simon Kuznets first exploited federal income tax returns and national income estimates with systematic and painstaking care. What Kuznets did for income shares, Robert Lampman (1962) soon did for wealth shares. These two studies by the National Bureau of Economic Research were based on federal taxes on income, which have been levied since 1913, and on wealth at death, which have been levied since 1916. For the post–World War II period, a richer data base has been established by the surveys of household income and wealth undertaken by the Census Bureau, the Federal Reserve System, and the Institute for Social Research at the University of Michigan. Building on this base, others have extended our knowledge of twentieth-century distribution trends.

Kuznets and Lampman found that the gap between rich and poor appeared to decline sharply between the 1920s and mid-century. Numerous studies of trends since World War II failed to find further significant leveling, although some have argued that a modest leveling took place across the postwar years. These twentieth-century distribution trends have quite naturally raised a number of important questions: Why was there a reduction in inequality before mid-century and hardly any since? Are the aggregate trends real, or are they just an artifact of demographic shifts in the age distribution or the rise of more fragmented households? If American income and wealth were much more unequal in the twenties than today, how did they get that way? Compared to the present, was

3

distribution always more unequal before 1929, or was there an earlier period that conforms to the more popular image of an egalitarian America?

It is not easy to illuminate early inequality experience. Data derived from tax returns on income and wealth for the years before World War I are sparse. Prior to 1913 America experimented with federal income taxes only briefly in 1866–1871 and 1894, and even then the tax affected only the very rich. Wealth was taxed only in some localities, such as the precocious states of Massachusetts and Wisconsin. Thus, to establish evidence for the years before 1913, scholars interested in American inequality have had to exploit less conventional data sources.

Several economic historians have risen to the task, finding usable data where none seemed at first to exist. Lee Soltow (1969, 1971a, 1971b, 1975) drew on mid-nineteenth-century census materials, most notably the manuscript censuses of 1850, 1860, and 1870, which recorded household real estate and personal estate holdings. Led by Jackson Turner Main (1965) and Alice Hanson Jones (1972, 1978, and forthcoming), colonial historians have used probate inventories and local tax assessments to explore wealth inequality before the Revolution.

Part One pulls these materials together and augments them with information on the structure of earnings. It also subjects these diverse estimates to some sophisticated technical adjustments suggested by the study of inequality over the last dozen years.

A host of scholars have recently added sobriety to public debate over inequality by noting the vagueness of the concept and the sensitivity of its magnitude to the mode of measurement. The normative importance of inequality is to some extent elusive, since almost everyone rejects the concept of enforcing complete equality yet no one has a clear answer to the question, How equal should an egalitarian society be? It has also been shown that there are various inequality statistics, and these can result in quite different income distribution rankings (Atkinson, 1970). Furthermore, several authors have stressed the possibility that spurious inequality trends can result from greater dispersion in adult ages or from a tendency of couples to separate. This potential for error exists because the usual data only reveal the inequality of income within a year, or of wealth at one point in time, and not the inequality of lifetime income or age-standardized wealth. Finally, conventional estimates only measure trends in the size distribution of nominal dollar incomes, without any adjustment for the possibility that the cost of living may be moving very differently for the poor and the rich, groups who perennially consume different items.

We find that there have indeed been important movements in inequality in America over the past three centuries, even when one has made all the possible technical adjustments to the raw data. The ratio of the income or wealth of the richest 10% to that of the poorest 10% does not display an eternal constant. Rather, certain epochs of American history stand out as ones of rising or falling inequality in income and wealth. Furthermore, it appears that these inequality epochs have about the same dates whether they are documented by the behavior of earnings, income, or wealth.

Our survey in Part One offers the tentative conjecture that inequality among *free* Americans before the Revolution was not too different from that which we experience today. Yet, inequality was hardly stable for the long period in between. It now appears that the main epoch of increasing inequality was the last four decades before the Civil War. The Civil War itself reduced inequalities within regions, but it also increased inequality between regions by opening a severe income and wealth gap between North and South. Although we can find no evidence of rising inequality across the remainder of the nineteenth century, trending inequality emerges once more between the turn of the century and World War I. World War I administered a brief, strong dose of equality, but the effects had worn off by 1929. The Kuznets–Lampman finding of considerable equalization in income and wealth between 1929 and mid-century appears to survive all the critical adjustments one might care to perform. After World War II, there was no sharp reversion to earlier high degrees of inequality, as happened after World War I. Instead, postwar distributions appear to us to exhibit a curious stability; a slight increase in pretax and pretransfer inequality has been offset by the impact of taxes and transfers such that "post-fisc" inequality has declined slightly since the Korean War.

Searching for Explanations

Now that these historic trends are evident, we must try to explain them. The task is challenging. Several intuitive explanations that quickly come to mind are just as quickly dispelled. The trends relate to income and wealth inequality *before* taxes and transfers ("pre-fisc"), a focus we shall retain throughout this book. Therefore, increased taxes on the rich and more generous transfers to the poor since the 1930s cannot directly account for pre-fisc trends toward inequality either before or after the 1930s. If the rise of government played a role in affecting American pre-fisc income inequality, we shall have to dig deeper to find it. The inequality movements also bear no simple relationship to boom and slump, or to full employment and underemployment. Unemployment rates were at about the same level before the antebellum period of rising inequality as after it, and before and after the income-leveling period between 1929 and the middle of the twentieth century. In both cases, the overall trend persisted during intervening business cycles. In Chapter 6, we shall see that other popular explanations also fail to account for these long-run trends.

Even more formidable obstacles hamper the search for explanations. Standard econometric tools cannot be employed for reasons that are tied to the long-run nature of the trends to be explained. First, there is the problem of assuming an error structure for an eclectically measured dependent variable. The inequality measures take different forms for different periods. Across the nineteenth century, the main available series relate to the structure of wages and the gap between skilled and unskilled workers. In the twentieth century this series is based on different underlying data for different periods, and other inequality series appear and disappear over the years. From these different threads we can weave a rich tapestry documenting what happened over the decades, but modern econometric methods are not equipped to work with such materials. Standard methods of statistical inference require specification of a systematic structure of error terms, or random components, over the entire sample period. We cannot determine that error structure when the data base keeps shifting so. This basic problem has yet to be resolved by economists and others wishing to test competing hypotheses about long-run trends.

A second difficulty relates to degrees of freedom. Each episode of rising, declining, or stable inequality seems to have lasted a decade or longer, with the exception of the sharp equalization during World War I. This pattern suggests that inequality forces work themselves out only very slowly, and that historical tests of competing models should use long stretches of time, say a decade or longer, as units of observation. But we are left then with precious few epochs of documented experience to sort out the influence of a dozen variables that intuition would offer as potential explanations. Given the state of the statistical arts, quantitative testing cannot be performed in any ordinary way.

We think plausible explanations for trends in inequality can be advanced, but to do so, Parts Two and Three resort to less fashionable quantitative methods. Part Two takes a straightforward look at some variables with which inequality has been correlated over American history. Several variables, such as technology, demography, and capital accumulation, are found to have high raw correlations with the inequality trends.

Part Three establishes a framework which can quantify the independent influence of each of these key forces. To quantify without the aid of standard regression techniques requires the use of some strong prior assumptions about the workings of the economy. Our approach is to assume that the influences of technology, demography, and accumulation can be adequately approximated in a three-sector, four-factor general-equilibrium model applied to long stretches of history. It turns out that when these few variables are allowed to influence inequality through the model, it predicts quite accurately what actually happened to pay ratios since the antebellum era. The model also yields predictions that conform well to actual trends in real wages, output growth, industrialization, and relative output prices. It has the further strength of revealing subtle patterns of structural change that were never clear to ordinary intuition.

The Equality–Growth Trade-off Debate

One view often advanced is that modern economic growth normally generates rising inequality in its earlier phases and declining inequality later, thereby tracing out an "inverted U" on a graph of inequality over time. This view was encouraged by Simon Kuznets when, in his famous presidential address to the American Economic Association (1955), he conjectured that something like this may have happened over the course of economic development in currently advanced economies. Several international cross-sectional studies (Paukert, 1973; Ahluwalia, 1976) have also encouraged the inference that countries in the middle of economic development have more income inequality than the least-developed nations, and much more inequality than the most-developed nations. The message would appear to be that any country seeking economic advancement must first experience growth with inequality, holding the faith that greater equality will eventually return.

A related but distinct position ties inequality to the rate of growth. According to this view, in order for a country to develop rapidly, it must accept wider inequalities to make the faster capital accumulation and growth possible. This position was stated with candor by the government of Pakistan in its five-year plans. The second plan proclaimed (Maddison, 1971, p. 136): "The tax system should take full account of the needs of capital formation. It will be necessary to tolerate some initial growth in income inequalities to reach high levels of saving and investment." The same message was delivered at the start of the fourth plan: "We cannot distribute poverty. Growth is vital before income distribution can improve." And in the third plan: "What is basic to Islamic socialism is the creation of equal opportunities for all rather than equal distribution of wealth."

A similar view was officially advanced during the first five-year plans of the Soviet Union and the People's Republic of China. Stalin stressed the need for unequal pay and privilege in the early 1930s, denouncing the notion of egalitarianism as a bourgeois atavism. Official Chinese press releases during the first plan (1953–1957) similarly stressed the need for material incentives and unequal pay according to productivity, a position scrapped in the Great Leap era but later revived.

This belief in a growth–equity trade-off has been challenged, with good insight and bad data, by William Cline (1972) and the World Bank (Chenery et al., 1974). They have stressed that growth can be stimulated by state policy that reduces inequality as well as by policy that raises it. Governments can forego special fiscal incentives to skill- and capital-intensive capital formation in favor of encouraging private or public projects enhancing the value of poor people's assets: investing in water control, public health, mass education, and so forth. According to the World Bank group, they could also redistribute income directly by means of taxes, transfers, and forced land redistribution, without harming aggregate growth performance.

American experience should be of value in the contemporary debate over growth and equality in the Third World. Many of the arguments about various investment strategies and forms of productivity change are given a partial test by the variations in American patterns of capital accumulation and growth in productivity during the nineteenth and the twentieth centuries. American experience also underlines the importance of another economic dimension barely mentioned in the debate: policies toward immigration and fertility. These are some of the contributions that emerge from a detailed study of what happened to inequality in America and why.

2

IN THE BEGINNING: THE DISTRIBUTION OF WEALTH IN COLONIAL AMERICA

The American Dream and the Revisionists

Visiting contemporary observers were unanimous in describing colonial America as a utopian middle-class democracy, where economic opportunities were abundant and egalitarian distributions the rule. After his 1764 visit to Boston, Lord Adam Gordon remarked, "The levelling principle here, everywhere operates strongly and takes the lead, and everybody has property here, and everybody knows it [Mereness, 1916, pp. 449–452]." A French visitor, Brissot de Warville, viewed Boston in 1788 and "saw none of those livid, ragged wretches that one sees in Europe."[1] Of colonial Philadelphia, visitors pronounced, "This is the best poor man's country in the world [Nash, 1976a, p. 545]." According to early America's most famous foreign observer, Alexis de Tocqueville, things were pretty much the same by the 1830s. Indeed, Tocqueville's hope coincided with the American dream that the New World could somehow continue to avoid the classic conflict between growth and equality, a conflict so painfully obvious in England and on the European continent when Tocqueville and his predecessors made their visits to America.

These early observers thought America was egalitarian by European standards, and modern social historians have done nothing to overturn these early impressionistic judgments. The modern quantitative evidence is effectively summarized by Alan Kulikoff's (1971) statement that "In the seventeenth century wealth in American towns was typically less concentrated than in sixteenth-century English towns, where . . . the richest tenth owned between half and seven-tenths. . . [p. 380]."

---

[1] Quoted by Kulikoff (1971, p. 383).

While comparative *levels* of European and American inequality have never been seriously debated, a lively and relevant debate has heated up regarding colonial *trends* in America.

Three competing hypotheses have emerged in the literature. Following Jackson T. Main (1976, p. 54), the first thesis holds that a European class structure and highly concentrated wealth distribution was exported to seventeenth-century America. The frontier made short work of the European model, however, and the Revolution eventually ensured its demise. Although this first thesis predicts an egalitarian trend for the economy as a whole in the colonial era, it is not clear that it predicts as well an egalitarian trend in the older eastern settlements, where the English model was first imported.

In contrast, the second thesis argues that the presence of the frontier made it possible right at the start to achieve equality in the distribution of land and thus wealth. As the readily accessible colonial frontier became exhausted, a trend towards inequality and wealth concentration emerged, and the Revolution served only to halt temporarily the retrogression. This second thesis has many proponents and, for simplicity, we shall label them "the revisionists." Kenneth Lockridge (1970, 1972), for example, uses his theory of colonial economic stress to describe increasing wealth concentration and diminished opportunities for accumulation in settled agrarian coastal regions. The ratio of men to land rose, land values shot up relative to wages, and since it became increasingly difficult for the landless to purchase an acre of farmland and earn rent, increased wealth and income inequality resulted. Lockridge assumes there were formidable barriers to migration out of the farm sector or to the western frontier. That is, he finds it convenient to view eastern settled colonial townships as nearly closed agrarian systems. His "crowding" thesis quite naturally predicts inequality as the European classic steady state emerged. There is another band of revisionists who share the rising-inequality view, but the city is their window on colonial America. Bridenbaugh (1955), Henretta (1965), J. T. Main (1965, 1971), Kulikoff (1971), and Nash (1976a, 1976b) have argued that poverty was on the rise in American cities, and that urban trends were toward propertylessness, swollen relief rolls, increasing stratification, declining opportunity, and general inequality. For these scholars, inequality trends in Boston and Philadelphia are far more important than colony-wide performance or even trends within settled coastal agrarian townships. They view these cities as the flash points for revolution, political change, and social reform. It matters little to the urban revisionists that these towns contained a small and sharply declining share of the total colonial population.

The third thesis is the one we adopt here: trends were mixed but *in the aggregate* colonial inequality was stable at low levels.[2] In some cities, inequality was on the rise. These were the fast growers, which attracted the young adult and/or the propertyless. In others, no rise in inequality can be observed. These were typically slow growers, which failed to attract the young and propertyless. Some settled agrarian regions exhibited inequality trends, others did not. Even frontier settlements exhibited some evidence of rising inequality. The colonial era exhibits a lack of consistent local behavior, in contrast to the consistency shown later, after 1820. Indeed, when the New England or middle colonies are examined as a whole, we believe there is no evidence to support the view of drifting colonial inequality.

It appears to us that participants in the colonial wealth debate have fallen victims of the fallacy of composition. Were there evidence of rising inequality in *all* town and rural communities, this would still fail to establish the case for aggregate colonial inequality trends. As we shall see, this apparent contradiction can be easily resolved if populations shift toward regions with both lower inequality and more rapid wealth accumulation per capita. These were in fact the ingredients of colonial extensive and intensive frontier development, ingredients that fail to characterize the nineteenth-century economy and thus fail to spare it from aggregate inequality trends produced by modern economic growth.

Wealth Inequality in the Colonies

A WORD ABOUT DATA

Colonial social historians have made great strides in establishing a broad data base documenting trends in wealth inequality in the New England and middle colonies. Whether based on tax assessments or probate inventories, these wealth distributions can be used as indicators of income inequality only with a solid understanding of their limitations. Since probate records are by far the best source of information on colonial inequality, what follows is primarily directed toward this type of information.

Measuring the wealth that individuals left at death gives us valuable

---

[2] Six years ago Lee Soltow (1971a) insisted that inequality and wealth concentration were high and stable during the nineteenth century, and that this had been a relatively permanent attribute of American experience before 1776 and after. That wealth inequality levels were high during the colonial era cannot be maintained on the basis of the enormous amount of data which has accumulated since 1971. (See J. T. Main [1976, p. 54], for a critical evaluation of Soltow's position).

clues about the inequality of current property income and past total income among the living. Research into colonial probate records has shown clearly that wealth inequality at death exhibits much the same trends (but different levels) as wealth inequality among the living, where both kinds of documentation are available. This is apparent in the studies by A. H. Jones (1970, 1971, 1972, 1978, forthcoming), G. Main (1976), J. T. Main (1976), G. B. Nash (1976a), and others, all of whom have been able to classify numerous extant colonial wealth distributions for decedents by age, so as to reweight the distributions to conform to the age distributions of the living (following the "estate multiplier" method, e.g., Mendershausen, 1956; Lampman, 1962). In no case do the resulting trends in wealth inequality among the living depart from those based on the dying. In short, while the first limitation of colonial wealth probate data is that they fail in theory to describe the living, past studies have established unambiguously that adjusting for age distribution affects only the levels and not the trends in wealth inequality.

It might seem that any colonial wealth distributions fail to gauge income inequality, which should be the relevant focus. Yet the links between income inequality and wealth inequality are quite strong. Wealth inequality measures will be monotonically related to income inequality measures when a few innocuous assumptions are satisfied. Wealth inequality *levels* are monotonically related to inequality in current property incomes (human and conventional) if rates of return on assets (including consumer durables) vary little across wealth classes. Even if rates of return rise with size of wealth holdings, the correlation still holds. Parallel inequality trends in property income and property values would still be assured in this case, although income inequality levels and trends would be magnified. Indeed, although contemporary twentieth-century evidence shows that property income is more highly concentrated than wealth, implying higher rates of return among the more wealthy, the temporal correlation between the two after 1929 can be established with ease. Compared with the twentieth century, colonial wealth distributions are likely to exhibit an even closer parallel to *total*, as opposed to only property, income distributions. After all, conventional property income is a far larger share of total income in early stages of growth, since human capital, and thus labor earnings above "subsistence," is less important. On these grounds alone, the distribution of wealth was more important in determining income distribution early in America's growth than later. Finally, wealth inequality trends will accurately reflect *prior* income inequality trends if average propensities to save do not decline with increases in income and if the income slope of the average-propensity-to-save function is relatively stable over time. Neither of these assumptions can be rejected on the basis of colonial and early national data.

We turn now to another problem in dealing with colonial wealth data. Due to small sample size, probate wealth distributions, appropriately deflated, must be averaged over several years to shed light on long-term trends in wealth distributions. Records drawn from only a year or two make wealth inequality statistics much too sensitive to the timing of death among the very rich. In response to this problem, some researchers report the full distribution from which have been subtracted the effect of the richest few. Although the latter procedure has been favored by some (e.g., J. T. Main, 1976, uses the "trimmed mean" in Connecticut colonial probates), we shall rely instead on multi-year averages.

Two remaining limitations on the probated wealth distributions are more important than those just mentioned. First, many persons failed to leave wills or to have their estates administered at death. The records that survive thus supply only a sample of all decedents. Fortunately, these samples are usually large enough to predict population wealth distributions. Though the samples are not free of coverage bias, colonial historians have been impressed at how well represented are both the very poor and the very rich in probate records. To be sure, samples may exhibit better coverage among estates of middle and high value, and those too poor to leave any wealth whatsoever are often seriously underrepresented. Yet these problems are hardly intractable, and consistent rules for augmenting colonial probate records have been well established (D. S. Smith, 1975; G. Main, 1976; J. T. Main, 1976; A. H. Jones, 1978, forthcoming), thus correcting for the propertyless and coverage bias. The essential point is that probate samples will accurately reflect *trends* in wealth inequality unless there were changes in coverage. Changing coverage does not appear to be a serious problem in judging trends in colonial inequality within regions, although they may be more serious in comparing levels of colonial inequality between regions. Whereas many social historians are interested in the latter, our interest is primarily in the former.

Second, probate records are limited in their coverage of assets and liabilities. As a rule, the middle and southern colonies did not include real estate (land, improvements, and buildings) in their records, but covered only personal estate. The New England colonies were more complete in asset coverage. In both cases, financial liabilities were rarely included. As we shall see, this variation in asset coverage is a serious defect only if we focus on comparisons across colonies or on short-term instability. The problem of limited coverage does not appear to be significant when evaluating long-run trends, since colonial wealth inequality measures normally trace out the same secular pattern regardless of probate asset coverage.

What, then, do these sources tell us about the distribution of colonial wealth and opportunity?

TRENDS IN COLONIAL WEALTH INEQUALITY

We have long time series on urban and rural areas, and the series yield a wide geographic representation. Appendix A collects estate and tax-list distributions from New England and the middle colonies, producing twenty-nine series in all. Connecticut and Massachusetts are both very well represented from the middle of the late seventeenth century to the Revolutionary War. The middle colonies are less extensively documented, but even in this case we have time series on Philadelphia and New York City as well as Maryland and rural Pennsylvania. The data have two limitations. First, they fail to supply summary descriptions of trends in aggregate performance for any colony or region, with the possible exception of Maryland. Although manuscript censuses for 1860 and 1870 yield returns on total personal wealth for America as a whole and for major regions, no such aggregates are available for the colonial era, with the exception of Alice Jones's benchmark for 1774 (A. H. Jones, 1970, 1972, 1978, forthcoming). This attribute of trends in colonial wealth concentration has the effect of producing an inherent upward bias and, as we shall see, invites erroneous inferences from the recent literature. Second, wealth distributions derived from tax lists must be treated with great caution. Since so much of the revisionist literature (Henretta, 1965; Lemon and Nash, 1968) was initially based on tax lists, it might be useful to discuss its limitations before proceeding further.

Some years ago, Henretta (1965) reported steep wealth inequality trends for colonial Boston. His pioneering work was based on very imperfect tax-list data. He thought he observed a striking trend towards wealth concentration, since the top 10% increased their share from 46.6% in 1687 to 63.6% and 64.7% in 1771 and 1790 (Appendix A, Col. (12)). Apart from the fact that Gloria Main's and Gary Nash's Boston probate data (Appendix A, Cols. (8) and (9)) now make it apparent that the 1680s and 1690s were decades of atypical low concentration ratios, the tax data have now been shown to be seriously flawed. Gerard Warden's adjustments (Appendix A, Col. (13)) suggest a much more modest rise from the atypical trough of the 1680s, from 42.3% to 47.5% between 1681 and 1771. Warden's adjustments deal with problems of undervaluation. Undervaluation ratios varied greatly across assets, the ratios varied over time, many assets escaped assessment altogether, and asset mixes varied over time and across wealth classes. Apparently, these valuation problems tend to yield a spuriously steep inequality trend for Boston. Although no one to our knowledge has yet attempted similar adjustments to the Philadelphia, Chester County (Pennsylvania), Hingham (Massachusetts), and New York City tax-list wealth distributions, they must by inference be treated with equal caution. It is for this reason that Figures 2.1–2.4 rely almost exclusively on probate data.

What do the probate wealth inequality trends tell us? Was the colonial

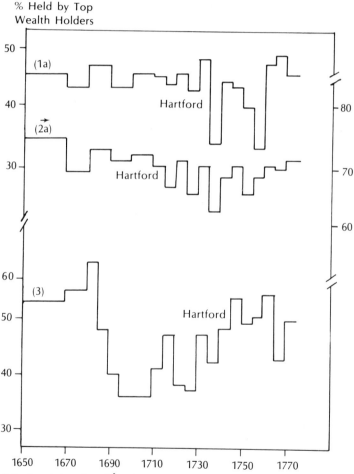

FIGURE 2.1. Trends in colonial wealth inequality: Connecticut. From Appendix A. (1a) = personal wealth held by top 10% in Hartford; (2a) = personal wealth held by top 30% in Hartford; (3) = real wealth held by top 10% in Hartford.

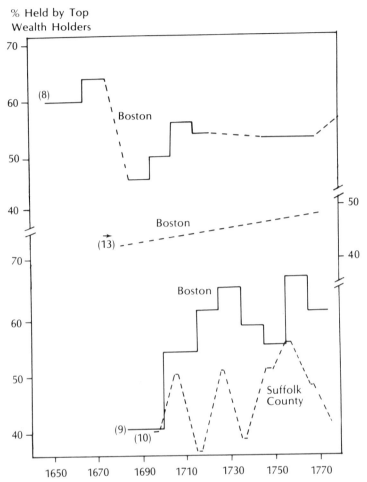

FIGURE 2.2. Trends in colonial wealth inequality: Boston and Suffolk County. From Appendix A. (8) = wealth held by top 10% in Boston; (9) = personal wealth held by top 10% in Boston; (10) = wealth held by top 10% in Suffolk County; (13) = wealth held by top 10% in Boston, "adjusted" tax lists.

era one of drifting inequality? If one were to take 1690 or 1700 as a base, the wealth inequality series reported in Figures 2.1–2.4 would suggest mixed trends, but, on average, a drift toward greater wealth concentration for the seven or eight decades prior to the Revolution. This characterization holds for rural Connecticut (but *not* for Hartford County), for rural Massachusetts (but *not* for rural Suffolk County), for Boston as well as Portsmouth (New Hampshire), and for Philadelphia as well as nearby Chester County. It does *not* hold for Maryland, however, which exhibits

% Held by Top
Wealth Holders

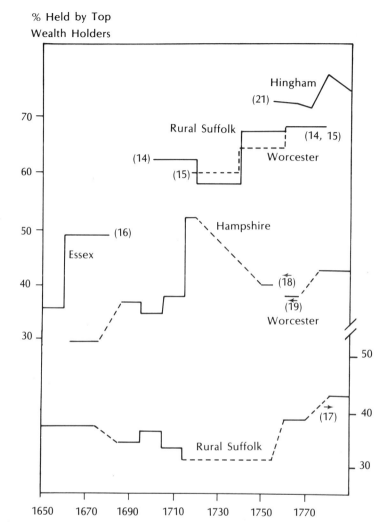

FIGURE 2.3. Trends in colonial wealth inequality: rural Massachusetts. From Appendix A.
(14) = wealth held by top 30% in rural Suffolk; (15) = wealth held by top 30% in
Worcester; (16) = wealth held by top 10% in Essex; (17) = wealth held by top 10% in rural
Suffolk; (18) = wealth held by top 10% in Hampshire; (19) = wealth held by top 10% in
Worcester; (21) = wealth held by top 30% in Hingham.

stability from the 1690s onward. New York City is another exception,
since it had a stable wealth distribution between 1695 and 1789 (Appendix
A, Col. (25)), but this inference is based solely on tax-list data.

Selection of benchmark dates is critical in evaluating colonial inequality
trends. Boston traces out inequality trends only if the 1690s are taken as a

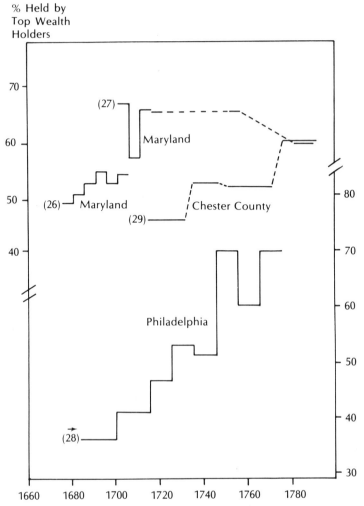

FIGURE 2.4. Trends in colonial wealth inequality: the middle colonies. From Appendix A. (26) = wealth held by top 10% in Maryland; (27) = wealth held by top 10% in Maryland, adjusted for underreporting; (28) = wealth held by top 10% in Philadelphia; (29) = wealth held by top 20% in Chester County.

starting point, whereas no perceptible trend can be identified when the 1770s are compared instead with the 1670s or 1730s. "Cycles" in wealth inequality are also reported by Gloria Main for both Boston and Suffolk County probates (Appendix A, Cols. (8)–(10)). Wealth concentration rose after a trough in the 1680s and 1690s, but far higher inequality was recorded in the colonial era beginning in 1650. If the 1690s were years of atypical economic conditions accounting for unusually low concentration levels, then the case for stability in colonial inequality trends in Boston would be reinforced. It hardly seems coincidental that New England imports were low and declining from 1697 to 1706, high and rising thereafter to 1771.[3] These episodes of "bust" correspond very well with periods of low inequality in Boston and Suffolk County (Fig. 2.2), a predictable result, since extended depression must have produced capital losses at the top of the distribution and thus a leveling in wealth concentration. Subsequently, the improvement in Boston trade (and associated capital gains) produced increased wealth concentration following c. 1705 and again following c. 1750. What we may be observing between 1700 and 1730 is not a pervasive secular shift in *physical* asset accumulation at the top of the wealth pyramid, but an uneven rise in average asset values among the very rich, who held mercantile capital in relatively high proportion. After all, real estate was far more equally distributed in mercantile Boston than was "portable" personal property (Nash, 1976a, pp. 552–553), and the latter included slaves, servants, currency, bonds, mortgages, book debt, stock in trade, and ships. Short-term capital gains and losses must have been more typical for these types of assets than for real estate, at least for a trading center like Boston, which was subjected to the whims of exogenous world commercial conditions. Since the very wealthy held land in relatively low proportions to total assets, their relative fortunes were far more sensitive to the vagaries of mercantile conditions. (For a twentieth-century example, see Robert Lampman's [1962, pp. 220–229] discussion of asset price changes and wealth inequality during the 1920s and 1930s.) Thus the "cycles" in wealth concentration can be readily associated with Boston's trade conditions, and since the 1680s and 1690s were years of atypically poor trade conditions, whereas the 1670s or 1710s were not, long-term stability (or decline) in Boston's wealth concentration seems the best characterization of the whole colonial era.

Mercantile centers were not the only colonial areas to exhibit wide instability in wealth concentration. Maryland supplies another example, and thus the choice of benchmark dates plays a crucial role here too. Although wealth concentration was remarkably stable after 1710 (Appendix A, Col. (27)), the social historian beginning his analysis with 1675 would have cited instead evidence of a slight drift toward inequality in Maryland throughout the colonial era. While Gloria Main's estimates

[3] The import values in pounds sterling can be found in *Historical Statistics* (1975, Part 2, Series Z-216, pp. 1176–1177). Unfortunately, the series does not extend back to the mid-seventeenth century. For further discussion of Boston's cycles, see Nash's (1976a, pp. 575–576) account of wartime boom, postwar recession and its "disfiguring effect on urban societies."

(Appendix A, Col. (26)) show a modest rise in Maryland wealth inequality from 1675 to 1690, Menard, Harris, and Carr (1974, p. 174) have shown that the 1670s were unusual, since a leveling in the wealth distribution had been at work for the quarter century following 1640, at least along the lower western Chesapeake shore. This pattern seems to correspond fairly well with tobacco fortunes: American tobacco prices fell sharply up to the late 1660s and bottomed out thereafter. Furthermore, the temporarily low wealth inequality recorded in 1705–1709 (Appendix A, Col. (27)) also appears to correspond with depressed tobacco exports.[4] So capital gains and losses from changes in export demand seem to account for Maryland's colonial wealth instability, too. The best tentative starting point for judging trends in wealth inequality in colonial Maryland thus seems to be the relatively normal 1690s, and from this decade to the 1750s there was no net change in wealth inequality in Maryland.

Hartford, Connecticut, will serve as a final example of colonial instability and the benchmark dating problem. J. T. Main's (1976) finding of long-term stability of wealth distribution for the Hartford probate district can be seen quite clearly in Figure 2.1. J. T. Main's trends for Hartford are confirmed by Daniels (1973–1974, pp. 129–131). Daniels also finds, however, that wealth inequality was on the rise in small and medium-sized Connecticut towns after the early 1700s. Daniels reports a steep trend in wealth concentration in Danbury, Waterbury, and Windham after 1700, and in the smaller frontier towns in Litchfield County after 1740 (Appendix A, Cols. (5) and (6)). Main's data, reproduced in Figure 2.1, show that the contrast between rural and "urban" Connecticut may be only apparent, not real. Although in Hartford, personal wealth inequality and total wealth inequality were stable throughout the eighteenth century (see Fig. 2.1 and Appendix A), *real* wealth inequality was not, for it rose between 1710 and 1740 or 1750. Since the smaller frontier towns had a far larger share of wealth in real estate (and thus land),[5] the rise in wealth concentration outside of the Connecticut trading towns following 1710 seems less anomalous. Indeed, had Daniels extended his analysis backwards to 1680, he might have discovered stable inequality in rural Connecticut too. J. T. Main's figures for real estate concentration in Hartford County (Fig. 2.1) show a very striking leveling in real wealth distributions from the 1680s to

---

[4] For tobacco prices and exports, see, e.g., Menard (1973) and Clemens (1974).

[5] For example, around 1700 "settled trading" towns in Connecticut had 52.2% of their wealth in real estate, whereas for the "new frontier" towns, the share was 62.1% (J. T. Main, 1976, Table IX, p. 78). Furthermore, land was the dominant asset in the real estate total—about 82%—if Hartford, Farmington, and Simsbury in the 1760s are typical (personal correspondence from J. T. Main, May 27, 1976).

1710. Had we, like Daniels, begun our analysis in 1700, we would have observed a real wealth inequality drift in Hartford up to 1774. If, instead, the analysis starts with the 1680s or earlier, no trend in real wealth concentration can be observed. By inference, it seems likely that at least some of the wealth inequality trends following 1700 noted by Daniels in rural Connecticut are spurious.[6]

To summarize, among those probate wealth inequality series that extend backwards before the 1690s, Worcester County (Massachusetts) and Philadelphia reveal the minority position: a clear secular drift toward inequality for the entire colonial era. Connecticut, Boston, rural Suffolk County (Massachusetts), and Maryland represent the majority: they do *not* reveal inequality trends. If, instead, one is content to start the analysis with 1700, then a modest drift toward inequality seems to characterize these colonial "local histories" best. We have tried to show, however, that the 1700 benchmark may impart a spurious upward trend to wealth concentration indices. Some readers may disagree with this interpretation, but those historians who have adopted the 1700 benchmark, and thus view the mixed "local history" trends as evidence of a colonial inequality drift, may be inadvertent victims of yet another bias—the fallacy of composition.

The Fallacy of Composition and the Trending Inequality Bias

NEW FRONTIERS, OLD SETTLEMENTS, AND COLONIAL WEALTH INEQUALITY

We have argued that probate and wealth-tax data for localities fall short of revealing wealth inequality trends for the thirteen colonies as a whole. Yet aggregate trends can be roughly inferred if we remember how overall wealth inequality depends on the distribution of population and wealth between groups as well as on the distribution of wealth within each group. As we have shown elsewhere (Williamson and Lindert, 1977), it is helpful to divide changes in the variance (or inequality) of wealth into changes

---

[6] Furthermore, concentration trends in real estate holdings follow closely rates of change in relative land values in Connecticut. Taking the ratio of prices of an acre of meadow (J. T. Main, 1976, pp. 101–102) to farm labor wages (U.S. Department of Labor, 1929, pp. 9, 51, 53, and 124), we find the relative price of land stable from the 1680s to 1710. It rises sharply to 1759 and then stabilizes thereafter. The index is 16.67 for 1680–1689, 36.30 for 1755–1759, and 44.12 for 1774.

arising from (a) changes in wealth inequality within groups; (b) changes in the differences in mean wealth between groups; and (c) changes in the population shares falling in the different groups.

To show how this decomposition-of-variance approach can be applied to colonial wealth trends, let us divide the colonies schematically into two regions, the older and more urban seaboard and the rural inland frontier. Trends in wealth inequality for all the colonies combined were determined by four proximate forces: (a) changes in wealth inequality within older regions; (b) changes in wealth inequality at the frontier; (c) changes in the ratio of average seaboard wealth to average frontier wealth; and (d) changes in the share of population at the frontier.[7] Clues about these four proximate forces allow us to put together a picture of the overall trends in wealth inequality for colonial America as a whole.

NEW ENGLAND'S DEVELOPMENT AND THE IRRELEVANCE OF BOSTON

Turning first to New England, we can use the decomposition-of-variance approach on the perspectives offered by past studies of inequality trends. Thus far, past studies have concentrated on trends within Boston and other seaboard regions—that is, on the first component of inequality change listed above. As we have mentioned, the wealth gap between rich and poor Bostonians widened before the Revolution only if we begin from the late 1680s or the 1690s. Even on these terms, any widening of the economic gap in Boston could not have had much effect on the overall distribution of wealth among colonial New Englanders. While Boston may have been a focal point for political change, its share of New England's population throughout the eighteenth century was less than 8%, as shown in Table 2.1. This means that the much-studied changes in inequality within Boston could not have had much effect on the trends in wealth inequality for all of New England.

Another salient fact about the wealth of colonial Bostonians is that it grew more slowly than the average wealth of the rest of New England. As documented in Appendix B, wealth per capita in 1687 was about 60% higher in Boston than in New England, but Boston's wealth advantage had dropped to about 34% by 1771. This convergence in wealth must have been a significant equalizing force and deserves further study.

[7] Some readers will note the obvious similarity between this discussion of colonial wealth and Simon Kuznets's (1955) decomposition of *income* inequality into urban and rural components. The same four forces were present in his analysis too: (a) urban inequality, (b) rural inequality, (c) urbanization, and (d) rural–urban income gaps. The framework has been used recently in a wide variety of circumstances. A general statement can be found in Lindert and Williamson (1976, p. 6) or Robinson (1976).

TABLE 2.1
Colonial Population Trends

Year	New England Colonies Population		(3) Percentage Population in Boston $(1) \div (2) \times 100$
	(1) Boston	(2) New England	
1680		68,400	
1690		86,900	
1700		92,800	
1710	8,665	115,200	7.5
1720		170,900	
1730	13,875	217,400	6.4
1740	16,800	289,800	5.8
1750	15,800	360,000	4.4
1760	15,631	449,700	3.5
1770	15,500	581,100	2.7
1780	10,000	712,600	1.4

Year	(1) Population	Period	Middle Colonies Population		(4) Percentage Population in Major Cities $(2)+(3) \div (1) \times 100$
			(2) Philadelphia	(3) New York City	
1700	83,200	1700–1710	2,450	4,500	8.3%
1710	112,300	1711–1720	3,800	5,900	8.7
1720	169,200	1721–1730	6,600	7,600	8.4
1730	238,100	1731–1740	8,800	10,100	7.9
1740	336,700	1741–1750	12,000	12,900	7.4
1750	437,600	1751–1760	15,700	13,200	6.6
1760	590,200	1761–1770	22,100	18,100	6.8
1770	758,500	1771–1775	27,900	22,600	6.7
1780	968,300				

Sources: New England and middle colonies totals are from *Historical Statistics* (1975, Part 2, p. 1168). The New York City and Philadelphia figures are from Nash (1976, Table 4, p. 13). The Boston figures are from Nash (1976, Table 4, p. 13) and Kulikoff (1971, Table V, p. 393).

An additional leveling force was the decline in Boston's share of the region's population. In 1710 an estimated 7.5% of New Englanders lived in Boston; by 1770 only 2.7% did so (Table 2.1). The eighteenth century was hardly a period of rapid urbanization. This population drift away from the city (and the seaboard) toward the less affluent and more egalitarian frontier again contributed to an aggregate equalizing of New England wealth.[8] So even if we start from the inequality trough of the late 1680s and the 1690s, there are good reasons to doubt rising inequality for the New England colonies as a whole.

MIDDLE-COLONY DEVELOPMENT AND THE DOUBTFUL RELEVANCE OF PHILADELPHIA

For the middle colonies, trends can again be clarified by reference to the decomposition-of-variance approach. Trending wealth concentration in old-settled regions has seemed clearest for Philadelphia, for which Nash's (1976a) figures imply a serious widening of the gap in the middle of the eighteenth century. The same was apparently not true for New York City, where the share of taxable wealth held by the richest 10% of wealth holders hardly changed between 1695 and 1789. Within the hinterland, inequality trends were mixed, to judge from fragmentary returns: Gloria Main's probate estimates for Maryland show declining inequality between 1700 and 1754, while an eighteenth-century rise in inequality appears for Chester County, Pennsylvania, in the studies by Duane Ball (1976) and by Lemon and Nash (1968).

Philadelphia thus stands out as the main theater of known wealth concentration in the middle colonies. Yet Philadelphia's share of the region's population was small: fewer than 4% of the middle-colony population lived there. It appears unlikely that a rise in wealth concentration within Philadelphia could have greatly raised wealth inequality for the entire region.

An offsetting leveling force was the de-urbanization of the middle colonies. Philadelphia's share of the region's population dropped from 3.9% to 3.7% between the 1720s and the Revolution. New York's share dropped more sharply, from 4.5% to 3.0% over the same period (Table 2.1). Since both urban centers had much higher average wealth and inequality[9] than the rural middle colonies, their decline meant a shrinking urban upper class in the region, a change tending to equalize the distribution of wealth for the region as a whole.

Although a firm judgment of middle-colony inequality trends must await

[8] For a quantification of this contribution, using decomposition-of-variance formulae, see Williamson and Lindert (1977, Section 2.3).

[9] In terms of taxable wealth, by the middle of the eighteenth century, the top 10% owned the following shares: in Philadelphia, 46.6% (1756) while in Chester County, Pennsylvania, 28.7% (1748). In terms of inventoried wealth, the top 10% owned the following shares: in Philadelphia, 70.1% (1746–1755); in rural Maryland, 65.8% (1750–1754). These estimates can all be found in Appendix A. Furthermore, A. H. Jones (1972, Tables 13 and 17) has documented net worth shares for 1774; the top 10% in Philadelphia County claimed 54.7% while in the middle colonies as a whole they claimed only 40.6%.

better data on rural wealth, there is no reason to reject the null hypothesis of stable wealth gaps across the colonial era.

AGE, WEALTH, AND SELECTIVE MIGRATION

Demographic forces may also have acted to produce a spurious drift in colonial wealth inequality. To judge what truly happened to life-cycle wealth inequality, an effort must be made to hold age distribution constant. After all, young adults have far smaller average wealth holdings (Table 2.2 and Figs. 2.5 and 2.6). On these grounds alone, if young adults are added to a static adult population through immigration or natural increase, wealth inequality may rise even though life-cycle inequalities change not at all. The larger the differential in average wealth levels by age, the more potent the effect. In addition, we must consider wealth inequality within age classes. Based on 1870 total estate and 1850 real estate census data, Lee Soltow (1975, p. 107) has shown that inequality was high in the age group 20–29, was much lower in the age group 30–39, and remained fairly stable in subsequent age groups. It would appear that as the share of adult males in their twenties rose over time, inequality would also appear to rise when no true inequality trend was present.[10]

What is the colonial evidence on wealth and age? We would be satisfied with either of two kinds of wealth concentration data: (*a*) measures of wealth concentration over time *within* fairly narrow age classes; (*b*) detailed information on changing age distributions, which could be combined with our knowledge of age profiles on wealth means and variances. Since the colonial data base does not yet fulfill these rigorous demands, we must be content with Soltow's 1850 estimates of wealth dispersion within age classes.[11] What about wealth by age class? Does the colonial

---

[10] In contrast with Gallman's (1974) cautious speculations on the early national period, some historians write as if the impact of age distribution on aggregate wealth inequality trends were fully understood for the colonial era. On the 1714–1790 period in Chester County, Duane Ball (1976) states:

> [The] distribution of wealth, though seemingly unequal, actually might be considered fairly egalitarian if we were to take the age of wealth holders into account. It is also possible that at least some of the increasing concentration . . . is attributable to a change in the age structure . . . from relatively younger to relatively older [p. 637].

All things are possible, but as far as we know there are no adequate colonial data which would allow exploration of the influence of changing age distributions.

[11] This is not entirely accurate. J. T. Main (1976, Table VI, p. 93) reports the distribution of decedents by wealth and age class for all Connecticut towns. Unfortunately, he pools observations drawn from the century ending in 1753, a sufficiently long period to make age–wealth analysis tenuous at best.

TABLE 2.2
Age and Wealth in the Colonies, 1658–1774: Various Estimates (*average wealth by age class relative to total average wealth*)

Age Class	(1) Maryland 1658–1705
25 or less	.246
26–45	.940
46–60	1.334
61+	1.021
All adult males	1.000

	(2) Hartford 1710–1714	(3) Hartford 1750–1754	(4) Connecticut 1700–1753
21–29	.340	.383	.264
30–39	.744	.767	.607
40–49	1.545	1.208	1.014
50–59	1.330	1.342	1.383
60+	.898	1.192	1.283
All adult males	1.000	1.000	1.000

	(5) Middle Colonies 1774 Net Worth	(6) Middle Colonies 1774 Physical Wealth	(7) New England 1774 Total Wealth	(8) New England 1774 Physical Wealth
25 or less	.121	.881	.184	.197
26–45	.770	.891	.731	.732
46+	1.338	1.295	1.270	1.269
All adult males	1.000	1.000	1.000	1.000

Sources: Col. (1) is the value of total estate (excluding land and improvements), inventoried at death, lower western shore of Maryland, from Menard, Harris, and Carr (1974, Table II, p. 178). Cols. (2) and (3) are for Hartford probate district, personal wealth only, from J. T. Main (1976, Table XI, p. 84). These are for periods for which Main's samples are relatively large. Col. (4) is all Connecticut inventoried wealth, including land, from J. T. Main (1976, Table XIX, p. 95). Cols. (5) and (6) are middle colonies, decedent wealth, from A. H. Jones (1971, Table 5). Cols. (7) and (8) are New England, decedent wealth, from A. H. Jones (1972, Table 4, p. 114).

age–wealth life cycle trace out a profile much like mid-nineteenth- and twentieth-century patterns? Table 2.2, Figure 2.5, and Figure 2.6 exhibit a remarkable consistency over time and across regions in the age–wealth profile. Whether late seventeenth-century Maryland, mid-eighteenth-century Hartford, or Revolutionary New England, the patterns are very similar to twentieth-century age–wealth profiles. It is a simple matter, therefore, to establish a *potential* role for demographic forces as a source

Relative Wealth
(1.0 = average)

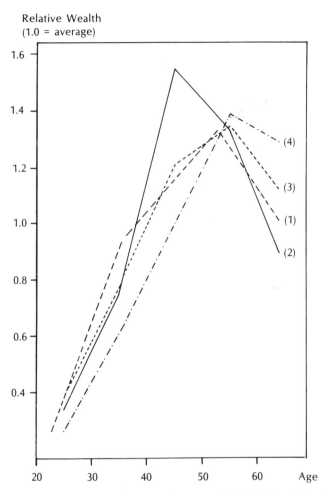

FIGURE 2.5. Age and relative wealth in the colonies, 1658–1753. From Table 2.2. (1) = Maryland, 1658–1705; (2) = Hartford, Conn., 1710–1714; (3) = Hartford, Conn., 1750–1754; (4) = Connecticut, 1700–1753.

of change in measured wealth inequality in pre-Revolutionary decades. All we require are early- and late-colonial age distributions.

The *actual* role of demographic forces is far more difficult to isolate. Demographic data for the colonial era are very skimpy, and the time series that are available rarely supply more than three age classes (most commonly under 16, 16–60, and over 60). What we do have suggests stability in colonial age distributions. Ignoring the Revolutionary War years, when (young) men in the army were undercounted or missed

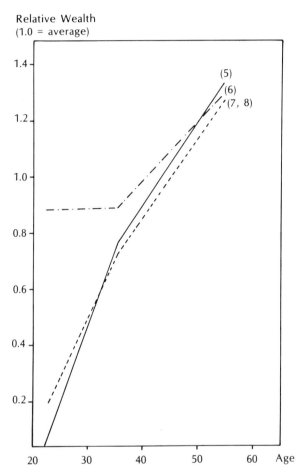

FIGURE 2.6. Age and relative wealth in the colonies, 1774. From Table 2.2. (5) = middle colonies (net worth); (6) = middle colonies (physical wealth); (7, 8) = New England (total and physical wealth).

entirely, the evidence suggests very little change in age distributions in New Hampshire between 1767 and 1773, in New York between 1712–1714 and 1786, or in New Jersey between 1726 and 1745.[12] Indeed, the age distribution of adult males (free *and* slave) was not much older or more dispersed even in 1860 than in colonial times.[13]

[12] These estimates can be found in *Historical Statistics* (1975, Part 2, p. 1170).

[13] This sentence is based on an examination of the following age distributions: New England white males, c. 1690 (Thomas and Anderson, 1973, p. 654); Westchester, Bedford, and New Rochelle, New York, adult males and both sexes, 1698 (Wells, 1975, p. 117); U.S. white and total males, 1800 (*Historical Statistics*, 1975, Part 1, p. 16).

The discussion here is motivated by a different set of issues than that motivating J. T.

While age distributions appear to have been stable colony-wide in the eighteenth century, and thus would impart no bias in an aggregate inequality index, the same cannot be said for colonial cities and more urbanized eastern settlements. A widening of inequality may have resulted if cities attracted the young. Rapid growth in colonial towns could not have been achieved in the absence of native immigration from the countryside as well as a foreign influx. These newcomers tended to be younger and, more frequently, single males. Thus, those towns enjoying the most rapid growth were likely to have exhibited the steepest inequality trends, not necessarily because average ages were declining there but rather because individuals were increasingly far more widely dispersed by age. To the extent that this relationship holds,[14] we would expect high positive correlation between rapidly growing colonial towns and trending inequality in the aggregate wealth distribution. One cannot help wondering, for example, to what extent the striking rise in Philadelphia's poor, documented by Nash (1976b), could be explained simply by the increased preponderance of youth in the city's population. A recent paper by B. G. Smith (1977) has quantified the unusually rapid growth in Philadelphia's eighteenth-century population not only by the standards of colonial America but also by English standards. Indeed, even by modern standards, Philadelphia's growth rates (as high as 4.02% annually in the 1760s) "were phenomenally high" (B. G. Smith, 1977, p. 885). Since Smith feels that the mass immigration created an unusually young age structure in Philadelphia, and increasingly so over time, increased aggregate urban inequality seems the inevitable consequence. After all, skewed age distributions imply skewed wealth distributions: "The city's age structure must have been very skewed, with children and the middle-age predominating greatly over those in the older groups. Colonial Philadelphia was, it seems, an unusual environment, characterized by high mortality, high fertility, and large-scale immigration of people in younger age groups [B. G. Smith, 1977, p. 889]."

There is yet another upward bias in the urban wealth concentration trends. Migration is, by definition, selective. Those who migrated *from* the cities had, in all likelihood, more middling wealth and age than those who migrated *to* the cities. Emigrants to the hinterland presumably had

---

Main's recent analysis of Connecticut eighteenth-century probates. He devotes considerable attention to the impact of age on wealth distribution from region to region and across occupations, but never across time. See J. T. Main (1976, pp. 77–97).

[14] J. T. Main (1976) thinks it could, at least based on Connecticut evidence: "Historians seem to have neglected this life-cycle. They have lamented a high proportion of nearly propertyless polls appearing on tax lists . . . without perceiving that most of these were just entering manhood . . . [p. 61]."

enough wealth to start a farm. From the hinterland and from Europe, meanwhile, the cities attracted a few rich and many unpropertied young males. This selective aspect of urban immigration imparts an upward bias to urban inequality trends beyond the bias imparted by age itself.[15]

One can only speculate, but it does seem likely that changing urban age distributions imparted an upward bias to eighteenth-century wealth inequality trends in Boston and Philadelphia. Although the same cannot be said for colony-wide trends, the fact remains that it is the experience of these two cities that has attracted much of the social historian's attention. This section suggests yet another reason for doubting trending inequality as a description of the colonial era.

Northern Quiescence and Southern Darkness

It could be argued that all the protagonists in the colonial wealth debate are correct, but none of them has articulated how local trends relate to trends for the thirteen colonies combined. Urban inequality *did* rise in some cities, perhaps supplying fuel for revolution and social change. Inequality and social stratification *did* rise to high levels in some settled agrarian regions along the Atlantic coast, especially those from which young men were slow to emigrate. Inequality even rose over time in some frontier settlements. The important point, however, is that new frontiers were being added at a very rapid rate. The opportunities for wealth accumulation were there in the interior, and they were exploited assiduously. The result was both extensive and intensive development in the interior of the northern colonies, where wealth per capita grew relative to the seacoast settlements. This produced a leveling influence, since the new settlements were comparatively poor to start with. Total wealth and population shifted to the interior as well, and this too had a leveling influence, since equality was more a frontier attribute.

The net effect was to produce quiescence in the wealth inequality among northern colonists, a quiescence that matches the absence of

[15] Take the case of Boston. Rapid growth early in the eighteenth century would imply a rise in the proportion of young adults in the adult population, increased age dispersion, and, given in addition migration selectivity, an inequality bias. We should count more poor, the percentage on relief should have risen, and probate records along with tax lists should produce rising concentration ratios. The opposite should have been true following the 1730s, when young people (without much wealth) must have fled Boston's stagnating economy. The Boston probate records document historical concentration trends that may be explained at least in part by these (alleged) age distribution changes. That is, some portion of the inequality trend from 1700 to 1730 (Fig. 2.2) must be accounted for by the presumed rise in the relative number of young adults.

strong per capita growth in income and wealth (Anderson and Thomas, 1978; Anderson, 1979; Kulikoff, 1979).

If future research is to uncover a widespread colonial trend toward more concentrated wealth, it will have to light up the statistical darkness surrounding southern wealth distribution trends. As we have noted, the only local long-run time series on colonial southern wealth come from the Chesapeake. There is a good chance that new southern data would reveal widening inequalities, even though southerners were already very unequal when they crossed the Atlantic in the seventeenth century. One source of rising inequality was the rise of slavery. Slaves were about 8% of the population of the thirteen colonies around 1690 and over 21% by 1770. If this massive influx of virtually propertyless households is counted as part of the southern population as well as part of the economic assets of slave owners, it must have imparted an upward trend to southern wealth inequality and to wealth inequality in the thirteen colonies as a whole. We suspect that later scholarship will conclude that southern inequality became more acute from Jamestown to the Civil War. And within the colonial period the high initial wealth of free southerners, particularly slave owners, suggests that the rise of slavery may well have significantly widened inequalities for the entire thirteen-colony population— especially, of course, if we count slaves both as people and as others' assets. It seems likely that the South, rather than northern towns, offered the largest contributions to rising aggregate inequality before the Revolution.

3

TRENDS IN WEALTH INEQUALITY SINCE 1774

Introduction

INEQUALITY TRENDS AND MODERN GROWTH

The inequality of American wealth holding has not been an eternal constant. While the colonial era was one of relative egalitarianism and stable wealth distribution, it was followed by an episode of rising wealth concentration lasting for more than a century. By the early twentieth century, wealth concentration had become as great in the United States as in France or Prussia, though still less pronounced than in the United Kingdom, to judge from some tentative comparisons of probate returns. This episodic rise in wealth concentration seems to have occurred primarily in the antebellum period, with the most dramatic shift toward concentration apparently taking place in the second quarter of the nineteenth century.

Wealth inequality declined in three periods, the most recent decline being the most pronounced. First, while northern wealth inequality remained almost unchanged during the Civil War decade, southern inequality was reduced dramatically by slave emancipation. This revolutionary leveling in southern wealth contrasted with, and outweighed, the opening of new inequalities in wealth (as well as income) between North and South. Second, the distribution of wealth leveled briefly but sharply during World War I. Third, the last period of declining wealth inequality coincided with the "income revolution" documented by Kuznets (1953) and proclaimed by Arthur Burns (1954). That is, wealth inequality declined between the late 1920s and the mid-twentieth century. In contrast with the previous periods of wealth leveling, the twentieth-century leveling has not been reversed.

American experience suggests a confirmation of Kuznets's hypothesis of an early rise and later decline in inequality during long-term modern economic growth. Furthermore, it appears that the inequality of wealth holding today resembles what it was on the eve of the Declaration of Independence.

Any effective theory of wealth distribution must deal with these long-term changes in concentration over time. The greatest challenge to existing theory, of course, will be the apparent episodic shifts in wealth concentration at two points in American history: First, the marked rise in wealth concentration in the first half of the nineteenth century following what appears to have been two centuries of long-term stability; second, the pronounced decline in wealth concentration in the second quarter of the twentieth century following what appears to have been six decades of persistent and extensive inequality with no clear evidence of trend. Furthermore, these episodic shifts in American wealth inequality were not merely the product of demographic-mix changes. Changes in age composition, for example, fail to account for either of these revolutionary shifts in aggregate wealth inequality. Thus, while the life-cycle model may help account for inequality levels at points in time, it fails to offer an explanation for inequality trends over time. In addition, it cannot be argued that American inequality trends have been influenced in any important way by changes in the size of the immigrant population stock.

These are the tentative findings of this chapter. Before we go further, however, two issues must be confronted: motivation and measurement.

MOTIVATION AND MEASUREMENT

Whereas some observers care about income and wealth inequality itself, others appear to be more concerned about justice, opportunity, and social mobility. Injustice, not inequality, is central to any debate over institutions that foster discrimination by race or sex. Immobility is central to those concerned with the impact of genes, inheritance, and other dimensions of family background, not unequal outcomes. Yet information on wealth inequality is crucial even to debates on economic justice, mobility, and opportunity. To judge the importance of discriminatory rules or other barriers to mobility in producing economic inequality, it is important to measure wealth gaps between rich and poor. If the richest 1% of households has always held only 20% more wealth than the poorest 1%, then being born male to rich parents can only buy a 20% ticket at most. By contrast, if the richest 1% has always held a thousand times more wealth than the poorest 1%, then investigating the extent and sources of injustice and immobility would have far more to recommend it.

Furthermore, inequality may itself help foster attitudes of contempt that exacerbate discrimination and socioeconomic immobility.

The problems of measurement are well known, and they involve the time interval over which income or wealth is to be measured, the income or wealth concept, the recipient unit, and the summary statistic for computing inequality. As for the time interval, it seems clear that the greatest welfare meaning can be attached to lifetime income from all sources, or its capitalized counterpart—total personal wealth—viewed from a given age. Such measures better capture material well-being than any one of those usually available: annual income, annual earnings, or the stock of nonhuman wealth. Like other researchers, however, we have been forced to retreat to less perfect measures. This and the previous chapter analyze the available data on the distribution of nonhuman net worth alone (including the ownership of slaves), in the knowledge that it sheds light on trends in lifetime income inequality in two ways. First, movements in nonhuman wealth inequality are likely to reflect movements in current property income if the slope relating the average rate of return to the size of household wealth does not change significantly over time. Second, wealth inequality trends are likely to correspond with earlier movements in overall income inequality if the marginal propensities to save and rates of return maintain stable relationships with levels of income and wealth, respectively. Time series on wealth inequality are valuable mainly because they relate to the inequality of lifetime income in these indirect ways, and also because wealth-distribution data exist from earlier time periods, well before household surveys and income tax returns were available to supply estimates for the distribution of current income.[1]

Ambiguity relating to the population unit selected and the summary inequality statistic employed also blurs, though it does not greatly obscure, the meaning of trends and levels in wealth inequality. Wealth is shared to varying degrees among relatives and coresidents, complicating the definition of just who it is that has access to that wealth. The "household" offers a unit of observation which is probably as satisfactory a

---

[1] One should resist the meritocratic temptation to single out nonhuman wealth as that part of total lifetime income or wealth that is of special interest because it is inherited and not based on individual productivity. The distribution of wealth is affected by much more than inheritance. Some people save a greater share of their earnings than others, giving rise to a component of wealth inequality that is less repugnant to most people than differences in inheritance. The present data do not allow us to separate the effects of differences in saving rates from those of differences in inheritance. The mixing of inheritance with individual accumulation also characterizes human capital and earnings, of course, since parental wealth and abilities are strong determinants of human investments. The case for studying the separate distribution of nonhuman wealth is not based on its having a separate welfare meaning, but on its greater accessibility.

resolution as can be had for the question "Whose wealth is it?" In addition, recent work has shown that the summary inequality statistic selected can influence the ranking of different distributions by inequality. One distribution may appear to reveal great inequality when a Gini coefficient is used, less inequality when an entropy measure is used, and virtual equality when top shareholder percentages are used (Atkinson, 1970). Behind this diversity in rankings of given distributions lie more basic differences in what aspects of inequality we care about most: Some observers care most about the gap between the richest and the median, which is featured by some statistics, and others care most about the gap between the median and the poorest, which is featured by competing statistics. In order to compare studies of wealth distribution in different time periods, this chapter concentrates on the three measures most commonly provided by these studies—the share of wealth held by the richest 1% of households, the share held by the richest 10%, and the Gini coefficient—with attention to variance measures where decomposition identities are useful. Our conclusions imply a belief that the major changes in wealth inequality revealed by American history would be evident regardless of the inequality statistic employed.

These comments set the stage. Measurement of inequality through historical time is fraught with problems, and thus this chapter is long. But the exercise is an essential prerequisite to any serious modeling of long-term inequality dynamics in America.

Wealth Concentration in the First Century of Independence

THE 1774, 1860, AND 1870 BENCHMARKS

For the century inaugurated by the Declaration of Independence, we now have benchmarks for nationwide distributions. A. H. Jones (1978) has constructed one set of estimates for 1774 using probate inventories and the estate-multiplier method, by which the wealth distribution of the living is reconstructed from that of decedents. For the end of the century, Soltow (1975) has used large manuscript census samples to derive size distributions of total assets for 1860 and 1870.

Table 3.1 reports that the top 1% of free wealth holders in 1774 held 12.6% of total assets, while the richest 10% held a little less than half of total assets. In 1860, the richest percentile held 29% of total American assets, and the richest decile held 73%.[2] Thus, the top-percentile share

---

[2] These dramatic trends can also be captured by shifts in the ratios of average wealth at the top to average wealth economy-wide. Between 1774 and 1860 the ratio of the average wealth

more than doubled and the top decile increased its share by half again of its previous level. Among free adult males, the Gini coefficient on total assets rises from .632 to .832. Equally dramatic surges are implied for the South and non-South separately.

The rise in wealth inequality is still evident if one includes slaves as part of the population. Counting slaves both as potential wealth holders and as wealth has the effect of raising estimated inequality before the Civil War. This follows from the reasonable assumption that slaves had zero assets and net worth. Adding extra ''wealth holders'' with zero wealth is equivalent to scaling down the share of the population represented by the same number of top wealth holders. This adjustment should be greater for 1774 than for 1860, since the slave-population share peaked at about 21.4% in 1770 and declined to about 11% by 1860. Thus counting slaves as both people and property, a defensible procedure, should have raised the inequality measure more for 1774 than for 1860. Nevertheless, Table 3.1 suggests that this adjustment has little effect on the net rise in inequality between these two dates.

The 1774 colonial wealth distribution bears a close resemblance to the (revised) distribution implied by the Federal Reserve survey for 1962, discussed later in this chapter. The share held by the richest 1% was apparently a little lower in 1774, both among the free and among the free plus slaves. On the other hand, the top-decile share appears to have been somewhat higher on the eve of the Revolution than it was nearly two centuries later.[3]

If the figures in Table 3.1 are allowed to stand without adjustment, then they reveal an epochal rise in wealth concentration between 1774 and 1860. Tocqueville (1839) anticipated this trend toward concentration, pointing to the rise of an industrial elite which he feared would destroy the economic foundation of American egalitarianism:

> I am of the opinion . . . that the manufacturing aristocracy which is growing up under our eyes is one of the harshest that ever existed. . . . The friends of democracy should keep their eyes anxiously fixed in this direction; for if a

---

of the top 1% of wealth holders to the average wealth of the lower 99% rose from 14.0 to 40.4. Over the same period, the ratio of the top decile's average wealth to that of the bottom 90% rose from 8.54 to 24.3. Both ratios nearly tripled.

[3] There is good reason to believe that the comparison between 1962 and 1774 *understates* relative equality in the mid-twentieth century. Human capital embodied in slaves is included as a portion of total wealth held by rich slaveholders in the colonial South. This capital was transferred to poor blacks with emancipation. Conventional wealth accounting, however, fails to include nonslave human capital. Thus, whereas the demise of slave wealth serves to lower inequality after the Civil War, the augmentation of human capital among the lowest wealth classes—the freed slaves—is not captured. In short, an important source of wealth leveling is ignored by our accounting conventions.

TABLE 3.1
Selected Measures of Wealth Inequality in the United States, 1774, 1860, 1870, and 1962

Period and Wealth-Holding Unit	Net Worth			Total Assets		
	Percentage Held by Top 1%	Percentage Held by Top 10%	Gini Coefficient	Percentage Held by Top 1%	Percentage Held by Top 10%	Gini Coefficient
1774 (13 colonies)						
Free households	14.3%	53.2%	.694	12.6%	49.6%	.642
Free and slave households	16.5	59.0	n.a.	14.8	55.1	n.a.
Free adult males	14.2	52.5	.688	12.4	48.7	.632
All adult males	16.5	58.4	n.a.	13.2	54.3	n.a.
Southern free households	10.7	47.3	.664	9.9	46.3	.649
Non-South, free households	17.1	49.5	.678	14.1	43.8	.594
1860						
Free adult males				29.0	73.0	.832
Adult males				30.3–35.0	74.6–79.0	n.a.
Southern free adult males				27.0	75.0	.845
Non-South, free adult males				27.0	68.0	.813

permanent inequality of conditions and aristocracy . . . penetrates into [America], it may be predicted that this is the gate by which they will enter [1963 ed., p. 161].

Jackson T. Main suspected that Tocqueville's fear was borne out by subsequent events, at least based on his early rough estimates of wealth inequality on the eve of the Revolution and Gallman's (1969) findings for 1860 (J. T. Main, 1971). Gallman suspected a rise in wealth inequality after 1810, though for different reasons. Edward Pessen took a similar position, debunking "the era of the common man" with evidence of rising wealth inequality and social stratification (1973). Soltow (1971b, 1975) has opposed this view, arguing instead that wealth inequality remained unchanged across the nineteenth century.

Did a marked shift toward wealth concentration really take place?

POSSIBLE BENCHMARK BIASES AND WEIGHT SHIFTS

There are several ways that the figures in Table 3.1 might be judged misleading. The obvious frontal assault is to claim that the underlying data are simply unreliable.

TABLE 3.1 (Continued)

Period and Wealth-Holding Unit	Net Worth			Total Assets		
	Percentage Held by Top 1%	Percentage Held by Top 10%	Gini Coefficient	Percentage Held by Top 1%	Percentage Held by Top 10%	Gini Coefficient
1870						
Adult males				27.0	70.0	.833
Southern adult males				33.0	77.0	.866
Southern adult white males				29.0	73.0	.818
Non-South, adult males				24.0	67.0	.816
1962						
All consumer units ranked by total assets, unadjusted	36.9	69.1–82.6	n.a.	26.0	61.6	.76
All consumer units ranked by total assets, revised	20.6	38.5–46.1	n.a.	15.1	35.7	n.a.

Sources and notes: The 1774 wealth distributions are from A. H. Jones (1978, Vol. 3, Table 8.1). We are grateful to Professor Jones for advice and access to unpublished calculations that were useful as cross-checks to our own computations. We also wish to thank Roger C. Lister for performing the 1774 computer calculations for this and the next table. The 1860 and 1870 figures are from Soltow (1975, pp. 99, 103). The 1962 figures are derived from Projector and Weiss (1966, Tables 8, A2, A8, A14, and A36).

The sample sizes on which these calculations are based follow. For 1774: 919 decedents, of whom 839 were males and 298 were from the South. For 1860: spin sample of 13,696 males; of whom 27.6% were from the South. For 1870: spin sample of 9823 males. For 1962: 2557 consumer units.

For definitions of net worth, total assets, and the population unit, see the sources cited above. It should be remembered that the 1774 and 1860 calculations include the asset values of slaves in the total assets and net worth of their owners.

The calculations referring to the total population, free plus slave, include slaves as households with zero assets and net worth as part of the population. In these calculations, slaves are thus both people and property. Their share of the 1770 population of households was estimated by multiplying both the total free and slave populations by a proxy for the ratio of households to population. This proxy was the share of negroes and mulattoes over 16 years of age in Maryland in 1755 in the case of slaves (*Historical Statistics*, 1975, Part 2, Chap. Z), and the share of white males over 16 for 1790 (*Historical Statistics*, 1975, Part 1, Series A119–134) for the free population. Assuming the same ratio of household heads to adults among slaves as among the free, and applying the adult-to-population ratios to the slave and free populations yields the estimate that slave households were 20.2% of all households in 1770, which is applied to 1774.

Point estimates (single values) are reported for cases in which we judged the range between high and low estimates based on different interpolations within wealth classes to be sufficiently narrow. Where the range implied by alternative methods of interpolation was wide, we have reported a range of values. The latter are not to be interpreted as true lower and upper bounds, since errors could arise from factors other than just interpolating shares within the wealth classes supplied by the underlying data.

Our results show lower inequality for 1774 than was reported by A. H. Jones (1978, Vol. 3) for two reasons. The first is that Professor Jones has concluded that her regional weights within the South require revision so as to reduce the weight of prosperous Charleston to 1% of the South, as she will report in her forthcoming volume for Columbia University Press. We have used her revised regional weights here and wish to thank her for informing us of the revision. The second relates to an apparent slight deviation in our procedure from hers in constructing the "$w*B$" weights used to convert the sample decedents to the estimated population of living wealth holders. The differences are slight, however, with Professor Jones's revised size distributions (forthcoming) resembling ours much more than they resemble her earlier (1978) size distributions.

Since her 1774 sample consisted of only 919 observations, as against the 13,696 observations used by Soltow for 1860, it is natural to point the finger of suspicion at Alice Hanson Jones. As far as the asset coverage and population unit are concerned, however, we see no clear bias. Although the probate inventories she used may well exclude some financial assets or liabilities, no clear effect on the size distribution of net worth or total assets is obvious. Unleased real estate was excluded from the inventories outside of the New England colonies, yet Professor Jones supplied the missing real estate values from predictions implied by regressions estimated on the New England observations. As for the population unit, Professor Jones tried to make the basic population that of all households in the thirteen colonies by assuming that a large majority of adult females were not household heads. Should one wish to compare an all-male wealth distribution in 1774 with that for 1860 or 1870, the comparison is reported in Table 3.1, with little difference in the implied trend toward concentration.

The most serious criticism of the underlying probate data is that they cover a biased sample of the population of potential wealth holders. We know that only a minority of decedent household heads left wills and inventories. We know that the set of decedents for whom no inventory survives includes people from all wealth classes. We also know that the main excluded group is the very poor, who left no inventory because they left no wealth to appraise. The net effect is likely to be an undersampling that is more serious for the poorest classes, producing a probate sampling bias that could make wealth inequality look misleadingly low. Given the extent to which probate records will remain a critical data base in future historical research, it is important that more detailed studies be devoted to cross-checking the probate inventory samples against other primary data identifying the wealth, occupation, and other attributes of the population from which the probates survive. It is especially important to identify the wealthiest and most prominent citizens in earlier centuries, to quantify the sampling ratio for the rich. Such research into probate bias has already begun (D. S. Smith, 1975; G. Main, 1976), but much remains to be done.

Professor A. H. Jones has already performed sensitivity analyses to determine the importance of the probate sampling bias. Her estimates reported in Table 3.1 are based on the assumption that the probate inventories undersampled the poorer wealth classes. In the net worth size distribution, for example, these "$w*B$" weighted results are based on an underlying assumption that the bottom net-worth decile includes from five to eighty times more nonprobated decedents than the top decile, the relative ratio varying from region to region. These multipliers are based in part on Professor Jones's own limited cross-checks between the probate samples and other source materials, such as local tax lists. The multipliers must, however, be characterized as guesses, and guesses that lack the guidance of any colonial contemporary judgments regarding which people were eluding probate.

Consider what kinds of errors in these probate sampling multipliers might have led to a serious underestimation of wealth inequality in 1774. Perhaps the poor have still been relatively undersampled, despite Professor Jones's attempt to augment their numbers. Although such undersampling is a possibility, an alternative set of weights that uniformly expanded the numbers in the bottom quarter of wealth holding (Jones's "$w*A$" weights) showed no greater inequality than the preferred "$w*B$" weights used here. Another possibility is that the very rich were undersampled as well. Yet, it must be remembered that the very wealthy would have had little incentive to hide their wealth from probate in 1774. There were no estate taxes to avoid, and even the local property taxes on the living were light enough to offer little incentive to keep property hidden from the probate appraiser, or to motivate *inter vivos* transfers.

One can also question the reliability of the 1860 census returns underlying Soltow's recent book. It might be argued that respondents gave very casual answers to the census takers. In particular, a large number of them may have reported zero wealth in order to avoid the bother of estimating asset value. Fully 38% of free adult males reported property less than $100 in the 1860 census sample, but it is hard to tell what share of these actually reported zero wealth. At the other end of the wealth spectrum, one might speculate that the very rich overstated their wealth in the 1860 and 1870 censuses, but this is a hard conjecture to sustain. Again, we know of no clear bias in the estimates, either for 1774 or for 1860.

Another common suspicion relates not to the quality of the data but to the potentially distorting effect of shifts in demographic weights, such as changes in the age distribution, changes in nativity, and changes in urbanization. Reflecting the sophistication with which economists approach measures of income or wealth inequality in the 1970s, many have expressed the view that the antebellum rise in wealth inequality may be a mirage caused by shifts toward an older population or by shifts in the share foreign-born or the share living in cities. To address such skepticism, we need to ascertain whether there was a rise in wealth inequality among people of given age, place of birth, and area of residence.

Elsewhere we have performed detailed calculations quantifying the direct contributions of aging, immigration, and urbanization to the nineteenth-century rise in wealth concentration (Williamson and Lindert, 1977, Sections 3.3–3.5). The overall result is unmistakable: these shifts in group weights do not account for the observed widening of the gap between rich and poor.

Changes in age distribution again fail to live up to their potential, as in the colonial era. In principle, a dramatic rise in the share of adults under 30 could have accounted for the nineteenth-century rise in wealth inequality, especially if the richest age group, 55–64, had risen relative to the middle-wealth age groups (30–54 and 65+). But no such dramatic age shift took place. In one experiment, using 1774 age–wealth patterns, we found that the small observed shifts in age distributions could account for less than 6% of the observed rise in wealth concentration between 1774 and 1860. In another, using Wisconsin 1860 age–wealth patterns, we found the age shifts would actually have lowered wealth inequality over the same period, raising the amount of antebellum widening to be explained.

The rise in the share of Americans born abroad might have widened wealth gaps both directly and indirectly. The direct effect could have come from the addition of relatively poor immigrants at the bottom of the wealth ranks. The indirect effect would have worked through the effects of immigration on factor rewards and income, thereby affecting wealth inequality: a surge of low-paid immigrants would lower wage rates even for native-born common laborers, widening income and wealth gaps throughout the economy. Soltow's (1975, Chap. 4) data for 1860 and 1870 cast doubt on the importance of the direct effect. The Gini coefficients for native Americans and for all Americans differ by only 2%, a very small share of the observed widening before 1860. The rising tide of immigration cannot directly explain rising wealth inequality. Its relevance to the nineteenth-century widening would have to lie in its indirect effects through rates of pay and income, a theme we pick up again in Chapter 9.

The antebellum wealth inequality trend is not a mirage induced by age and nativity forces, but perhaps urbanization accounts for the aggregate trends. The motivation here is somewhat different from that in the case of age and nativity, since even if we found the inequality surge to be solely urban based, this would *not* diminish its importance. After all, while nativity and age-distribution changes may be viewed in large part as exogenous variables in American antebellum development, urbanization surely cannot be so viewed. In any case, it would be of some value to sort out the key sources of the antebellum inequality trend along urban–rural lines, especially given the conventional wisdom that urbanization can "account for" the vast majority of inequality trends during early modern growth.

In a separate experiment (Williamson and Lindert, 1977, Section 3.5) we found that while urbanization served to raise inequality in the first three-quarters of the nineteenth century, its contribution to the aggregate inequality surge appears to have been minor. This again implies that the vast majority of the antebellum wealth inequality surge in America showed itself *within* sectors and regions.

WHEN AND WHERE DID WEALTH BECOME MORE CONCENTRATED?

Other independent measures of wealth inequality trends between these 1774 and 1860 benchmarks are essential to test the implications of the A. H. Jones and Soltow–Gallman research.

Gathering data on the estates of the very richest families and comparing their aggregate value with rough estimates of the wealth of the entire nation, Gallman (1969, Table 2) found that the share held by top .031% rose from 6.9% in 1840 to 7.2–7.6% in 1850, and then to 14.3–19.1% in 1890. The suggestion that inequality between the super-rich and the rest of the nation rose across the 1840s supplies a valuable clue, even though Gallman's data do not allow a comparison between middle- and low-wealth shares.

Soltow reaches the opposite conclusion, based on real estate distributions in 1850 and 1860. For both these years, and for 1870, census marshals asked respondents to state the value of their land and buildings gross of lien. Sampling these returns, Soltow (1975, Chap. 4) has found no net change in real estate inequality across the 1850s, the top quantile shares almost exactly matching the same shares of total estate in 1860. Stability in the inequality of real estate would surely limit inequality trends for the 1850s, given that real estate was nearly 60% of the total value of wealth in 1860. Still, firm conclusions about inequality in total estate cannot be reached from the distribution of real estate alone.

The remaining time-series evidence comes from regions and cities. For the late antebellum South, Gavin Wright (1978, pp. 29–37) has presented data on the inequality of improved acreage, farm real estate values, farm physical wealth (land, buildings, slaves, implements) and cotton output from the Parker–Gallman farm sample in cotton counties. Wright found only a slight rise in inequality for the 1850s, though the second and third deciles from the top gained noticeably at the expense of the top decile and the lower 70%. This result seems to reinforce Soltow's finding of no net change in real estate concentration for the South (as well as for the nation) across the 1850s.

Enough data do exist to construct size distributions for slaveholding over a much longer portion of the antebellum period. Soltow's work with the slave-owning data has led to the summary figures shown in Table 3.2. Soltow himself (1971a) concluded that there was no change in slavehold-

TABLE 3.2
Unequal Slaveholding in the South, 1790–1860

	1790	1830	1850	1860
Five regions on the eastern seaboard				
No. of slaves per slaveholder	8.3	9.6	9.8	10.2
No. of slaveholders per family	.35	.36	.30	.25
No. of slaves per family	2.9	3.5	2.9	2.6
Gini coefficient, among				
slaveholders only	.572	.573	.582	.597
Share held by top 1%				
of slaveholders	13.4%	13.0%	14.2%	13.7%
of families	22.5%	26.7%	27.9%	30.5%
Four regions on the eastern seaboard				
Share held by top 10%				
of families	74.0%	75.2%		
Entire South				
Share held by top 10%				
of families		71.5%		82.3%

Source and notes: Soltow (1971a, Tables 1 and 2) draws on both official census publications and his own sample of families and slaveholders from the manuscript censuses.

The regions consisted of most of Maryland, the District of Columbia, and North Carolina, plus parts of South Carolina. The fifth region added to these was most of Virginia, with some property tax returns for 1780 educating the underlying estimates for Virginia.

Professor Soltow's tables of size distributions across numbers-of-slaves classes reported some of the assumed class means. We have assumed others using what seem to be comparable procedures.

ing inequality among slaveholders. Yet the more relevant measure is one that examines inequality among *all* families, not just slaveholders. As Soltow notes, slaveholders were a declining share of all free families. Therefore what is at most a modest rise in inequality of slaveholding among slaveholders after 1830 becomes a pronounced rise in slaveholding inequality among all families (Table 3.2). Contrary to the findings of G. Wright for the cotton South, the entire South shows a rise in the 1850s in slaveholding inequality, apparently part of a longer-term trend. The years after 1830, and perhaps even after 1790, exhibit rising inequality in southern slaveholding.

The remaining antebellum observations on wealth distributions are mainly from northeastern cities.[4] The tax and probate data for these areas

[4] This state of affairs need not continue. For the 1850s, more can be done from the manuscript federal and state census returns on real estate value, farm acreage, and farm implements, either with the Bateman–Foust and Soltow samples, or with new samples. Local tax returns can also be exploited more fully. In addition, Gallman's procedure of tracking down the wealth of the richest individuals for comparison with rough wealth aggregates can be extended to other dates and to regions. Above all, as we shall mention in the text, the vast numbers of probate inventories, a few of them collected and referenced in

% Held by Top
Wealth Holders

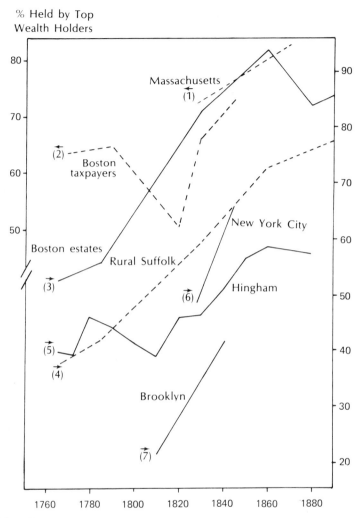

FIGURE 3.1. Dating the rise of antebellum wealth concentration: Northeast. From Appendix C. (1) = top decile shares of net worth among all decedents, Massachusetts; (2) = top decile shares of taxable wealth among taxpayers, Boston; (3) = top decile shares total wealth among adult males, Boston; (4) = top decile total wealth among adult males, rural Suffolk County, Mass.; (5) = top decile shares of total taxable wealth among property taxpayers and adult males without property, Hingham, Mass.; (6) = share of nonbusiness wealth held by top 4%, New York City; (7) = share of nonbusiness wealth held by top 1%, Brooklyn.

the Library of the Genealogical Society of the Church of Jesus Christ of Latter-Day Saints near Salt Lake City, promise better perspectives on wealth distributions from the colonial period until the onset of estate tax returns in the 1920s.

have yielded the top quantile shares displayed in Figure 3.1. These supply a valuable corroboration on the 1774 and 1860 benchmarks, since they are derived by different scholars, with possibly different sampling techniques, and in some cases with different kinds of data (e.g., tax returns).

Two striking patterns emerge from Figure 3.1. First, it suggests when the steepest trend toward concentration set in. The local tax returns from Boston and neighboring Hingham show troughs in the 1810s and 1820s. William Newell reports similar findings among testators in Butler County, Ohio (Newell, 1977, Fig. 2, p. 9). The two top quantile shares from this period for New York City and Brooklyn are also much lower than those for the 1840s. Each series shows steep increases after 1830, as did the southern slaveholding returns, and as do estate data for Butler County, Ohio (Newell, 1977, p. 9). Second, rates of increase in the top decile shares per decade seem to average about the same as that derived for total assets among all free households between 1774 and 1860 (about 4.6% per decade as a percentage of the share itself, according to Table 3.1 above). It appears, therefore, that the movement toward wealth concentration occurred *within* regions, just as it seems to have occurred within given age groups, among native or foreign born, and within rural and urban populations.[5]

Although no rich empirical feast can be prepared from such scraps, the appetizer should certainly stimulate further expeditions into early nineteenth-century archives. The working hypothesis seems now to be that wealth concentration rose over most of the period 1774–1860, with especially steep increases from the 1820s to the late 1840s. It should also be noted that these two or three decades coincide with early industrial acceleration, and, as we shall see in Chapter 4, with a period in which wage gaps between skilled and unskilled occupational groups seemed to widen.

The Uneven High Plateau: Civil War to Great Depression

TIME-SERIES CLUES

The seven decades following the Civil War mark a period for which wealth inequality remained very high and exhibited no significant long-

---

[5] It would be interesting to explore the extent to which the rise in urban inequality was due to the influx of immigrants from other countries and from the U.S. countryside, thus paralleling the experiments we performed on the effects of immigration at the national level. The data for doing so were not available at time of writing however.

TABLE 3.3

Top Decile Shares of Total Wealth among Adult U.S. Males, 1860 and 1870 (in percentages)

	1860 Free	1860 All	1870 White	1870 All
United States	73%	74.6–79.0%	68%	70%
South	75	(very high)	70	77
North	68	68	67	67

Sources: Table 3.2 and Soltow (1975, p. 99).

term trend. This judgment is based on slim evidence, since the period is illuminated statistically only near its start and finish. The half-century between the 1870 census and the onset of modern estate tax returns— begun in 1919 and reported after 1922—is an empirical Dark Age for wealth distributions. It need not remain this way. Probate records are rich for most of this pretax era. For the moment, however, we must rely on a data base which is less extensive for this half-century than for 1860 or even 1774.

The manuscript censuses have allowed Soltow to compare the distribution of total assets in 1860 and 1870. The dominant intervening event during the decade was slave emancipation, a massive confiscation from the richest strata of southern society. Thus, the net change across the 1860s was a shift toward more equal wealth holding for the United States as a whole, whether we count slaves as part of the wealth-holding population or not. The movement of top-decile shares is shown in Table 3.3. The leveling within the South was apparently sufficient to outweigh the contribution to total U.S. wealth inequality implied by the opening up of a

TABLE 3.4

Holmes's Estimated Wealth Distribution for American Families in 1890

Class	Number of Families (thousands)	Net Worth (millions of dollars)
Lowest	1,440.0	$ 216.0
	752.8	1,359.7
	1,756.4	5,309.6
	5,159.8	2,579.9
to	720.6	1,142.5
	1,764.3	6,749.1
	1,092.2	30,643.2
Highest	4.0	12,000.0
Total	12,690.2	60,000.0

Source: Holmes (1893, pp. 591–592).

new wealth gap between North and South. Within the North, meanwhile, there was either no change or a slight leveling across the 1860s.

The next set of clues is offered by the census year 1890. As we noted above, Gallman's richest .031% increased their share of total wealth to 14.3–19.1% in 1890, from 7.2–7.6% at mid-century. The rest of the Lorenz curve for 1890 has been estimated by Holmes (1893). The 1890 census supplied data on farm and home ownership in twenty-two states and Holmes extrapolated this sample to the national distribution. Furthermore, using reported mortgage debt in the census, Holmes was able to approximate net worth as opposed to gross wealth, thus making the distributions more comparable to Lampman's 1922 net estate benchmark (1959). Holmes estimated a full distribution of wealth from this data base and, by the imaginative use of other information, generated the distribution for 1890 reproduced in Table 3.4.

Holmes's guesses imply that the top 1% and 10% of American families held, respectively, 25.76% and 72.17% of the wealth. Interpolation suggests that the top 1.4% claimed 28.13% of the total wealth. By comparison, Lampman (1959, Table 6, p. 388) calculated that the top 1.4% of families held 29.2% of the total wealth in 1922.[6] To the extent that comparability holds, wealth concentration increased only slightly between 1890 and 1922.[7]

Better estimates of national wealth distributions around World War I are offered by the Federal Trade Commission's early research. In 1926 the commission published the results of a special survey in which 43,512 probate estate valuations were collected from 23 counties in thirteen states plus the District of Columbia. The survey covered the years 1912–1923.[8] Table 3.5 exploits the FTC data, though it should be emphasized

---

[6] Lampman's modern estimates for 1922 are to be preferred, of course, but King (1927, p. 152) estimated a wealth distribution for 1921 from which it can be inferred that the top 1.4% of *persons* held 31.51% of the total wealth. Lampman and King are remarkably close, it seems to us, and either estimate for the early 1920s implies the same mild upward drift in concentration following 1890.

[7] Professor Lampman (1959) was apparently in error when he rejected Holmes's estimate of the 1890 wealth concentration with the statement: "It is difficult to believe that wealth was actually that highly concentrated in 1890 in view of the 1921 and 1922 measures [p. 388, n. 14]." This statement is apparently based on the mistaken impression that Spahr's (1896) allegation that the top 1% held 51% of 1890 wealth could be attributed to Holmes as well. On the contrary, Holmes's results are quite in line with Lampman's estimates.

[8] In addition, the commission sampled 540 estates of $1 million and over from New York, Philadelphia, and Chicago for 1918–1923, using the earliest estate tax returns.

The data work sheets underlying the entire FTC income and wealth study are currently available in the Washington National Records Center in Suitland, Maryland. The 1912–1923

that these distributions relate to those dying in the sampled counties, and the sample contains only one major city, Washington, D.C. If the sample had contained a more accurate representation of the urban eastern seaboard, inequalities at death would look even greater for these years. On the other hand, both King's and our procedures for including the nonprobated decedents may tend to overstate the wealth inequality of decedents. These potential biases make it hazardous to compare these size distributions with ones that attempt to estimate wealth inequality among the living.

The FTC results for 1912 and 1923 can, however, be used to reveal the likely net change in net worth inequality between these dates. Table 3.6 reveals a sharp drop in wealth inequality across World War I, either in terms of the top quantile share or in terms of the Gini coefficient. The wealth leveling replicates findings emerging from two other strands of research. First, it appears that World War I was a pronounced leveler of incomes and wage ratios (see Chap. 4). Second, Stanley Lebergott's evidence suggests that mobility into and out of the ranks of top wealth holders was great across the same era (Lebergott, 1976b). The First World War was a sharp but brief leveler, perhaps because of its sudden inflation, perhaps because of its effects on labor supply and product demand.

Wealth inequality trends across the 1920s can be gauged by the application of estate-multiplier methods to the returns of the estate tax initiated in 1916. Lampman (1962) performed that task some time ago, and his figures show an unmistakable rise in the shares held by the richest between 1922 and 1929. The top percentile share among all adults rose from 31.6% of total equity in 1922 to 36.3% in 1929. As we shall see in Chapter 4, here again the top quantile measures of wealth inequality display positive correlation with movements in income inequality. The 1920s were years in

---

probate sample has the file designation Tab 5 Cou 5. Our colleague Victor Goldberg has kindly sampled these files for us and reports that the counties sent varying details back to the FTC. Although they all provided the size distributions the commission requested, they did not provide the individual wealth data in all cases, and apparently there is no consistency in further detail volunteered by the county officers. Some gave the names of the decedents, some did not; some broke down wealth into asset categories, some did not; and so forth.

Scholars in serious pursuit of further data on historical wealth should also consider two other potential sources in addition to the FTC data files. One is the Composition of Estates Survey of about 100,000 probated estates, collected by the WPA, but not analyzed by them because federal funds ran out (Mendershausen, 1956, p. 279n). The other is an unsampled set of files at the National Bureau of Economic Research in New York marked "W. I. King data files," the existence of which was kindly reported to us by Geoffrey H. Moore of the bureau.

TABLE 3.5

The Distribution of Wealth from FTC Sampled Estates, 1912 and 1923: Two Estimates

	1912				1923			
	King		Williamson–Lindert		King		Williamson–Lindert	
Wealth Class	No. of Individuals	Value	No. of Individuals	Value	No. of Individuals	Value	No. of Individuals	Value
Not probated	4,624	$ 448,528	5,914	$ 573,658	4,805	$ 494,915	6,146	$ 633,038
< $500	469	119,353	469	119,353	462	124,775	462	124,775
500–1,000	360	255,070	360	255,070	406	287,638	406	287,638
1,000–2,500	599	983,480	599	983,480	817	1,334,301	817	1,334,301
2,500–5,000	486	1,715,689	486	1,715,689	731	2,607,015	731	2,607,015
5,000–10,000	370	2,613,262	370	2,613,262	643	4,585,009	643	4,585,009
10,000–25,000	316	4,822,552	316	4,822,552	623	9,411,982	623	9,411,982
25,000–50,000	140	4,966,955	140	4,966,955	242	8,464,878	242	8,464,878
50,000–100,000	54	3,699,454	54	3,699,454	136	9,064,680	136	9,064,680
100,000–250,000	42	6,464,171	42	6,464,171	62	9,824,211	62	9,824,211
250,000–500,000	12	4,135,571	12	4,135,571	27	8,718,762	27	8,718,762
500,000–1,000,000	4	2,521,647	4	2,521,647	9	6,198,199	9	6,198,199
1,000,000 <	2	8,165,326	2	8,165,326	2	5,599,535	2	5,599,535
Total	7,478	40,911,058	8,768	41,036,188	8,965	66,715,900	10,306	66,854,023

Sources and notes: The FTC data are reported in U.S. Congress (1926, pp. 58–59). King assumed that those not probated had, on average, $100 at death. The estimates here allow instead for the same average among those not probated, but for a rise from $97 in 1912 to $103 in 1923, the observed rate of increase in the less-than-$500 class. In addition, numbers not probated are estimated as a residual from mortality data in the Williamson-Lindert estimates. The mortality statistics are for registered states reported in U.S. Department of Commerce (1918 and 1923). These supply a trend in crude death rates which is then applied to the FTC aggregate estimate of 184,958 for the whole 1912–1923 period to supply annual estimates for 1912 and 1923. This figure is distributed by sex using U.S. Department of Commerce (1921) proportions. Total potential wealth holders at death are then estimated assuming 25.3% of deceased females were potential wealth holders. The 25.3% figure is derived from FTC 1944 estate tax returns (Mendershausen, 1956).

TABLE 3.6

Wealth Inequality Statistics, 1912 and 1923: Two Estimates

	1912		1923	
Inequality Statistic	King	Williamson–Lindert	King	Williamson–Lindert
Gini coefficient	.9186	.9252	.8878	.8988
% Share of top				
1%	54.38%	56.38%	43.10%	45.68%
5	77.69	79.83	70.18	72.44
10	88.08	90.03	81.24	84.10

Source: Table 3.5.

which the top percentile share of income, the ratios of skilled to unskilled wage rates, and the inverse Pareto slope of income inequality among top income groups also rose.

The period from 1860 to 1929 is thus best described as a high uneven plateau of wealth inequality. When did wealth inequality hit its historic peak? We do not yet know.[9] We do know that there was a leveling across the 1860s. We also know that there was a leveling across the World War I decade (1912–1922), which was reversed largely or entirely by 1929. This leaves three likely candidates for the dubious distinction of being the era of greatest inequality in American personal wealth: c. 1860, c. 1914, and 1929. That each of these pinnacles was followed by a major upheaval— civil war and slave emancipation, world war, or unparalleled depression—suggests interesting hypotheses regarding the effects of these episodic events on wealth inequality (or perhaps even the impact of inequality on these episodic events).

INTERNATIONAL COMPARISONS

The quality of the available wealth distribution data around the turn of the century makes comparisons between shaky U.S. figures and shaky figures from other countries hazardous. Yet a rough comparison can at least be suggested, since the early years of this century were ones for which several countries reported information on one particular kind of wealth distribution, the distribution of wealth among probated decedents.

The comparison in Table 3.7 pivots on the FTC probate distribution of 1912, which shows more inequality than any other measure of wealth dispersion from our history. It may be a biased indicator, but, as we have argued, it is not clear which way the bias runs. The FTC probates understate inequality with their underrepresentation of large cities, yet the assumptions used by King and ourselves to include nonprobated estates may overstate inequality. With all of these qualifications, it appears that America had joined industrialized Europe in terms of its degree

---

[9] We have a few time series of more limited scope, and they also give conflicting indications of trends across the late nineteenth century. The suggestion of a gentle rise in wealth inequality planted by Gallman's (1969) top shares receives some slight support from the gentle rises in the Gini coefficients for Indiana real estate appraisals for 1870–1900 and for U.S. real estate mortgage values for 1880–1889. On the other hand, the various Massachusetts probate and tax series given in Appendix C fail to agree on any trend after 1860, and Soltow feels that wealth inequality in Wisconsin showed a net decline between 1860 and 1900 (1971b, pp. 11, 12). We cannot identify any trends between 1870 and World War I, either in these limited series or in the national wealth distributions available.

TABLE 3.7
Wealth Shares Held by the Top 1% and 10% of Decedents and the Living, Four Nations,
1907–1913

	Wealth Share of	
Country	Top 1%	Top 10%
Among decedents		
United States, 1912: FTC probate sample	56.4%	90.0%
United Kingdom, 1907–1911, succession		
duty returns for males over 25	57.8–64.3	91.9
France, 1909, all probated estates	50.4	81.0
Among the living		
England and Wales, 1911–1913, persons		
over 25 (estate-multiplier method)	70.0	n.a.
Prussia, 1908, family wealth		
(based on tax assessments)	49.1	82.3

Sources and notes: The sources are Table 3.6, King (1915, pp. 86–95), and Lampman (1962, pp. 210–215), citing an earlier study by Kathleen Langley. In constructing the probate size distribution for the United Kingdom, King assumed that the estates in the poorest class of men averaged 60 pounds ($292) each, and that women owned the same fraction of the number and value of estates as in Massachusetts in 1890. It should also be noted that the British estate duty returns are likely to be distorted by a peculiar cause for tax avoidance. The British succession duties were a step function of total estate, making the duty jump by large numbers of pounds as one's estate gained the extra few pennies that put that estate into a higher tax bracket. Our preliminary inspection of summary returns suggests that in high wealth brackets the average declared wealth was noticeably above the midpoint, while this was not true of lower tax brackets. This is not the pattern one would expect of a distribution that rises and then falls with size.We suspect that rich heirs prevailed on themselves and their assessors to pull down their taxable estate into lower wealth brackets, thus understating British wealth inequality.

King felt the French returns appeared to list all estates, and left the probate-tax-return distribution unadjusted. He estimated the lower 86% of the Prussian distribution assuming ''that the curve for small properties would resemble in form that known to exist for France [p. 91].''

of reported wealth inequality. Whatever leveling effects the American ''frontier'' and her more rural orientation may have imparted, they did not show up in the form of a clearly lower degree of wealth inequality. By the eve of World War I, wealth—or at least decedents' wealth—was as unequally distributed here as in Western Europe. Tocqueville was right; less than a century after his visit, the American egalitarian ''dream'' had been completely lost.

If further studies confirm this tentative comparison, several corollaries demand attention. First, it is important to establish whether differences in age distribution and urbanization affect the international comparison. If Gallman's mid-nineteenth-century comparisons between America, Britain, and France can be used as a guide, international differences in age distribution may matter a great deal (Gallman, 1974). Second, was the trend toward wealth concentration as strong in Europe as in the United States across the nineteenth century? Since it is well established that American wealth in the seventeenth century was more equally distributed than English wealth (Kulikoff, 1971), it follows that America underwent far more pronounced inequality trends over the subsequent two centuries. But what about the nineteenth century and "modern economic growth"? Third, who migrated from Europe in the late-nineteenth century, and did the arrival of these migrants serve to raise wealth inequality in America but lower it in Europe? Theil has shown us a way to attack the problem (Theil, 1967, pp. 114–120), but the historical evaluation has yet to be made. Finally, what became of the European–American comparison after the First World War? This last question has already been explored by Lydall and Lansing (1959), as well as by Lampman (1962, pp. 210–215). They find that the top quantile shares among living wealth holders in England and Wales dropped with each decade from 1911–1913 to mid-century, yet wealth inequality remained more pronounced there than in the United States from the 1920s on. Either the prewar comparison is misleading, or the age adjustment from the deceased to the living serves to raise American inequality more markedly, or there was an even more dramatic leveling of wealth in the United States across World War I than the available figures have revealed. This issue has yet to be resolved.

Twentieth-Century Leveling

THE POST-WORLD WAR I ESTIMATES

Our understanding of levels and trends in wealth inequality since World War I rests on two kinds of data. One source relies on estimates of shares of top wealth holders using estate tax returns and estate-multiplier methods (Lampman, 1962; J. D. Smith and Franklin, 1974). The other main source is the Federal Reserve Board's oft-cited Survey of Financial Characteristics of Consumers, taken on December 31, 1962 (Projector and Weiss, 1966).

The top quantile shares reported in Table 3.8 reveal unambiguous and well-known trends. Top wealth holders increased their share markedly between 1922 and 1929, apparently recovering their pre–World War I position. Their share then dropped over the next twenty years, hitting a trough around 1949. This leveling in wealth distributions also parallels the "revolutionary" income leveling over the same period, about which more

TABLE 3.8

Share of U.S. Personal Wealth Held by Top Wealth Holders, 1922–1972 (in percentages)

Year	(1) Top 1.0% of Adults	(2) Top 0.5% of Population	(3) Top 1.0% of Population	(4)
1922	31.6%	29.8%		
1929	36.3	32.4		
1933	28.3	25.2		
1939	30.6	28.0		
1945	23.3	20.9		
1949	20.8	19.3		
1953	24.3	22.7	22.0%	27.5%
1954	24.0	22.5		
1956	26.0	25.0		
1958			21.7	26.9
1962			21.6	27.4
1965			23.7	29.2
1969			20.4	25.6
1972			20.9	26.6

Sources: Cols. (1) and (2) are from Lampman (1962, pp. 202, 204). Cols. (3) and (4) are from J. D. Smith and Franklin (1974, and unpublished estimates).

will be said in Chapter 4. Furthermore, as with incomes, the wealth leveling is not solely a wartime phenomenon, since an equally dramatic leveling took place early in the Great Depression. Whereas this revolutionary change in the distribution of wealth has become a permanent feature of the mid-twentieth century, the postwar period has not recorded any further trend toward wealth leveling.

ADJUSTMENTS AND ANOMALIES

So say the unadjusted estate tax series. But when these are compared with the 1962 Federal Reserve Board survey, the estimates begin to reveal serious gaps. The survey implies that the top 1% of all consumer units held 36.9% of net worth at the end of 1962. In contrast, the top 1% of total population held only 27.4% in the same year, according to Smith and Franklin. This significant gap must be explained.

Elimination of the gap between these inequality estimates may well begin with standardization of population units. The Federal Reserve Board survey dealt with households, or, more accurately, "consumer units." The estate tax studies could not easily follow the same convention, however. Given data on top individual wealth holders, they projected these top wealth holders onto the total population or the total adult population. Converting the estate tax results into a size distribution among households is of course impossible in the absence of data on the wealth of other family members. It is crucial to know, for example, the frequency with which male and female millionaires estimated from the decedent returns are married to each other. If they tend to be, then wealth inequality among households is higher than that implied by calculations which treat them as living in separate households.

Although point estimates of wealth inequality among households are elusive, we can establish ranges. Table 3.9 performs an exercise of this sort, accepting the underlying wealth data and converting the aggregates for top wealth holders from an individual to a household basis. These estimates cannot be proved to bound the true top percentile shares, but it is our judgment that the truth lies within the range given here. In any case, Table 3.9 suggests that twentieth-century inequality trends are not much affected by converting the top-share estimates to a household basis. The rise in wealth concentration between 1922 and 1929 persists, a somewhat larger decline from 1929 to mid-century emerges, but the stability since the early 1950s remains.

While the revisions fail to change trends by much, they *do* add to the anomalous discrepancy between the estate tax and the Federal Reserve Board survey estimates. It now appears that the top 1% of households held only 19.2–21.1% of 1962 net worth according to the estate tax estimates, whereas the 1962 Federal Reserve survey reports 36.9%. The anomaly grows.

Perhaps the discrepancy lies in different definitions or measurements of wealth. Yet, the two studies seem to have used similar definitions, though Lampman's economic estate and J. D. Smith and Franklin's net worth are not exactly the same as the Federal Reserve Board's definition of net worth.

Our attention turns quite naturally to the reporting of wealth to the estate tax authorities. Tax avoidance certainly must be considered, since top wealth holders face estate taxes now rising to marginal rates as high as 77%. Perhaps the richest have simply been much more adept at hiding their wealth from fiscal authorities and increasingly so as the marginal tax rates rose with time. Perhaps the survey of 1962 is correct and there is much less to the wealth leveling since World War I than meets the eye.

The difficulty with this obvious possibility is that it does not offer a clear explanation of why the Federal Reserve Board survey got such different results. Inheritance tax avoidance by the rich implies large transfers to heirs *inter vivos* and through trusts, some of which go unreported altogether (Mendershausen, 1956; Lampman, 1962; J. D. Smith and Franklin, 1974). Yet if the rich are doing so in much greater pro-

TABLE 3.9

Top Percentile Shares of Estimated Net Worth among Households, 1922–1972 *(in percentages)*

Year	Low Estimates	High Estimates	
		Lampman Procedure	Alternative Procedure
1922	22.8%	26.0%	
1929	27.7		
1953	17.65	22.4	
1962	19.2	21.1	
1969	17.9	20.4	26.2%
1972	18.9		

Sources and notes: These estimates refer to the national wealth held by top 1% of wealth holders. The sources are Lampman (1962), J. D. Smith and Franklin (1974), and, for the total number of households, *Historical Statistics* (1975) and *Statistical Abstract of the United States* (various issues).

The low estimates of top wealth holders' shares of wealth were based on the following definitions:

$$\begin{array}{l}\text{Percentage of top wealth}\\\text{holders (those with wealth}\\\text{above \$x) in population of}\\\text{households}\end{array} = \frac{\begin{array}{l}\text{No. of individual estates above \$x}\\\text{(among estimated living population)}\end{array}}{\text{No. of households in the United States}}\,(\times\ 100)$$

$$\begin{array}{l}\text{Their percentage}\\\text{wealth share}\end{array} = \frac{\begin{array}{l}\text{Total value of estates}\\\text{individually above \$x}\end{array}}{\begin{array}{l}\text{Wealth of the entire}\\\text{household sector}\end{array}}$$

Note that this low estimate intentionally ignores the fact that more than one personal estate can exist in the same household.

The Lampman procedure (1962, pp. 204–207) generates what is probably a high estimate of the top wealth holders' share by subtracting the number of married women among individual top wealth holders from the ranks of the top wealth holders, with no other adjustments. This amounts to dividing the husbands with individual estates above the top wealth holders' threshold into two groups. The first group is married to wives also having more than the threshold individual wealth. The second group has wives and children with zero personal wealth.

The alternative procedure for developing a high estimate marries all the top wealth-holding husbands off to the richest possible wives and gives them all the children with individual estates. That is, this procedure uses the following definitions:

$$\begin{array}{l}\text{Percentage of top wealth}\\\text{holders (those households}\\\text{with wealth above \$x)}\end{array} = \frac{\begin{array}{l}\text{No. of individual estates}\\\text{above \$x, excluding all}\\\text{wealth holders under age}\\\text{20 and all married women}\\\text{with wealth above \$x}\end{array}}{\begin{array}{l}\text{No. of households in the}\\\text{United States}\end{array}}$$

$$\begin{array}{l}\text{Their percentage}\\\text{wealth share}\end{array} = \frac{\begin{array}{l}\text{Total value of estates over}\\\text{\$x among adult males plus}\\\text{adult females not currently}\\\text{married plus estates of all}\\\text{minors plus estates of the}\\\text{richest married women equal}\\\text{in number to the married}\\\text{males with estates over \$x}\end{array}}{\begin{array}{l}\text{No. of households in the}\\\text{United States}\end{array}}\,(\times\ 100)$$

portions that the poor, why did they have such a larger share of total wealth still in hand to report to the interviewers in the 1962 survey? Alternatively, if we believe they are hiding vast sums from the assessors, why would they be so much more candid when interviewed by the Federal Reserve in 1962? We can well believe that people might lie to avoid a 77% marginal tax rate, but it is not yet clear how or why their lying was so inconsistent. There must be another explanation for the discrepancy.

There are only small gaps between the amounts of wealth reported for top wealth holders to the survey, to the Internal Revenue, and in the Smith–Franklin modification of the IRS data. For either the top million wealth holders or the top two million, the estimated amounts of wealth in the survey run something like 10% above the amounts implied by the Smith–Franklin estimates. The discrepancy is not large enough to explain the top share gap already noted. Furthermore, the same top million or two reported even more to the IRS itself, according to its own estimates (U.S. Department of the Treasury, 1967). Differences in the amounts of wealth attributed to top wealth holders apparently do not account for the differences in the 1962 share estimates.

The key to the 1962 puzzle must lie with competing estimates of the total net worth of the entire personal sector. The 1962 survey never reported its estimate of total personal wealth, but the mean net worth and the estimated population size imply an aggregate net worth of $1198 billion. This is very close to Kendrick's recent estimate of the personal sector's gross assets of $1175 billion for the same date (1976, p. 70). However, both figures are well below the $1779.9 billion total net worth used by Smith and Franklin—and supplied to them by Helen Stone Tice of the Federal Reserve Board. It appears that the Federal Reserve survey somehow erred by using a total net worth estimate which is only 56% of the figure later disseminated by the Federal Reserve Board itself. A look at the Projector–Weiss technical notes to the survey reveals that these authors (Projector and Weiss, 1966, pp. 61, 62) were already aware of a serious underestimation of total assets and net worth. If we conclude that the better estimate of total net worth was that later supplied by the Federal Reserve Board to Smith and Franklin, then the 1962 survey itself implies a top percentile share of only 20.6% of net worth, well within the range estimated in Table 3.9 above.

AGING IN THE TWENTIETH CENTURY

If the estimates are now consistent with each other, they still do not reveal what made wealth inequality decline between 1929 and mid-century. We must take care to subject this aggregate leveling to the same

kind of scrutiny applied to the nineteenth-century trends in wealth concentration. In particular, could the leveling just be an artifact of changes
in the age distribution? Between 1930 and 1940 or between 1930 and 1960,
there was indeed an aging in the population of male household heads, but
it takes a different form from the antebellum aging discussed above. Over
the nineteenth century young adult males declined in relative numbers
over time, thus imparting a downward drift to aggregate inequality indicators as the age distribution compressed. The twentieth-century experience appears to be somewhat different. While young adults (under 35)
decline in relative numbers from the 1920s to the 1960s, the percentage of
adults at the other end of the age distribution increases (aged 55 and
above). The net life-cycle impact on aggregate wealth concentration
trends is unclear. To resolve the issue, we applied the age distributions
for male household heads in the censuses of 1930 through 1960 to the 1962
age–wealth pattern (Williamson and Lindert, 1977, Section 5.2), with two
noteworthy results. First, in sharp contrast to the implications of the
"Paglin debate" (Paglin, 1975, and the subsequent exchange in later
issues), age/life-cycle effects appear to be a trivial component of aggregate
wealth concentration trends in the mid-twentieth century. Regardless of
the time span selected, Gini coefficients vary hardly at all in response to
these demographic forces. Second, the impact—although very small—is
to produce *increased* wealth concentration over time. Thus, it appears
that the post-1929 leveling in wealth distribution is *understated,* and
proper adjustment for life-cycle effects would serve to make the trend
toward greater wealth equality even more pronounced.

TOWARD SIZE DISTRIBUTIONS OF TOTAL WEALTH: HUMAN CAPITAL,
SOCIAL SECURITY, AND PENSIONS

Thus far we have addressed only the size distribution of nonhuman
wealth (inclusive of slaveholding), and have ignored the distribution of
total wealth. The latter augments "conventional" wealth by the capitali-
zation of all expected future income streams accruing from human capital
as well as claims on retirement income. So basic an omission is easily
justified for the nineteenth century and earlier, when human capital was a
far less important mode of accumulation and pensions were uncommon.
For this century, however, we should at least begin the task of discerning
what better measures of total wealth would show, since better measures
should soon be available.

It is well known that earnings are far more equally distributed than
conventional property income or total income. The implication for wealth

distributions is straightforward: *Total* personal wealth must be far less concentrated than conventional wealth, and intangible human capital must, by inference, be more equally distributed. Frequency distributions of adults by formal schooling are certainly consistent with that inference, and a recent publication by Lillard (1977, p. 49) supplies more specific support. Lillard reports an explicit calculation of the distribution of human capital for a male cohort born between 1917 and 1925. Gini coefficients are calculated for the cohort between ages 35 and 44 (e.g., over the years 1943 to 1970), taking on an average value of .45 and ranging between .39 and .53. By comparison, Projector and Weiss (1966, Table 8, p. 30) report a Gini coefficient of .71 for "conventional" 1962 wealth in the same age class. What is true for the age class 35–44 is likely to be even more pronounced for adult potential wealth holders as a group.

From the properties of variance, we also know that the coefficient of variation describing the concentration of *total* wealth can be decomposed into three parts: (*a*) the coefficient of variation describing human capital concentration weighted by the share of human capital in total wealth economy-wide; (*b*) the coefficient of variation describing conventional capital concentration, weighted by the share of conventional capital in total wealth economy-wide; and (*c*) a covariance term. It follows that total wealth will become more equally distributed over time for any of four reasons, singly or in concert: (*a*) a leveling in human capital distribution; (*b*) a leveling in conventional capital distribution; (*c*) an economy-wide rise in the importance of human capital in total wealth; and (*d*) a diminution in the (presumably positive) correlation between conventional and human wealth holdings.

Table 3.10 explores the potential impact of the third item, namely the shift in the economy-wide portfolio mix toward human capital following 1929. For net national wealth held by *persons,* John Kendrick estimates that the intangible human capital share in total wealth rose from 50.3% to 58.7% between 1929 and 1969. Based on the tentative estimates supplied by T. W. Schultz and Denison, 1929 was a watershed, since there is very little evidence supporting a shift in portfolio mix prior to that date. Indeed, it appears that conventional wealth was a *higher* share of total wealth in 1929 than in 1896. The implication would appear to be that the trend toward less concentrated wealth holdings following 1929 is significantly understated by our inattention to this fundamental shift in the wealth portfolio mix during the middle third of the twentieth century.[10]

---

[10] Proximate causes of the portfolio shift following 1929 are not hard to find. Kendrick's estimates (1976, p. 240; 1974, p. 465) suggest that net rates of return on human capital,

TABLE 3.10
The Composition of Wealth, 1896–1973: Three U.S. Estimates (*percentage shares*)

	Schultz		Denison–Schultz		Kendrick		
Year	Education Stock	Reproducible Nonhuman Stock	Intangible Human Capital Stock	Reproducible Nonhuman Stock	Education Stock	Intangible Human Capital Stock	Tangible Nonhuman Stock
1896			32.1%	67.9%			
1899			33.3	66.7			
1900	18.3%	81.7%					
1909			33.4	66.6			
1910	18.9	81.1					
1914			32.5	67.5			
1919			31.9	68.1			
1920	19.4	80.6					
1929	19.2	80.8	29.8	70.2	42.9%	50.3%	49.7%
1930	19.7	80.3					
1940	24.7	75.3					
1948			34.3	65.7	45.1	51.7	48.3
1950	27.0	73.0					
1957	29.6	70.4					
1969					50.5	58.7	41.3
1973					n.a.	60.7	39.3

Sources and notes: Schultz: The education stock refers to members of the labor force with ages greater than 14. The reproducible nonhuman wealth stock is Raymond W. Goldsmith's estimates for the U.S. economy as a whole. Both series are in constant 1956 prices (T. W. Schultz, 1961, Table 14, p. 73; and 1963, Table 4, p. 51).

Denison-Schultz: Denison's labor quality input index 1896–1948 is applied to Schultz's educational capital stock benchmark for 1929. Reproducible nonhuman stock is private domestic economy capital stock, from Kendrick for 1896–1909 and from Denison for 1909–1948 linked (Denison, 1962, Tables 11 and 12, pp. 85 and 100; Kendrick, 1961, Tables A-XV and A-XXII, pp. 320–322 and 333). All series are in 1929 prices.

Kendrick: Net national wealth held by persons, in current dollars. Estimates exclude intangible nonhuman capital (e.g., research and development) and tangible human capital (e.g., rearing costs) (Kendrick, 1976, Tables 2–9, 2–10, 2–11, and C–7, pp. 50–51 and 239).

roughly measured, have exceeded those for nonhuman capital from the 1930s through the 1960s:

Private Domestic Economy Rates of Return

	to Human Capital	to Nonhuman Capital
1929	10.1	10.0
1937	9.6	8.9
1948	12.6	14.2
1953	14.8	11.4
1957	13.4	9.9
1960	12.9	9.2
1969	12.2	8.9

Conventional wealth estimates also exclude the present value of contingent claims to social security benefits. Since its introduction in 1937, the Social Security System has expanded dramatically. Because this form of wealth has markedly increased in relative importance, and given its more equal distribution, we have reason to expect that its exclusion from wealth concentration statistics tends to bias upwards total wealth inequality trends since the 1920s. Furthermore, if low- and middle-class groups have tended as a result to shift out of conventional accumulation much more dramatically than the rich, then the measured concentration of "conventional" wealth has an upwards bias over time as well.

Feldstein (1974) has estimated that in 1971 social security wealth increased wealth of the entire population by 37%, net of the present value of social security taxes paid by those currently in the labor force. A similar calculation for 1962 yields an estimate of 31%, while for those households in which there is a man aged 35–64 the figure is 35% (Feldstein, 1976). J. D. Smith (1974) has estimated that pension fund reserves amounted to about 7% of individual net worth in 1962. Not all pension plans are fully funded, of course, so this figure might be viewed as an understatement. Who benefits from the presence of pensions and social security? On the face of it, wealth held in these contingent forms must be most important for middle- and low-income individuals with little conventional nonhuman wealth except for house equities and consumer durable stocks.

Feldstein (1976) has made an explicit calculation of the impact of social security wealth on the distribution of total 1962 wealth reported by Projector and Weiss. The calculation is based on the assumption that social security taxes reduce human wealth but not nonhuman wealth, so that his results are gross of taxes. Feldstein thus estimates (1976, Table 2) that the share of the top 1% of wealth holders, aged 35–64, falls from 28.4% of fungible wealth to 18.9% of total wealth when social security wealth is included. No doubt somewhat less striking results would be forthcoming if the calculation were expanded to include all adults, but what does that 9.5% difference suggest regarding "conventional" wealth concentration trends offered by Lampman (1962) and J. D. Smith and Franklin (1974)? As a share in adult population, the top 1% had their share in conventional wealth decline from 31.6% to 26.0% between 1922 and 1956 (Table 3.8). If the Feldstein 1962 adjustment was roughly applicable to 1956 as well, the true decline would have been from 31.6% to 16.5%.[11]

[11] Drucker and others have guessed that the inclusion of pension plans would result in a "distribution of total wealth [that] would probably turn out to be very similar to . . . the distribution of personal income [Drucker, 1976, p. 12]," but no one to our knowledge has attempted a calculation for pensions like Feldstein's for social security. In any case, it is not clear how such an accounting would affect the post-1929 trends in income and wealth

There is, of course, an active debate (Feldstein, 1974; Munnell, 1976; Barro, 1977) over the response of *total* private saving to the presence of pension and social security plans, a debate which extends to labor supply and the retirement decision. However, no one has appeared to challenge the view summarized above that these mid-twentieth-century plans have induced a pronounced shift in wealth portfolios in such a fashion as to understate significantly the wealth leveling as reflected in "conventional" wealth measures.

Overview

Chapter 2 argued that colonial wealth inequality exhibited stability and low levels of wealth inequality from the mid-seventeenth century to the Revolution. Between 1774 and the outbreak of the Civil War, the distribution of wealth appears to have undergone an episodic change. Our nationwide estimates point to a near tripling in the ratios of the average wealth of the top 1% or 10% of wealth holders to the average wealth of all other groups. Estimates from local probates and tax return sources seem to confirm this dramatic trend toward concentration. Furthermore, regional estimates suggest that most of the antebellum shift to wealth concentration occurred from the 1820s to the late 1840s, though the supply of such shorter-run data is still very inadequate. In addition, our calculations show that the apparent rise in wealth inequality before the Civil War cannot be explained by mere shifts in the age distribution, by the increasing share of foreign born, or by urbanization, though this last factor does contribute noticeably to the rise of wealth concentration.

We still know little about wealth inequality trends within the long period from the Civil War to World War I. Slave emancipation unambiguously leveled wealth inequality within the South and for the nation as a whole across the 1860s. For the half century after 1870 we are in the dark, so that we cannot with confidence identify peak wealth inequality with 1929, 1914, or 1860. Nevertheless, it is apparent that no significant long-term leveling took place during the period and that inequality persisted at very high levels.

The twentieth-century figures suggest a clear pattern. Wealth inequality, like income inequality, dipped across World War I and rose across the 1920s, though it is hard to say whether 1929 wealth was more or

---

distribution. Lampman's total wealth variant, upon which the trends in top shares are based, *includes* reserves of private pensions (Lampman, 1962, Table 97, p. 209), although the 1962 Projector and Weiss estimates do not.

less equally distributed than that of 1912 or some nearby year. From 1929 until mid-century, wealth inequality seems to have undergone a permanent reduction, again paralleling the movement in income inequality. After mid-century, neither wealth nor income inequality has shown a trend that can be judged significant on existing data. The American record thus documents a "Kuznets inverted-U" for wealth inequality, and it appears that significant wealth inequality did not become a part of the American scene until the onset of modern economic growth in the early nineteenth century.

TRENDS IN INCOME AND EARNINGS INEQUALITY SINCE 1816

Measuring Income Inequality

As we pointed out in Chapter 3, any measure of income inequality requires choosing an income concept, a recipient unit, a length of time over which income flows, and a summary statistic for quantifying "overall" inequality. Inequality of what kind of income? Among whom? Over a year or over a lifetime? Is inequality rising or falling when both the top 20% and the bottom 20% experience the same percentage point gains relative to the middle-income group? Economists have revealed just how sensitive our perceptions of inequality are in response to these conceptual questions. Yet there is more to gain from the available facts than just the knowledge that inequality measurement is a complicated business.

Two concepts of aggregate income inequality relate especially well to popular intuition, and both can be traced through the historical data. One is the inequality of the distribution of *real* income among individuals before it is altered by government policy (pre-fisc distribution). If we wish to document how an economy rewards individuals, we need a distributional index based on nominal incomes, before taxes and government spending, including capital gains and imputed rents, and deflated by a class-specific cost-of-living index. This concept coincides with common notions of what is meant by the distribution of earning power, although the focus on individual labor force participants is blurred in the data, since property incomes are often earned by families or by individuals outside of the labor force. The other workable concept of inequality followed in this chapter is the post-government (post-fisc) distribution of real income per person (or per adult-equivalent consumer unit) among households. This concept reflects our concern with living standards after transfers and taxes have had their influence.

Regardless of the inequality measure one selects, its movements can be divided into three distinct components relating to specific population groups or social classes: (a) inequality trends due to changing income inequality within groups; (b) inequality trends due to relative changes in groups' average incomes; and (c) inequality trends due to population shifts, or shifts in the shares of the overall population belonging to different groups. This breakdown is relevant whatever the groups chosen: classes, occupations, age groups, or regions. This decomposition can also be applied to income by source. For example, labor earnings can be separated from property incomes, so that aggregate inequality trends can be decomposed into those due to wage stretching (e.g., rising pay ratios by occupation and increasing wage differentials by skill), increasing profit rates, and thus to changes in the relative returns on human and nonhuman assets; those due to changes in human and nonhuman wealth distributions; and those due to shifts in the share of property income (nonhuman wealth) in total income (total wealth).

Separating inequality trends into these component parts is valuable for two reasons. First, it supplies additional clues about the sources of inequality change. Any hypothesis aimed at explaining overall income inequality must be consistent with the historical behavior of these component parts. Second, the breakdown serves to isolate those inequality movements that society cares about most. Many would be alarmed if increased inequality were explained solely by the fact that the average pay of executives and professionals rose relative to unskilled workers. Indeed, most of the shouting has been about movements in "class" pay rates. Increased inequality within groups may also generate social concern. We tend to get less excited, however, about movements in aggregate inequality produced by mere population shifts. For example, rising inequality might be viewed as spurious if it resulted merely from the voluntary shift in population from large-family households to separate living quarters for individuals and couples, or from the increased dispersion of household heads by age associated with a previous baby boom or immigrant influx. It is important, therefore, to separate true changes in pay structure from mere population shifts.

What follows is a historical chronology of income inequality episodes in America since the early nineteenth century, years when some of the necessary documentation becomes available. These episodes are delineated notably by changes in trend but, alas, also by changes in data quality and coverage. Each period is introduced with an examination of the available inequality indicators. Each section also compares inequality movements with shifts in occupational pay ratios to judge the extent to which inequality changed because of a shift in the pay structure itself.

The central question, of course, is whether income inequality indicators and factor distribution statistics trace out trends which replicate our findings on wealth inequality presented in Chapter 3. Were increasing inequality of both income and wealth by-products of modern economic growth? How closely does the wealth leveling following 1929 correlate with an income leveling? Does income inequality also exhibit a "Kuznets curve" much like that of wealth inequality? Are trends in income inequality primarily the result of changes in the concentration of human and nonhuman wealth, or are they also influenced by changes in rates of return, skill premia, and the pay structure?

Wages, Earnings, and Income Inequality, 1816–1880

THE ANTEBELLUM SURGE IN WAGE INEQUALITY

Shortly before World War I, the premium on skilled labor was extraordinarily high in America. Skills were very expensive even by West European standards. Phelps-Brown (1968, p. 47) notes that the ratio of skilled to unskilled wages in American building trades, for example, was 2.17 in 1909, while just two years earlier the ratio was as low as 1.54 in the United Kingdom.[1] In contrast, English visitors a century earlier characterized America as a nation endowed with cheap skills and expensive "raw" labor. Habakkuk (1962) supplied extensive contemporary comment on the abundance of skilled labor in America during the 1820s. Estimates for the 1820s by Zachariah Allen (Rosenberg, 1967) suggest that American skilled workers had slightly less pay advantage over common labor than in Britain. In short, compared to England (and the Continent[2]), skilled labor may have been relatively cheap in America at the start of modern industrialization. A century later conditions had reversed, and skilled labor was relatively expensive in America.

While these pay ratios and wage relatives have considerable intrinsic interest, one may doubt that their trends are likely to capture long-term overall distribution changes. After all, there are many skill categories and age–experience groups within each occupation. Furthermore, no one occupation can be trusted to reflect the same percentile position on the

---

[1] This was the dominant view of contemporary analysts, too. Taussig (1927, pp. 58–60), for example, found the "comparatively low rate of pay for the unskilled" prior to World War I "markedly peculiar."

[2] Comparisons with the Continent can be found in Uselding (1975), where this characterization is generalized.

income spectrum year after year, even though some are always more highly paid than others. The nature of any one job also drifts with time— neither doctors nor the "unskilled" do the same things they did a century ago. In spite of all these reservations, pay ratios do indeed trace out trends that coincide with "true" inequality measures. Later in this chapter we shall supply more detailed evidence of the correlation based on twentieth-century observations. This section will serve only to make the following point: We have seen that an extraordinary rise in wealth concentration may have been compressed within the last four antebellum decades. The same impression of an inequality surge between about 1820 and the Civil War reappears when we look at trends in occupational pay structure.

Figure 4.1 presents five annual time series documenting movements in the pay structure. Pay ratios in Massachusetts building trades reveal a downward drift between 1771 and 1820, yielding some confirmation of the wealth inequality trends discussed in Chapter 3. This trend appears to reinforce the view that colonial distributional "quiescence" continues after 1774 up to about 1820. The Massachusetts pay ratios surge thereafter, peaking in the 1850s. Pay ratios in northern cities, skilled to common labor, also rise steeply over the antebellum period, from a low in 1816 to a high in 1856. The ratio of public school teachers' salaries to pay for unskilled common labor, urban or rural, also rises prior to the Civil War, as does the ratio of engineers' to common labor wages. All of these series document a brief but sharp decline in the skill premium during the Civil War itself, a finding which is repeated in both twentieth-century world wars. However, Figure 4.1 offers a mixed picture on trends in pay structure following the Civil War. The urban skilled-worker series remains relatively stable up to the early 1890s, and the same is true for the Massachusetts building trades. The remaining three series show somewhat steeper trends in pay ratios up to the late 1870s before stabilizing. Generally, it appears that skill premia, pay ratios, and earnings differentials trace out the same "uneven plateau" that is apparent in the late-nineteenth-century wealth distribution statistics discussed in Chapter 3 as well as in the late-nineteenth-century income distribution statistics to be discussed below in this chapter.

What is most remarkable about Figure 4.1 is the striking surge in the relative price of skills and an abrupt widening in the pay structure from 1816 to 1856. The movements after 1856 pale by comparison. In four short decades, the American Northeast was transformed from the "Jeffersonian ideal" to a society more typical of developing economies with very wide pay differentials and, presumably, marked inequality in the distribution of wage income. True, the sharp rise following 1816 may be somewhat exaggerated by our choice of 1816 as a base year. It was in the midst

Ratio of Wages
by Occupation

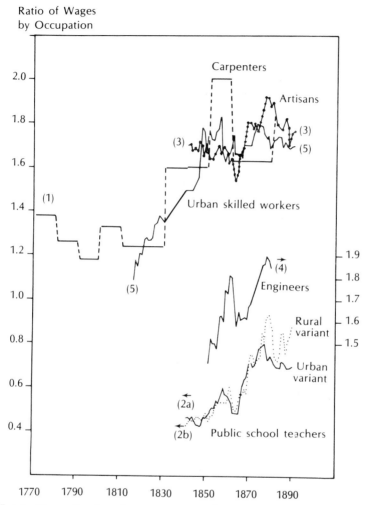

FIGURE 4.1. Occupational nonfarm pay ratios, 1771–1870. From Appendix D. (1) = carpenters to unskilled workers in building trades, Massachusetts; (2a) = public school teachers to common laborers, urban; (2b) = public school teachers to common laborers, rural; (3) = artisans to laborers; (4) = engineers to common laborers; (5) = urban skilled workers to unskilled workers.

of hard times in the urban Northeast following readjustments in the wake of the War of 1812. But the post-Revolutionary wage structure (1781–1790) was quickly regained by the early 1820s, when social overhead construction and capital formation resumed and skilled labor was put back to work. In short, even if we select the 1820s as a base, a surge in antebellum pay differentials is still apparent in our series.

The linked urban skilled-workers series in Figure 4.1 is based primarily on manufacturing data from the *Aldrich Report* following 1840. Prior to that date, the series is even more limited, based as it is on payroll data from iron-producing firms in eastern Pennsylvania.[3] Since the series suggests an inequality surge of such dramatic proportions even prior to the Irish immigrations in the late 1840s, it might be wise to pause and consider whether evidence other than the Massachusetts building trades is consistent with our characterization of sharp widening in the early antebellum pay structure. We have only the sketchiest data for the 1830s, but none of it is inconsistent with the upward drift suggested by Figure 4.1. Indeed, we may have understated the rise. For example, when Layer (1955, Table 14, p. 52) computed daily earnings of cotton mill employees by department, he found that the dressing department was consistently the highest paid in the antebellum period, while spinners were the lowest. The pay differential rose by 13% from the period 1830–1834 to 1840–1844, whereas our "linked" index rose by 9% over the same period. Further confirmation can be found in Erie Canal payrolls and civil engineers' earnings on internal improvement projects.[4] Between 1830 and 1845, the "skilled-labor wage premium" on internal improvement projects rose by 13.9–15%, while our linked series registers a rise of 14.2%.

Though we encounter no difficulty in confirming a surge in pay differentials during the 1830s, how about the 1840s? Do other wage indicators confirm the epic spreading in pay differentials during the 1840s? Apparently so, since other data fragments from the *Aldrich Report* document the following (Williamson, 1975, pp. 12–15): Compared with common laborers, the daily rate for New York bricklayers rose by 18% from 1840 to 1850, while that of carpenters and joiners rose by 37% over the same period; compared with common laborers, "best" machinists' wage relatives in New York increased by 37%, boilermakers' by 8%, and iron molders' by 13%; in Massachusetts, railroad conductors' wage relatives rose by 10% when common labor is used as a base, and by 14% when teamsters are used as a base.

We have dealt at length with the 1830s and 1840s, since measures of pay differentials during these decades of early industrialization are important in dating the nineteenth-century inequality surge in America and thus to economic interpretations of the sources of capitalist inequality. It seems appropriate, therefore, to conclude this section by examining some wage

[3] Zabler (1972, pp. 109–117) is preferred to Adams (1968, pp. 404–426). The two document conflicting trends to 1825. They coincide thereafter.

[4] Erie Canal common-labor wage data are taken from W. B. Smith (1963, Table 1, pp. 303–304). The earnings data for civil engineers working on canals and other internal improvements can be found in Aldrich (1971, Table 1, p. 201).

data drawn from a New England state where it all began, Massachusetts. Rosenberg's (1967) use of Zachariah Allen's data confirmed that in 1825 the average British machinist was paid a premium above common labor of some 105% while his American counterpart earned only a 50% premium. Cheap skills and expensive raw labor are consistent with relative earnings equality in America about 1825. However, the premium on skills surged to 85% by 1837, to 90% during the 1840s, and to 120% by the 1850s. That is, the wage structure in urban Massachusetts in the 1850s was almost exactly like that in England in 1825. It never again reached that height in the three decades that followed.[5]

It should be emphasized again that the pay differentials discussed above relate to *urban* workers in the Northeast. There is some evidence to suggest that *all* workers would be described by a pay-structure index not entirely unlike the northeastern urban index itself. The missing data, of course, relate to "wage gaps" between urban and rural employment, as well as to wage differentials between regions. The development literature makes much of these wage gaps (e.g., Todaro, 1969; Kelley, Williamson, and Cheetham, 1972, pp. 241–252, 271–273), the prevailing view being that they rise during early industrialization and growth, thus contributing to nominal wage stretching and inequality economy-wide. Some contrary evidence from New England is presented in Figure 4.2. From the 1770s to the 1820s, the nominal pay differentials between urban common labor and hired farm work declines, thus contributing to the egalitarian drift over the early national period. More to the point, however, the Massachusetts wage differential suggests a fair degree of stability between 1820 and 1880. Since there is no reason to believe that things were different for other states, then by inference the economy-wide pay structure must have followed closely the northeastern urban pay structure in the antebellum and Reconstruction episode of wage stretching. Furthermore, what is true for intersectoral wages is also true for interregional wage differentials.[6]

Table 4.1 offers even stronger evidence that intraregional wage differentials were trivial in late antebellum America, both North and South. With the exception of Vermont during the 1840s and 1850s, no region

[5] The following ratio of machinists' daily wages to those of common labor are gleaned from C. D. Wright (1889, pp. 22, 54, 55, and 185):

1825	150.0%	1841–1850	190.1%
1831–1840	154.8	1851–1860	220.5
1837	185.2	1871–1880	168.2
1845	169.0	1881–1883	171.8

[6] Evidence confirming stability in money wage differential trends *between* regions can be found in Coelho and Shepherd (1976) for the period 1851–1880.

Ratio of Wages
by Occupation

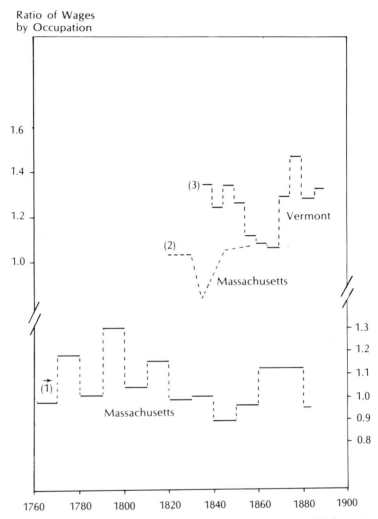

FIGURE 4.2. New England "wage gaps," 1761–1889. From Appendix E. (1) = urban over farm nominal daily wages, Massachusetts (decade average); (2) = urban over farm nominal daily wages, Massachusetts (annual); (3) = urban over farm nominal daily wages, Vermont.

exhibited pronounced farm–nonfarm wage gaps for labor of comparable skill. The average of these ratios for the North and for the United States as a whole is 0.99.[7] Furthermore, since both of these low-wage occupations are quoted including board, cost-of-living differentials are unlikely to matter much, a supposition consistent with the negligible nominal wage

[7] These issues are pursued in far greater detail in Williamson (1977b, pp. 41–43).

TABLE 4.1
Intrasectoral Wage Differentials, Nominal Daily Earnings, Urban Common Labor Relative to Farm Labor, 1850

Region	(1) 1850 Farm Labor with Board (per day)	(2) 1850 Common Labor with Board (per day)	(3) 1850 Ratio (2) ÷ (1)
New England	$.72	$.77	1.07
Maine	.76	.76	1.00
New Hampshire	.72	.63	.88
Rhode Island	.70	.72	1.03
Connecticut	.69	.76	1.10
Mid Atlantic	.62	.60	.97
East North Central	.58	.58	1.00
Indiana	.56	.55	.98
West North Central	.61	.56	.92
Missouri	.61	.55	.90
South Atlantic	.47	.48	1.02
Georgia	.52	.50	.96
East South Central	.55	.49	.89
West South Central	.65	.70	1.08

Sources and notes: Calculated from Lebergott (1964). His farm labor average monthly earnings with board (Table A–23, p. 539) is converted to a daily basis using the conversion factors implied by his Table A–30 (p. 546). The urban common labor series is taken from his Table A–25 (p. 541).

differentials for unskilled labor. We thus focus on rising skill premia and increasing earnings inequality *within* sectors.

Regional income gaps need not behave the same way as wage differentials for labor of homogeneous skills. Indeed, Easterlin (1960) and Williamson (1965, 1977b) have shown that regional divergence in per capita income was characteristic of the American economy in the nineteenth century after 1840. That is, the weighted coefficient of variation based on state per capita income rises sharply from .279 in 1840 to .355 in 1880 and .322 in 1900 (Williamson, 1965, pp. 25–27). Yet, Table 4.2 suggests that these trends can be fully accounted for by southern Civil War losses, since there is *no* evidence of an increased dispersion between 1840 and 1880 in northern state labor productivities, regardless of the regional definition, the income concept, or the inequality statistic utilized. Furthermore, there appears to be little evidence to support the view that southern incomes fell behind during the last two decades of the antebellum period (Engerman, 1971; Fogel and Engerman, 1974; Williamson, 1977b), although that conclusion is crucially influenced by the unusually good crop conditions for cotton in the year 1859/1860 and the poor

TABLE 4.2
Measures of Regional Income Inequality in the North, 1840–1900

Year	Northeastern States (N = 11)			Northern States (N = 18, 22)		
	Agricultural Income	Nonagricultural Income	Total Income	Agricultural Income	Nonagricultural Income	Total Income
	Weighted Coefficient of Variation (V_W)					
1840a	.153	.080	.157	.222	.128	.256
1840b		(.204)	(.186)		(.261)	(.276)
1880	.191	.075	.127	.212	.078	.172
1900	.127	.087	.113	.215	.086	.139
	Theil's Entropy Index (Hg)					
1840a	.012	.004	.012	.026	.010	.033
1840b		(.020)	(.016)		(.033)	(.037)
1880	.020	.003	.009	.021	.003	.015
1900	.008	.004	.007	.023	.004	.010

Sources and notes: The weighted coefficient of variation, (V_W), is calculated as

$$V_W = \frac{\left[\sum_i (Y_i - \bar{Y})^2 l_i^{1/2}\right]}{\bar{Y}} ,$$

where Y_i = income per worker in the ith state; $\bar{Y}$ = income per worker, total region; l_i = share of ith state's labor force in total regional labor force.
Theil's entropy index (Hg), calculated as

$$Hg = \sum_i y_i \ln (y_i/l_i)$$

where, in addition, y_i = share of ith state in total regional income.
The data are taken from Easterlin (1960, Tables A–1, A–2, pp. 97–104). The variant 1840a includes commerce, and 1840b excludes commerce. The northeastern region refers to the eleven New England and middle Atlantic states. The northern region refers in addition to the eleven north central states.

conditions for that key crop in 1839/1840 (Ransom and Sutch, 1977; G. Wright, 1978).

We do not have the necessary data to explore regional inequality experience over the most relevant period, 1820–1850, and such data may well document increased regional inequality over the first half of the nineteenth century, a period when other inequality indicators were on the rise. We know, for example, that regional inequality was already part of the American scene as early as 1840. After all, the weighted coefficient of variation across states was higher in 1840 than in 1948, a century later (Williamson, 1965, Table 4, p. 25). Furthermore, the 1840 figure for America was about the same as for France in either 1864 or 1951, a country where "pôle de croissance" had its intellectual beginnings. The figure exceeds by far that of Canada in 1935, or 1960, a country now beset with regional conflict bordering on secession. The figure is, in fact, almost comparable to that of interwar Italy, a nation with perhaps the most studied "North–South problem" (Williamson, 1977b, p. 39). In short, America was already beset by regional inequalities in 1840, and they were marked either by present American standards, or by the international standards of the late nineteenth or early twentieth century. Furthermore, what is true for America as a whole is also true for the northern states by themselves (Table 4.2).

To summarize, during the nineteenth-century surge in wealth inequality, wage stretching, and earnings dispersion, there is no evidence of increasing *spatial* occupational pay differentials. Furthermore, when Civil War effects are accounted for, there is little evidence of increased disparities in *average* regional incomes and labor productivities following 1840, although such disparities may have been on the rise prior to 1840. These findings coincide with the wealth inequality trends discussed in Chapter 3: The sources of the nineteenth-century inequality surge were not simply manifested by rising income differentials across regions and sectors. Indeed, the sources of the nineteenth-century inequality surge are as likely to be found *within* regions as between them.

The Uneven Plateau: Civil War to Great Depression

INCOME INEQUALITY CLUES

The best information documenting income inequality between 1860 and 1929 is summarized in Figures 4.3 and 4.4, combined with what we know about movements in prices and unemployment. Our indicators seem to mark out the entire period from Civil War to Wall Street crash as one of far greater income inequality than today. This plateau contains three episodes that may have seen the highest income inequalities in American history: (*a*) the end of the Civil War decade and the early 1870s; (*b*) the eve of the First World War, especially 1913 and 1916; and (*c*) the eve of the Great Crash, or 1928 and the first three-quarters of 1929. Let us first examine the evidence for high income inequality at these three junctures, and then explore what may have happened in between.

The federal government collected income taxes from the very top income groups in and around each of these three periods of high inequality. The tax returns yield two kinds of income inequality measures: the shares of national income received by the very top income recipients (Fig. 4.3 (5)) and an index of income inequality *among* those at the top

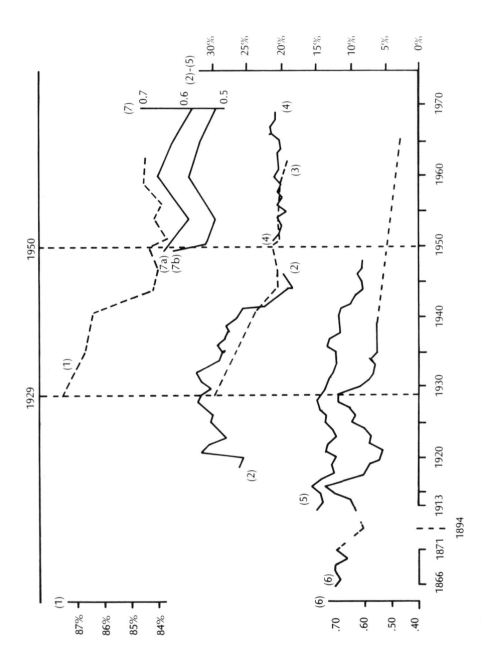

FIGURE 4.3. Selected measures of income inequality in the United States since 1913 and in seven earlier years. From Appendix F. (1) = share of income received by top 60% of households (OBE–Goldsmith); (2) share of income received by top 5% of recipient units (Kuznets, economic variant); (3) = share of income received by top 5% of recipient units (OBE–Goldsmith); (4) = share of income received by top 5% of recipient units, social security population (Brittain); (5) = share of income received by top 1% (Kuznets, basic variant); (6) = coefficient of inequality among richest taxpayers (Tucker–Soltow); (7a) = variance in the log of personal income, males 25–64 (Chiswick and Mincer); (7b) = variance in the log of personal income, males 35–44 (Chiswick and Mincer).

(Fig. 4.3 (6)).[8] Both measures show peak inequalities on the eve of America's entry into World War I and again just before the Great Crash. There was no federal income tax before the Civil War, but the tax returns do continue for the early Reconstruction Era (1866–1871).

These limited income tax data suggest a plateau of high income inequality from the Civil War to 1929. They also reveal pronounced deviations around that plateau which deserve brief citation. Although America drifted along at high inequality levels up to the 1890s, this period of quiescence ended around the turn of the century. This is suggested by the Tucker–Soltow coefficient of inequality among the richest taxpayers (Fig. 4.3 (6)). Trending inequality seems to have been more an urban phenomenon, since the nonfarm inequality indicators exhibit a much more pronounced inequality trend after 1900 than do the economy-wide indicators. This result is attributable to two factors: (a) a decline in the farm–nonfarm income gap after about 1900, and/or (b) the absence of trending inequality within the farm sector itself.

Although World War I had a remarkable egalitarian impact on America, its influence was short lived, since by 1929 the high post–Civil War inequality levels had been reestablished. Other studies offer similar results. Soltow's annual series on the inequality of Wisconsin incomes shows a steep drop in inequality for 1913–1920, and a steep rise for 1920–1929 (Soltow, 1971b, pp. 14, 135–139). The same pattern is shown in the estimates of factor shares, which show the property-and-profit share falling from 1913 to 1920 and rising over the next decade, both for the economy as a whole and for each major nonfarm sector (Williamson, 1974a).

These medium-term swings and long-term trends in income inequality are also reproduced by estimates of regional per capita income derived

[8] This index, the inverse Pareto slope given in Figure 4.3, measures the percentage by which income must rise to achieve a 1% drop in the proportion of the population having more than that income in the year in question. It turns out in practice that this slope is virtually constant over most ranges above the mean income but is not useful in describing inequality below the mean income.

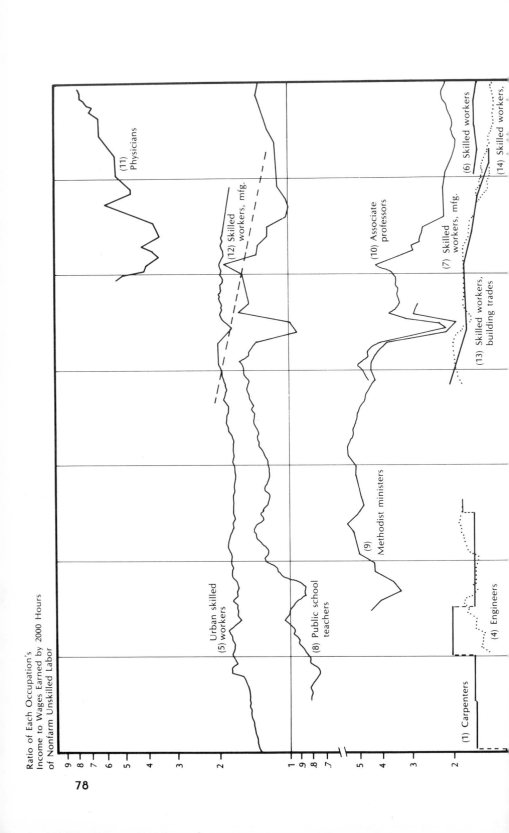

Ratio of Each Occupation's
Income to Wages Earned by 2000 Hours
of Nonfarm Unskilled Labor

(11) Physicians

(12) Skilled workers, mfg.

(5) Urban skilled workers

(8) Public school teachers

(10) Associate professors

(9) Methodist ministers

(7) Skilled workers, mfg.

(6) Skilled workers

(14) Skilled workers,

(13) Skilled workers, building trades

(1) Carpenters

(4) Engineers

78

FIGURE 4.4. Occupational pay ratios in nonfarm United States since 1830. From Appendix D. (1) = carpenters to unskilled workers, daily wage, Massachusetts; (4) = Engineers to common laborers, United States; (5) = urban skilled workers to unskilled workers; (6) = skilled workers to unskilled workers; (7) = skilled workers in manufacturing to unskilled workers; (8) = public school teachers to industrial unskilled laborers; (9) = Methodist ministers to unskilled workers; (10) = associate professors to unskilled workers; (11) = physicians to unskilled workers; (12) = skilled workers in manufacturing to unskilled workers; (13) = skilled workers in building trades to unskilled workers (Ober–Miller); (14) = skilled workers in building trades to unskilled workers (BLS).

from state production data taken at census years. One such statistic of regional inequality (a weighted coefficient of variation) follows:[9]

1840	0.279	1920	0.331
1880	0.355	1921	0.373
1900	0.322	1929	0.369
1910	0.324	1948	0.214
1919	0.276		

No doubt the high regional inequality reached in 1880 is closely related to southern Civil War defeat and its economic consequences. Nonetheless, there is evidence of a modest convergence in state per capita incomes in the late nineteenth century. Furthermore, regional inequality trends also undergo a reversal from the turn of the century to World War I. The war itself favored poor agricultural states, but the convergence was brief, since by 1929 regional inequality levels had returned to, or perhaps even exceeded, the levels of 1880. As with other inequality indicators, there is no evidence of long-term convergence in state per capita incomes over the half century 1880–1929.

While the six decades following the Civil War clearly registered persistent inequality levels far in excess of mid-twentieth-century standards, and although no dramatic long-term trends like the antebellum surge or the post-1929 collapse can be identified, we might be a bit more precise in dating America's peak inequality watershed. For the "Income Tax Age," the years of greatest income inequality were 1916 and 1929, with size distributions more skewed in 1916 than in 1929. The share of the top 1% in personal income was slightly higher in 1913 than in 1928–1929, and the 1916 figure is considerably higher. The same is true of the coefficient of inequality among richest taxpayers, at least when 1916 and 1928–1929 are

[9] For measures of the overall inequality of state and regional incomes per capita spanning this and other eras, see Williamson (1965, Table 4, p. 25; 1977b), Theil (1967, p. 103), and Lindert (1974, Table 1, Series (7)). Some of this information is incorporated in Appendix F, Series (8).

compared. Soltow's (1971b) annual series on Wisconsin incomes also shows greater inequality for 1913 than for 1929.

MOVEMENTS IN PAY RATIOS

Information on taxed incomes before 1929 relates mainly to the top income groups. They tell us little about inequality among the lower- and middle-income groups, and we have been reminded by Atkinson (1970) and others that inequality among those below the top matters for overall size distribution trends. Although we lack size distributions covering middle- and low-income groups for years other than the 1929 and later benchmarks, we do have information on trends in occupational pay ratios from which we can infer how rates of pay among various wage-earning classes moved over time. As long as the groups whose rates of pay are being compared were large and separated by fairly stable percentage points in the total income distribution, then occupational pay ratios should be fair proxies for the degree of income inequality.[10] Pay ratios are of interest in their own right. Since they may also reveal what is happening to overall income inequality when direct observations on the latter are limited, it might be useful to explore more carefully the correlation in time periods when both series are available.

The correlation between simple pay ratios and direct measures of income inequality can be explored for the period 1913 to 1934, the first date marking the twentieth-century income tax era and the second date preceding the first truly adequate income survey in America (1935/1936).[11]

[10] The urban unskilled and skilled wage categories underlying our "linked" series in Figure 4.4 do occupy positions in the income distribution that are usually separated by fairly stable differences in percentiles. The term "usually" is stressed, since the statement seems to hold from 1918 to 1929 and from 1950 to 1970. It does not hold during the leveling from 1929 to 1950, however. Unfortunately, we do not have adequate data for any of the years prior to World War I to extend this analysis backwards.

[11] Regressions were run on annual data for the period 1913–1934. PARETO refers to the Tucker–Soltow inverse Pareto slope among taxpayers, while TOPPER is Kuznets's basic variant, top 1%. WGP, or wage gap, refers to Williamson's (1975) linked series on the ratio of skilled to unskilled wages. The nonfarm civilian unemployment rate, u, is calculated from Lebergott (1964, Table A-3) for the 1913–1921 period. The remaining years are from Coen (1973, Table 2, p. 52):

$$PARETO = -0.13422 + 0.00422[WGP] - 0.00446[u]$$
$$\quad\quad\quad\quad (.48370) \quad\quad (2.87349) \quad\quad\quad (3.10692)$$

$$\bar{R}^2 = .3756, \quad DW = .5738$$

$$PARETO = -0.38302 + 0.00588[WGP] + 0.12293\log[1/u]$$
$$\quad\quad\quad\quad (1.30677) \quad\quad (3.63376) \quad\quad\quad (3.31096)$$

$$\bar{R}^2 = .4029, \quad DW = .6650$$

During World War I, unskilled nonfarm workers, and to a lesser extent farmhands, gained greatly on higher-paid occupations. The war effort made unskilled labor especially scarce, and its wage rates jumped. The wages of skilled and professional groups, by contrast, were bid up much less, partly because contracts in these occupations are always longer-term and slower to adjust to unanticipated inflation. The net result was an unprecedented contraction of pay scales between 1916 and 1920. This leveling was then undone in the 1920s, with higher-paid groups increasing their pay advantage over both the urban unskilled and farm labor. By 1929, the gaps between traditionally high-paid and low-paid jobs were almost as wide as in 1916, when the widest gaps in American history seem to have prevailed. This is exactly the same chronology that one finds in the fortunes of the top income recipients in Figure 4.3. The shares of total income going to the top 1% dropped between 1916 and 1920 and re-bounded strongly across the 1920s. The return to inequality in the 1920s was so great that, according to one recent calculation (Holt, 1977), the real income gains for the top 7% of the nonfarm population alone matched the increase in real personal income, leaving no apparent net gain for the rest of the population. The parallelism between simple pay ratios and income inequality measures even extends to the dispersion in incomes among the very rich. Before viewing the data, one would not have guessed that the pay ratios of machinists to unskilled urban workers should have followed the same time path as the dispersions of income among the top 5% or even the top .05% of families. Yet it turns out that way. The available data for the years since 1913 clearly show that occupa-tional pay ratios can be good proxies for overall inequality, especially during full-employment periods.

This striking parallelism between pay ratios and income inequality suggests that we could use the former to suggest how inequality moved between 1860 and America's entry into World War I. The pay ratios in Figure 4.4 imply a chronology that closely conforms to that told by the regional data as well as the federal income tax reports: Intraregional income gaps narrowed a bit during the Civil War, returned to something

---

TOPPER = −1.40900 + 0.08208[WGP] − 0.07299[u]
     (.31006) (3.41267)   (3.10375)

$\bar{R}^2$ = .4229, DW = 1.2920

TOPPER = −4.81580 + 0.10470[WGP] + 1.80650log[$1/u$]
     (.95174) (3.75064)   (2.81846)

$\bar{R}^2$ = .3868, DW = 1.2360

Figures in parentheses are t statistics, and it is these rather than the $\bar{R}^2$ which matter to our argument. DW denotes the Durbin–Watson statistic.

like their prewar levels by about 1873, drifted very modestly toward convergence up to 1896, and then widened—at least in urban areas—from 1896 to 1916. Furthermore, like our measures of income dispersion, the pay ratios show a generally counter-cyclical pattern. The pay ratios tend to drop in booms and to rise in recessions. This tendency is much more pronounced when the boom or contraction comes rapidly than when it takes a few years to gather momentum. This tendency is also a little more pronounced for teachers, whose pay contracts are longer in term. Thus the sharpest oscillation is in the ratio of teachers' to unskilled labor's wages (Fig. 4.4) during the price level swings of World War I and its wake, when the unskilled wage rate shot up and down with the volatile cost of living while teachers' nominal salaries were fixed for a year or two. The more controlled, or at least less sudden, inflations of the Civil War, World War II, Korea, and Vietnam lowered pay ratios more gently.

This chronology must be modified slightly by what we know about movements in the rate of unemployment. Unskilled labor tends to have unemployment rates twice or three times the average rate in nonfarm sectors. This means that the relative income position of bottom groups will be worse in periods of high unemployment than one would have gathered by looking just at ratios of pay per unit of time worked among those who remained employed. It also means that recovery from serious depression will register egalitarian trends as the unskilled become fully employed, in much the same way that Kuznets argued that perhaps a third of the observed trend toward equality from 1939 to 1944 might be explained by the sharp elimination of unemployment,[12] or that Chiswick and Mincer (1972) stressed the weeks-worked variable in explaining trends in log variance of male personal incomes between 1939 and 1965. How should we apply these twentieth-century findings to nineteenth-century pay ratio trends? Between 1860 and World War I nonfarm unemployment was apparently most severe in the periods 1874–1879 and 1893–1897 (Lebergott, 1964, pp. 164–189; Williamson, 1974c, Table C-5, p. 304). Knowing this, one should be prepared for the possibility that the modest leveling, now dated from 1873 to 1896, should perhaps be dated from the end of the 1870s to the turn of the century.

Twentieth-Century Leveling

THE INCOME REVOLUTION, 1929–1951

Since the beginning of federal income tax returns in 1913–1914, and

---

[12] Kuznets (1953, Table 119, p. 607). See also Williamson (1974a) for similar calculations relating to World War I and its aftermath.

especially since the 1940 census, more and more data have become available on the overall size distribution of income. Shortly after World War II, Simon Kuznets and others (Kuznets, 1953; S. F. Goldsmith, 1967) began to supply estimates, based on these early federal returns, which showed that income inequality had diminished sharply between the late 1920s and the late 1940s. .

Defenders and critics of capitalism both used this ammunition to renew the perennial debate: Is increasing inequality an inevitable by-product of modern economic growth? Arthur Burns (1954, p. 137) viewed this leveling as solid evidence that private enterprise led to a just and equal distribution of economic rewards, and counted the transformation "as one of the great social revolutions of history. . . ." Burns was defending only *mature* capitalism as an income leveler, and even he might have concurred with the Kuznets's (1955) conjecture—now confirmed here and in Chapter 3—that incomes are equalized only late in the process of capitalist development, following long episodes of increasing inequality. But the critics would not accept even this weak and tardy defense of capitalism. In fact some *still* deny that income has really become more equally distributed. They charge that Burns's "social revolution" is based on statistical legerdemain: that since the 1920s the rich have become more adept at concealing their incomes and social statisticians have distorted the data even further to produce a false equalization. If the truth were known, say the critics, inequality rises at the onset of capitalist development and fails to reverse thereafter. Furthermore, say the critics, aggregate inequality statistics hide more fundamental distribution indicators. In particular, the critics assert that class pay differentials have not collapsed since the 1920s (Perlo, 1954; Kolko, 1962, Chaps. 1 and 2). The time is ripe for a reassessment.

There does appear to have been a dramatic and pervasive shift toward more equal incomes between the Wall Street crash and the Korean War. The entire income spectrum seemed to converge, since every series in Figure 4.3 tells the same tale of pronounced leveling in income. The net change is impressive. The only factual question requiring a closer look is whether the Great Depression saw more or less leveling than World War II. The classes gaining in relative shares differed between the two decades. During the Depression, higher-paid employees, such as skilled and white-collar workers and professionals, suffered less than others simply by keeping their jobs at negotiated nominal wage rates that were less sensitive than others to the cycle. Meanwhile, the urban unskilled, farmers, and profit recipients all suffered an erosion of incomes. While the top 5% of all income recipients suffered a drop in their relative share across the 1930s, the shares of the top 5% of *employees* and the top-income *regions* actually peaked at the bottom of the Depression and were still no worse in 1940 than in 1929. The 1940s, by contrast, saw a clear contraction of the entire income spectrum. The shares of top-percentile individuals dropped again, but this time the biggest gainers were those at the bottom—farm workers, blacks, southern states, women, and unskilled urban white males.

The greatest changes over the two decades as a whole were the rise of the share received by the poorest fifth and the decline in the share received by the top fifth (especially the top 5%). In 1929, the average income of the richest fifth was 15.5 times that of the poorest fifth. By 1951 this ratio had dropped to 9.0.[13] An impressive leveling also occurred in regional inequality as revealed by estimates of personal income per capita derived from state production data. The North–South gap in average incomes dropped dramatically, in part owing to the heavy migration of low-income workers from the South to northern urban centers.[14] In no other extended period of American history did the available indicators swing so sharply toward equality.

This leveling was remarkable in two respects. First, it spanned a 22-year period that was far from uniform. Between these two full employment dates, America sank into its greatest depression, surged back with the help of World War II, had a postwar boom, and then entered the Korean War. Such turbulent times might be expected to have brought reversals in inequality trends, but the leveling appears to have continued unabated throughout, although it seems to have accelerated during World War II. Second, the trends reported in Figure 4.3 are all the more remarkable, since they document a leveling of incomes *before* the effects of government are included. Furthermore, this decrease in pre-fisc inequality appears to have been as great as the entire equalization achieved by all government programs in 1950 and almost as great as the total equalizing effect of government programs in 1970.[15] This last statement bears repeating: The leveling in pre-fisc incomes between 1929 and 1951 was as great as the difference berween the distribution of pre-fisc and

[13] Budd (1967, Table I) citing the same OBE–Goldsmith series used to plot Series (1) and (3) in Figure 4.3.

[14] The regional data are summarized in Appendix F, Series (8). See Williamson (1977b) for a more detailed discussion of the twentieth-century experience with regional convergence of incomes.

[15] The Gini coefficient produced by the OBE–Goldsmith data dropped by about .110 between 1929 and 1951. By comparison, M. Reynolds and Smolensky (1975) have estimated that the total redistributive effect of all government spending and taxation was on the order of .079 for 1950, and about .110 for 1970. To improve comparability, transfer payments should be subtracted from the OBE–Goldsmith data. Doing so would bring the pre-fisc equalization of 1929–1951 down to about the 1950 estimate of government redistribution.

post-fisc incomes in 1950, the latter including *all* state, local, and federal tax–transfer expenditure policies.

So say the available series. Would the egalitarian trend be reinforced or eliminated by correcting these series to better conform with our "ideal" concepts of inequality? The corrections run in both directions. One adjustment would magnify the "income revolution." Professor Kuznets has estimated that the capital gains actually realized through the sales of assets would have raised the share of the top 5% by 3.60% in 1929, by 0.17% in 1940, and by 1.86% in 1946 (Kuznets, 1953, Table 88). The top 5% so adjusted fell by 3.43 percentage points more across the 1930s, and 1.74 percentage points more over the entire period 1929–1946, than the shares plotted in Figure 4.3 would imply. The inclusion of capital gains magnifies the egalitarian trend for the whole period and shifts more of the leveling back to the 1930s.

Adjustment for changes in the age composition would also reinforce the egalitarian trend, at least among adult males. As we argued in Chapter 3, a population that has a wider age dispersion will also have a greater dispersion of incomes for any given set of life-cycle opportunities. Incomes rise steeply across the adult age groups until about age 50 and fall more gradually for those still in the labor force. Thus, if an older population has more widely varying ages, it will show greater inequality, and the adult population did age considerably between 1929 and 1951. The age-dispersed population may have high income inequality for another reason: The dispersion in incomes tends to be higher among the very young and very old. Using T. P. Schultz's (1971) data on the log variance of 1950 incomes by age classes (males, 20+), we computed the effect of the 1930–1950 age-distribution shift on inequality. Whether one excludes those under 25, those over 65, or both, the effect of age-distribution changes between 1930 and 1950 was to *raise* inequality. Although these demographic influences were never very large, we must conclude that the measured equalization tends to understate the equalization of life-cycle incomes.

Thus far, it appears that the leveling of pre-fisc income was indeed as great as the conventional estimates had implied all along, and that the leveling of post-fisc incomes was much greater. The direct measures of aggregate inequality are not the only kind of evidence of this leveling, however. The same impression could have been conveyed by data on pay ratios. Occupational pay ratios like those in Figure 4.4 reveal the same leveling, even though they are drawn from different survey data from those used in measuring aggregate pre-fisc inequality. Between 1929 and 1951, unskilled nonfarm workers reaped far greater percentage gains in pay than all of the major groups above them on the income scale. Unskilled workers gained ground not only on skilled blue-collar workers but also on lawyers, dentists, engineers, army officers, teachers, professors, and even physicians.[16] What is true for the urban unskilled also seems to be true of farm labor, although the former may have slightly widened their real pay advantage over farmhands. In 1929 the ratio of the (National Industrial Conference Board) hourly wage rate for unskilled nonfarm labor to the hourly farm wage rate (averaged across seasons) was 2.016; the 1951 ratio of janitorial to farm wage rates was virtually the same. Furthermore, trends in the civilian economy are mirrored in the military as well.[17]

The message clearly emerging from an examination of pay ratios is the same as that from the aggregate direct measures of income inequality: The pay structure shifted toward greater equality between 1929 and 1951. Another message is also conveyed by both the pay ratios and the direct inequality measures: The egalitarian trend was not confined to World War II, but was spread over the entire era, with middle-income groups losing less than the richest groups in the Depression and the lowest-paid groups gaining dramatically on all others across the 1940s.[18]

LYING AND LEVELING

For all the above evidence on the narrowing of pay and income gaps, the view persists that the whole "income revolution" was a lie. This view,

[16] For time series on the pay of these professional groups, see Stigler (1950, Tables 28, 29, 46, D, and the sources cited there), Stigler (1956, Table 51), Blank and Stigler (1957, Table 11). Pharmacists appear to have gained as fast in average income as did unskilled workers for the decade 1939–1949, to judge from their income gains reported in Blank and Stigler (1957, Table 12).

[17] When basic pay is adjusted by allowances, the ratio of annual earnings of officers to enlisted men declined from 3.101 to 2.380 between 1918 and 1945 (*Historical Statistics*, 1975, p. 176). Unfortunately, our source fails to supply estimates for the late 1920s.

[18] The leveling also manifested another notable social change: the decline of the domestic servant, the barber, and the beautician. Repeating World War I experience, the numbers employed in each of these occupations dropped in World War II. What these occupations have in common, of course, is that buyers tend to be concentrated in the top income groups, while the sellers are at the bottom. With incomes equalizing, the prosperity of the 1940s was accompanied by a drop in the quantities of these services consumed. Though several factors may have contributed to the decline, the main explanation seems to be simply that the top income groups could no longer afford so many servants, barbers, and beauticians, now that the pay gap between rich and poor had narrowed. And after World War II (unlike the aftermath of World War I), the trend toward declining numbers and higher pay for domestic servants, like the greater equality of income, was not reversed. See Stigler (1956, pp. 93–105) and *Statistical Abstract of the United States* (1974, pp. 350–356, 754, 766, plus earlier issues).

presented in detail by Perlo (1954), has been echoed by Kolko (1962) and, most recently, by Bronfenbrenner. Ignoring the evidence of pay ratios and household income surveys, Bronfenbrenner focuses on the tax returns and proclaims that "America's 'income revolution' of 1930–1950 reduces in retrospect . . . largely to superior tax avoidance" by the rich, whose "learning by doing" allows them to find better hiding places for their income faster than tax collectors can uncover the old ones (1978, p. 1462). This serious charge demands an answer in terms of the tax-return evidence itself, in addition to our above survey of evidence from nontax sources.

Dismissing the income leveling as a tax-dodger's lie requires stronger assumptions about tax avoidance than anyone has acknowledged. It is not enough to argue that the rich avoid taxes. Nor is it enough to argue that they do so by income concealment, as well as by reporting incomes in lighter-tax forms such as capital gains. No, the tax-lie denial of leveling must assume a double differential: It must assume that the percentage *difference* between the income concealments of the rich and the rest of us *grew* enough between 1929 and the postwar era to cancel out the apparent leveling.

We have a good set of clues about the formidable problem of hidden income. National product estimates allow an aggregate view of personal income based not on individuals' statements but on total amounts of factor incomes generated in businesses, farms, and other units of production. S. F. Goldsmith (1951, 1958; see also Kuznets, 1953, pp. 435–468) has made detailed comparisons between these factor-income aggregates and the amounts of personal income reported by individuals in surveys and tax returns. As shown in Columns (2) and (3) of Table 4.3, it is indeed the case that some kinds of income more characteristic of the rich are more hidden from individual returns. This is especially true of interest income, though it is also true of farm incomes received by the not-so-rich.

To judge the link between lying and leveling from 1929 to, say, 1946, let us make some strong assumptions in favor of the view that the leveling is a statistical mirage. Let us focus only on Kuznets's estimates, which trust tax-return figures for the rich but which use national-income aggregates for the incomes of the total population. (Household surveys, by contrast, use underreported figures for both high and low incomes.) And to minimize the 1929–1946 income leveling, let us also assume that high-income taxpayers were perfectly honest back in 1929—a strained assumption about the generation of business leaders that cooked up Teapot Dome and sold house lots in Florida swamps. Let us further assume that in 1946 the groups reporting top incomes lied just as much about any one type of

TABLE 4.3
The Underreporting of Personal Income by Type, 1946

(1) Income Type	Income Reporting Ratios, All Households		(4) Share of This Type of Income in Total Reported Income of Top 5%	(5) Ratio of Adjusted ("True") Value to Reported Income of Top 5% (4) ÷ (3)
	(2) In Census Surveys	(3) In Income Tax Returns		
Wages and salaries	.91	.94	.4020	.4277
Nonfarm entrepreneur-ial income	.59	.85	.4031	.4742
Farm income	.67	.41	(neglig.)	(0)
Dividends	.23	.80	.1262	.1578
Interest		.34	.0429	.1262
Rent	.63	.50	.0257	.0514
All types	.78	.86	1.0000	1.2373 = 1/.8082 (i.e., 80.82% of all income was reported by the top-5% group)

Sources and notes: Cols. (2) and (3) are from S. F. Goldsmith (1958, pp. 76–79). Col. (4) is from Kuznets (1953, p. 671). The ratios for nonfarm entrepreneurial income and farm income in Col. (3) refer to 1951 rather than to 1946.

income (dividends, profits, etc.) as all other persons having that type of income. Table 4.3 shows that under these assumptions the top 5% of persons ranked by reported income[19] abandoned their honesty and re-ported only 81% of their income in 1946. Uncovering this new dishonesty would make the income share of the top 5% fall only 60% as far as the Kuznets estimates imply for the period 1929–1946. Thus even under a strong assumption about changes in the pattern of lying, most of the leveling remains unobscured.

[19] Note that we are here dealing with the top 5% ranked by reported income, and not the preferable concept of the top 5% ranked by true income. This should not make any significant difference to our present argument, because the two relevant biases offset each other more or less: (a) By following the true incomes of the top 5% by reported income, we may be missing the wider margins of underreporting by persons who should be in the top 5% but do not appear to be there in 1946; yet (b) the higher margins of underreporting by these people are to be added onto their lower reported incomes, making the share of true income received by the true top 5% not much more than that received by the top 5% ranked by reported income. This same argument applies, of course, back in 1929 as well as in 1946, again leading us to suspect no serious optimistic bias in the statements of the text.

THE ORIGINS OF THE "NO-CHANGE" VIEW

The post-1929 leveling seems so pervasive that we are led to ask how anyone could have advanced the view that income inequality remained unchanged across this century. The answer seems to lie in the belief that pre-fisc income was far more equally distributed very early in this century than it was by 1929. This view can be traced to the use of older, unreliable estimates for years just before World War I. Once the drawbacks of these older estimates are understood, it becomes apparent that income inequality just prior to World War I was far closer to the high inequality of 1929 than to the more equal distributions of pre-fisc incomes after World War II.

In his much-cited book, *Wealth and Power in America* (1962), Gabriel Kolko went out of his way to show that "A radically unequal distribution of income has been characteristic of the American social structure since at least 1910, and . . . no trend toward income equality has appeared [p. 13]." Among others, Tom Christoffel et al. (1970, p. 9) and Robert Heilbroner (1974, p. 123) have recently identified with the Kolko view. Kolko repeated Perlo's criticism of the Kuznets and OBE–Goldsmith estimates, mixing the point that many reported incomes get lightly taxed with the assertion that some incomes go unreported altogether, while omitting any corrections that might reinforce the equalizing trend after 1929. He thought his case for no shift toward equality was clinched by presenting a table of distributions going back to 1910, when income looked even more equal than in 1959 (Kolko, 1962, p. 14). The distributions for 1941–1959 were taken from the Survey Research Center and Federal Reserve surveys. These show degrees of inequality very close to the other main series. The difficulty lies in Kolko's estimates of the early years, those covering the period 1910–1937.

When linking statistics drawn from different points in time, one must be sure they measure the same thing. One obvious way of checking the comparability of two series is to examine estimates for an overlapping year. Kolko could not do this, since the earlier series ended in 1937 and the new one picked up only with 1941. Kolko's early estimates can be compared, however, with the OBE–Goldsmith series, the latter yielding results like those of the Survey Research Center for the years following 1941. In 1929, Kolko's richest fifth of the population had an average income only 9.5 times as high as that of the poorest fifth, while the OBE–Goldsmith figures suggest a ratio of 15.5. Among the series available to him, Kolko seems to have selected early estimates that minimize the post-1929 income leveling. Where did Kolko find these series, and why have we rejected them?

The source of Kolko's 1910–1937 estimates is a volume written by the National Industrial Conference Board to tell "the story of the American enterprise system and its contribution to prosperity and public welfare."[20] Kolko did not criticize this source, sparing it any charges of having omitted capital gains or of having underreported high incomes. It is a mysterious set of estimates. The NICB notes under the key table: "Source: Data from Official Sources: Estimates by the Conference Board," and supplies no further information. It is hard to imagine what these official sources could have been. Income tax returns never covered more than the top 7% or 8% of the population until World War II, yet the NICB figures confidently stated the shares of each tenth of recipient units from top to bottom.

Doubts about "official sources" become most acute for Kolko's crucial year 1910, a year in which there was no national income or wealth tax, no official Bureau of Labor Statistics cost-of-living survey, and no decennial census of personal income or wealth. The only estimated distribution of income for 1910 is that of Willford I. King (1915), who wove 1901 worker survey data, 1902 Chicago wages, 1914 tax returns on top incomes, Wisconsin state income tax returns, and other odds and ends into a detailed set of estimates, using methods that were "mainly graphic and . . . too varied to describe here [p. 221]." King's 1910 estimates cannot be accepted or criticized without our knowing more about his underlying procedure. It should be noted, however, that King dropped these estimates from his later published work and coauthored a volume in 1921 that gave figures showing considerably greater inequality around 1910 than his 1915 book had revealed.[21] It should also be noted that even compared to

[20] National Industrial Conference Board (1939, Table 1, p. 125). The book's foreword elaborates on its intent: "The purpose was to focus the attention of the business community and the public upon the problems of preserving and improving the enterprise system, and to create a clear, common consciousness of its underlying principles, the condition of its effective operation and its past and potential accomplishments [pp. v–vi]."

[21] Greater inequality is implied at a couple of points in Mitchell, King, et al. (1921, pp. 112, 116). There it was estimated that 96% received less than $2000 for 1910, versus only 94.86% in King's book. The 1921 study also estimated the 1913 share of income going to the top 5% at 33%, far enough above King's figure of about 27.6% for 1910 to make the latter look suspiciously low.

King's estimates for 1910 also appear to have overestimated the incomes of low-income groups. In 1910, a nonfarm unskilled worker received about 18.1¢ per hour, to judge from the BLS samples. If he was fully employed, he earned $471.47 annually, based on the all-manufacturing average of 2604.8 hours per worker per year. Over half of industrial common laborers and almost all farm laborers, or a total of 14.4% of the gainfully employed in the 1910 census, must have earned less than this figure. Yet King places this annual income down at the 4th percentile in his distribution, which, to repeat, shows more inequality than the NICB estimates.

King made no mention of the pioneering 1910 estimates in his *National Income and Its*

the early King estimates the NICB–Kolko figures give a lower share to the top 10% of families and a higher share to the next 40%.[22] King himself probably understated the true 1910 inequality. Nevertheless, if King's estimates had been used instead of NICB's, Kolko would have found the 1910 income distribution more "radically unequal" than 1959. He would have seen a greater secular decline in the share of the top 10% during the half century following 1910.

Like Kolko, Irving Kravis (1962, pp. 202–236, Appendix 2.1) also concluded that income inequality was no greater between 1900 and World War I than it had been since World War II.[23] Unlike Kolko, Kravis was critical of his sources. He distrusted King's 1910 numbers and reported some of them only "for whatever they are worth."[24] He also recognized that the Bureau of Labor Statistics cost-of-living surveys for such early years as 1888–1890 and 1901 seriously understated the true inequality, since the surveys covered only a very narrow part of the income spectrum. He went to some length to search for subsamples from a 1950 survey that were comparably narrow in coverage, but we doubt that he succeeded.[25] More serious is the fact that Kravis then cast aside his own precaution and used raw King and early BLS figures to splice together "indexes of inequality" spanning the period 1888–1958 (Kravis, 1962, pp. 213–216).

The belief in no twentieth-century change is thus rooted in some eclectic size-distribution guesses for 1900–1910. It is better to pass over these,

Purchasing Power (1930). He did, however, continue making eclectic estimates of the entire income distribution. Two of his unpublished detailed estimates, one for 1921 and one for 1928, existed in the files of the National Bureau of Economic Research as of 1939 and may, if recovered, give important clues to his procedure. (See Merwin, 1939, pp. 11n., 12n., 38–45.)

[22] King's Tables XLIII and XLIV place the top-decile share of income in the range 35.36–35.42%, whereas the NICB and Kolko report only 33.9%. The King estimate is higher than all their top-decile shares for later years except those for 1921 and 1929.

[23] Bronfenbrenner's (1971, pp. 67–72) book is often cited in the recent literature, and he relied on Kravis and Kolko when summarizing income distribution trends in the United States.

[24] Kravis (1962, pp. 208, 209). Actually, Kravis understated the inequality of income reported by King in one respect: He reported that the top 5% of recipients got 26.3% of the 1910 income, whereas King's own figures (Tables XLIII and XLIV) gave the top 5% about 27.6%.

[25] The pre–World War I BLS surveys were designed to "be representative of the conditions as to cost of living of persons employed as wage workers and at small salaries [U.S. Commissioner of Labor, 1904, p. 15]." The "normal family" subset picked up by Kravis consisted of families with husbands currently employed at nonprofessional jobs, with wives present, and with earnings below a cutoff point making them "representative" of working families. By contrast, Kravis's "comparable" 1950 groups included some professionals and managers. Kravis also seems to acknowledge that differences in the top income cutoffs and in earnings by secondary breadwinners made the earlier surveys still narrower in population coverage than his 1950 counterparts (see Kravis, 1962, pp. 34, 35).

and to form tentative conclusions based on series that are at least comparable with data from after World War I. These remaining clues, surveyed
above, imply that inequality levels on the eve of World War I resembled
the wide gaps of 1928–1929 much more than the narrower gaps prevailing
after World War II.

Distributional Stability since World War II

Although the twentieth-century "income revolution" has survived our
scrutiny unscathed, it does seem clear that the leveling ceased by 1950.
By almost any yardstick, inequality has changed little since the late 1940s.
If there has been any trend, it is toward slightly more inequality in pre-fisc
income and toward slightly less inequality in post-fisc income. This stability has been extraordinary even by twentieth-century standards.

The data that yield this conclusion differ greatly from one another.
Several series are available: the Statistics of Income reported by the
Internal Revenue Service, the Survey of Consumer Finances, the Census
Bureau's Current Population Survey, the income distributions of the Social
Security Administration, and the benchmark consumer surveys of the
Bureau of Labor Statistics. Apart from the fact that they are gathered for
tax purposes, the IRS data stand out by their exclusion of transfer payments from money income. The anonymous survey data differ from one
another in their coverage of income and especially in their definition of the
recipient unit. One would expect such diversity to produce a variety in the
estimates, but in fact none of the inequality measures exhibits any dramatic trend.[26] In other words, each available series shows the same
stability displayed by the share of the top 5% of income recipients in the
Social Security population, shown in Figure 4.3.

The main available series do not exactly coincide with either of our
"ideal" concepts of income inequality. To infer trends in the *pre-fisc*
inequality among individuals, we must ask what changes would result if
the original series were forced to conform to pre-fisc distribution defi-

---

[26] In some cases a slight trend toward inequality is statistically significant. Sheldon
Danziger and Eugene Smolensky are currently conducting a detailed examination of the
available annual series on income inequality since 1947. In addition to their work and the
sources cited in Appendix F, summary measures of postwar income inequality can be found
in the following: Budd (1970), Katona (1971 and earlier annual volumes from the Survey
Research Center covering the years 1959–1969), T. P. Schultz (1971), Chiswick and Mincer
(1972), Gastwirth (1972, using IRS data for 1955–1969), and Henle (1972, for 1968–1970).

Danziger and Smolensky have found that the IRS data (1947–1971 or 1955–1969), Brittain's
Social Security series, and Henle's subset of the CPS data show significant trends toward
greater inequality, while the overall CPS series lacks a significant trend.

nitions. If transfer payments were excluded from money income, then the resulting statistics documenting truly pregovernmental income inequality would rise a bit faster over the postwar years,[27] as in fact is the case with pre-fisc income as measured in the official IRS numbers. The trend toward more unequal incomes before the effects of government would be further reinforced by another adjustment: It has been argued that if we could document what fringe benefits were received along with regular paychecks, then the trend toward income inequality would in fact be stronger than the numbers at hand suggest (Henle, 1972, p. 18). In short, these adjustments serve to increase the likelihood that the trend in pre-fisc income inequality was significantly but not dramatically upward in the postwar period.

On the other hand, it has been argued that what looks like a slight trend toward inequality may have been due just to population shifts, like the trend toward more fragmented households or the shift in age distributions. For example, Rivlin (1975) has suggested that people have tended toward separate living arrangements, a development fostered by changes in attitudes towards work by women and also by such programs as Social Security and Aid to Dependent Children. This may be, but correcting for changes in household type or in the share of earners who are women does not affect the inequality trend very much. Studies that have held demographic composition constant still have found a slight trend toward greater inequality of pre-fisc income. Similarly, holding age distribution constant also fails to eliminate the slight trend toward more unequal incomes.[28]

The trend in income inequality *after* taxes, transfers, and the estimated incidence of government purchases has been either steady or slightly toward equality between 1950 and 1970. In other words, the government has become a slightly more income-equalizing force across the 1950s and 1960s. Although the tax system has had a less "progressive" effect, government purchases and transfers have had an increasingly equalizing

---

[27] M. Reynolds and Smolensky (1975, Table 2) have estimated that the income-equalizing effect of transfer payments has risen across the postwar period. Removing that part of transfers included in some income-distribution series would produce a steeper upward trend across the postwar years in pre-fisc income inequality.

[28] Henle (1972) found a similar slight upward inequality trend when restricting his view to full-time adult male workers. T. P. Schultz (1971) documented steady or modest trends in inequality for most age–sex groups, though less so than for all hosueholds in the aggregate. Danziger and Plotnick (1975) also found that the modest inequality drift between 1965 and 1972 remained even after they controlled for various demographic factors. These results contradict Paglin's (1975) assertion that when the effects of changes in age composition are subtracted out, a residual decline in life-cycle inequality is left between 1947 and 1972. A critique of Paglin's approach can be found in Danziger, Haveman, and Smolensky (1976).

effect.[29] The net result is a degree of income leveling that has risen through government action, leaving the post-fisc inequality of income in 1970 almost the same as in 1950.

If demographic adjustments fail to influence the postwar inequality drift much, then the stability or slight rise in inequality should also show up in an examination of occupational pay ratios. Figure 4.4 seems to confirm this hunch, since pay ratios do indeed trace out postwar trends that coincide with the "true" inequality measures. Since the Korean War there has been no change in the pay advantage that industrial skilled workers have over unskilled workers.[30] Nor was there any change in the pay advantage of these unskilled nonfarm workers over farm workers.[31] On the other hand, blue-collar and farm workers appear to have fallen a little further behind the higher-paid professional and nonfarm managerial groups.[32] The series relating to teachers, professors, and physicians in Figure 4.4 show some variations on this theme. Physicians have succeeded in widening the income gap between themselves and low-skilled workers, a privileged pay position obviously maintained with the help of barriers to entry. The relative fortunes of teachers and college professors peaked about 1967 but have sagged since then. In general, then, occupational pay ratios exhibit the same slight drift toward greater pre-fisc inequality displayed by the direct measures of overall inequality.

The Long View, Backward

What can we conclude from this excursion through 150 years of American income inequality trends?

The evidence, particularly for the twentieth century, strongly suggests that movements in the size distribution of income are paralleled by

---

[29] M. Reynolds and Smolensky (1975). The "impact of government purchases" is restricted to an assessment of the distribution of direct benefits from government expenditures. It does *not* include a full general-equilibrium analysis of the induced production effects. On the pre-fisc–post-fisc demand influence see Williamson (1976c) and Chapter 8.

[30] A ratio of skilled and unskilled, based on union-prescribed pay scales in the building trades, shows a drop of 10% in the 1950s, followed by stability thereafter (Lindert, 1974, Table 2).

[31] This sentence is based on a comparison of the hourly pay of janitors and custodians in the BLS occupational wage surveys with the USDA series on farm hourly wage rates. The former was consistently a little over twice the latter in the postwar period.

[32] Between 1951 and 1966 the median earnings of "professional, technical, and kindred workers" and those of managers, officials, and proprietors (nonfarm) rose by 12.8% and 18.2%, respectively, relative to the wage rates for janitors and custodians.

movements in the basic pay structure. When measures of overall inequality were on the rise, so too were measures of dispersion in the rates of pay for occupational groups. Trends in skill premia, occupational wage differentials, earnings dispersion, and thus in rates of return to human capital seem to correlate well with size-distribution trends. This finding is very important to theorizing about distribution dynamics, since it suggests that previous changes in human and nonhuman wealth distributions have never been necessary to yield changes in current income distributions. In addition, however, we *do* observe a remarkably close correspondence between trends in income inequality and in wealth inequality. The causal link between these trends has yet to be established, however, and the possibilities are varied. For example, those forces which have been responsible for trends in pay ratios may also account for at least some of the observed trends in wealth distributions through their impact on asset values. Alternatively, it may be changes in the distribution of income which induce, through saving behavior, changes in the distribution of wealth, rather than vice versa.

Our survey opens anew the issue of inequality's relation to economic growth. Inequality in income and wealth rose sharply in America between 1820 and 1860. An inequality drift continued after the Civil War, although at a much diminished rate. The upward drift accelerates from the turn of the century up to America's entrance into World War I. Inequality fell between 1929 and the early years after World War II. It has changed little since. To repeat the conclusion to Chapter 3, this long-run pattern seems to confirm Simon Kuznets's (1955) conjecture that inequality first rises and then falls with modern economic growth. We stress "modern," since Chapters 2 and 3 showed that colonial and early antebellum growth failed to generate any trends in American inequality.

What does our chronology imply about the link between inequality and growth? Was modern economic growth either a necessary or a sufficient condition for trending inequality? Was trending inequality a prerequisite for rapid accumulation and modern economic growth? We submit that the answers are far from obvious, and Part Three of this book will make our position apparent. In any case, before we can proceed further, the historical behavior of *absolute* standards of life must be distinguished from *relative* standards. Income- and wealth-distribution statistics focus on the latter, and all of the statistics used in this and the previous two chapters follow in that tradition. Since we feel that any explanation of the correlation between inequality and growth must simultaneously account for the historical performance of both absolute and relative standards of life, Chapter 5 will devote considerable effort to the documentation of prices and absolute living standards since the early nineteenth century.

5

PRICES, INEQUALITY, AND ABSOLUTE LIVING STANDARDS

Forging a Link between Incomes and Prices

Real pay differentials between top and bottom socioeconomic classes will widen most dramatically when, on the income side, the nominal differential itself rises or, on the expenditure side, the cost of living for the poor undergoes the sharpest increase. Thus far we have examined trends in nominal differentials, whereas class cost-of-living differentials have been ignored. It is possible, of course, that prices played a systematic and important role in generating inequalities, but we have few theoretical guidelines to help us formulate some expectations. On the one hand, periods of stretching in the pay structure, swelling profit shares, and increasing concentration in income and wealth may also have witnessed a relatively sharp rise in the living costs of the poor compared with the rich. Based on early English industrial growth, T. S. Ashton (1954) certainly thought so:

> For those endowed with little or no skill, marginal productivity, and hence earnings, remained low. A large part of their income was spent on commodities . . . the cost of which had hardly been affected by technical development. . . . There were, however, large and growing sections of skilled and better-paid workers whose money incomes were rising and who had a substantial margin to spend on the products of the machine, the costs of which were falling progressively [p. 51].

Ashton's thesis may fail, of course, in which case episodes of trending nominal inequality would have been moderated by the relative improvement in the cost of living for the poor. An evaluation of distribution performance in America hinges on answers to these questions, since the distributional impact of these price movements could be as influential as the trends in inequality of nominal income and wealth that we conventionally measure.[1]

But there is more at stake than simply judging the adequacy of statistics on nominal distribution as social welfare indicators. Even more important is the possibility that the historical behavior of these relative prices may shed light on the determinants of trends in income distribution themselves. Indeed, Parts Two and Three of this book will argue that trends in nominal factor rewards, income distributions, *and* relative commodity prices are likely to have been determined by similar exogenous forces. In this chapter we shall in fact illustrate how historical trends in relative prices may help suggest promising hypotheses that could account for America's extraordinary distribution experience since 1820. We shall examine the evidence connecting prices and inequality in urban situations, then cast our net out farther to capture farm–nonfarm performance. We shall then examine aspects of regional inequality. Yet, our interest is not limited solely to the *relative* welfare performance of classes in American history. To prove the point, we shall supply evidence on absolute living standards of the low-income majority over the past century and a half. Our purpose, at least in part, is to explore the correlation between trends in absolutes and relatives, that is, between trends in the real income of the poor and trends in inequality.

American Prices and Urban Inequality

THE PEACETIME MODEL

Let us begin with the observation that the urban poor have always devoted a very large share of their budgets to traditional commodities, and that these commodities have always been produced by technical

___

[1] There appears to be an empirical void on this topic, despite the fact that cost-of-living indices abound for isolated regions and occupational groups. For example, the 1890–1929 period supplies at least five such indices for "average urban workers." Rees's (1961) index (1890–1914) was preceded by the contributions of King and Douglas, and Douglas (1930, pp. 656–667) himself cites seventy-three publications dealing with cost-of-living estimates limited to the 1890–1926 period alone. With the exception of King, however, not one of these studies attempts to compare cost-of-living changes by socioeconomic class. King (1930, Chap. III, pp. 65–72) supplies indices for five socioeconomic classes, 1909–1928. To our knowledge, his is the only serious attempt to confront the issue prior to the 1930s. King's pioneering contribution has been all but ignored by subsequent researchers.

For a masterful overview of the nineteenth-century behavior of relative prices, see Brady (1964).

TABLE 5.1
Expenditure Elasticities: American Urban Workers, 1875–1950

Sample	Rent	Fuel and Light	Food	Apparel	Dry Goods Sundries Miscellaneous
1875 Mass. urban	1.436	0.876	0.607	1.821	1.406 2.041
1888–1891 U.S. industrial	1.130	n.a.	0.680	1.210	1.290
1901 U.S. urban	0.839		0.712	1.435	1.561
1916 Washington, D.C.	0.930	0.730	0.670	1.360	1.480
1950 U.S. large northern cities	0.764		0.693	1.399	1.367

Sources and notes: Total expenditure elasticities are based on double logarithmic functions which offer joint estimates of expenditure and family-size elasticities. The 1875 and 1916 estimates are from Williamson (1967, Table 6, p. 119); the 1888–1891 estimates are from Fishlow (1973, Table 3.5, p. 65); and the 1901 and 1950 estimates are from Houthakker (1957, Table II, p. 541).

processes intensive in natural resources and unskilled labor, for example, food, fuel, and lighting.[2] High-income families—the skilled, the educated, and the wealthy—have always been heavy consumers of semidurables and durables. Most historians would concur that, compared with traditional necessities, production of these luxuries has always required the more intensive use of skills and machines—human and nonhuman assets owned primarily by upper-income groups. The classification of commodities by (modern) luxury and (traditional) necessity has been well established, but some notion of the remarkable stability of this classification over the past century in America can be seen in Table 5.1. Apparel, dry goods, and sundries consistently exhibit urban-family-expenditure elasticities far in excess of unity. The opposite has always been true of food, fuel, and light. The result is consistent, of course, with the fact that the urban poor have always been heavy consumers of traditional commodities, intensive in low-wage unskilled labor and "land," while the urban rich have always tended to favor modern commodities, intensive in high-wage labor and machines. Given the wide divergence in budget

[2] More generally, socioeconomic groups tend to consume heavily commodities produced by their own class. For example, in 1899 food used almost twice as much low-wage labor as consumer durables, apparel, and consumer services. Taking all consumption expenditures 1899 as a base of 100, the unskilled-labor intensity of food ranked 180, whereas apparel, consumer durables, and miscellaneous services ranked 102, 79, and 51 respectively (Table 8.6). Chapter 8 will supply further twentieth-century evidence supporting this characterization.

shares, any systematic long-run movement in the prices of either of these two commodity types will impart a welfare bias in favor of one class at the expense of another. Increasing land scarcity implies a rise in the relative price of food over time and thus a bias against its heaviest consumers, the poor. Relatively rapid technological change in the production of modern factory goods and a lagging technology in the production of traditional goods would impart a similar bias: the relative price of food and other traditional wage goods would rise. This theoretical speculation is certainly consistent with Brady's (1964) observations on the antebellum period: "Between the 1830s and 1860, the number of machine-made items that could be procured for a pound of pearlash, or a pound of the best rags, about doubled [p. 172]." To the extent that increasing land scarcity and rapid (and unbalanced) technical change are associated with modern economic growth and inequality, we might expect increasing nominal inequality to understate real inequality trends.

There is an additional complexity to consider. Up to this point we have focused on *commodities*. Suppose the budgets of upper-income groups were also dominated by unskilled-labor *services*, for example, domestic servants, seamstresses, laundresses, and coachmen. If nominal wages of the unskilled tend to lag during dramatic growth episodes, then the rich may derive an added cost-of-living benefit to their already large relative nominal income gains. We shall have more to say about the correlation between real wage performance of unskilled labor and inequality trends later in this chapter. For the moment, we simply note that systematic movements in the relative price of unskilled labor may also have an influence on relative cost-of-living trends by class.

These remarks should suffice to introduce the empirical report which follows. Have prices played any systematic distributional role during American peacetime development?

The Late Antebellum Years

The data are sparse for the early nineteenth century, but some very rough estimates of class living costs are presented in Table 5.2. They are based on Brady's (1972) urban budget share estimates for the 1830s. The resulting indices are certainly flawed: for example, they exclude shelter expenditures, they are restricted to purchased items, and they make no allowance whatsoever for different rates of quality change—rates that were far higher for luxury commodities. With these qualifications in mind,[3] we note that the price of necessities apparently rose a bit more

---

[3] In an earlier version of this chapter (Williamson, 1976a, Table 2), estimates of class cost of living were also presented for the period including 1820–1843. They were based on data which we now feel to be much too skimpy to warrant reproduction here.

TABLE 5.2
Cost of Living in Eastern Cities, 1844–1860, by Socioeconomic Class ($1860 = 100$)

Year	(1) Cost of Living Poor (Unskilled)	(2) Cost of Living Rich	(3) Ratio of Cost of Living of Poor to Rich (1) ÷ (2) × 100
1844	83.0	84.7	98.0
1845	84.5	85.3	99.1
1846	84.1	83.4	98.5
1847	99.3	94.3	105.3
1848	92.2	89.6	93.5
1849	92.5	90.0	102.8
1850	90.9	91.3	99.6
1851	90.7	91.4	99.2
1852	98.6	95.8	102.9
1853	103.0	99.9	103.1
1854	118.9	110.7	107.4
1855	122.8	110.3	111.3
1856	116.1	107.8	107.7
1857	122.3	112.5	108.7
1858	101.3	101.7	99.6
1859	102.0	100.1	101.9
1860	100.0	100.0	100.0

Sources and notes: The cost-of-living index for some jth class is

$$COL_j(t) = w_{Fj}P_F(t) + w_{Cj}P_C(t) + w_{Sj}P_S(t) + w_{Oj}P_O(t),$$

where the weights are computed from Brady (1972, Table 3.7, p. 79) for the 1830s:

	Unskilled	Rich
w_{Fj}	.65	.30
w_{Cj}	.15	.21
w_{Sj}	0	.20
w_{Oj}	.20	.29

Urban family income ranges were classified as follows: Poor = \$0–\$200 and Rich = \$2000–\$3000. The price of purchased foods (P_F) is taken from *Historical Statistics* (1960, E–3, p. 115) (The Warren–Pearson wholesale price). The price of clothing (P_C) is taken from the same source (Warren–Pearson wholesale price of textiles, E–5). The price of servants (P_S) is the nominal daily wage for common labor, taken from Appendix G.

In addition, the following price index for "sundries" is applied to both classes:

$$P_O(t) = .26 \, P_{FL}(t) + .74 \, P_{HF}(t).$$

The price of fuel and light (P_{FL}) and house furnishings (P_{HF}) are taken from *Historical Statistics* (1960, E–6 and E–10, p. 115) (Warren–Pearson wholesale). These two items together account for 45% of "sundries less church and charity" in the \$1000 range.

rapidly than that of luxuries over the period between 1844 and 1860. Living costs of the poorest urban workers rose more rapidly than costs of rich families during the inequality surge which, according to Chapter 4, peaked in 1856 (see Fig. 4.1 and Series (5), Appendix D); the opposite was true during the brief pay-ratio leveling from 1856 to 1860; the net effect was a modest rise in the poor man's relative living costs over the seventeen years as a whole.[4] The cost of living of the urban poor was changing in such a fashion as to cause a double deterioration in their relative economic position—a deterioration on both the income and expenditure side.

Up to this point we have been content simply to establish whether high-income families suffered smaller cost-of-living increases than poor families during this antebellum phase of trending nominal inequality. It seems that any urban measure of the nominal wage structure, pay differentials, or income distribution will understate real antebellum trends. How can we translate this finding into a *quantitative* measure of the importance of price changes on real income differentials? As we have seen in Chapter 4, the requisite size distribution of income data is available only for the twentieth century. While we shall utilize such data below, our nineteenth-century calculations must be limited exclusively to pay ratios. These supply only the most limited earnings ranges. Obviously, the impact of differential cost-of-living patterns will depend on the range of income classes examined; the wider the range, the greater the variance in budget weights, and thus the larger the difference in cost-of-living performance. Since we wish to make broad inferences about trends in antebellum urban inequality, it seems sensible to apply the "rich" cost-of-living index to the "top" of our nominal pay structure in assessing the likely quantitative importance of urban prices. What does the exercise tell us? While the nominal skill differential rose by 21.5% between 1844 and 1856 (Series (5), Appendix D), the real differential rose by 33.5%. Indeed, the real wage of the urban unskilled had declined to four-fifths of its 1844 level by 1856 (Appendix G). Similar forces were at work during the brief leveling of pay ratios in the late fifties. Whereas the nominal index diminished by 8.2% between 1856 and 1861, the real index declined by twice as much—16.3%, and the real wage of unskilled urban workers rose by almost 18%.

---

[4] A linear time trend (using $y = a + bt$), fitted to the relative cost-of-living data in Table 5.2, Col. (3), yields the following estimates:

$$1844–1860 \quad b = +0.212 \ (1.864),$$
$$1844–1856 \quad b = +0.262 \ (3.431),$$

where the figures in parentheses are t statistics.

The Quality Bias

The surge of urban inequality following 1844 was reinforced by cost-of-living movements that penalized the poor. Changes in the relative prices of consumer goods worked to favor the rich, the highly skilled, and the professional, thus making the urban inequality surge worse in real terms. While the nominal income forces seem to be far more potent than the supportive cost-of-living movement, our calculations do contain a downward bias. We have ignored the obvious fact that quality improvements were more typical of luxury modern products than traditional necessities. The relative cost-of-living gain to the rich is understated in Table 5.2, but by some unknown factor. If twentieth-century rates of quality improvement of consumer durables are assumed to have prevailed from 1844 to 1855 as well, then the relative rise in the cost-of-living ratio, poor to rich, would have been 18.4% rather than the 13.6%, as measured in Table 5.2.[5] Such estimates of the quality bias are only guesses at best, but they do illustrate the likely size of our understatement of the relative inflation of living costs for the poor in the antebellum period.

The Emergence of a Peacetime Model

Antebellum inequality trends were reinforced by the unequal incidence of cost-of-living changes, and all the more so when the quality bias is considered. Does this vindicate Ashton's thesis? Did the price of *all* traditional wage goods rise rapidly compared with other consumption goods? Perhaps one commodity dominated these trends. Perhaps the decline in real wages (the relative price of services) from 1844 to 1856 was doing all the work. The incidence of relative price changes over the 1844–1861 swing is summarized in Table 5.3, where class differences in cost-of-living changes are decomposed into commodity groups. It should be apparent that the impact of changing commodity prices on the relative cost of living of a class depends on the relative importance of that expenditure in its budget as well as the magnitude of the price change. Thus, the decomposition in Table 5.3 tells us precisely what the sources of living-cost changes by socioeconomic class were: *All* of the excessive rise in the cost of living of the urban poor (over and above that of the rich) between 1844 and 1856 can be attributed to the relative rise in food prices. The story is even more convincing from 1855 to 1861. The relative decline

---

[5] The rate of quality improvement is assumed to apply to all nonfood and nonservice expenditures. Gordon (1971, Table 4, p. 144) tells us that consumer durables improved in quality at a rate roughly equal to 2.5% per annum, 1935–1953. The size of the downward bias on the antebellum relative cost of living of the poor is simply $(.50 - .35) \times 2.5\% = +.38\%$ per annum. The two figures in parentheses refer to budget weights of the rich less those of the poor; they roughly conform to the weights reported in Table 5.2, $w_{sj} + w_{oj}$.

TABLE 5.3
Cost-of-Living Incidence by Class and Its Components, Cities, 1844–1948 (*in percentages*)

	Inequality Trends				Equality Trends			
	Peacetime		Postwar Stabilization		Peacetime	Wartime		
Components	1844–1856	1896–1914	1865–1874	1919–1929	1855–1861	1862–1864	1914–1919	1936–1948
Total: $\left[\dfrac{COL(t)}{COL(t-1)}\right]_{POOR} - \left[\dfrac{COL(t)}{COL(t-1)}\right]_{RICH}$	+12.7	+7.0	+3.7	+3.1	−3.6	−7.9	−10.7	+2.4
Due to relative price change in								
Food	+19.6	+5.3	−5.7	−1.8	−2.0	+15.0	+8.4	+14.8
Clothing	−0.2	+1.0	+10.6	+3.9	0	−22.0	−13.2	−5.0
Rent	n.a.	+0.2	−0.6	+0.8	−0.8	−0.4	+0.7	+1.0
Fuel and light	n.a.	+0.5	−0.7	+0.5	−0.5	+0.7	+1.4	+1.6
Home furnishings	n.a.	n.a.	n.a.	+0.4	n.a.	n.a.	−2.5	−1.1
Domestics	−5.3	n.a.	n.a.	n.a.	n.a.	n.a.	n.a.	n.a.
Miscellaneous	−1.4	0	+0.1	−0.6	−0.3	−1.2	−5.5	−8.8

Sources and notes: The decomposition is achieved by the expression

$$\left[\frac{COL(t)}{COL(t-1)}\right]_{POOR} - \left[\frac{COL(t)}{COL(t-1)}\right]_{RICH} = \sum_j \frac{1}{r}\left[P_j(t) - P_j(t-1)\right]\left[\frac{w_{jPOOR}}{COL_{POOR}(t-1)} - \frac{w_{jRICH}}{COL_{RICH}(t-1)}\right]$$

The underlying data are taken from Tables 5.2, 5.4, 5.5, 5.6 and Williamson (1976a, Table 9, p. 330).

of food prices did indeed tend to favor the urban poor, and the decline accounted for the majority of their relative cost-of-living improvement. But note the consistency with which *every* wage good underwent price movements to favor the poor—rent, fuel, light, and food—while luxuries were rising in relative price.

The Pre–World War I Years

The stretching in the nominal pay structure between 1896 and 1914 reflects the last great surge in American urban inequality. The forces making for inequality were so strong, in fact, that hardly any increase in real wages took place for the urban unskilled; even if one uses Rees's revisions, the real wage rose at the paltry rate of 0.42% per annum in the eighteen years following 1896 (Appendix G). Cost-of-living movements again favored the rich—even ignoring the potent influence of the quality bias in consumer-goods prices—thus making for even sharper real pay differentials. Table 5.4 (which is based on Rees's price data and 1901 budget weights) shows that while urban laborers faced a 22% cost-of-living rise over the 18 years,[6] highly skilled workers and professionals suffered a rise of only 15%. Furthermore, Table 5.3 suggests that *all* relative prices were contributing to this cost-of-living trend (with the exception of unskilled-labor services, whose prices had a neutral effect on the "miscellaneous" category). The key driving force, however, was the relative price of food.

The pre–World War I years conform to the nineteenth-century "peacetime" pattern. Relative prices reinforced nominal income trends. Trending nominal inequality always coincided with sharper cost-of-living increases for the poor, and food prices were the main influence.

THE WAR-INFLATION AND POSTWAR-STABILIZATION MODEL

Civil War and "Catching Up"

The first modern expenditure and income survey, based on an 1875 sample of Massachusetts urban workers, falls in this period. In addition, the 1890/1891 budget detail in the *Aldrich Report* is available, along with Coelho and Shepherd's (1974) analysis of *Weeks Report* retail prices. Table 5.5 presents some fruits of this harvest, and they must be viewed as vastly superior to the antebellum estimates. Three Middle Atlantic urban family indices are reported: unskilled ($400 income in 1875 dollars);

---

[6] The rise is even more dramatic on the farm. The farm cost-of-living index rose by 41%, reinforcing the urban bias. See discussion below.

TABLE 5.4
Cost of Living, by Socioeconomic Class, Cities, 1890–1914 (*1914* = *100*)

Year	Cost-of-Living Indices		(3) Ratio of Low to High Cost of Living
	(1) Low (Unskilled)	(2) High (Skilled)	(1) ÷ (2) × 100
1890	91	99	91.9
1891	91	98	92.9
1892	90	97	92.8
1893	90	96	93.8
1894	86	92	93.5
1895	83	88	94.3
1896	82	87	94.3
1897	81	86	94.2
1898	82	86	95.3
1899	82	85	96.5
1900	83	86	96.5
1901	84	87	96.6
1902	85	87	97.7
1903	87	89	97.8
1904	87	89	97.8
1905	86	88	97.7
1906	89	90	98.9
1907	93	94	98.9
1908	91	92	98.9
1909	91	92	98.9
1910	94	95	98.9
1911	95	95	100.0
1912	97	97	100.0
1913	98	99	99.0
1914	100	100	100.0

Sources and notes: The underlying prices are taken from Rees (1961, Table 22, p. 74). Five commodities make up the indices: food (P_F), clothing (P_C), fuel and light (P_{FL}), rent (P_R), and sundries (P_M). The weights are taken from the 1901 urban survey reported in U.S. Commissioner of Labor (1904, p. 101):

	Low (Unskilled) ($200–$300)	High (Skilled) ($1,200)
w_{FJ}	.473	.365
w_{CJ}	.087	.157
w_{MJ}	.188	.254
w_{RJ}	.180	.174
w_{FLJ}	.072	.050

The report of the 1901 urban survey suggests that $200–$300 was typical of janitors, construction laborers, and manufacturing common labor, while the top "working" class at $1200 would have been skilled workers with seniority and professionals.

TABLE 5.5

Cost of Living by Socioeconomic Class, Middle Atlantic Cities, 1855–1880 (*1860* = *100*)

Year	Cost-of-Living Indices			(4) Ratio of Low to High Cost of Living (1) ÷ (3) × 100
	(1) Low (Unskilled)	(2) Middle (Skilled)	(3) High (Rich)	
1855	109.1	107.2	106.2	102.7
1856	104.2	104.5	104.6	99.6
1857	109.9	109.1	108.7	101.1
1858	101.6	102.3	102.6	99.0
1859	104.0	104.8	102.2	101.8
1860	100.0	100.0	100.0	100.0
1861	102.3	103.0	103.4	98.9
1862	110.1	111.6	112.4	98.0
1863	131.0	136.0	138.5	94.6
1864	177.0	184.9	188.9	93.7
1865	186.4	189.5	191.1	97.5
1866	186.3	185.6	185.2	100.6
1867	175.2	173.8	173.2	101.2
1868	175.2	172.2	170.8	102.6
1869	163.5	161.9	161.2	101.4
1870	159.3	158.3	157.9	100.8
1871	155.8	154.1	153.4	101.6
1872	155.6	153.3	152.3	102.2
1873	152.3	150.2	149.2	102.1
1874	147.2	144.9	143.8	102.4
1875	141.3	139.1	138.4	102.1
1876	135.1	132.8	131.8	102.5
1877	133.1	130.4	128.6	103.5
1878	123.7	121.5	120.5	102.7
1879	118.3	116.7	116.0	102.0
1880	120.0	118.5	117.8	101.9

Sources and notes: The data are slightly revised versions of Coelho and Shepherd (1974). Professor Coelho kindly supplied the price data used here for clothing (P_C), food (P_F), fuel and lighting (P_{FL}), and rent (P_R). They are based on *Weeks Report* prices and *Aldrich Report* fixed 1890–1891 weights. "Miscellaneous" (P_M), the fifth category, is a weighted average of house furnishings and domestic wages. The cost-of-living index for some *j*th class is

$$COL_j(t) = w_{Fj}(t) + w_{Cj}P_C(t) + w_{FLj}P_{FL}(t) + w_{Rj}P_R(t) + w_{Mj}P_M(t),$$

where the weights are derived from linear Engel functions in Williamson (1967, Table 4, p. 116):

	Low (Unskilled)	Middle (Skilled)	High (Rich)
w_F	.689	.549	.479
w_C	.041	.142	.193
w_{FL}	.070	.058	.051
w_R	.136	.163	.177
w_M	.064	.088	.100

The "low" income class refers to $400 total annual expenditure, about the average income of unskilled urban workers in Massachusetts (1875). "Middle" income refers to $800 total expenditure, the average income of skilled workers. "High" refers to $1600 total expenditures, the highest income reported in the 1875 sample.

107

skilled ($800); and "rich" ($1600). The "rich" income class is hardly at the pinnacle of the 1875 income distribution, but it surely falls in the top Massachusetts quintile.

Note that the unskilled workers' cost of living underwent a relatively sharp decline in 1855–1861, confirming the earlier results based on sketchier data. The peacetime contraction in earnings differentials was even more impressive in real than in nominal terms. Furthermore, the narrowing of pay differentials during the Civil War was accentuated by the much sharper inflation in living costs among high-income classes. Consider the most dramatic inflationary Greenback episode, 1862–1864. While the nominal skilled-wage premium fell by 4.6% over these three years, the real premium fell by 9.5%—almost twice as much. Once again, movements in relative prices reinforced trends in nominal income distribution.[7] Postwar "catching up" generated an impressive stretching in pay differentials, along with other attributes of increasing inequality. It also produced relative price behavior which reinforced these nominal distribution trends. While the nominal skill premium rose by 8.7% from 1865 to 1874, it rose almost twice as much in real terms.

An extraordinarily consistent historical pattern is emerging from this examination. Whether peacetime, wartime, or return to normalcy, whether inflation or deflation, the relative price structure *always* behaved in a fashion that reinforced trends in nominal income distribution. Surely the same forces could not have been at work in each case. Indeed, Table 5.3 makes it clear that very different models must be used to explain peacetime, wartime, and postwar-stabilization episodes. From 1855 to 1861 we have the conventional peacetime pattern: The relative decline in food prices accounted for the lion's share of the improved cost-of-living position of the poor, so that the narrowing of nominal pay differentials was even more pronounced in real terms. A further narrowing of nominal wage differentials took place during the Civil War, and the trend was also

---

[7] This paragraph may appear to argue that real wages of unskilled labor rose during the Civil War. On the contrary, taking 1860 = 100, the real wage for unskilled workers was 77.5 in 1864; for skilled workers it was 74.5. Thus, these new cost-of-living indices by socioeconomic class do not erase "Mitchell's Paradox" of falling real wages. (While real wages declined during the Civil War, Appendix G shows that they rose during World Wars I and II. Family annual earnings is another matter entirely.) Nor should the decline in real wages imply that the "wages share" diminished during the war. In sharp contrast to twentieth-century wars, Civil War financing relied far more heavily on indirect taxes (both internal and external). As a result, real disposable income fell for *all* social classes as public military expenditures rose markedly as a share in GNP. Furthermore, *family* incomes among poor urban households may have behaved differently from average earnings of the employed unskilled—depending on who entered the military. The point remains that unskilled workers fared better in real terms than did skilled workers and professionals, or perhaps even property income recipients.

more pronounced in real terms. The causes were surely very different, however, since the trends in food prices were working in the opposite direction. It was the enormous (and oft-quoted) rise in clothing prices that accounted for the relatively more dramatic deterioration in the cost of living of the rich. Similar contrasts appear during the postwar "catching up" and stabilization (or, more commonly, pre-Resumption deflation). When nominal inequality measures were on the rise from 1865 to 1874, the poor suffered an even greater diminution in their relative real income position. Yet the causes cannot be attributed to surging food prices, nor to fuel, light, and rents, since they all had exactly the opposite influence. Once again, clothing and durable-goods prices were doing the trick—the latter increasingly dominating "miscellaneous" and "sundries" as the century progressed.

To summarize nineteenth-century experience, the prices of traditional, "necessary" commodities were the major factor influencing the relative cost of living by socioeconomic class during peacetime. The relevant peacetime model appears to be one of increasing land scarcity and technological imbalance: Since agriculture lagged behind during dramatic surges of technological change, the relative price of foodstuffs tended to rise, and the nominal inequality trends associated with early capitalist development were reinforced on the expenditure side. During wartime and subsequent return to normalcy, the prices of durables and semidurables dominated the relative cost-of-living movements. This latter performance has long been treated as a unique phenomenon associated with the Civil War cotton famine. Perhaps there were more systematic forces at work. An examination of the twentieth-century experience should indicate how far we have come in our quest for a general, wartime model.

World War I and the Roaring Twenties

The previous chapter noted that while twentieth-century experience with income distribution has always attracted attention, serious analysis usually starts only with 1914, since distribution data are so sparse prior to this point. We emphasized three phases which have attracted special interest: (a) a narrowing in wage structure and movements toward equality during World War I; (b) a return to postwar normalcy during the twenties with related trends toward greater inequality; and (c) the "revolutionary" egalitarian drift from 1929 to the late forties. Here we focus on the first two periods. Did cost-of-living movements tend to reinforce trends in nominal pay differentials during the 1914–1929 period?

Nominal wage differentials declined by 13.4% from 1914 to 1919, a very sharp contraction for such a short period of time. Indeed, there is no period in the preceding century that compares with this wartime collapse in wage differentials. This trend must have been reinforced by cost-of-living movements (Table 5.6), since the index for the poor rose more modestly than for the rich during the wartime inflation. Furthermore, all of the divergent cost-of-living changes were centered on the most inflationary years 1916–1919, a condition that held for nominal wage differentials as well. These changes also coincided with America's first experiment with price controls:

> The war-time rise in the prices of staples prior to our entrance into war was tolerated without complaints by the labor and middle classes. . . . A general discontent developed, however, when prices mounted higher after mobilization began reducing thousands of family budgets. . . . Many believed it the duty of the government to protect them from exorbitant charges for the staple commodities, and urged this course until the Congress set up the machinery for a control over food and fuel prices [Garrett, 1920, p. 35].

Table 5.6 suggests that the middle class and rich had more cause for complaint. Indeed, while the real wages of the urban unskilled rose by almost 10% between 1914 and 1919 (Appendix G), those of skilled workers *fell* by 11%, and most of these remarkable changes occurred in the last three years of the period.

Modeling these wartime forces is now a simple enough task. Wars require a heavy reliance on *commodity* production—food to some extent, manufactured nondurables as well, but especially durables. Skill-intensive private capital goods production and urban service activities (the most notable of which is private construction) tend to contract as a consequence. Skilled labor and professionals are in low demand as the output mix shifts. The enormous restriction on the supply of unskilled labor available to the private economy strongly reinforces these effects.[8] The prices of consumer durables, semidurables, and low-skill personal services rise at a rate exceeding the inflation in food and the prices of other traditional wage goods. The net result is to penalize the rich on both the income and expenditure side.[9]

Presumably, these forces are reversed as the economy returns to normalcy. Who paid for postwar stabilization during the twenties? These new cost-of-living indices have much to tell us not only about increasing relative inequality during the 1920s, but also about the *absolute* real income position of the urban poor. The facts are that it was 1927 before the real wages of the unskilled achieved the level they had reached in 1920 (Appendix G). Real wages of skilled workers rose by 11% during the same

[8] A more extensive argument can be found in Chapter 12 and in Williamson (1974a, 1974e, 1976b), where the demand effects for the 1914–1929 period are discussed in detail.

[9] Some may well argue that the rich could easily absorb the penalty, but this book avoids such judgments.

TABLE 5.6
Cost of Living by Socioeconomic Class, Cities, 1914–1929 (1914 = 100)

Year	Cost-of-Living Indices		(3) Ratio of Low to High Cost of Living (1) ÷ (2) × 100
	(1) Low (Unskilled)	(2) High (Skilled)	
1914	100	100	100.0
1915	102	102	99.3
1916	115	115	99.7
1917	138	140	98.9
1918	167	172	97.0
1919	190	201	94.7
1920	191	202	94.7
1921	169	175	96.5
1922	164	169	97.1
1923	168	173	97.2
1924	167	172	97.5
1925	176	178	98.7
1926	173	176	98.4
1927	169	173	98.1
1928	168	171	98.0
1929	169	172	98.1

Sources and notes: All underlying prices are December BLS quotations reported in *Statistical Abstract of the United States* (1951). Six prices are used to construct these indices: food, clothing, fuel and light, rent, house furnishings, and sundries. The weights are taken from the 1918–1919 BLS urban budget survey reported in U.S. Department of Labor (1924, Table 2, p. 5). "Low (Unskilled)" refers to families earning income below $900 in 1918–1919 prices. "High (Skilled)" refers to those earning in excess of $1500. Relative to the 1918–1919 survey average, these groups maintain the same standardized dispersion as those used in Table 5.4 for 1901. The weights are

	Low (Unskilled)	High (Skilled)
w_F	.441	.349
w_C	.132	.204
w_{FL}	.068	.041
w_R	.145	.106
w_{HF}	.036	.053
w_M	.178	.247

period. Lean years for urban workers at the bottom of the distribution, indeed. Not only did the distribution of real earnings shift toward greater inequality following 1919 and 1920, but the absolute real wage for the urban unskilled declined until 1926.

In contrast with our nineteenth-century analysis, we no longer need limit ourselves to the wage structure in making judgments regarding the quantitative impact of these cost-of-living changes. Table 5.7 uses Simon Kuznets's limited size-distribution information dating from World War I. Consider the share in nonfarm income of the top 10% of nonfarm families.

TABLE 5.7
Deflation of Relative Income Shares, Nonfarm, 1917–1948 (*in percentages*)

Year	Top 10%		Top 5%	
	Money	Real	Money	Real
1917	34.5%	34.5%	25.6%	25.6%
1920	30.3	29.3	22.6	21.8
1920	30.3	30.3	22.6	22.6
1929	35.4	36.3	26.1	26.8
1929	35.7	35.7	26.3	26.3
1939	33.0	32.0	22.9	22.3
1939	33.0	33.0	22.9	22.9
1948	25.4	25.7	18.3	18.5

Sources and notes: The nominal income shares are Kuznets's nonfarm estimates (Kuznets, 1953, pp. 610–614). The real income shares are derived by deflation using relevant cost-of-living indices. The commodity price data are December BLS quotations reported in *Statistical Abstract of the United States* (1951). The weights are estimated from double logarithmic expenditure functions: 1917–1929 uses 1918/1919 weights; 1929–1948 uses 1935/1936 weights.

During the wartime egalitarian drift, the *real* income share of the top tenth dropped from 34.5% to 29.3%, that is, 5.2 percentage points. Approximately one-fifth of this enormous redistribution can be attributed to the cost-of-living effects that tended to tax the rich. During the twenties, about 1 percentage point out of the 6% rise in the real share of the top tenth can be explained by cost-of-living changes that penalized the poor. Given the extraordinary quality developments during the so-called "consumer durables revolution" of this decade, this estimate must be viewed as a lower bound.

Furthermore, the underlying sources of the cost-of-living performance almost exactly duplicate those of the Civil War (1862–1864) and catching-up phase (1865–1874) a half century earlier. The wartime relative price behavior of food, fuel, light, and rent all tended to tax the poor, but the behavior of the relative prices of clothing, house furnishings, and "sundries" imparted a far heavier penalty on the rich (Table 5.3). These conditions reversed during the twenties, just as they reversed following 1865.

THE LAST HALF CENTURY: OLD WINE IN NEW BOTTLES[10]

Obviously, inflation or deflation cannot have different expenditure effects by socioeconomic class unless *relative* prices of consumption goods

[10] This section is taken from Williamson (1977a), where American post–World War II experience is examined in more detail and also compared with England.

exhibit some variance. While this condition was fulfilled in the century before 1929, apparently it was unfulfilled for the first two decades of post–World War II American experience. Hollister and Palmer (1969) found that only medical care had changed significantly in relative price from 1947 to 1967. Prices of food, housing, clothing, transportation, personal care, and durables tended to conform closely to the overall consumer price index. In spite of a very wide range in the budget shares from poor to rich, differential effects of postwar inflations have been relatively small on the expenditure side, at least prior to 1967. Hollister and Palmer concluded that relative prices of consumer goods had only a trivial influence on real distributions and that nominal-distribution statistics were quite adequate social indicators. Lest the reader conclude that the pre-1929 experience discussed above is in conflict with the Hollister and Palmer results, he should be reminded that American postwar growth has also been accompanied by remarkable stability in the distribution of nominal income (Chap. 4). Thus, one wonders if the Hollister and Palmer finding would hold from 1929 to 1948 during the "great leveling," or even after 1967, when inequality was on the rise. It does not. Rather, we shall see that the nineteenth- and early-twentieth-century pattern is repeated once more.

Since size distributions of income become abundant following 1929, we can now apply more sophisticated measures to our price and inequality problem. Contemporary economists use a bewildering variety of inequality statistics. Among those most commonly used are the coefficient of variation, the relative mean deviation, the Gini coefficient, and the standard deviation (or variance) of logarithms. A few years ago Atkinson (1970, p. 257) proposed a more general index which encompasses all of these, and we shall use it here. Our real inequality index is written as

$$I = 1 - \left\{ \sum_j \left[\frac{\overline{y}_j^*}{\overline{y}^*} \right]^{1-\epsilon} f(y_j) \right\}^{1/(1-\epsilon)},$$

where

$$\overline{y}_j^* = \frac{\overline{y}_j}{\sum_i w_{ij} P_{ij}} = \text{mean real expenditure of the } j\text{th income class,}$$

$$\overline{y}^* = \sum_j \left\{ \frac{\overline{y}_j}{\sum_i w_{ij} P_{ij}} \right\} f(y_j) = \text{economy-wide mean real expenditure,}$$

and w_{ij} = fixed expenditure share on the ith good in the jth income class. Furthermore, $0 \leq I \leq 1$, and $\epsilon > 0$ is a parameter measuring the degree of

TABLE 5.8
Prices and Urban Inequality: The 1914–1920 Egalitarian Episode *(using 1935/1936 weights)*

	Atkinson's Inequality Index		
	$\epsilon = +1.5$	$\epsilon = +2.5$	$\epsilon = +4.0$
Nominal expenditure distribution			
(urban, 1935/1936)	.1706	.2592	.3574
Impact of historical price changes, 1914–1920 (using 1935/1936 weights)			
All prices	.1602	.2447	.3399
Food	.1868	.2814	.3836
Rent	.1736	.2631	.3618
Fuel and light	.1785	.2703	.3710
Furnishings	.1665	.2534	.3504
Clothing	.1576	.2409	.3351
Miscellaneous	.1465	.2253	.3160

Sources and notes: The nominal distribution index is for urban families, 1935/1936, as are the expenditure weights. See Table 5.9 for sources and methods. The prices used in the calculations are December BLS quotations reported in *Statistical Abstract of the United States* (1951).

inequality aversion. This is a very attractive general statistic, since it allows us to examine inequality experience while applying various weights to the relative importance of different intraclass transfers. As ϵ rises, transfers to lower-income groups are given heavier weight and transfers among top-income recipients are given lighter weight. In the empirical analysis that follows, we shall consider values of ϵ in the range 1.5 to 4.0. Based on Atkinson's experiments (1970, pp. 260–262) with U.S. 1950 size-distribution data, this range encompasses such popular distribution statistics as the Gini coefficient and the variance of log income.

The Twenties Again

In Table 5.7 we calculated that as much as a fifth of the 5.2 percentage point decline in the top 10% real income share could be explained by relative cost-of-living movements from 1917 to 1920. Similar results were apparent for the 1920s: While the top 10% share in real income rose by 6 percentage points, one of these percentage points was due to the favorable cost-of-living changes facing the rich. Since the reader may have been skeptical about the relevance of a calculation based only on the top 5% or 10%, it might be useful to repeat the calculation using our new index proposed by Atkinson. Unfortunately, we do not possess good urban size-distribution data prior to 1935/1936. The data problem can be partially surmounted, however, by asking the following question: What would have been the impact of the 1914–1920 relative price changes on the 1935/1936 distribution of (real) expenditures among urban families? Three values of ϵ are used in Table 5.8, and they tell a story quite consistent with our earlier calculation. That is, those relative price changes served to lower the incidence of urban inequality from 1 to 1.7 percentage points.

The "Great Leveling"

Table 5.9 documents the impact of prices on inequality during the 1930s and 1940s, a period of impressive nominal leveling in the distribution. Look first at the longer term, the two decades from one full-employment year to another, 1929–1948. There does seem to be a continuation of our "empirical law of living costs," since relative prices were tending to contribute to the egalitarian drift. The impact is hardly as great as during the more volatile first third of the twentieth century: Atkinson's index is lowered by only 0.5 to 0.7 percentage points in response to the price changes, and the index falls hardly at all when estimates of quality improvements are introduced. Nevertheless, nominal and real distribution once again move together.

Curiously enough, the "law" fails for the shorter-term period following 1935. The rise in food prices was sufficiently large to reverse the correlation: While nominal inequality indicators were falling—primarily in response to full-employment effects, according to T. P. Schultz (1971) and Chiswick and Mincer (1972)—living costs were rising most dramatically for the poor. This is the *only* such correspondence in a century of American experience. It should be emphasized, however, that the more relevant long-term experience, between the full-employment points 1929 and 1948, yields the more conventional result: While nominal inequality indicators were falling, living costs were also rising most dramatically for the rich.

Prices and Inequality in the 1970s:
A Recurring Theme

Income inequality was on the rise between 1967 and 1973. No doubt expenditure distributions would exhibit a less steep inequality trend, but Table 5.10 confirms that relative price movements were contributing significantly to the inequality drift. Assuming $\epsilon = 2.5$, the historical price changes from 1967 to March 1975 would have raised urban inequality from a .3165 base (the 1960/1961 figure) to .3298, a rise of 1.33 percentage points. This is no small matter when judged by the actual increase in nominal income inequality from 1967 to 1973. At $\epsilon = 2.5$, Atkinson's

TABLE 5.9
Prices and Urban Inequality, 1929–1948

	Atkinson's Inequality Index		
	$\epsilon = +1.5$	$\epsilon = +2.5$	$\epsilon = +4.0$
Nominal expenditure distribution (urban, 1935/1936)	.1706	.2592	.3574
Impact of historical price changes, 1935–1948			
All prices	.1735	.2632	.3622
Food	.1922	.2887	.3921
Housing	.1722	.2613	.3598
Fuel and light	.1737	.2635	.3627
Furnishings	.1681	.2556	.3530
Clothing	.1622	.2473	.3430
Miscellaneous	.1565	.2395	.3336
All prices: quality-adjusted	.1766	.2676	.3674
Furnishings	.1693	.2573	.3551
Miscellaneous	.1593	.2435	.3385

	Atkinson's Inequality Index		
	$\epsilon = +1.5$	$\epsilon = +2.5$	$\epsilon = +4.0$
Nominal expenditure distribution (urban, 1935/1936)	.1706	.2592	.3574
Impact of historical price changes, 1929–1948			
All prices	.1662	.2532	.3504
Food	.1838	.2774	.3790
Housing	.1693	.2575	.3554
Fuel and light	.1724	.2617	.3604
Furnishings	.1687	.2565	.3542
Clothing	.1646	.2507	.3471
Miscellaneous	.1586	.2424	.3372
All prices: quality-adjusted	.1714	.2604	.3590
Furnishings	.1703	.2588	.3569
Miscellaneous	.1630	.2487	.3448

Sources and notes: The nominal distribution indices are for urban families, 1935/1936. These data are taken from the U.S. National Resources Planning Board (1941) and refer to total family expenditures over twelve income classes ranging from $0–$500 (excluding those on relief) to $5000–$10,000. The impact of prices on inequality uses the nominal I (1935/1936) as a base, and the w_{ij} are estimated from double logarithmic expenditure functions (total family expenditures the sole independent variable). The P_{ij} are taken from *Statistical Abstract of the United States* (1951, pp. 282–283). The "adjusted house furnishings" price index attempts to introduce a quality-change estimate. The rate of quality improvement estimated for refrigerators (1935–1948) is assumed to apply to all house furnishings over the period (R. J. Gordon, 1971, Table 4, p. 144). The "adjusted miscellaneous" price index does the same for automobiles. The quality improvement rate is taken from Griliches (1939–1947, low-priced automobiles: see R. J. Gordon, 1971, Table 4, p. 144). In 1935/1936, the "average" urban family spending $1750 annually devoted 23.9% of miscellaneous expenditures to automobile purchases. This fixed budget weight is utilized to get the "adjusted" price series used in the table.

TABLE 5.10
Prices and Urban Inequality, 1967–1975

	Atkinson's Inequality Index		
	$\epsilon = +1.5$	$\epsilon = +2.5$	$\epsilon = +4.0$
Nominal expenditure distribution (urban, 1960/1961)	.1913	.3165	.4618
Impact of historical price changes, 1967– March 1975			
All prices	.2004	.3298	.4773
Food	.2178	.3573	.5097
Housing	.1944	.3206	.4659
Fuel and light	.1924	.3180	.4633
Furnishings	.1889	.3125	.4565
Clothing	.1869	.3097	.4536
Miscellaneous	.1780	.2959	.4367
All prices: quality-adjusted	.1982	.3273	.4748
Furnishings	.1899	.3142	.4587
Miscellaneous	.1752	.2918	.4320

Sources and notes: The nominal distribution indices are for urban families, 1960/1961. These data are taken from the 1960/1961 survey of consumer expenditures (U.S. Department of Labor, 1964), and refer to total family expenditures over ten income classes ranging from "under $1000" to "$15,000 and over." The impact of prices on inequality uses the nominal I (1960/1961) as a base, where w_{ij} are estimated from double logarithmic expenditure functions (total family expenditures the sole independent variable). All prices are taken from annual December issues and June 1975, *Monthly Labor Review*. The "adjusted house furnishings" price index attempts to introduce a quality-change estimate, as does "adjusted automobiles." The former is an estimate based on 1954–1968 for refrigerators, and the latter is an estimate based on 1960–1966 for "low-priced" autos (R. J. Gordon, 1971, Table 4, p. 144).

index rises by 5 percentage points (see Williamson, 1977a). That is, price trends have had at least one-quarter as much effect as nominal income trends in contributing to inequality trends in recent years. We conclude that prices have been a significant regressive force since the late 1960s, just as they were during all other periods of trending nominal inequality since 1844.

Which wage goods have been most responsible for the regressive impact of prices since 1967? Table 5.10 confirms in quantitative terms what we have found to be true for the past 130 years in America. Virtually all of the regressive price impact can be traced to food. While overall inflation acted to raise Atkinson's index ($\epsilon = 2.5$) by 1.33 percentage points, food prices by themselves contributed to a 4.08 percentage-point increase. Similar patterns emerge for the 1929–1948 period (Table 5.9) and earlier (Table 5.3).

Certainly the strategic role of food is explained in part by its extraordinary rise in price after 1972. But its dominance can also be explained by the relative sensitivity of inequality measures to a given change in food prices compared with an identical change in any other price. The computations reported in Table 5.11 reveal the impact of a 25% change in some consumer goods prices—holding all other prices constant—on Atkinson's index. The strategic wage goods are food, whose price has by far the largest potential regressive impact, and "miscellaneous," whose price has by far the largest potential progressive impact. The latter includes

TABLE 5.11
Sensitivity Analysis for U.S. Urban Families: "Strategic" Commodities, Inflation, and Inequality

	Atkinson's Inequality Index			
	1935/1936	1960/1961		
	$\epsilon = +1.5$	$\epsilon = +1.5$	$\epsilon = +2.5$	$\epsilon = +4.0$
Nominal expenditure distribution: I	.1706	.1913	.3165	.4618
Impact of a 25% change in P_j, holding all other P_k constant: $I - \hat{I}$				
Detail, $j = 1,...,6$				
Food	+.0062	+.0099	+.0156	+.0190
Housing	+.0018	+.0011	+.0015	+.0015
Fuel and light	+.0023	+.0004	+.0006	+.0006
Furnishings	−.0006	−.0007	−.0011	−.0014
Clothing	−.0022	−.0028	−.0042	−.0051
Miscellaneous	−.0073	−.0077	−.0122	−.0150
Detail, $j = 1,...,15$				
Food	+.0063	+.0103	+.0161	+.0194
Housing	+.0019	+.0012	+.0016	+.0016
Fuel and light	+.0023	+.0004	+.0006	+.0006
Furnishings	−.0006	−.0007	−.0011	−.0014
Automobile	−.0041	−.0053	−.0078	−.0088
Household operations	−.0018	−.0004	−.0008	−.0011
Clothing	−.0021	−.0027	−.0043	−.0051
Other transport	0	−.0001	−.0003	−.0004
Medical care	−.0004	+.0007	+.0009	+.0010
Recreation	−.0012	−.0011	−.0017	−.0020
Personal care	+.0001	0	0	−.0001
Tobacco	+.0003	+.0001	+.0002	+.0002
Education	−.0005	−.0004	−.0006	−.0007
Reading	+.0001	0	0	0
Miscellaneous	0	−.0025	−.0039	−.0046

Source: Williamson (1977a, Table 10, p. 40).

such important durables as car purchases, as well as general services. Table 5.11 also reports the surprising result that the strategic role of food and durables has not diminished over time. If anything, these commodities may have become more important since the 1930s.

THE GRAND DESIGN: A BRIEF GLIMPSE AT THINGS TO COME

While this section has established that nominal and real inequality indicators almost always move together, the differential impact of prices by class has never been as large as the nominal inequality movements themselves. One can hardly dismiss them on these grounds, however, since any serious macroeconomic distribution theory must confront these curious price facts. Why the consistent historical correlation between the relative prices of outputs and inputs? That is, why do periods of stretching in the pay structure and increasing nominal inequality in the size distribution *always* contain relative price changes which inflate the cost of living for the urban poor faster than for the rich? Why is the opposite *almost always* true for periods of leveling in the nominal size distribution? The correspondence seems to extend over periods far longer than could be accounted for simply by aggregate demand instability. It seems to us that any macrodistribution theory which purports to explain American inequality experience since 1820 must simultaneously account for the behavior of the commodity output price structure as well. The "peacetime" and "war-inflation–postwar-stabilization" models suggested here are only the most tentative beginning. Parts Two and Three of this book will attempt to go far beyond that start.

Meanwhile, Back on the Farm

TWENTIETH-CENTURY PATTERNS OF FARM INCOME AND RURAL COST OF LIVING

The cost-of-living issue seems sufficiently important to warrant an expansion of our investigation to include the farm sector. Information on farm cost of living appears all the more relevant given the preponderance of farm families in the lowest income classes. Have farm families suffered the same relative movements in their cost of living as the low-income urban poor? Our inquiry is limited to the eight decades following 1890, for which the data are of good quality. The period covers three episodes during which the farm cost-of-living issue is crucial, but thus far almost ignored in the literature. The first of these is the boom in farm products up to and including World War I. The second is the economic collapse of agriculture during the 1920s. The third includes the income-distribution revolution up to 1948. How does the farm cost of living measure up during these episodes?

The Pre–World War I Years

The only continuous farm cost-of-living series available prior to 1910 appears to be a Vermont farm laborer index (T. M. Adams, 1944, Table 47, p. 97).[11] The resulting indices are presented in Table 5.12.

Earlier in this chapter we argued that the marked surge in urban inequality between 1896 and 1914 was reinforced by relative cost-of-living behavior. During this mild inflationary episode, urban low-income ($200–$300, 1901 prices) families suffered a 22% rise in their cost of living, while high-income professionals (approximately $1200, 1901 prices) faced only a 15% increase. Table 5.12 illustrates how farm families did by comparison; the farm cost-of-living index rose by 41%! Obviously, prices had a strong inequality bias from 1896 to the outbreak of the First World War, both in urban areas and economy-wide.

The Turning Point, 1910–1929

The USDA began collecting and reporting prices paid by farm families in 1910. USDA treatment of farm house rents is quite imperfect, however, and our revised cost-of-living index is utilized in all subsequent calculations. Table 5.12 compares the farm cost-of-living index with urban low- and high-income households. While the year 1920 appears to be an aberration, a clear secular decline in relative farm living costs is apparent up to 1929. Much of the decline is centered on the five years 1914–1918, but a gradual diminution persists during the 1920s. That is, while the farm cost-of-living index rose by 50 points from 1914 to 1929, the index for "high-income" urban families rose by 72 points. The wartime inflationary figure (1914–1918) for farm families was 59 points, while that for "high-income" urban families, 72 points.

These trends obviously have important distributional implications. Chapters 3 and 4 have shown that the period 1913–1929 is a turning point for America. All the *nominal* distribution statistics indicate (a) an abrupt short-term income leveling up to 1919; (b) a sharp inequality trend during the 1920s; and (c) stability or a very modest longer-term leveling between 1913 and 1929. The farm cost-of-living data would appear to reinforce these nominal trends. Between 1914 and 1929, the urban poor found their

---

[11] The index has been revised to include rents. Between 1910 and 1929, the USDA and the Adams series have very similar trends.

cost of living declining by 3 points compared to the urban rich. Farm families underwent a relative decline of some 13 points.[12] Real incomes of poor urban families *and* farm families were improving relatively over the fifteen years as a whole.

The Great Leveling, 1929–1948

Nathan Koffsky (1949) related farm to city purchasing power for the year 1941. Koffsky compared prices paid by farmers and city workers "at the lowest significant income levels, $500–$1,000 per city family and $250–500 per farm family [p. 158]." Food prices exhibited by far the greatest discrepancy. Using 1935/1936 weights, Koffsky found the urban cost of living some 27% higher using farm expenditure weights, and some 14% higher using urban expenditure weights. Judging from Table 5.12, conditions were almost exactly the same in 1936 and in 1929, although there was extraordinary instability in the cost-of-living ratio of farm to city during intervening depression years.

Table 5.12 also documents a very sharp rise in farm cost of living following 1941. The ratio of farm to low-income urban indices surged by 12.5% between 1941 and 1945. This figure is very close to that reported by Koffsky.[13] In short, the wartime inflation tended to erode farm purchasing power far more seriously than elsewhere in the economy. While there was a minor deterioration in low-income urban family cost of living compared to the urban rich, there was a major deterioration in farm family cost of living. Examination of the longer period between 1929 and 1948 does not reverse these conclusions. The cost-of-living index rose by 52% for farm families, by 34% for the urban "poor" ($500–$700, 1936 prices), and by 38% for the urban "rich" ($4000–$5000, 1936 prices). In summary, while the price structure of consumer goods was shifting to reinforce nominal distribution trends in urban areas (the urban poor suffering the smallest cost-of-living rise over the two decades), the same may not be true economy-wide, since the farm sector faced a relatively sharp rise in living costs.

FARM COST OF LIVING AND "WAGE GAPS"

Labor economists, historians, and development economists have long maintained an interest in the functioning of factor markets when such

---

[12] Appendix H shows that a revolutionary change in prices paid by farmers took place from 1914 to 1922, a change which continued at a more gradual pace up to 1929. With the exception of clothing, every commodity and service purchased by farm families (USDA) fell in price relative to urban (BLS) prices. The explanation appears to lie with the automobile.

[13] Koffsky (1949, pp. 174–175) reports data suggesting an 8 percentage point rise from 1941 to 1945.

TABLE 5.12
Farm Cost of Living, Absolute and Relative, 1890–1948

Year	(1) Farm Cost of Living	(2) Ratio of Farm to (Low) Urban Cost of Living	(3) Ratio of Farm to (High) Urban Cost of Living
	(1914 = 100)		
1890	80.6	88.6	81.4
1891	78.6	86.4	80.2
1892	76.7	85.2	79.1
1893	77.7	86.3	80.9
1894	72.8	84.7	79.1
1895	72.8	87.7	82.7
1896	70.9	86.5	81.5
1897	72.8	89.9	84.7
1898	72.8	88.8	84.7
1899	74.8	91.2	88.0
1900	75.7	91.2	88.0
1901	77.7	92.5	89.3
1902	77.7	91.4	89.3
1903	81.6	93.8	91.7
1904	82.5	94.8	92.7

Year	(1) Farm Cost of Living	(2) Ratio of Farm to (Low) Urban Cost of Living	(3) Ratio of Farm to (High) Urban Cost of Living
1925	157.8	89.7	88.5
1926	155.9	90.3	88.8
1927	152.0	89.8	88.1
1928	152.0	90.7	88.9
1929	150.0	89.0	87.3
	(1936 = 100)		
1929	125.4	99.0	102.9
1930	118.0	95.9	99.0
1931	101.6	91.3	92.2
1932	86.1	86.8	85.9
1933	86.9	93.1	91.8
1934	96.7	100.3	99.5
1935	98.4	99.4	99.4

Year	(1)	(2)	(3)	Year	(1)	(2)	(3)
1905	84.5	98.3	86.0	1936	100.0	100.0	100.0
1906	84.5	94.9	93.9	1937	103.3	99.7	99.7
1907	87.4	94.0	93.0	1938	99.2	97.8	96.9
1908	91.3	100.3	99.2	1939	98.0	97.9	96.8
1909	92.2	101.3	100.2	1940	98.4	97.5	96.6
1910	95.1	101.2	100.1	1941	104.9	99.0	98.6
1911	96.1	101.2	101.2	1942	119.7	102.3	102.4
1912	97.1	100.1	100.1	1943	131.1	105.7	106.6
1913	98.1	100.1	99.1	1944	137.7	109.8	109.1
1914	100.0	100.0	100.0	1945	142.6	111.4	110.4
1915	102.0	100.4	99.7	1946	156.6	113.0	113.1
1916	110.8	96.5	96.2	1947	181.1	114.7	116.0
1917	134.3	97.3	96.2	1948	191.0	112.4	114.0
1918	158.8	95.0	92.2				
1919	184.3	96.9	91.7				
1920	209.8	109.8	103.9				
1921	160.8	95.4	92.1				
1922	149.0	91.0	88.4				
1923	152.9	91.0	88.4				
1924	153.9	91.9	89.6				

Sources and notes: Col. (1), for 1890–1914, is from T. M. Adams (1944, Table 47, p. 97) revised to include imputed rents. The period 1915–1948 is based on a revision of U.S. Department of Agriculture (1962, Table 3, p. 5). Expenditures on building materials are taken as living expenditures by the USDA. We have replaced this with a more relevant cost component. Cols. (2) and (3) are from Col. (1) and Tables 5.4, 5.6, and 5.9.

markets are subjected to the strain of economic growth, structural change, western settlement, and urbanization. The key statistic utilized to evaluate the secular performance of labor markets—and the presence or absence of "market failure"—seems to be trends in nominal wage differentials or "wage gaps."[14] Thus, the argument has often been made that during rapid industrialization, the relatively rapid contraction of agriculture places such severe pressure on the efficient operation of labor markets that the gap between rural and urban wages widens. Symmetrically, when the relative pace of urbanization, farm contraction, and the city exodus all slow down, the wage gap tends to collapse. Much to our surprise, the evidence presented in Chapter 4 seemed to be inconsistent with this hypothesis: Antebellum labor markets were quite efficient in the sense that gaps between farm and nonfarm wages were small and exhibited no trend. What is the evidence after 1890?

Tables 5.13 and 5.14 offer data which appear at first blush to confirm the "market failure" or "disequilibrium" view of American labor markets. The golden age of agriculture, from 1896 to the end of World War I, was a period of relatively slow migration from rural areas to the cities, when the farm sector maintained its relative position in the American economy while the last great surge of unskilled European immigrants flooded American cities. These conditions are reflected in Table 5.13 by the relative collapse in the wage gap. Farm wages gained very rapidly on the urban wages of the unskilled. As we have seen in Chapter 4, this favorable farm income performance served to minimize economy-wide inequality trends up to 1916, thus making the inequality surge more an urban phenomenon. In contrast, with the collapse of farm prices following 1920, the wage gap reappears with a vengeance (Table 5.14), never regaining wartime "parity," even by 1929. Thus, lagging farm earnings tended to reinforce urban inequality trends during the 1920s.

Now how do these gaps fare when they are converted to *real* dollars? Tables 5.13 and 5.14 confirm that much of the observed instability in nominal gaps is eliminated when cost-of-living deflators are applied. This is especially apparent from 1890 or 1896 to 1914. Almost all of the relative improvement in nominal farm wages is illusory, since the relatively rapid rise in farm living costs offsets the majority of that gain.[15] The rural–urban cost-of-living deflators seem to make a difference in an evaluation of labor market allocative efficiency during the two decades prior to the Great War. The real wage gap was quite stable over the period. The

[14] The literature is enormous. For a general survey see either Reynolds and Taft (1956) or Kelley, Williamson, and Cheetham (1972, Chaps. 7 and 8). The American historical experience can be sampled in Williamson (1974b, Chap. 3).

[15] This result is consistent with Coelho and Shepherd (1976) and Coelho and Ghali (1971, pp. 932–937).

TABLE 5.13

Ratio Farm to Nonfarm Wages, Nominal and Real: Douglas, 1890–1914 (*1914* = *100*)

Year	Nominal Wage Ratio	Real Wage Ratio
1890	85.7	96.8
1891	85.9	99.4
1892	88.3	103.6
1893	85.7	99.2
1894	80.3	94.8
1895	81.6	93.0
1896	82.9	95.9
1897	84.2	93.7
1898	84.4	95.1
1899	88.3	96.8
1900	89.7	98.4
1901	91.3	98.7
1902	92.6	101.3
1903	95.2	101.5
1904	97.6	102.9
1905	101.2	103.0
1906	102.3	107.7
1907	100.0	106.4
1908	102.2	101.9
1909	100.0	98.7
1910	103.2	102.0
1911	103.2	102.0
1912	104.2	104.2
1913	103.0	103.0
1914	100.0	100.0

Sources and notes: These figures represent the ratio of farm wages to unskilled manufacturing wages. The nominal wage data are taken from Douglas (1930, Tables 59 and 63, pp. 177 and 186). The manufacturing wage deflator for unskilled labor is that for "low-income" urban households.

same cannot be said of the extraordinary years of wartime disequilibria and subsequent agricultural collapse. From 1914 to 1918 and relative to unskilled urban workers, farm laborers' earnings rose even more dramatically in real than in nominal terms. Furthermore, the relative deterioration in farm laborers' earnings from 1918 to 1921 is just as pronounced in real as in nominal terms. Over the longer-term period 1914–1929, the relatively rapid decline in farm cost of living did help alleviate rural distress: the increase in the wage gap is somewhat less pronounced in real terms.

SUMMARY

Urban cost-of-living movements have a systematic bias by socio-economic class. Every nineteenth- and twentieth-century episode of ris-

TABLE 5.14
Ratio Annual Earnings (Full-Time Employees) Farm to Nonfarm, Nominal and Real: Lebergott, 1910-1929 (1914 = 100)

Year	Nominal Earnings Ratio	Real Earnings Ratio
1910	101.9	98.6
1911	105.9	103.7
1912	106.0	104.9
1913	101.9	102.0
1914	100.0	100.0
1915	106.2	106.2
1916	102.6	106.5
1917	110.1	113.0
1918	107.7	113.2
1919	106.5	109.8
1920	102.5	93.3
1921	76.0	79.9
1922	76.8	84.5
1923	78.9	86.7
1924	78.2	84.9
1925	78.3	87.3
1926	77.8	86.3
1927	76.6	85.2
1928	74.6	82.5
1929	72.8	81.6

Sources and notes: These figures represent the ratio of annual farm to nonfarm earnings for full-time employees. The nominal earnings data are from Lebergott (1964, Table A–18, p. 525). Nonfarm earnings are deflated by that of ''low-income'' urban households.

ing nominal urban inequality prior to 1929 was accompanied by relative price changes which reinforced the inegalitarian bias. Every episode of nominal urban income leveling was also accompanied by relative price changes which reinforced the egalitarian bias. This section has explored this remarkable historical symmetry in the rural–urban dimension. The results are fairly consistent with the urban distribution patterns. Farm price movements had an inegalitarian bias from the 1890s to 1914, a period of nominal urban inequality trends bordering on the episodic. So too for the 1918–1921 collapse. During the Great War itself and over the longer term, 1914–1929, periods of nominal egalitarian trends, cost-of-living trends favored farm families.

The exception to this ''historical law'' seems to be the distribution revolution 1929–1948. As in the case of urban cost of living by income class, farm prices had a sharp inegalitarian bias from the late 1930s to the late 1940s. In contrast with the urban cost-of-living trends, however, farm prices had a sharp inegalitarian bias from 1929 to the late 1940s as well.

Prices, Living Costs, and Regional Incomes[16]

Chapter 4 reviewed American experience with regional inequality. Though we concluded that the variance of incomes across regions does not seem to have been an important component of the total variance of incomes in America, some have argued that even that position is exaggerated. Critics have suggested that nominal inequality indicators grossly overstate *real* inequality over regions and that cost-of-living deflators would to a large extent erase both the levels and trends in state per capita income differentials in America since 1840.

Since comparisons of labor productivity and income per capita differentials across American regions are used to make welfare and distributional judgments, the relative prices that matter most are cost-of-living differentials. That being the case, we begin with the assertion that conventional wage goods—food, fuel, light, and rent—should have lower relative prices in backward regions. If this assertion holds, then it follows that the deflation of regional nominal performance measures by local cost-of-living indices should tend to raise the measured real income of the backward region relative to the more affluent.

Is it true that the cost of living is lower where nominal incomes are lower? Would convergence in nominal income be accompanied by a convergence or by a widening in the cost-of-living gaps between high- and low-income regions? While published cost-of-living data have always been available for twentieth-century tests, to our knowledge no such tests have ever been performed. In addition, Coelho and Shepherd (1974, 1976) have now supplied the data necessary for a nineteenth-century test.

Table 5.15 offers some initial evidence. The table reports what we call "Koffsky adjusted" cost-of-living indices across nine census divisions and for the period 1840–1970.[17] Each regional cost-of-living index is expressed in terms of New England = 100, and Appendix I describes their construction in detail. It does seem apparent that much of the wide variance in regional cost of living observed in 1840 had dissipated a century later, but considerable variance persists even today. The convergence did not take place smoothly and without a hitch, but some impressive examples stand out in the historical record: the abrupt decline in the South Atlantic relative between 1840 and 1880; similar declines in the Mountain and Pacific regions after 1920; and the steady upward drift in

---

[16] An extended version of this section can be found in Williamson (1977b).

[17] The indices convert urban regional price relatives to region-wide cost-of-living indices by applying estimates of farm–nonfarm cost-of-living differentials to the urban prices. Employment shares are used as weights in constructing the aggregate regional indices.

TABLE 5.15
"Koffsky-Adjusted" Regional Cost-of-Living Indices, 1840–1970 (New England = 100)

Region	1840	1880	1900	1920	1929	1950	1970
New England	100.0	100.0	100.0	100.0	100.0	100.0	100.0
Mid. Atlantic	98.5	95.7	99.1	101.3	101.3	100.0	98.4
East North Central	80.2	82.5	88.0	96.1	99.0	100.0	95.9
West North Central	100.8	93.4	93.0	98.8	92.7	95.9	94.3
South Atlantic	123.3	100.4	95.7	99.5	91.6	95.9	91.0
East South Central	83.5	80.6	90.6	97.2	84.0	94.5	88.5
West South Central	92.1	81.9	87.3	94.6	86.1	91.8	87.7
Mountain	n.a.	n.a.	n.a.	117.6	94.0	98.6	95.1
Pacific	n.a.	n.a.	n.a.	103.1	97.7	100.0	97.5

Source: Appendix I.

the relatives for the East North Central. Table 5.16 documents the price convergence for some key commodity groups, quoted in urban centers, and for three points in time. While space precludes presentation of the complete data here, Table 5.16 supplies some confirmation of the position that all prices tended towards convergence after 1840, but that the behavior of rents, fuel and light, and food mattered most, since these were the items whose prices varied the most at every point in time (and in the order given).

Have the poorest states always undergone the most dramatic cost-of-living increases? The evidence in Table 5.15 is mixed. For example, between 1880 and 1970 while most southern regions experienced a rise in relative living costs, it was not true of the South Atlantic. Between 1920

TABLE 5.16
Urban Cost-of-Living Indices, by Region and Commodity Group, 1851–1935 (New England = 100)

Region	Food			Clothing			Fuel and Light			Rent		Other	
	1851	1890	1935	1851	1890	1935	1851	1890	1935	1851	1935	1890	1935
New England	100	100	100	100	100	100	100	100	100	100	100	100	100
Mid. Atlantic	98	97	98	127	105	97	123	106	88	88	112	93	110
East North Central	83	95	95	127	103	104	32	79	85	91	107	87	114
West North Central	96	85	94	127	110	100	n.a.	92	94	66	104	88	104
South Atlantic	n.a.	106	100	n.a.	110	95	n.a.	85	85	n.a.	105	94	102
East South Central	85	98	94	111	104	92	35	75	78	134	87	87	100
West South Central	n.a.	95	95	n.a.	105	94	n.a.	104	78	n.a.	90	91	101
Mountain	n.a.	107	98	n.a.	118	105	n.a.	160	98	n.a.	96	112	100
Pacific	n.a.	104	95	n.a.	113	110	n.a.	163	98	n.a.	87	103	112

Source and notes: Appendix I. Observations for rents in 1890 and "other" in 1851 are unavailable.

TABLE 5.17
Cost-of-Living Impact: Coefficient of Variation in State Income per Worker, Nominal and Real, 1840–1970

Year	North Nominal	North Real	North & South Nominal	North & South Real	United States Nominal	United States Real
1970	.087	.067	.119	.081	.117	.086
1950	.087	.074	.183	.156	.177	.156
1929	.178	.154	.325	.273	.312	.262
1920	.149	.138	.275	.265	.268	.259
1900	.140	.120	.380	.364	.383	n.a.
1880	.173	.157	.381	.366	.396	n.a.
1880*	.155	.135	.380	.365	n.a.	n.a.
1840*	.255	.192	.313	.317	n.a.	n.a.

Source and notes: The cost-of-living data used in the calculations can be found in Appendix I where New England = 100 in each year. Appendix I also supplies the definitions of regions and the data sources used. Weighted coefficient of variation used throughout. 1840* and 1880* refer to comparable regional groups with state observations in both years (e.g., excluding Minnesota, the Dakotas, Nebraska, Kansas, Texas, and Oklahoma).

and 1970, the South Central and South Atlantic states all underwent a further decline in relative living costs. Thus the issue can only be resolved by the explicit introduction of relative regional weights, that is, the question can only be answered by applying the cost-of-living data directly to the estimates of the state (nominal) income per worker themselves.

If regional nominal income per capita dictates regional cost of living, then we should expect real incomes to converge more slowly than nominal incomes across regions. Tables 5.17 and 5.18 suggest the contrary. From 1880 to 1970, convergence is steeper in *real* terms. Thus, *nominal*

TABLE 5.18
Cost-of-Living Impact: Changing Coefficient of Variation in State Income per Worker, Nominal and Real, 1840–1970

Year	North Nominal	North Real	North & South Nominal	North & South Real	United States Nominal	United States Real
1950–1970	0	−.007	−.064	−.075	−.060	−.070
1929–1950	−.091	−.080	−.142	−.117	−.135	−.106
1900–1929	+.038	+.036	−.055	−.091	−.071	n.a.
1880–1900	−.033	−.037	−.001	−.002	−.013	n.a.
1880–1970	−.086	−.090	−.262	−.285	−.279	n.a.
1840–1880	−.100	−.057	+.067	+.048	n.a.	n.a.

Source: Table 5.17.

income understates the "true" convergence in America over the past century, a result consistent with all the previous findings in this chapter. Furthermore, the phenomenon is not simply manifested in North–South comparisons, since the same finding appears within the North itself. Over shorter-term periods, however, regional inequality trends behave pretty much the same way, whether nominal or real income measures are utilized. The only significant exception to this generalization would appear to be in the North from 1840 to 1880.

Finally, consider the regional inequality indices presented in Table 5.17. There we see that living costs have always been lower in backward regions. For *every* year documented in Table 5.17, the variance in real regional incomes per worker is smaller than the variance in nominal incomes, and in some years the variance is much smaller. Furthermore, it is *not* a North–South "sunshine" effect we are observing, since the same holds within the North. The essential point is that cost-of-living advantages in low-income areas have always been quite pronounced, and that these advantages persist to the present.

Prices, Poverty, and Living Standards

For some, the relevant question is not the *relative* performance of class or regional incomes—that is, distribution trends—but rather the performance of *absolute* living standards. The great debate over early English industrialization, for example, has almost exclusively focused on the latter: "The basic issue being debated seems straightforward. Did the per capita real incomes of the working classes rise or fall during the Industrial Revolution [Hartwell and Engerman, 1975, p. 190]?" We intend to leave the choice between relatives and absolutes for others to debate, since our interests lie with explanations rather than ethics. Our position hardly implies a lack of interest in the trends in real wages and living standards, however. Indeed, a full understanding of the historical forces which drove American inequality obviously requires an explanation of the historical forces which drove real wages among the working poor. We are sufficiently confident of the link between real wage behavior and inequality to predict unambiguously that episodes of trending inequality coincided with unimpressive growth in absolute living standards at the bottom of the income distribution.

The inverse correlation between the growth in real wages and trends in inequality is given abundant documentation in Table 5.19. There we measure per annum growth rates in real wages and annual earnings of the urban unskilled—the standard of living of the working poor. Real annual earnings of full-time, urban, unskilled labor grew at about half that of real

TABLE 5.19
Trends in Real Wages and Earnings: The Urban Working Poor, 1820–1948 (per annum rates)

Period	Real Wages: Period of Trending			Real Annual Earnings: Period of Trending		
	Inequality	Stability	Equality	Inequality	Stability	Equality
1820–1856	+0.84			+0.80		
1820–1880	+0.91			+0.72		
1844–1856	−1.51			−1.65		
1844–1880	+0.17			−0.13		
1856–1896		+1.35			+0.98	
1880–1896			+1.86			+1.54
1896–1916	+0.34			−0.25		
1916–1929		+1.79			+0.74	
1929–1948			+2.25			+1.45
1820–1948		+1.23			+0.79	
1844–1948		+1.04			+0.49	

Sources and notes: Real wages for urban common labor are taken from Appendix G. The real-annual-earnings series applies hours worked per year for full-time manufacturing employees to the real-wage series. The hours-worked series estimates are 1820, 3266.6; 1844, 3279.8; 1856, 3224.4; 1860, 3159.0; 1880, 2930.5; 1896, 2793.5; 1916, 2485.4; 1929, 2171.0; 1948, 1870.0.

wages and for obvious reasons: Over the century 1840 to 1950, the average workweek declined from 64 to 38.7 hours, and the weeks worked per year declined from 51.2 to 48.5 over the same period. Nonetheless, the inverse correlation between absolutes and relatives is maintained whether we look at wages or earnings. Real wages grew at very low rates during both the antebellum and the pre–World War I inequality surge. Indeed, from 1844 to 1880 and from 1896 to 1916 real wages rose at the paltry per annum rates of 0.17% and 0.34% respectively. They grew most rapidly by far during the great leveling following 1929, 2.25% per annum. They grew at intermediate rates during periods of stability or modest leveling, that is 1856–1896 and 1916–1929.

How about "numbers in poverty"? Shortly before the turn of the century, there was an extraordinary outpouring of social reformist literature and empirical attention to cost of living, standards of life, poverty, and the poor. Yet, in spite of the classic works by Rowntree, Booth, and Bowley in England, and Chapin, Nearing, Hunter, and Riis in America, time-series estimates of absolute poverty are very scarce. By absolute poverty, we mean the proportion who fall below some absolute living standard which is held constant over time. Hartley (1969), for example, uses BLS data from 1908 to derive a poverty line. The line is revised only to reflect changes in prices. Hartley's absolute measure is to be contrasted

TABLE 5.20
The Incidence of Poverty, 1870–1914, 1929–1944, 1947–1955 (*in percentages*)

Year	"Mfg. Population" Hartley	Total Population Hartley	Ornati	CEA
1870	62.08%	45.31%		
1880	61.56	46.86		
1890	40.53	35.30		
1900	38.63	31.60		
1904	36.77			
1909	43.89	34.77		
1914	41.87			
1929			43%	
1935/1936			46	
1941			32	
1944			15	
1947				30%
1955				26

Sources and notes: Hartley (1969, p. 19) uses fixed 1908 budget with variable prices. Ornati (1966, p. 158) uses variable "minimum adequacy" budget, but budget standards remained relatively unchanged up to 1944. U.S. Council of Economic Advisers (1969, p. 154) uses fixed poverty line.

with, for example, Ornati's (1966), which is based on a relative standard of "minimum decency" or "adequacy."[18] Obviously, standards of minimum decency or adequacy tell us more about changing attitudes towards poverty than about a society's success in eradicating it.

What little evidence we have on the percentage of households in poverty is presented in Table 5.20. The proportion of the population that is poor tends to decline over time, of course, since even periods of very modest real earnings improvement among the working poor recorded some success in moving out of poverty. The *rate* of decline in the percentage poor is more relevant for our purposes. The decline was fairly steep between 1870 and 1890, a period of relative quiescence among the inequality indicators presented in Chapters 3 and 4. The rate was even steeper between 1929 and 1944, during the revolutionary leveling in the distribution of income. In contrast, the rate of decline slowed down during the 1890s and in fact the percentage poor increased between 1900 and 1909 or 1914, a result fully consistent with the inequality trends prior to World War I.

It appears that absolute living standards, numbers in poverty, and relative inequality trends have always exhibited a high correlation in American history.

[18] For a useful discussion of these points, see Weinstein and Smolensky (1976, pp. 13–22).

Part Two
POTENTIAL EXPLANATIONS

6

COMPETING HYPOTHESES

Monocausality and History's Complex Stage

What explains the long-run trends in pay ratios, factor shares, and income distributions? What forces were most important in accounting for the nineteenth-century inequality surge and the twentieth-century leveling? This chapter will list those explanations which seem to match some common intuitions. The list is not meant to be exhaustive, and, furthermore, the minor actors will be accorded only brief appearances, never to reappear on our stage. Some are rejected outright because of their blatant inconsistency with any plausible model of growth and distribution. Others are rejected as *ad hoc* explanations, unique to some particular episode in American historical experience. Still others can be shown to be endogenous results of more fundamental macro forces at work in the economy. No monocausal explanation of American inequality experience will emerge from our effort, however, since inequality trends are too complex for us to expect simple explanations to survive empirical tests on historical evidence. But we can identify the four central players: (*a*) biased technological progress, (*b*) labor supply, (*c*) capital accumulation, and (*d*) the rise of government. Whereas this chapter only attempts to establish their plausibility, the remainder of this book will evaluate their likely quantitative influence on observed trends in American inequality since the early nineteenth century. They will, in effect, become the key components in accounting for the sources of inequality.

The main thrust of this initial theorizing is to account for trends in occupational pay ratios, skill premia, factor shares, and earnings distributions. It seems to us that the evidence presented in Part One argues quite persuasively for such an approach, namely, that an understanding of the forces driving factor incomes will take us a long way toward understanding trends in more complex size distributions of income. Furthermore, we do not think it helpful or accurate to view changes in the distribution of wealth as an independent force driving the distribution of income. Instead we find it more persuasive to view changes in the distribution of wealth either as an outcome of previous changes in the distribution of income or as a simultaneous solution, since those forces driving quasi-rents (income streams) on assets surely had a concomitant impact on the *value* of wealth holdings (asset prices) and their distribution as well. Finally, we should stress that these competing theories must be capable of explaining more than just historical trends in distribution. General-equilibrium theory warns us that each of these competing hypotheses must also account for changes in the patterns of production and the structure of commodity prices.

The Minor Actors and Supporting Roles

INFLATION, EQUITY, AND WAGE-LAG

If one ignores the employment and price twists of the Great Depression, there is a weak correspondence between periods of rapid inflation and periods of leveling in incomes and pay ratios. The correlation is far stronger if we restrict our focus to major inflations. In sharp contrast with the simple—and apparently inaccurate—"wage-lag" thesis (Mitchell, 1903, 1908; DeCanio and Mokyr, 1977), each of the three major inflations between 1820 and 1970 has been associated with egalitarian trends, and each has been tied to war.

It has been argued that inflation levels incomes and rates of pay in several ways. First, the post–World War II data clearly show a short-run cyclical relationship between inflation and measures of overall income inequality. The reason is simple enough: Inflation has been accompanied by reductions in unemployment great enough to govern short-run inequality movements (Kuznets, 1953; T. P. Schultz, 1971; Chiswick and Mincer, 1972). The link between extra jobs and more equal distribution, however, is an aggregate demand influence which lacks the scope to account for long-run trends.

A second variation on the inflation theme is the argument that higher-level salaries are more rigid in nominal terms than the wages of the unskilled. Higher-level salaries are often negotiated in long-term contracts and adjust only very slowly to unforeseen changes in the rate of change of prices. This argument is supported by the fact that teachers' salaries, to take an example documented in Figure 4.4, failed to keep pace with the cost of living and wage rates for unskilled labor during sudden inflations, and correspondingly failed to drop as fast when prices fell off, for example, during the early 1930s. The difficulty with this sticky-salary variant of the inflation argument is that it fails to explain why the equalizing produced by sudden inflation should persist long after the inflation has ceased and all salaries have been renegotiated many times. This was true of the late 1860s, the early 1920s, and especially the 1950s.

There is yet a third variant on the war-inflation theme. It has been argued that during periods of wartime inflation the public considers it "only fair" that rates of pay should advance most rapidly for the poor. The argument appears to rely on the fear that, since the poor can least afford to be damaged by inflation, public sentiment shifts in favor of more egalitarian pay settlements when the nation needs wartime unity. The argument suggests that major wars call for a sharing of national burdens inconsistent with prewar economic inequalities. This wartime-sharing thesis has the strength of explaining the persistence of egalitarian pay structures years after the war has ended. Once the principle of equity has become accepted during wartime, it may seem plausible to argue that the spirit should linger on in postwar pay settlements. It is difficult to imagine, however, how such a shift in attitude could still be a prime determinant of the pay structure a decade later. Competition and profit-maximization would soon reward those firms and workers who agreed on rates of pay reestablishing the old inequalities. The new attitudes could persist only if something else in the postwar setting made lower pay differentials profitable to tens of thousands of employers. Equity must be profitable to persist in the private sector.

All of the theories connecting inflation and equity suffer from the additional defect that inequalities failed to drop during some wars and some peacetime inflations. Pay ratios and income inequality drifted upward during the gentle 1900–1913 inflation, and they surged during the peacetime inflation from the 1840s to the 1850s. Inequalities and pay ratios were not greatly affected by the Vietnam War, except that the approach to full employment brought extra income to the poor. The inflation of the 1970s has not been characterized by leveling, as less than full employment persists and the relative rise in food and fuel prices takes a greater toll on budgets of the poor than of the rich. Inflation has failed, therefore, to have a consistent impact on inequality trends.

The inflation theories suffer a final flaw. They do not offer an explanation for the movements in relative prices and output mix associated with changes in pay differentials. Of course, if one is prepared to take a "structuralist" or "demand-pull" position, which stresses the behavior of certain key components of aggregate demand, then the inflation theory would be subsumed under the more comprehensive analyses of trends in the structure demand offered below.

In short, it does not seem wise to search for explanations of long-run inequality trends by appeal to macroeconomic models linking price inflation with pay differentials.

GOVERNMENT POLICY AND GROWTH STRATEGY

It could also be argued that government policy induced major historical shifts in the pattern of demands which favored the relatively rich during industrialization. Indeed, there is an extensive development literature that makes much of this point (Morawetz, 1974; Cline, 1975). Government wage manipulation, loan subsidies, and exchange rate policy, it is argued, encourage firms to use capital- and skill-intensive technologies, a tendency which surely exacerbates inequality in the developing economy. Since such tools were not part of American policy in the nineteenth century, we can readily dismiss them in our quest for explanations of our inequality experience. Yet America did pursue other policies which favored industry, tariff policy being the classic example. General-equilibrium models suggest that agriculture and the extractive export industries should have contracted while industries competing with imports should have expanded. To the extent that industry was far more intensive in skills and machines than in unskilled labor, pay ratios should have risen, the poor should have suffered, and inequality trends should have been reinforced. Furthermore, government policy favored capital formation both directly, through social overhead investment, and indirectly, by fostering private accumulation. To the extent that the production of capital goods generally, and producer durables specifically, required relatively small amounts of unskilled labor, inequality trends would have been reinforced on those grounds too.

We have no theoretical argument with this appeal to the inherent distributional bias in growth–industrialization strategies. But to attribute a significant portion of American inequality experience during the nineteenth century to such policy is to assign a far greater role to the state than the historical evidence can possibly support. For example, while iron and steel and textiles were supported by nineteenth-century tariffs, the prevailing view seems to be that tariffs were not of decisive importance in shaping their long-run growth (Temin, 1964; Zevin, 1971). In addition, it could be argued that such policy lagged behind private economy forces in the same direction, and that the growth strategy itself was a reflection of more fundamental endogenous influences.

UNIONIZATION

The greatest reductions in twentieth-century wage differentials and overall inequality came during a period of rising union power. Although unions have lacked an explicit policy for changing wage differentials, their demands appear to have been more favorable for lower-skill workers after the 1930s than before. As a result, it seems reasonable to ask whether unions have raised the relative wages of the unskilled while raising all wages at the expense of profits. Does it seem plausible, therefore, to assign to union strength a key role in accounting for the income leveling since 1929? There is, of course, a related literature that dwells on monopoly power, market structure, and weak unions in accounting for trending inequality prior to 1916 and during the 1920s. This thesis (Baran and Sweezy, 1966; Keller, 1973) emphasizes the merger movement between 1919 and 1930, and, in particular, cites the fact that the merger and new acquisition rate tripled between 1924 and 1929 and was almost twice as high as any year in the 1950s. During this merger wave, labor unions found their power on the wane. From a peak membership in 1920, the American labor movement lost 1.5 million members by 1929. Does it seem plausible, therefore, to assign to union weakness a key role in accounting for the inequality trend up to 1929?

One can easily find local cases where the impact of unions on the wage structure was profound. For example, the patternmakers at the McCormick Works were able to win a handsome hike in their pay advantage vis-à-vis unskilled workers during World War II, at a time when wage premia for skilled labor were dropping in most sectors (Ozanne, 1962, pp. 293, 296, and 298).

At the aggregate level, however, the union impact on wage rates and income inequalities has been minor at most. Union members still comprise less than 30% of the labor force, and pay differentials have moved together in unionized and nonunionized industries. Changes which weakened union power provide no explanation for the antebellum inequality surge, or the apparent reduction in some measures of inequality between 1913 and 1929, or the tendency of pay differentials and earnings distributions to stabilize after the Korean War, when union membership was greater than ever before. Furthermore, even if unions had won for their members the maximum possible influence allowed by H. G. Lewis's (1963) study, they could not have reduced aggregate measures of inequality anywhere near as much as they have in fact declined. Unions, after all, offer no relative gains for the larger numbers of unskilled nonunion workers. Indeed, these groups may well be hurt by the labor displacement back onto nonunionized sectors, thus implying an ambiguous impact on economy-wide income distribution. At best, therefore, whatever influence unions may have had in the short run must be denied them in the longer run when one recognizes that union power can level rates of pay over decades only if one of two conditions holds. The government must somehow conspire with the private sector to maintain the demand for, or restrict the supply of, unionized labor. Alternatively, unions may serve to replicate the results of a competitive factor market, in which case their long-run "power" is endogenous to an economic system being driven by more fundamental demand and supply forces. That is, unionization and union strength may be only a manifestation of strong market demands for labor in general and unskilled labor in particular—demands which themselves must be explained.

These considerations, reinforced by other studies of wage structure (e.g., Hildebrand and Delahanty, 1966; Evans, 1971, pp. 185–191), lead us to conclude tentatively that changes in union power account for little if any of the long-run aggregate trends in pay ratios or overall income inequality.

Another form of union impact also fails as an explanation for trends in pay ratios and overall inequality. Unions have successfully pushed for the passage of minimum wage legislation ever since the New Deal. Might this account for the leveling in the 1940s? Since the long-run demand for unskilled labor is not totally inelastic, minimum wage legislation which successfully drives up the relative price of unskilled labor should also generate a sustained rise in unemployment specific to the unskilled or a retardation in the rate of migration from legally exempt sectors. Neither of these developments occurred in the 1940s and early 1950s, when wage differentials were shrinking. If one wishes to argue that government aggregate demand management was aimed at preserving full employment along with legal minimum wages, it must be shown that the net result of this policy would somehow have kept skilled-labor wage rates and profits from rising during an inflationary boom designed to employ all of the unskilled at the minimum wage rates. The minimum wage hypothesis would at that point become equivalent to the inflation argument already examined and rejected.

THE SUPPLY OF LAND

One frequently encounters the argument that rapid expansion of available land before 1900 must have had a considerable democratizing and leveling influence. An unskilled worker who faced poor prospects in eastern industry could flee to the opportunity of developing a farm on good soil relatively unencumbered with obligations to landlords and governments. Perhaps more accurately, he could flee to western urban employment, replacing a western migrant who moved to the frontier, thus creating a vacancy in his wake. The argument would suggest that as more farmland became economically accessible, incomes would have felt a leveling influence, as would have wealth.

What is possible in theory was apparently never important in the nineteenth and twentieth centuries. Although the model may serve to explain much of colonial experience with wealth inequality (Chap. 2), it appears that land expansion was never the predominant variable driving the distribution of income among Americans after 1820. While the supply of land grew rapidly in the nineteenth century, the distribution of wealth and pay ratios moved toward inequality. Two decades after the rate of growth of farm acreage dropped off at the start of this century, income and wealth started to become more equally distributed. What we know about the supply of land complicates, rather than resolves, the problem of explaining the historic trends in income distribution.

ENGEL'S LAW

Engel's Law has established that increases in income reduce the share of household income spent on food. Largely (but not exclusively) for this reason, resources have been shifting out of agriculture for two centuries. Since agriculture tends to employ unskilled labor far more intensively than elsewhere in the economy (Chap. 8), it appears plausible to argue that variations in the rate of shift in demand away from agriculture might affect the relative income of unskilled labor, thereby contributing to an explanation of inequality trends. Others have pointed out that a growth-induced shift of resources out of agriculture can affect overall inequality in a variety of complex ways. The shift in demand away from farm products tends to raise the wages of skilled labor and profit rates relative to the wages of the unskilled for the factor intensity reasons already given. Furthermore, the shift should also induce a decline in farm rents relative to profits on industrial capital, and since farmland and farm rents are more equally distributed than other forms of property income emanating from the nonfarm sector, aggregate inequality would rise on this score too. On the other hand, the shift should also induce a decline in farm rents by more than the decline in the wages of unskilled labor, a countervailing force that might help reduce inequalities, since farmland ownership (and farm rental income) is less equally distributed than unskilled labor power (and unskilled labor's earnings).

There are other influences which complicate the impact of agriculture's demise on inequality trends. Kuznets (1955), for example, has suggested that the steady movement of population out of agriculture, even with rates of pay held constant, can first raise and then lower inequality. Under certain conditions (Theil, 1967, pp. 114–120), Kuznets is correct. While elegant two-sector models have been developed to replicate Kuznets's results (Robinson, 1976), the following simple example will serve to illustrate the process. Suppose that everyone employed in agriculture earns $5000 a year and everyone employed outside of agriculture earns $10,000. (Robinson's [1976] model allows for income variance within sectors, but the results are much the same.) Start from a situation in which everyone is employed in agriculture. The migration of the first person to the new higher-paying sector creates inequality where none had existed before. Further migration will for a while continue to raise most measures of inequality, such as the share earned by the top 5% of individuals. In this simple example, migration must ultimately bring a return to equality. When the last farmer has migrated, perfect equality would again be restored, since everyone would be earning $10,000. The process would generate an "inverted U," inequality rising and then falling over time.

It turns out that this possibility is not only mathematically fragile[1] but also not very helpful in accounting for American distribution trends. The data presented in Part One make it clear that American inequality trends appear *within* sectors and regions. They are not just an aggregate artifact of migration between sectors. Indeed, changes in inequality within sectors and regions appear to have been quantitatively far more important in accounting for trends in aggregate inequality than either changes in sectoral income gaps or changes in the distribution of population across sectors. Thus, forces that first widened and then narrowed inequalities were much more pervasive than these simple migration examples imply. In any case, both migration and the distribution of income within sectors are taken as exogenous forces in the Kuznets model and it is clearly a serious error to treat them so. After all, had *no* migration taken place, inequality would have risen in the countryside and income differentials between the two sectors would have widened. Thus, migration itself is an endogenous response to economy-wide forces, and the simple statistical models supply little insight into the nature of those forces.

Engel effects do supply one such force, however, and we accept the conventional assertion that agriculture's demise should generate inequality on the following grounds: Its demise should raise the demand for

---

[1] The model contains fragile assumptions regarding economic behavior as well. It assumes that recent immigrants to urban employment receive earnings equal to average urban incomes. The characterization is grossly inaccurate. Rather, new immigrants off the farm normally secure employment at low-wage jobs, wages which in real terms are quite comparable to those received for farm labor.

skills and machines while lowering the demand for unskilled labor. Skill premia should rise relative to unskilled labor's wages, as should profit rates, and these inegalitarian trends are likely to prevail, since the impact on farm rents has an ambiguous influence on these inegalitarian tendencies.

Yet the argument has two weaknesses, one theoretical and one empirical. In terms of theory, an appeal to Engel effects fails to isolate a key exogenous force. After all, Engel effects are an endogenous result of whatever exogenous forces may be raising income per capita; technological progress and capital accumulation being the traditional prime candidates. Engel effects are an exogenous variable only if one seeks to compare actual experience with a hypothetical world in which Engel's Law does not hold. The pervasiveness of Engel's Law makes such a comparison uninteresting. Yet, the empirical flaws in the argument may be even more serious than the theoretical ones. Growth in per capita income induces a variety of changes in household demand mix, among them an increase in personal services. It is quite possible that attention to the declining share of income devoted to foodstuffs may be misplaced, since other labor-intensive expenditures may take the place of food as incomes rise. This empirical issue will be confronted in Chapter 8. Most important, it is not at all clear that the demise of agriculture is to be explained solely or even largely by Engel effects. After all, in a world where international trade in commodities was extensive, Engel effects may have had a potent impact on domestic demand but only a very modest impact on shifts in output mix and thus on changes in factor demands as well. Indeed, under those more realistic nineteenth-century conditions, change in the relative size of agriculture was more likely to have been determined by episodic changes in transport costs and differential rates of productivity performance across sectors. We shall return to this issue below.

The Leading Actors

BIASED TECHNOLOGICAL PROGRESS

A potentially powerful determinant of the distribution of income is the degree to which the course of modern technological progress tends to economize on certain factors of production and to favor the use of others. A bias toward saving on unskilled labor can widen income gaps by worsening job prospects and relative wage rates for the unskilled while bidding up rates of return on skills, machines, and land. Furthermore, these macro laborsaving forces are magnified over time, at least according to most micro models of accumulation. Any macro laborsaving force which increases inequality will foster even higher relative rates of wealth accumulation at the top of the income distribution if one believes that saving rates and rates of wealth accumulation rise with income. Inequality breeds further inequality.

If we can find a mechanism which ensures a laborsaving bias during modern economic growth, we would indeed have a plausible explanation for the inequality trends which start during the first phases of antebellum industrialization. The mechanism would also require an explanation for the reversal of nineteenth- and early twentieth-century labor saving during World War I and the late 1920s. Furthermore, the mechanism must offer an explanation for the observed variety in *rates* of labor saving for, as we have seen, inequality trends have moved in fits and starts since 1820. The mechanism is sufficiently attractive to have motivated detailed attention to labor saving by both economists and historians for some time. Although Chapter 7 will pursue the issue at length, some introductory remarks here will set the stage for a good portion of the remainder of the book.

Econometric estimates of the aggregate bias in twentieth-century technological change encourage the belief that economists may have discovered one of the keys to trends in American inequality. For the economy as a whole, each of several studies has found a strong laborsaving bias from about the start of this century to 1929, followed by either neutrality or a labor-using bias from 1929 to World War II. There has been considerable debate over whether a strong laborsaving bias has in fact resumed in the postwar period (David and van de Klundert, 1965; Brown, 1966, Chap. 10; Morishima and Saito, 1968). None of these studies actually distinguished between unskilled and skilled labor, making inferences about the distribution of income somewhat difficult, but it may be surmised that any era of labor saving was likely to be especially unskilled-labor saving. The econometric literature thus suggests that the equalization of incomes following 1929 may have been due to a switch in the bias of aggregate technological progress from labor saving to labor using. The absence of any further equalization within the postwar era might be tied to the tendency of technology to return to the nineteenth-century pattern of labor saving once again.

To understand the causal role of technological bias, one must take care in identifying exactly what part of the observed saving on labor is in fact exogenous, and what part is endogenous and thus simply a result of other forces already measured independently. The aggregate laborsaving bias can be decomposed into the following component parts:

1. Aggregate bias due to shifts in sectoral output shares (e.g., the contraction of agriculture in aggregate economic activity).
2. Aggregate bias due to differences in the rate of neutral technological advance between sectors using labor in various intensities.
3. Aggregate bias due to labor saving within firms, industries, and sectors in response to the secular rise in labor's price and increasing scarcity.
4. Aggregate bias due to exogenous labor saving within firms, industries, and sectors in response to the discovery of new technologies.

Development economists would appear to agree that systematic changes in output mix are critical determinants of labor saving and thus distribution trends (Kelley, Williamson, and Cheetham, 1972; Morawetz, 1974; Cline, 1975). Yet even this first source of aggregate technological bias cannot be called a true causal influence. The expansion of other sectors at agriculture's expense, for example, may look like aggregate unskilled-labor-saving technological change, since the favored sectors use unskilled labor far less intensively than agriculture. But the observed resource shift between sectors is not an exogenous determinant of the process that determines incomes, factor prices, and pay ratios. It is instead an endogenous result of the same process and requires explanation. It may be that some other dimension of technological change, such as a rapid rate of technological progress outside of agriculture, is the cause of the shift between sectors, but the point remains that the sectoral shift itself is not a causal influence on the income distribution. The same point can be made about the third force listed above: an apparent bias toward labor saving that is simply a response to rising wages does not deserve to be counted as a factor influencing wage rates and other factor incomes. On the contrary, it is a response to the increased scarcity of labor over time. Thus, to identify technological biases that are independent influences on the distribution of income, we must isolate empirically the second and fourth sources above.

Some authors have taken care to provide measures of technological bias that succeed in isolating some of its exogenous components for the United States in this century. Kendrick (1961, 1973) has presented sectoral estimates of total factor productivity growth for several periods between 1889 and 1969. Morishima and Saito (1968), Keller (1973), and Williamson (1974a, 1976b) have all examined the decomposition of technological bias into the working parts listed above. One outcome of these studies is to show that most of the apparent aggregate bias is due to shifts in sectoral shares plus sectoral differences in rates of neutral productivity advance. It turns out that a prime determinant of relative factor demand has been the difference in neutral productivity advance between sectors. For example, Keller and Williamson have shown that what looked like a jump in laborsaving bias from the years around World War I to the 1920s was the result of a jump in the difference between productivity growth in manufacturing and agriculture. With productivity advancing much more rapidly in manufacturing, which used unskilled labor much less intensively than agriculture, aggregate measures recorded a bias toward techniques—actually, toward a sector—that used unskilled labor much more sparingly.

Over the longer period, the productivity estimates of Kendrick and others show that productivity continued to advance more rapidly in manufacturing, transportation, and utilities than in agriculture until shortly before World War II. There is some evidence that this intersectoral gap in neutral productivity advance favored the nonfarm sector more during periods of rising income inequality—1889–1909 and 1919–1929—than during periods of declining inequalities—1909–1919 and 1929–1953. The nineteenth-century evidence on unbalanced rates of productivity advance is, of course, far less abundant, but the thesis seems to us sufficiently promising to pursue it at length in Chapters 7 and 10.

In summary, imbalance in the rates of technological progress by sector appears to be an excellent candidate as a causal force driving American inequality experience since the early antebellum period. It supplies an exogenous source of aggregate growth; it supplies an exogenous source of industrialization, urbanization, and structural change; it supplies an exogenous source of the systematic movements in relative commodity prices documented in Chapter 5; and it offers an explanation of aggregate laborsaving and nominal inequality trends. Perhaps in combination with exogenous labor supply forces, it may provide an adequate theory of American macro inequality experience.

FERTILITY, IMMIGRATION, AND LABOR SUPPLY

Hypotheses regarding macro distribution performance over time can be readily classified as related to factor demand or factor supply. Thus far, we have focused on factor demand forces. What about factor supply? Have these two forces been competitive or have they been mutually reinforcing throughout most of American history?

The factor supply thesis in general (and the labor supply thesis in particular) has often served as a popular explanation for inequality trends. After all, theory tends to favor the argument that fertility and immigration should be linked positively to inequality. Most general-equilibrium models imply that a rise in the labor force—from earlier fertility increases or from current immigration—would lower wage rates and raise returns to land and capital. Since earlier fertility increases translate first into an expansion of the labor force at young ages, the relative price of the unskilled (new, young entrants) should undergo especially large declines, thus raising skill premia and earnings inequality as well. What is true for lagged fertility increases is even more true for current immigration, if, as it is commonly thought, relatively young unskilled males dominated the immigrating labor force in the century between the 1820s and the 1920s. If it can be shown that the labor supply, specifically immigration, is primarily an exogenous force in American development—rather than an endogenous response to rising real wages—then we have an influence on inequality which certainly warrants our careful attention. (On the dominance of "push" forces underlying nineteenth-century immigration, and thus the exogeneity of labor supply growth, see Williamson, 1974b, Chap. 11; 1974d.)

The labor supply thesis has other attractions as well. Econometric models also suggest that an exogenous fall in the labor force should accelerate the advance of wages even in the short run (Metcalf, 1972). Furthermore, there are additional microeconomic effects that should strengthen the impact of declining fertility on subsequent leveling of incomes. These micro forces are similar to the accumulation responses outlined earlier in this chapter where we invoked the hypothesis that saving rates and rates of accumulation rise with family income. Here, these forces would be manifested through the effects of family inputs on child achievement (Kuznets, 1974, p. 144; Lindert, 1974):

1. A reduction in fertility lowers the dispersion of family sizes, since birth restriction typically reduces the number of children born into very large families by a greater percentage than it reduces the number of first and second children. Since larger family size seems to be a factor that should retard the development of earning capacity in individual children, the reduction in family size differences ought to reduce later earnings inequality.

2. Since about 1910, birth restriction has on balance reduced the proportion of children born into poor and less-educated families. Birth restriction should thus tend to lower income inequality by cutting down on the relative number of children born into the extreme disadvantage of being unwanted members of large low-income families.

3. Another reason for suspecting that lower fertility means less inequality is that large families tend to create overcrowding in public schools. If the total amount of philanthropic and taxpayer support for schooling is characterized by inertia, then the strain on school systems

should be directly related to the share of the population that is of school age. Reducing births may reduce the ratio of children to adults more than it reduces public (and philanthropic) school expenditures per adult, so that the smaller cohort of school-age children enjoys greater public educational outlays per child. To the extent that this public-support effect is more relevant below college than it is for public funding of higher education, the extra public expenditures per child should help the most disadvantaged children the most. This should reduce inequalities of schooling and income.

The first-order macroeconomic impacts deserve the greatest stress, however. It might prove helpful to repeat the two strictly supply-related forces already mentioned:

4. A drop in fertility now implies fewer labor force entrants a generation later, and a current fall in immigration implies fewer new entrants today. These events should tend to accelerate the rise in all wage rates—for the skilled and unskilled—relative to profit rates and to rates of return on property. Since conventional property is distributed less equally than human capital (Chap. 3), a relative rise in wage rates and wage income shares tends to make for more equally distributed incomes.

5. Birth reduction should reduce the dispersion of skills and raise their average levels for the microeconomic reasons given (the first three points above). A reduction in immigration, if biased toward the unskilled, should do the same. Thus, a diminished rate of growth in the labor supply for either reason should tend to reduce earnings inequality by bidding down the premia earned by higher-paid, skilled employees. That is, reductions in fertility and immigration should tend to raise the wage rates of the unskilled (and/or the young) by more than the skilled (and/or the old).

Other macroeconomic effects may be offsetting to the extent that population influences the composition of demand. Extra children and extra (young) immigrants tend to shift demand toward agricultural products, especially food, and toward ''population-sensitive'' investment. A decline in immigration and fertility should tend to have the opposite effect. This suggests that labor supply should have a two-sided demand effect on overall inequality:

6. By shifting demand away from food and population-sensitive investment, reductions in immigration and fertility may lower the relative price of these products. This would tend to reduce inequalities in real purchasing power to the extent that food and housing are a greater share in the cost of living of poor families than of rich.

7. The same shift in demand would cause both agriculture and construction to decline as a share of national income, two very unskilled-

labor-intensive activities, especially in the nineteenth century (Chap. 8). This might weaken the relative nominal pay position of unskilled laborers, causing a counter-tendency toward inequality. These induced and conflicting demand effects are almost certainly of lesser magnitude than the initial labor supply impact and thus are unlikely to influence the outcome of the initial labor supply effect.

Although the link between labor supply and inequality has always been a popular device for understanding "labor surplus" economies (W. A. Lewis, 1954; Fei and Ranis, 1964), only recently has it been applied systematically to more advanced economies. Kindleberger (1967) has applied the framework to postwar Europe, Minami (1973) has applied it to post–World War II Japan, Kelley and Williamson (1974) have applied it to pre–World War I Meiji Japan, and Lindert (1974, 1978) has applied it to America. With the exception of the Japanese studies, however, these earlier efforts have relied on the raw correlation between inequality and labor supply. They do not supply a quantitative accounting of the portion of the observed inequality experience to be explained by labor supply forces. We hope to do so in Part Three, after Chapter 9 has documented the American correlation itself.

THE RATE OF CAPITAL ACCUMULATION

If the economy-wide rate of accumulation of human and nonhuman capital were truly an exogenous force, it would offer an attractive additional explanation for the observed trends in inequality. Between 1840 and 1912, when inequalities were widening, the capital stock grew at the rapid rate of 5% per annum (Davis et al., 1972, p. 34). The subsequent leveling of incomes was accompanied by a rate of capital accumulation of only 2% between 1912 and 1950, while the rate rose to 3.3% during the 1950s, when the equalizing trend ceased. These swings in the rate of accumulation were sufficiently wide so that the capital stock per man-hour grew faster during the drift toward inequality than during the leveling period. This correlation suggests that more rapid accumulation of nonhuman capital may raise earnings inequalities and occupational pay ratios by bidding up the return to skills of all sorts while displacing unskilled labor. That surmise is encouraged by the findings of Griliches (1969), Berndt and Christensen (1973), and Fallon and Layard (1975): capital and skills tend to be complementary inputs, while both tend to be substitutes for unskilled labor. It would appear, therefore, that whatever causes an acceleration in the rate of capital accumulation would also produce a concomitant increase in the relative demand for skills. Furthermore, since the production of human and nonhuman capital is skill- and machine-intensive (Chap. 8), rising saving rates and rates of capital formation may offer a further source of increased inequality.

Yet the rate of capital accumulation is a variable that no explanation of trends in income inequality can afford to leave unexplained and exogenous. Intuition and recent developments in growth theory both suggest that income distribution and capital accumulation are simultaneously determined. It is just as easy to argue that income inequality fosters rapid capital accumulation as it is to argue the reverse. As we shall see, it is also possible to argue that other exogenous forces were driving *both* and that their correlation over time is spurious (Chap. 11). To make good use of the information we have about trends in the rate of capital accumulation, one must identify the secular influences that altered both the rate of accumulation and the degree of income inequality together. Two basic forces could have caused the rate of accumulation, the trend in inequality, and the rate of profit all to take a long-run plunge shortly after World War I. The same two forces could account for the simultaneous acceleration in accumulation and the surge in inequality during the antebellum decades. One is the shift in the growth rate in the labor force. The other is the unbalanced rate of total factor productivity growth across sectors.

If one believes that saving is the active constraint on accumulation and further that aggregate saving is linked to inequality (the rich are the predominant savers even on the margin), then the role of labor supply on accumulation might seem obvious. For example, the drop in the rate of growth of the labor force during World War I and again at the end of the 1920s would have tended eventually to squeeze profits, compress wage and salary differentials, and reduce capital accumulation simultaneously. Since the slower labor force growth tended to accelerate the rise in average skill levels, the restriction in labor supply must have been more severe in low-skill job markets. Faced with this slower supply expansion, firms found it difficult to keep profits up. The pressure on profits tended in turn to cut into firms' ability to use inside funds to finance real accumulation. Since borrowed funds are in fact seldom available at the opportunity cost of inside funds, the reduction in profits should have cut investment through the total supply of savings as well as through its influence on expectations about future returns to accumulation. If this argument is correct, then the slowing of labor supply growth lowered the pay advantage of skilled labor in two ways: directly, by encouraging the growth of the average skills of those entering the labor force, and indirectly, by cutting into the accumulation of nonhuman capital, which is complementary in use with skills.

Suppose instead one believes that the active constraint on physical accumulation is not just nominal savings, but also the capacity of the capital goods sector to fill those accumulation requirements. Suppose further that the capital goods sector exhibits the most dramatic variety over time in the rate of total factor productivity growth, so that when unbalanced rates of productivity growth were most apparent—that is, during phases of trending inequality—they were most rapid in the capital goods sector. The spectacular decline in the relative price of producer durables during the antebellum period (Williamson, 1974b, 1974c), for example, would have fostered accumulation even if the nominal savings rate had remained constant. The far greater rise in the antebellum savings ratio in constant than in current prices furnishes support for the position. Furthermore, those sectors using the cheapened (but higher-quality) machines intensively would expand, that is, capital- and skill-intensive industrial activities. In addition, the cheaper machines would tend to replace labor throughout the economy, diminishing the relative demand for unskilled labor (a substitute for machines) while augmenting the demand for skills (a complement to machines). The net result is both greater accumulation and greater inequality. (We intend to pursue this theoretical narrative in far greater detail in Chapters 10, 11, and 12.) The argument can also be made in a somewhat different way. We shall establish in Chapters 7 and 11 that productivity apparently advanced much faster in those industries using unskilled labor least intensively during the period 1889–1909 and 1919–1929, though this was not true during the 1909–1919 decade or after 1929. We noted above that this pattern roughly corresponds with inequality trends, and that the correlation appears to hold for the nineteenth century as well. It could be argued, therefore, that the change in total factor productivity growth favoring sectors using unskilled labor intensively (agriculture, in particular), especially after 1929, not only depressed the pay advantage of skilled labor, but also may have cut into profits and capital accumulation to the advantage of farmers as well as unskilled labor. Similarly, the impressive rates of unbalanced total factor productivity growth prior to the Civil War must have fostered structural change that was biased against unskilled labor, raising inequality and accumulation rates simultaneously.

Capital accumulation adds another channel through which movements in the labor supply and unbalanced rates of productivity growth seem likely to have influenced trends in inequality. Furthermore, this tentative theoretical account has made only casual reference to another potential force contributing to the link. Chapter 8 will explore the hypothesis that the *production* of both human and nonhuman capital requires relatively heavy inputs of skills. To the extent that this hypothesis survives the test, then the accumulation–inequality link is reinforced.

The era in which inequalities shrank was also one in which the share of national product consumed by government rose. The wars were, of course, the main influence on government's growth, but after each war government expenditures failed to return to their prewar shares in GNP. How might the rise of government have fostered the leveling of personal incomes measured *before* taxes? One way is by raising the proportion of the labor force drafted or induced into the armed forces, thereby bidding up wages in the private sector. This influence can be viewed as either a form of labor supply restriction to the private sector or as a shift in final demand favoring unskilled and young labor economy-wide. Its importance during wars reinforces the labor supply argument already discussed. The other type of government impact is to shift the composition of demand for final products in both war and peace. If it can be shown that the government's purchases of goods and services create a much greater demand for unskilled labor than the same amount of displaced private demand, then the twentieth-century rise of government may have been a leveling influence on incomes even aside from its effects on troop levels, aggregate demand, and the progressivity of taxation. This proposition will be explored in Chapters 8 and 12.

The Agenda

This chapter has set the stage for the remainder of the book. In our search for systematic, exogenous forces which might jointly explain American distribution experience since 1820, we have identified four factors that seem to us most promising: (*a*) unbalanced rates of technological progress, (*b*) labor supply growth, (*c*) capital accumulation, and (*d*) the rise of government. Like the trend in distribution itself, capital accumulation is really an endogenous variable. It seems wisest, however, to treat it separately, especially given the attention it receives in the "growth–equity trade-off" literature and the continued debate over its determinants. Some might argue that the rise of government is also endogenous, but that position extends the scope of political economy beyond our expertise. In any case, we doubt that knowledge would be advanced by our entry into that debate. We do not deny that other forces may have been at work as well, but they seem to us minor and unsystematic when examined over the broad sweep of inequality history.

The remainder of this part of the book is an empirical exploration of the debatable assertions made above. Chapter 7 will deal with labor saving and unbalanced growth. Chapter 8 will supply estimates of sectoral factor intensities and the impact of final demand shifts, including the impact of government and capital accumulation on derived factor demand. Chapter 9 will explore the role of labor supply, both in quantity and quality. When these chores are completed, we shall then be ready in Part Three to decompose the sources of American inequality.

7

UNBALANCED GROWTH AND LABOR SAVING

The broad correlation between income inequality and the relative pay of the unskilled suggests the wisdom of searching for the sources of inequality movements in the determinants of the demand and supply of unskilled labor. Chapter 9 explores the labor supply side, whereas this chapter and the next explore the demand side.

Aggregate Labor Saving

Economists and historians have long been concerned with the possibility that modern technology has a laborsaving bias, with new technologies replacing labor with man-made nonhuman inputs. Presumably, it is the income-distributional consequences of labor saving that have made these technological innovations a topic of heated debate since Marx gave them so much of his attention. If such a bias is truly exogenous, as opposed to an endogenous response to rising labor scarcity, it is a source of income inequality worth worrying about.

Modern labor saving has become such a firmly rooted "stylized fact" that it has given rise to a series of theoretical and historical narratives designed to explain *why* labor saving prevails during modern economic growth. In Marxian analysis, capitalists have few means of augmenting profits other than by seeking ways to reduce their direct demands for labor, especially when profit rates and accumulation rates are taken as monotonically linked. A neoclassical literature has also emerged in which laborsaving inventions and innovations, like ordinary shifts along production-function isoquants, are induced by prior trends toward labor scarcity. The theoretical quest was carried into economic history by H. J.

Habakkuk's classic on American and British technology in the nineteenth century (Habakkuk, 1962). Habakkuk pondered at length and with great imagination just why it was that American technological advances had such a pronounced trend toward mechanization and standardization. Prior to the more recent econometric analysis, most economists shared his presumption that labor saving was a basic fact of life, that it had occurred at both the firm and industry level as well as in the aggregate, and that it had proceeded at a relatively stable rate across time.

In the 1960s, economists began to raise empirical questions about the extent of and stability in the laborsaving bias. In pursuing production-function estimates, an econometric methodology was developed to measure the extent to which observed increases in the capital–labor ratio were a response to changes in factor prices as opposed to true changes in technology. Using (or assuming) prior information on a few key parameters, numerous regressions involving factor–use ratios, factor shares and/or factor–price ratios have appeared in the literature. These supplied estimates of factor substitution elasticities as well as of the exogenous factor-saving bias. The search was conducted at both the industry and the aggregate level. The aggregate results were presented under the implicit assumption that they summarized what was happening at both the industry and firm level.

The econometric literature appears to confirm that labor saving is significant at the aggregate national level as well as within industries. David and van de Klundert (1965) estimated the aggregate laborsaving bias to have raised American capital–labor ratios between 0.49% and 0.72% per year over the period 1899–1960.[1] Murray Brown (1966) divided

---

[1] David and van de Klundert report laborsaving biases of 0.72% and 0.86% per year from their Models II and III, but these figures require adjustment before they can be interpreted as shifts toward higher capital-labor ratios for given factor–price ratios and given states of other variables. The adjustment is required, since David and van de Klundert, like later authors (Asher, 1972; Abramovitz and David, 1973), estimated the laborsaving bias from regressions of factor–use ratios on factor–*share* ratios, rather than on factor–*price* ratios. The adjustment is necessary, since an exogenous shift toward labor saving would affect these shares as well as factor–use ratios. Using symbols to be introduced below in this chapter, these authors have run regressions of the form

$$\ln(K/L) = a_o + a_1\ln[\theta_L/(1 - \theta_L)] + B't + \text{(other terms)} + e.$$

Since the factor–share ratio $\theta_L/(1 - \theta_L) = wL/rK$,

$$\ln(K/L)(1 + a_1) = a_o + a_1\ln(w/r) + B't + \text{(other terms)} + e,$$

or

$$\ln(K/L) = \frac{a_o}{1 + a_1} + \frac{a_1}{1 + a_1}\ln(w/r) + \frac{B'}{1 + a_1} + \frac{\text{(other terms)}}{1 + a_1} + \frac{e}{1 + a_1}.$$

The coefficient in front of the log of the factor–price ratio (w/r) is by definition the elasticity

the twentieth century into subperiods and found much more pronounced labor saving in the 1920s than in the periods before or after. Morishima and Saito (1968) confirmed this result, estimating the time path of labor saving shown in Figure 7.1. Here again the 1920s stand out as years of pronounced labor saving. A more recent contribution by Abramovitz and David (1973, p. 434) extended these estimates back across the nineteenth century. The aggregate rate of labor saving in the nineteenth century was estimated at the much higher rate of 1.36% per year, a rate that also exceeded those estimated for American and British textile industries in the late nineteenth century (Asher, 1972). In short, the literature offers three conclusions: (a) labor saving has been the rule over the past century and a half; (b) labor saving was much higher in the nineteenth century; and (c) the 1910s and the period after 1929 witnessed an episodic reversal, or at least cessation, in the laborsaving bias.

Taken at face value, these estimates of aggregate labor saving might seem to fit neatly into an explanation of inequality movements. The periods in which labor saving seemed most pronounced—the nineteenth century as well as the 1920s—are periods in which income inequality was

---

of capital–labor substitution, σ. This coefficient can be rearranged to show that $1/(1 + a_1) = 1 - \sigma$. Therefore, the estimated factor-bias drift coefficient $B'/(1 + a_1) = B'(1 - \sigma) = B$. But it is this B that represents the factor-use bias in the equation in which the dependent variable, $\ln(K/L)$, is purged from the right-hand side.

It is for this reason that we have adjusted the David and van de Klundert factor bias estimates by multiplying them by $(1 - \sigma)$: $.0072 \times (1 - .3165) = .0049$ and $.0086 \times (1 - .1626) = .0072$. The Abramovitz–David (1973, p. 434) estimate for the laborsaving bias of the nineteenth century has been similarly adjusted, $1.7\% \times (1 - .20) = 1.36\%$, in the text above. No such adjustment is needed on the Morishima–Saito factor bias estimates, which used factor–share ratios as the dependent variable and factor–price ratios as one independent variable.

There is no basic problem in interpreting the coefficients for factor bias drift and the elasticity of substitution as empirical tendencies. Yet, as unpublished works by Peter A. Diamond and Daniel McFadden have stressed, great care must be taken in interpreting the estimated coefficients as revealing the parameters of an underlying production function. Only if the researcher imposes limiting assumptions about the form of technological change can production-function parameters be identified.

One set of assumptions that identifies the parameters of a CES production function using regressions like that given here is to assume that we know the functional form of factor-augmenting technological change. If, for example, we knew that the production function were of the convenient form

$$y = \gamma[\delta K^{-\rho} + (1 - \delta)L^{-\rho}]^{-1/\rho}$$

and that the distributional parameter $\delta/(1 - \delta)$ grew at the constant exponential rate B/σ, so that $\delta/(1 - \delta) = e^{(a_0 + Bt)/\sigma}$, then this production function would yield the regression equation introduced in the text. We interpret the David–van de Klundert, Asher, and Morishima–Saito studies as making assumptions like these when they report a long-run factor-saving bias.

Index of Labor-Capital
Ratio for Constant
Factor-Price Ratio

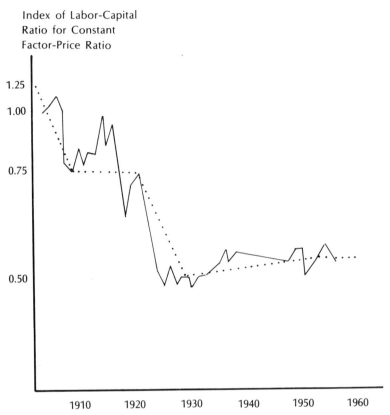

FIGURE 7.1. The Morishima–Saito index of U.S. labor saving, 1902–1955. From Morishima and Saito (1968, p. 438).

on the rise, whereas the decade beginning 1910 and the post-1929 era have both been characterized by income leveling. Yet there are three important reasons why these estimates should not be taken at face value: (*a*) the aggregate estimates are almost certainly too high; (*b*) they are unlikely to be primarily the result of intraindustry labor saving, as is generally assumed; and (*c*) they do not measure "savings" of *unskilled* labor—low-wage workers whose relative pay is most relevant to inequality trends.

The estimates of labor saving are probably too high because they contain a simultaneity bias and it may be especially serious at the aggregate level. In regressing capital-labor ratios on either factor–price ratios or factor–share ratios, the empirical literature has in effect assumed that factor prices are fixed by infinitely elastic factor supplies, so that factor-use ratios can be interpreted as demand curve observations. Yet the

American manufacturing sector rarely faced fixed prices in factor markets, and the entire American economy certainly never did. When factor demand curves shift, either through random components or through changes in any argument within the demand functions, factor prices are obviously influenced. With price ratios and quantity ratios thus simultaneously affected by demand and supply behavior, regressions on factor quantities will yield biased estimates of both the elasticity of substitution and the rate of factor-saving bias.

The issue is analogous to the problem of identifying demand and supply curves from price and quantity data in an individual market. To underline this analogy, consider the common case in which the factor-saving bias and elasticity of factor substitution are being estimated by regressing changes in capital–labor ratios on changes in wage–rental ratios:

$$(\overset{*}{K} - \overset{*}{L}) = - \sigma(\overset{*}{r} - \overset{*}{w}) + B + \text{(other terms)} + e,$$

which is equivalent to the more frequently used natural-log equation

$$\ln(K/L) = b_o - \sigma\ln(r/w) + Bt + \text{(other terms)} + e',$$

where $\overset{*}{K}$ is the rate of capital accumulation, $\overset{*}{L}$ is the rate of labor force growth, σ is the elasticity of capital–labor substitution in response to factor–price ratios, $\overset{*}{w}$ is the rate of growth of wage rates, $\overset{*}{r}$ is the rate of growth of rental rates on capital, B is the bias per year toward labor saving, and e' is a normally distributed error term with zero mean. If the investigator were lucky, $(\overset{*}{r} - \overset{*}{w})$ would be fixed in each time period by the position of an infinitely elastic set of factor supply curves. Such good fortune is unlikely, so the estimates are likely to suffer from the kind of simultaneity bias shown in Figure 7.2. There it is imagined that random elements exist on both the demand and supply sides of factor markets, varying in such a way that the demand curve spends half its time at position D_1 and half its time at position D_2 while the supply curve alternates equally between S_1 and S_2. History will produce four quantity-price observations, the four intersections indicated by a, b, c, and d.

Minimizing the sum of the squares of horizontal deviations will yield the biased "demand" curve $\hat{D}$, where the circumflex refers to the estimate. In the case portrayed here, this curve underestimates the elasticity of factor substitution, just as single-equation estimates of import demand chronically underestimate the price elasticities of import demands (Orcutt, 1950; Leamer and Stern, 1970, Chap. 2). At the same time, the degree of labor saving is overstated.[2] Whether the secular variance in the rate of labor

[2] Understatement of σ and overstatement of B are likely to prevail, even though strong positive correlation between demand-curve and supply-curve shift terms could reverse the

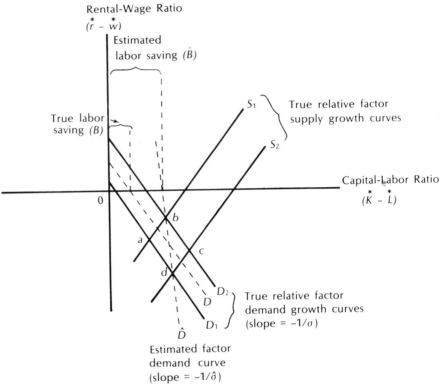

FIGURE 7.2. An example of biased estimation of factor saving and the elasticity of factor substitution.

saving is also affected remains a separate issue. It could very well be that the size of the bias is sufficiently stable that our judgments regarding *changes* in the rate of labor saving would remain untarnished.

Unbalanced Output Growth and Labor Saving

The *source* of shifting rates of aggregate labor saving has not received the attention it deserves if we are to understand and predict the degree of labor saving in the future. Morishima and Saito (1968) have presented results suggesting that changes in twentieth-century labor saving are

---

direction of bias. In Figure 7.2, for example, ordinary least-squares estimation would overstate σ and understate B if the observations alternated only between a and c owing to perfect correlation between the positions of the two curves.

explained entirely by changes in America's output mix rather than by laborsaving forces within sectors. They found that the economy-wide shift from labor saving to labor using between 1902–1929 and 1929–1955 was almost exactly matched by the shift one would have predicted from knowledge of sectoral growth rates and relative labor intensities of agricultural and nonagricultural sectors. For the entire period 1902–1955 the observed aggregate labor saving was more than accounted for by the output-mix effect, with the intrasectoral bias actually moving in the wrong (labor-using) direction.[3] This theme has also been stressed by development economists (Williamson, 1971; Morawetz, 1974), who consider "output composition" effects to have been an important source of labor saving in the Third World over the past quarter century.

To ignore the link between unbalanced growth and factor demand in explaining trends in the relative wages of men, skills, and machines is to miss a potentially important mechanism helping drive American income distribution. Simple general-equilibrium theory tells us so, and this section will add quantitative evidence to the theory. The next section will then explore one likely determinant of output-mix changes: sectoral differences in productivity advance.

EARLY MODERN GROWTH: 1839–1899

Since the antebellum period has always been characterized as the first and most spectacular phase of American structural change, it should occasion no surprise that we expect to find a causal link between the first great surge in inequality and the abrupt change in output mix which took place over these three or four decades. Gallman's data show that agriculture declined as a share in total commodity output from 72% to 56% between 1839 and 1859; manufacturing rose from 17% to 32% over the same two decades; mining, quarrying, and construction combined rose from 11% to 12% (Table 7.2). The rapid rate of structural change resumed

[3] Morishima and Saito (p. 435) give the following breakdowns of the total "technology effect," or the movements in factor shares toward labor not explained by factor price movements:

Period	Total	Due to changes in agriculture's output share	Due to intra-sectoral biases
1902–1929 (excl. '19, '21, '22)	−2.2%/yr.	−2.5%	0.4%
1929–1938 (excl. '32, '33)	2.4	2.3	0.2
1938–1955 (excl. '41–'46)	−0.1	−1.8	1.8
1902–1955 (all exclusions)	−0.9	−1.6	0.7

(Details may not add up to totals due to rounding.)

TABLE 7.1
Unbalanced Rates of Nineteenth-Century Output Growth, 1879 Prices

	Per Annum Rates of Output Growth in		
Period	Agriculture ($\overset{*}{A}$)	Manufacturing ($\overset{*}{M}$)	$\overset{*}{M} - \overset{*}{A}$
1839–1849	2.31	9.92	7.61
1849–1859	4.20	5.82	1.62
1859–1869	1.44	2.29	.85
1869–1879	4.22	6.17	1.95
1879–1889	2.22	7.79	5.57
1889–1899	1.92	4.18	2.26
1839–1859	3.25	7.83	4.58
1859–1879	2.82	4.22	1.40
1879–1899	2.07	5.97	3.90

Source: Gallman (1960, p. 43).

following the Civil War (see Engerman, 1966; Williamson, 1974c), but Table 7.1 shows that unbalanced output growth was most dramatic in the antebellum period. Furthermore, there is considerable macro evidence (David, 1967) as well as micro detail (Zevin, 1971) confirming equally dramatic industrialization between 1820 and 1840.

Nineteenth-century agriculture was far more intensive in unskilled labor than was manufacturing or construction. This assertion is based on an examination of 1899 industrial cost shares. Those sectors in which wage payments to unskilled labor loomed large as a share in total value added were clearly activities that utilized unskilled labor intensively. During periods of unbalanced sectoral output growth which favored industrial activities with low unskilled-labor requirements, the economy-wide demand for unskilled labor diminished compared with skills and machines. Increasing skill premia, wage stretching, rising pay ratios, income inequality, *and* aggregate labor saving should be observed as a result.

The impact of unbalanced output growth on the relative demand for unskilled labor can be estimated by combining observed shifts in sectoral value-added shares with observations on unskilled labor's wage share in each sector's value added. Let us define the economy-wide unskilled labor share as $\theta_L = wL/V$, where the numerator is simply aggregate wage payments to unskilled workers[4] and V is aggregate value added. The share

---

[4] As we shall note again in Appendix J and Chapter 8, payments to unskilled labor can be measured as the product of the base-period wage rate and either of two measures of employment. The first measure of employment is simply total national employment of all labor. Using this times the unskilled-labor wage rate implies viewing each member of the

of unskilled labor in national product can also be written as a weighted average of base-period sectoral value-added shares, θ_{Lj}:

$$\theta_L = \sum_j \theta_{Lj} v_j,$$

where the v_j are the sectoral value-added shares in GNP and $\sum_j v_j = 1$. Holding these θ_{Lj} constant, the impact of the changing output mix on the economy-wide unskilled labor share can be estimated by the expression

$$\Delta\theta_L = \sum_j \theta_{Lj}(\Delta v_j), \qquad \text{where } \sum_j \Delta v_j = 0.$$

Growth (or decline) in the relative demand for unskilled labor attributable to unbalanced output expansion can then be calculated as $[\overset{*}{\theta_L/(1 - \theta_L)}]$, where the asterisk denotes proportionate rates of change of the form $(dX/dt)/X = \overset{*}{X}$. Negative values imply labor saving.

The earliest base period available for the unskilled labor-share weights, θ_{Lj}, is the year 1899. Antebellum America could hardly have been very different from America in the 1890s, at least with regard to relative factor intensities, and stability in the *relative* magnitudes sector by sector is all we require for the calculations reported below. To the extent that factor-intensity differentials across sectors were likely to have been even greater early in the century, the calculations which appear in Table 7.2 must be viewed as an understatement of the magnitude of labor saving, but the time path is probably quite accurate.

Shifts in the value-added mix of the economy in the nineteenth century implied a large shift toward labor saving. Between 1839 and 1899, the ratio of unskilled labor to other factors—here measured by $\theta_L/(1 - \theta_L)$—declined at the rate of 1.06% per year. This tentative calculation is quite striking. Recall that Abramovitz and David (1973) have estimated the aggregate nineteenth-century laborsaving rate at 1.36% per annum. Thus, it appears that something like three-quarters of the aggregate labor saving in the nineteenth century may be due to output-mix changes alone, a finding much like that offered by Morishima and Saito on the twentieth century.

Furthermore, the figures reported in Table 7.2 bear remarkable similarity to the inequality trends reported in Part One. First, we note that the most impressive decline took place between 1844 and 1849, a period of

labor force as receiving returns to unskilled labor up to the unskilled-labor wage rate, with remaining earnings attributed to skills. The second, and somewhat preferable, measure of earnings by unskilled labor multiplies the unskilled-labor wage rate by employment only of persons in low-skilled occupational groups. Chapter 8 uses both measures at different times. The present calculations use only the first, which is far easier to document for the nineteenth century.

TABLE 7.2
The Impact of Changing Output Mix on Unskilled Labor's Share, 1839–1899

	Gallman's Value Added, 1879 Prices (*millions of dollars*)					Unskilled Labor's Share, Using 1899 θ_{Lj}
Year	Agri-culture	Mining	Manu-facturing	Construc-tion (A)	Total (A)	$(\theta_L = \sum \theta_{Lj} v_j)$
1839	$787	$7	$190	$110	$1,094	.477
1844	944	14	290	126	1,374	.464
1849	989	17	488	163	1,657	.428
1854	1,316	26	677	298	2,317	.420
1859	1,492	33	859	302	2,686	.413
1869	1,720	70	1,078	403	3,271	.404
1874	1,977	105	1,692	523	4,297	.377
1879	2,599	153	1,962	590	5,304	.388
1884	3,001	227	3,215	857	7,300	.358
1889	3,238	346	4,156	919	8,659	.342
1894	3,273	389	5,480	1,116	10,258	.320
1899	3,918	551	6,262	1,020	11,751	.325

Sources and notes: Value-added data are from Gallman (1960, Table A-1, p. 43), using variant A. The underlying θ_{Lj} weights are taken from Chapter 8 below. The figures for 1899 θ_{Lj} are the following:

Agriculture	.580	Manufacturing	.177
Mining	.277	Construction	.277.

five years which encompassed an "epic surge" in wage differentials. The decline continued up to 1854, as did the trends in wage stretching. Second, the half decades 1839–1844 and 1854–1859 apparently induced very mild declines in our predicted labor share. The trend corresponds with similar movements in pay ratios documented in Chapter 4. Third, while the predicted labor share continues its downward drift after the Civil War, the rate of decline tends to slow down considerably. This can be seen most clearly when the decline in the predicted labor share is reported for fifteen-year intervals: 1839–1854, 5.7%; 1854–1869, 1.6%; 1869–1884, 4.6%; and 1884–1899, 3.3%. We shall have more to say about this retardation below, but it is repeated in our distribution statistics covering the late nineteenth century.

There are grounds for believing that the calculations reported in Table 7.2 understate the laborsaving impact of nineteenth-century unbalanced output growth. First, we have already pointed out that the 1899 θ_{Lj} are likely to understate the relative differences in factor intensity that prevailed in the early nineteenth century. Second, data limitations make it impossible to expand the commodity output analysis to include services. The service sector (transportation, finance, personal services, wholesale and retail trade) was a very large share of urban employment then as now.

During this period of extraordinary urbanization and structural change nonfarm value-added shares were rising at least as rapidly as the share of manufacturing and construction in commodity output. If the θ_{Lj} for such urban services also tended to be far lower than agriculture, then we have additional grounds for believing that Table 7.2 understates the role of unbalanced growth. In 1921, at least, services did have far lower unskilled-labor content than agriculture. Indeed, trade, transportation, and communications all had lower unskilled-labor intensities than even manufacturing, and *every* service activity had lower unskilled-labor intensities than construction.[5]

In short, there is a presumption that a large share of the nineteenth-century inequality surge was attributable to sharply changing conditions in the relative demand for factors, such that skills and machines were favored at the expense of unskilled labor. These demand conditions must have created large quasi-rents on human and nonhuman assets of all sorts. One must surmise that the economy could only begin to eliminate these rents when the additional disequilibrating conditions introduced by Civil War and "catching up" had dissipated. Note too that the output-mix hypothesis, in conjunction with inflation and wage lags for skilled labor, may also help account for the Civil War episode. The low and declining skill premia from 1862 to 1865 may be explained, at least in part, by the cessation of capital formation activities and the expansion (or diminished relative rate of decline) in farm production, in a fashion similar to America's twentieth-century wars. These conditions are reversed during the postwar stabilization and up to the mid-1880s.

THE LATE NINETEENTH CENTURY: 1882–1906

Gallman's deflated sectoral output data cease with 1899. Similar twentieth-century data (King, 1930)—which have the added advantage of service sector coverage—do not begin until 1909. However, Kuznets's constant-price final demand estimates, which also cover services, fill the gap up to 1906. The laborsaving impact of changes in final demand mix is presented in Table 7.3 for the period spanning the turn of the century. The results confirm that the output mix continued to shift against unskilled labor during the late 1880s, but this trend ceased entirely for the remainder of the century. As we shall see, the laborsaving drift does not clearly reappear until the 1920s. This observation around the turn of the century

[5] Including services might have raised the rate at which factor demand was being shifted away from unskilled labor, but this effect would be reduced by the fact that including services would lower the aggregate importance of agriculture, the sector with clearly outstanding use of unskilled labor.

TABLE 7.3
The Impact of Changing Final Demand Mix on Unskilled Labor's Share, 1882/1886–1902/1906

| | | | Kuznets's GNP Components, 1929 Prices (billions of dollars) | | | | | Unskilled Labor's Share Using 1899 $\hat{\theta}_{LJ}$ |
Period	Gross Construction	Gross Investment Durables	Services	Durables	Semidurables	Perishables	GNP	$(\theta_L = \sum \hat{\theta}_{LJ} v_J)$
					Consumption			
1882/1886	$3.1	$1.4	$5.1	$1.5	$2.5	$7.1	$20.7	.292
1887/1891	4.4	1.5	5.7	2.0	2.9	7.5	24.0	.285
1892/1896	5.5	1.9	6.6	2.1	3.2	9.0	28.3	.286
1897/1901	5.5	3.2	8.7	2.6	4.0	11.4	35.4	.286
1902/1906	7.0	3.8	11.8	3.3	5.0	14.1	45.0	.283

Sources and notes: GNP in constant prices is taken from *Historical Statistics* (1975, Part 1, p. 231). The underlying $\hat{\theta}_{LJ}$ weights are taken from Chapter 8 below. They differ from those used in Table 7.2. The latter dealt with national income originating by sector and thus used θ_{LJ}, direct labor cost shares in value added. The θ_{LJ} used here include direct and indirect payments impact, the latter generated by input-output relationships. The 1899 $\hat{\theta}_{LJ}$ (see Table 8.6) are

Consumer durables	.2130	Consumer services	.1360
Consumer perishables	.4834	Investment durables	.2083
Consumer semidurables	.2754	Construction	.2037

where food is equated to perishables and semidurables to apparel. The calculation reported in the table was also performed using 1919 $\hat{\theta}_{LJ}$, and the results are similar.

166

supplies one episode when labor saving induced by output-mix change correlates poorly with trends in the occupational pay gaps. Pay gaps changed very little across the 1880s, though they widened from 1890 to 1916 (Chap. 4). The labor saving generated by changes in the output mix would have implied the opposite pattern in pay ratio trends.

THE TWENTIETH CENTURY

Within the twentieth century we have access to more frequent estimates of the factor content of value added in different sectors, allowing more frequent revision of the factor-share weights that help us judge the effects of output composition on the demand for unskilled labor. Table 7.4 reports several calculations taking advantage of the more recent data. The table underscores three reversals within this century. Changes in the output mix favored unskilled labor in the period 1910–1920, with an unknown share of the credit going to World War I. Output shifted sharply away from the unskilled-intensive sectors across the 1920s, then swung back in their favor between 1929 and 1948. The postwar period, on the other hand, exhibits approximate neutrality. This chronology corresponds roughly with the timing of occupational pay gaps and income inequality trends. Although World War I may have added some spurious improvement to the correlation, it is noteworthy that laborsaving trends attributable to output-mix changes behave much like distribution trends.

TABLE 7.4
The Impact of Changes in Output Mix on Unskilled Labor's Share, 1909–1975

Period	Rate of Change in Unskilled Labor's Relative Share Implied by Changes in Output Mix $\left(\dfrac{*}{[\theta_L/(1 - \theta_L)]} \right)$	Base Year and Source for Unskilled-Labor Shares (θ_{Lj})	Number of Sectors Represented
1909–1919	+0.35%/yr.	1909 King	7
	+0.05	1919 King	7
1919–1929	−0.43	1919 Kuznets	8
	−1.12	1929 Kuznets	8
1929–1948	+0.36	1948 Commerce	12
1948–1966	+0.01	1948 Commerce	12
	−0.32	1963 Commerce	12
1966–1975	−0.11	1963 Commerce	12

Sources and notes: King (1930, pp. 56, 57, 60–62, 94 and 95); Kuznets (1941, various tables); U.S. Department of Commerce (various tables). Value-added shares were calculated from current-dollar figures, owing to the lack of a consistent series of sectoral value-added deflators.

The last 140 years of American experience therefore supply a correlation between movements in factor shares implied by sectoral output shifts and movements in pay gaps. The correlation offers an excellent potential candidate for explaining inequality movements. It also prompts a search for the sources of the unbalanced output growth. Three obvious proximate sources suggest themselves: changes in the growth rates of sectoral productivity, exogenous demand shifts, and changes in relative factor supplies. We turn to each of these potential sources in order, in this and the next two chapters.

Unbalanced Productivity Growth

It is intuitively clear that sectoral differences in the rate of total factor productivity growth can influence economy-wide factor demands. But which sectors and factors are favored? As we shall see, productivity has usually improved faster in capital- and skill-intensive sectors than in labor- and resource-intensive sectors. This could either raise or lower the demand for capital and skills relative to the demand for unskilled labor. It would raise the relative demand for capital and skills if the intersectoral effect predominated, with the faster improvements in the capital- and skill-intensive sectors drawing so many resources away from the labor-intensive sectors as to reduce the total relative demand for unskilled labor. The opposite happens when intrasectoral factor saving predominates. If outputs remain unchanged, the main effect of productivity growth in the capital- and skill-intensive sectors would be to reduce the amounts of these factors needed to produce the same output. Chapters 10 and 12 show that U.S. pay experience is well explained under the assumption that intersectoral productivity effects dominate the intrasectoral effects. Thus, productivity improvement in sectors using little labor per unit of output should actually be viewed as laborsaving technological change.

TOWARD A HISTORY OF PRODUCTIVITY: IMBALANCE AND CONVERGENCE

Total factor productivity growth is not an easy concept to measure, either for a national economy or for individual industries. The pioneering work by Kendrick (1961, 1973) and Denison (1962, 1974) announced fairly high rates of U.S. productivity growth, only to draw extensive criticism. The critics stressed that high apparent rates of productivity growth may be largely the result of underestimating improvements in the quality of inputs. Revised estimates reduced, but did not eliminate, the positive productivity growth. The measurement difficulties revealed by the recent productivity growth debate are seriously compounded for earlier periods. Calculations of total factor productivity growth for any time before World War I measure labor input by persons employed or man-hours, with little or no adjustment for changes in labor quality. Similarly, capital input estimates must rely on capital stock figures derived from census valuations and price deflators for new capital goods, with little attention to the subtleties of capital service rental rates or vintage quality.

Yet we are led to examine the historical productivity growth estimates, warts and all, by the intriguing overall patterns they imply. Taken at face value, the "crude" estimates suggest steadily accelerating rates of total factor productivity growth since at least the early nineteenth century, and possibly over the whole of U.S. economic history (e.g., Abramovitz and David, 1973). This conclusion is likely to stand even if the early estimates were subjected to the same adjustments that have been applied to the post-1929 estimates.

Another productivity pattern is far more important to our present purposes: The sectoral estimates of productivity growth seem to diverge early in economic development and to converge later on. This fact requires explanation if we are to understand the forces governing technological diffusion.[6] It is also relevant to an understanding of trends in income distribution because the intersectoral gaps in rates of productivity growth imply a laborsaving bias in economic growth.

For the colonial era, there is little evidence of significant total factor productivity growth or of large intersectoral gaps in such growth. All observers seem to agree that agriculture, the dominant sector, grew only through the growth of conventional inputs. Land was cleared and settled, and farm buildings were erected, but techniques changed little. Tentative and local estimates of agricultural productivity in Pennsylvania from the late seventeenth century through the Revolutionary era give growth rates near zero.[7] It appears unlikely that productivity growth was much more impressive outside of agriculture. Even the most spectacular example of the era—shipping services—seems to have experienced a rate of total factor productivity growth of only 0.8% per year over the period 1675–1775 (North, 1968; Shepherd and Walton, 1972, p. 72), and even this is

[6] While the long-run American pattern of early divergence and later convergence has not received attention in the literature, useful analysis of the recent gaps in productivity growth among U.S. industrial sectors has been offered by Kendrick (1961, pp. 134–147; 1973, Chaps. 5, 6). Unbalanced productivity growth has a much longer tradition in the literature on economic development. See Kelley, Williamson, and Cheetham (1972, Chap. 1).

[7] See Ball and Walton (1976), the accompanying rebuttal by Russell Menard, and the sources they cite.

TABLE 7.5
Total Factor Productivity Growth in Agriculture, 1800–1860 *(percentage per annum)*

	From				
To	1800	1810	1820	1830	1840
1810	−0.31%	—	—	—	—
1820	0.01	0.36%	—	—	—
1830	0.39	0.76	1.11%	—	—
1840	0.60	0.92	1.19	1.40%	—
1860	0.43	0.59	0.60	1.18	0.08%

Source: Gallman (1972, p. 208).

primarily due to improved safety and ship design rather than efficiency per se.

Total factor productivity continued to stagnate in agriculture across the first half of the nineteenth century. So say Robert Gallman's rough estimates reported in Table 7.5. This impression is reinforced by Gallman's later confession that his earlier estimates of agriculture's productivity growth were too optimistic (Gallman, 1975). The best guess now seems to be that agricultural total factor productivity growth became positive only around mid-century and accelerated thereafter.

In contrast, productivity was far from stagnant in manufacturing and transportation in the early nineteenth century. In the case of cotton textiles, major breakthroughs in mechanization and factory organization brought considerable productivity gains. The estimates cited in Table 7.6 imply that productivity growth rates above 2% a year prevailed until the mid-1850s. High rates have also been estimated for the antebellum transportation sector, as shown in Table 7.7. Fogel and Engerman (1971, pp. 159–161) offer estimates for the iron industry between 1842 and 1858 that imply rates as high as 6% per annum. What little we know about other

TABLE 7.6
Total Factor Productivity Growth in Cotton Textiles, 1815–1859 *(percentage per annum)*

	From			
To	1815	1833	1839	1855
1833	5.50%	—	—	—
1839	4.76	2.60%	—	—
1855	3.89	2.60	2.60%	—
1859	3.65	2.38	2.31	1.17%

Sources and notes: Zevin (1971, p. 146) gives a rate of 5–6% per year for 1815–1833. The remaining estimates are from David (1975, pp. 136, 162, and 186). Lower rates (1.0–1.5% per year) have been estimated for 1834–1860 by Nickless (1979), although hers are still provisional.

TABLE 7.7
Total Factor Productivity Growth in Transportation, 1815–1859 *(percentage per annum)*

To	From			
	1815	1833	1839	1849
1833	7.15%	—	—	—
1839	6.09	2.70%	—	—
1849	5.74	4.19	5.66(7.19)%	—
1859	4.68	3.02	3.42(4.29)	1.15(1.38)%

Sources and notes: For 1815–1859, an unweighted average of Mak and Walton (1972, p. 639) and North (1968, pp. 968–969). For 1839–1859, the figures in parentheses are unweighted averages including Fishlow (1966, p. 631) as well.

modern sectors reinforces the view that productivity might have grown at something like 3% a year in antebellum manufacturing and transportation. Furthermore, it seems to have grown most rapidly in the machine-tool sector specifically and in the producer durables sector generally.[8]

The available estimates should be handled with care. If skills per man-hour improved, then productivity advanced more slowly than the estimates imply, since the estimates rarely make any reckoning of the quality of labor input. As we argue in Chapter 9, however, labor quality in the nonfarm sector probably remained unchanged between 1839 and 1859, so that no labor quality adjustment needs to be made for this twenty-year period. Adjustments are in order, though, if we are to extrapolate from the modern sectors covered by the available estimates to the entire nonfarm sector. Within the industrial sector (mining, manufacturing, transportation, communications, and utilities), the available estimates may have focused on subsectors where productivity was growing extraordinarily rapidly. Furthermore, productivity growth was probably much slower in the service sector, which accounted for 38% of nonfarm product around 1850 (Gallman, 1960, p. 43; Gallman, 1966, pp. 26 and 27). Therefore we shall take the conservative stance that productivity growth in the indus-

[8] Production-function regressions by Uselding (1972, p. 305) suggest that total factor productivity growth at the Springfield Armory was between 3.8% and 7.4% per year for 1820–1850.

The pronounced decline in the relative prices of investment goods and of ferrous metals in particular suggests that a price-dual measure of total factor productivity growth would also find faster growth in these sectors than in agriculture. The relative decline of investment goods prices is noted in Chapters 10 and 12. The productivity gains in ferrous metals are hinted at by the following per annum rates of change in iron and steel prices compared to changes in two inputs between 1847 and 1860: bar iron, -2.89%; steel rails, -2.79%; common labor, $+0.98\%$; anthracite coal, -1.29% (*Historical Statistics*, 1960, Series D718, E129, E130; Temin, 1964, p. 283).

trial sector was only 2% per annum over the period 1839–1859, and that productivity in the tertiary sector (construction, trade, finance, private services, and government) grew at only 0.8% per annum, the lowest rate observed for this sector over long periods after 1869.

For the century following 1869, we lean heavily on Kendrick's estimates of sectoral productivity growth. His procedures have drawbacks (e.g., the capital stock is used as a proxy for capital services, and virtually no adjustment is made for changes in labor quality). We have added a crude adjustment for the growth contribution of improvements in the quality of the labor force to his figures.

Table 7.8 summarizes this unbalanced productivity growth evidence. A striking change has appeared in the position of agriculture since the

TABLE 7.8
Total Factor Productivity Growth in Major Sectors, 1839–1973 *(percentage per annum)*

Period	(1) Agriculture	(2) Industry	(3) Tertiary	(4) Productivity Growth Gap (2) − (1)
1839–1859	0.00%	2.00%	0.80%	2.00%
1869–1899	0.79	1.70	0.84	0.91
1899–1909	− 0.24	0.98	1.70	1.22
1909–1929	0.02	2.44	0.84	2.42
1929–1948	2.06	1.45	1.58	−0.61
1948–1966	1.44	2.35	0.77	0.91
1966–1973	1.02	2.28	1.04	1.26

Sources and notes: Agriculture: For the first two periods we have used Gallman's (1972, 1975) judgments on agricultural productivity, which seem to have given closer attention to the detail of agricultural inputs than Kendrick's (1961) estimates, which implied growth at 1.02% a year for the farm sector between 1869 and 1899. For 1899–1909 we fell back on Kendrick's farm sector estimate. For the years since 1909 we have used the USDA productivity series for the farm sector. It has the virtue of greater attention to input differentiation than Kendrick, but shares the drawback of not including agricultural services, forestry, or fisheries.

Industry and tertiary: For 1839–1909, the industrial sector consists of mining, manufacturing, transportation, communications, and utilities, and the tertiary sector consists of construction, trade, finance and real estate, private services, and government. For 1909–1973, the transportation sector is included in the tertiary sector.

The productivity growth rates for the industrial and tertiary sectors in the antebellum era (1839–1859) are the guesses of 2% and 0.8% respectively, defended in the text. For 1869–1966, we started with Kendrick's (1961, 1976) sectoral estimates, the number of sectors rising from six to ten. Kendrick made only a slight allowance for growth in labor quality, allowing labor inputs per man-hour to rise only owing to a shift from lower-paying to higher-paying industries. We made a further crude adjustment for growth in labor quality per man-hour within sectors using a procedure described in Chapter 9 below. That is, we multiplied the skills share of sectoral product by the growth rate in skills input per man-hour minus the quality growth Kendrick had already incorporated, and then subtracted this product from Kendrick's estimate of sectoral productivity growth. For 1966–1973, we replicated Kendrick's procedure as nearly as we could, using Department of Commerce estimates, and applying our skills growth adjustment once again.

mid-nineteenth century. Before 1929 its rate of productivity improvement continued to lag behind that of more modern sectors. This imbalance was dramatically reversed in the second quarter of this century, when total factor productivity grew faster in agriculture by any of the available comparisons. Since mid-century the old gaps have reappeared, but they remain far smaller than before 1929.[9]

This historic pattern of early divergence and later convergence in rates of total factor productivity growth is fascinating in its own right. It poses a tough question for anyone wishing to theorize about the process of technological diffusion. We have models of how a single idea, such as the mechanical reaper or hybrid seed varieties, gets diffused across firms in a single industry. But how is it that something so heterogeneous as technological progress diffuses across sectors, spreading from industry to agriculture? The answer is not obvious, but the question seems important if technological progress and other sources of productivity growth are to be forecast.

TECHNOLOGICAL IMBALANCE AND PAY GAPS

The history of unbalanced technological progress offers considerable promise in unraveling trends in income inequality. After all, periods in which sectoral productivity growth rates have been most dispersed have also been periods in which the sectoral productivity growth pattern has favored those sectors using unskilled labor least intensively. The antebellum surge in total factor productivity growth came in the more skills- and capital-intensive manufacturing and transportation sectors. The wide gaps of the early twentieth century favored such sectors as communications, transportation, and utilities, which were again relatively sparing in their use of common labor. The convergence of sectoral productivity growth rates after 1929 was achieved in large part by an acceleration in agriculture, a sector that still uses low-skill labor more intensively than the rest of the economy, despite the relative rise in the application of skills and schooling to farm activity during the mid-twentieth century.

---

[9] We are aware of a possible bias which may overstate the degree of unbalancedness in sectoral total factor productivity growth rates. Value-added data are normally used to measure total factor productivity growth when a superior alternative appears to be the gross output measure. Star (1974) has shown that the use of value-added data introduces biased estimates of total factor productivity growth, the bias being greater the more important are raw materials to the industrial production process in question. It follows that agriculture would be best estimated, and thus that the total factor productivity growth gaps reported in the text are overstated. It seems unlikely, however, that the *trends* in the gaps would be seriously affected by the bias.

The measure best able to capture the impact of sectoral imbalance in productivity growth on the demand for unskilled labor is

$$\Pi_L = \sum_j \overset{*}{T}_j \lambda_{Lj} \qquad (\sum_j \lambda_{Lj} = 1),$$

where Π_L is the measure of increase in output per unit of unskilled-labor input implied by the sectoral locus of productivity improvement, $\overset{*}{T}_j$ is the rate of factor-neutral total factor productivity growth in the jth sector, and λ_{Lj} is the share of the total employment of unskilled labor employed in the jth sector. Similar measures can be constructed for other factors of production as well (e.g., for land (Π_J), skills (Π_S), and capital (Π_K).

Comparison of Π_i for different factors of production offers insight into the impact of technological imbalance on the distribution of income. In Part Three we shall examine the likely effects of all sorts of factor biases on our convenient proxy for movements in earnings inequality, the rate of change in the pay premium earned by more skilled employees. As a first step in that direction, Table 7.9 documents the "relative skills bias" ($\Pi_S - \Pi_L$) and the "relative capital bias" ($\Pi_K - \Pi_L$). Since they have moved in much the same direction, we shall focus on ($\Pi_S - \Pi_L$) in what follows.

Figure 7.3 compares factor biases in the intersectoral productivity growth differences with movements in the skilled-labor wage premium, drawing on a measure of skills developed in Appendix J. Here we see that the early divergence and later convergence of rates of productivity growth may be very relevant to our task of explaining the early widening and later narrowing of pay gaps. The correlation between the relative skills bias and the increase in pay gaps is unmistakable in Figure 7.3.[10] The antebellum period and 1899–1909 stand out as the main examples of widening pay gaps, of greatest productivity growth gaps, and of the highest "relative skills bias." At the other extreme, the leveling era 1929–1948 was also a period of extraordinary balance in productivity growth and thus no "relative skills bias."

Here, then, is an important issue to pursue. Does the correlation between the relative skills bias and increasing wage premia for skilled labor mean that the evolution from unbalanced to balanced patterns of productivity growth accounts at least in part for America's early inequality trends and later reversal? Part Three extends this issue into the realm of quantitative accounting. We need to stress a productivity paradox, how-

---

[10] As the detail in Table 7.9 shows, the correlation would be damaged if one broke up the period 1909–1929 at 1919. This is simply because the wage rates for 1919 were still distorted toward abnormal equality by the short-run leveling effect of the rapid World War I inflation. One would not expect the reasoning embodied in the longer-run Π_i measures to account well for all such short-run departures.

Factor-Augmenting Biases Implied by Estimates of Sectoral Total Factor Productivity Growth Rates, 1839–1973

Rate of Augmentation (*percentage per annum*)

Period	Farmland (Π_J)	Other Property (Π_K)	Unskilled Labor (Π_L)	Relative Capital ($\Pi_K - \Pi_L$)	Nonfarm Skills (Π_S)	Relative Skills ($\Pi_S - \Pi_L$)	Rate of Increase in Skilled-Labor Wage Premium ($q^* - w^*$)
1839–1859	0%	1.30%	0.55%	0.75%	1.05%	0.50%	1.48%
1869–1899	0.79	1.25	1.05	0.20	1.14	0.09	0.35
1899–1909	−0.24	1.19	0.77	0.42	1.43	0.66	0.97
1909–1929	0.02	1.26	1.06	0.20	1.32	0.26	−0.09
(1909–1919)	(0.16)	(1.03)	(0.89)	(0.14)	(1.14)	(0.25)	(−2.28)
(1919–1929)	(−0.12)	(1.50)	(1.22)	(0.28)	(1.50)	(0.28)	(2.15)
1929–1948	2.06	2.25	2.01	0.24	2.01	0.00	−1.99
1948–1966	1.44	1.12	1.36	−0.24	1.47	0.11	0.35
1966–1973	1.02	1.00	1.18	−0.18	1.35	0.17	−0.21

Sources and notes: Π_i is calculated according to the formula given in the text, namely

$$\Pi_i = \sum_j T_j^* \lambda_{ij}.$$

The underlying sectoral rates of total factor productivity growth (T_j) were calculated from the estimates of Kendrick and others, using methods described in the notes to Table 7.8 and in Appendix J.

For the first three periods (i.e., up to 1909) the economy was divided into the three sectors described in Table 7.8. For 1909–1948 six sectors were used: agriculture (including agricultural services, forestry, and fisheries for sector weights, but using the farm sector productivity growth rates), mining, manufacturing, transportation, communications–utilities, and a national-economy residual. For 1948–1973 ten sectors were used: manufacturing was broken down into durables and nondurables, communications were separated from utilities, and construction and trade were added to the original six sectors.

The sectoral shares of each factor's employment (λ_{ij}) came from a variety of sources. The 1849 shares used for 1839–1859 and the 1899 shares used for 1869–1899 and 1899–1909 are introduced in Chapter 10. For 1909 through 1948 we used shares derived from Kuznets's (1941) estimates of sectoral product, employee compensation, and employment, using a Lebergott farm wage rate inclusive of supplements to split total employee compensation into skilled and unskilled parts, according to procedures sketched in Appendix J. For 1948 through 1973 the sectoral shares are derived according to the same procedures from 1963 data in the national income and product accounts (U.S. Department of Commerce, 1966).

The rates of change in the skilled-labor wage premium ($q^* - w^*$) are percentage rates expressed as a percentage of the gap between the rates for skilled and unskilled labor, rather than as a percentage of the unskilled-labor rate. (For example, a rise in the skilled-labor wage ratio from 1.50 to 1.75 means a percentage jump of .25/.50 × 100, or 50%.) This convention is appropriate, since the underlying data come in a form that makes it easier to measure skills as only that part of the return to a higher-paid job that exceeds the return to common labor (see Appendix J).

For a further discussion of the estimate of the 1929–1948 drop in the skilled-labor wage premium, see the notes to Table 11.1.

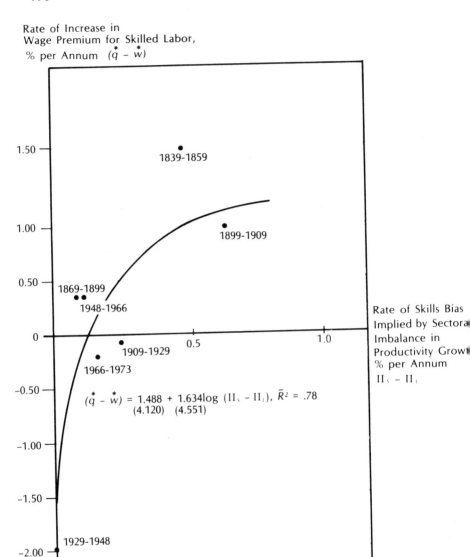

Rate of Increase in
Wage Premium for Skilled Labor,
% per Annum $(\overset{*}{q} - \overset{*}{w})$

1.50 —

　　　　　　　　•
　　　　　1839-1859

1.00 —

　　　　　　　•
　　　　1899-1909

0.50 —
1869-1899
　　••
1948-1966

Rate of Skills Bias
Implied by Sectoral
Imbalance in
Productivity Growth
% per Annum
$II_{\backslash} - II_{l}$

0 —
　　　•　　　0.5　　　　　　　1.0
　　1909-1929
　　•
1966-1973

-0.50 —
$(\overset{*}{q} - \overset{*}{w}) = 1.488 + 1.634\log\ (II_{\backslash} - II_{l}),\ \bar{R}^2 = .78$
　　　　(4.120)　(4.551)

-1.00 —

-1.50 —

　　1929-1948
-2.00 — •

FIGURE 7.3. Changes in wage premium for skilled labor compared with the relative "skills bias" implied by the imbalance in sectoral productivity growth, 1839–1973. From Table 7.9.

ever. We have found that periods characterized in other studies as highly labor saving in the aggregate were also periods in which the sectors economizing on factor inputs fastest were the more capital- and skill-intensive sectors rather than those using unskilled labor intensively. If this imbalance had left sectoral outputs unchanged, the factors laid off most by productivity growth would have been capital and skills, not labor. It is essential to stress that the other effect of productivity growth imbalance—the intersectoral effect—is the one more likely to have dominated. By drawing output and factor demands toward the more capital- and skill-intensive sectors, productivity imbalance may have made a major contribution to aggregate *unskilled-labor* saving—and possibly also to our understanding of what has changed relative factor rewards in the past.

8

THE FACTOR INTENSITY ISSUE: WHO BUYS THE SERVICES OF AMERICA'S WORKING POOR?

Commodity Demand, Derived Factor Demand, and Distribution

The previous chapter was organized around the following question: Had the composition of output changed in a systematic way since 1820 so as to offer support for a factor demand explanation of American inequality? The answer was most certainly, Yes. America's nineteenth-century output mix shifted in a way which saved on unskilled labor, diminished the relative demand for the services of the working poor, and thus tended to generate wage stretching and inequality. The reverse was true following the 1920s. Uncovering the link between inequality trends and rates of aggregate labor saving is one thing, offering an explanation for the observed rates of labor saving is another. We are taught in simple general-equilibrium theory that changes in output mix are an endogenous result of a number of forces. These forces can emanate from either the supply side of the commodity market or the demand side. The trick is to identify which of those forces played a major role in history.

One such force might be the change in commodity demand induced by income growth, that is, Engel effects. The list could easily be expanded to include changes in commodity demand induced by tax and tariff policy, the rise in big government, shifts in taste, and changes in the rate and mode of private accumulation. These forces have one thing in common: Each has an influence which begins by shifts in the structure of commodity demands.[1]

---

[1] It should be emphasized that nowhere does this chapter concern itself with cycles in *aggregate* demand. The main recent contribution to this active literature on distribution over the cycle seems to be Crotty and Rapping (1975).

What, then, have been the factor intensities of various "market baskets" demanded in America? Who has placed the heaviest demands on
the services of America's working poor? This chapter is organized around
these two questions. In it we present the evidence on sectoral unskilled-
labor intensities for the 1960s and explore three alternative sources of
shifting factor demand mix which are potential candidates in accounting
for some portion of America's income-distribution history since 1820. We
then examine the historical stability of the factor intensity relationships
uncovered for the 1960s. Where good documentation is available, from
1899 to 1963, we find remarkable stability in the rankings of sectors by
factor intensity, and our conclusions on output mix drawn from the 1960s
need not be qualified in the least when applied to our earlier history.
Indeed, our conclusions seem to be reinforced as we venture farther back
into the nineteenth century, where the data are thinner. The chapter
concludes with some alternative measures of labor intensity that have
more cosmetic appeal to the purist but, with one important exception,
turn out to add very little to empirical understanding.

The Unskilled-Labor Content of Commodities

Our mode of analysis is conventional: the open, static input–output
model. Stocks of capital goods are not linked to capital goods production
but rather new capital goods and consumer goods expenditures are
treated as components of exogenous final demands. Heterogeneous labor,
capital, and land are also taken as exogenous endowments. In contrast
with Chapter 7, our purpose here is to derive the primary direct *and*
indirect resource requirements to deliver alternative bills of final demand.
Chapter 7 was concerned primarily with observed, *ex post* changes in the
output mix. The relevant calculation there involved an accounting of
direct resource requirements only. Here we focus on the impact of
changes in final demand composition and thus we must trace the total
impact on output mix and resource requirements through the input–
output system. Moreover, we continue to emphasize the resource requirements in one dimension only, unskilled labor. Our approach will
contrast with the work of Carter (1970) and others in two ways: First,
"labor intensities" are measured as wage costs per dollar of output. The
use of cost shares, rather than physical man-hours per dollar of output,
better conforms with our interest in distribution as opposed to production
relationships per se. Second, "labor" is restricted solely to the unskilled,
and thus only the cost component of total payments which is attributed to
the wages of unskilled labor is considered. We argued in Chapters 4 and 5

that the relative performance of unskilled-labor's earnings seems to account for much of the observed historical trends in aggregate inequality. Thus, our focus here on the derived demand for unskilled labor requires little further defense.

How then do we measure unskilled labor's share, or "raw" labor intensity, by industry? We appeal to the well-developed postulates of human capital theory at this point. Following Chiswick (1974), Mincer (1974), and others, we could have estimated earnings functions from cross-section data and utilized the intercept in

$$Y_{Nl} = w \prod_{l=1}^{N} (1 + r_l k_l), \tag{8.1}$$

where Y_{Nl} are gross wage earnings in the lth period after N periods of on-the-job training, formal schooling, and other modes of human capital creation. The annual reinvestment rate of earnings into human capital formation is k_l, r_l is his average rate of return on that investment, while w is his full-year's earnings had he received no training. The latter may result, of course, because he is too young ($l = 0$), because the rate of return to training and skills is zero (an unlikely case), or because his reinvestment rate has been close to zero. In any case, the resulting estimated intercept, $\hat{w}$, from the logarithm-of-earnings regression would indeed be an unambiguous estimate of "raw" labor's annual rental price. Obviously, shifts in that intercept estimated from cross sections drawn from various points during a decade would reflect changes in the equilibrium "raw" wage over time. No one in the American labor force is restricted to the abysmal state of no human capital at all, of course. Yet the working poor do have the lowest human capital component, and thus they come closest to fulfilling the requirement. The human capital component of earnings is simply the residual, $Y_{Nl} - w$, and an expansion of the expression to include all sources of income could easily yield the total "non-raw-labor" component of income. What is true for the individual or the household is also true for the firm or the nation. To compute the portion of total costs per unit of output that is the wages of unskilled labor, we simply perform the calculation

$$\theta_j(t) = \frac{\hat{w}(t)L_j(t)}{C_j(t)}, \tag{8.2}$$

where $L_j(t)$ is the reported annual man-hours in industry j in year t, C is their total costs (including intermediate inputs), and $\hat{w}$ the wage of unskilled labor presumed common to all industries but variable over time. Alternatively, for the economy as a whole we could compute the unskilled-labor share as

$$\theta(t) = \frac{\hat{w}(t)\sum_j L_j(t)}{\sum_j C_j(t)}, \tag{8.3}$$

or, if C' is defined as value added,

$$I(t) = \frac{1}{\theta(t)} = \frac{\sum_j C'_j(t)/\sum_j L_j(t)}{\hat{w}(t)} = \frac{c'(t)}{\hat{w}(t)}. \tag{8.4}$$

What do we gain by this elaborate application of the human capital model above and beyond that of some far simpler alternative? We could just as well arbitrarily substitute \$3000, or some other poverty-subsistence line, for $\hat{w}(t)$ in Expression (8.2). The *relative* raw labor intensities by sector would not be affected. Nevertheless, it seemed esthetically more appealing to select some unskilled occupation as our yardstick for the average wage of the working poor. In what follows, we use the average annual wage earnings of hired farm labor as our $\hat{w}$ index, but later in this chapter we shall explore some alternatives. This wage is assumed to be uniform throughout the economy at any point in time. In fact, we know otherwise. The presence of rural–urban cost-of-living differentials (Chap. 5) ensures that the application of nominal farm wages to urban employment understates the true "raw" labor content of non-farm activities and thus exaggerates farm relative labor intensities. Unions introduce further anomalies, but the direction of bias is far less clear in this case. Factor market disequilibrium is a third labor market reality ignored in our analysis. Our hope is that none of these influences is sufficiently important to obfuscate our attempts to supply a cardinal ranking of sectors by raw-labor intensity.

The sources and notes to Appendix K supply detail on methods and sources but a summary might be helpful. Table 8.1 lists by industry the direct and indirect unskilled-labor intensity of 79 of the sectoral activities listed by the Department of Commerce (1969) in their 1963 input–output matrix. The items in Table 8.1 can be read as unskilled-labor intensities or as the payments impact on the working poor from a \$1 final demand expenditure on outputs of industry j. Call this payments impact $\bar{\theta}_j$:

$$\bar{\theta}_j = l\hat{w}Qy_j, \tag{8.5}$$

where y_j is the final demand for j, Q is the Leontief inverse for 1963 and each q_{ij} element measures dollar amounts of the ith good required directly and indirectly to deliver the dollar's worth of y_j, l is a vector of 1963 labor coefficients, each element of which denotes the number of persons engaged per dollar of the jth output, and $\hat{w}$ is a vector of 1963 wages of unskilled labor (annual earnings), by assumption constant across all j.

The reader will note the wide variance in $\bar{\theta}_j$ across sectors. Among the commodity-producing sectors, for example, the figures range from 0.11 for iron mining to 0.29 for livestock and crops, the latter two-and-one-half times the former. The spread is even greater among service sectors, from finance and real estate, 0.11, to hotels and personnel services, 0.33, and household services, 0.64. For comparison, Table 8.1 also supplies the value-added share of unskilled labor by sector. The latter ignores intermediate purchases, ranks sectors by the unskilled-labor share in primary factor payments, and thus estimates *direct* labor intensity only. While the value-added shares tend to be higher than $\bar{\theta}_j$, the ranking is closely preserved. The relative sectoral differences in unskilled-labor intensity tend to be lower among the $\bar{\theta}_j$, however, than among the value-added shares.[2] This confirms the position of Carter (1970) and others, that sharp differences in *direct* factor intensities between sectors tend to diminish when indirect factor requirements are considered. Nonetheless, wide variance in $\bar{\theta}_j$ persists.

Now then, what happens to this variance when these sectors are aggregated to more meaningful final demand categories?

Who Buys the Services of America's Working Poor?

To derive some appropriate final demand weighting scheme, Expression (8.5) need only be expanded to read

$$\bar{\theta}^f = l\hat{w}Qy^f, \tag{8.6}$$

where y^f is now a final demand vector, the elements of which are $\phi_j^f y_j$ such that $\sum_j \phi_j^f y_j = \$1$, and thus the "budget weights" sum to one, $\sum_j \phi_j^f = 1$. We denote each "final demand experiment" by the superscript f, and the adding-up constraint is introduced so that we can focus solely on *demand mix*. The results appear in Tables 8.2 and 8.3, and they shed light on three potentially important sources of output-mix change which might have had an impact on American inequality trends: changes in investment expenditures, consumption expenditures, and government expenditures.

---

[2] The following unweighted regression was estimated between the value-added share, θ_j, and the payments impact variable, $\bar{\theta}_j$, for the 79 sectors:

$$\bar{\theta}_j = .074 + .528 \theta_j, \quad \bar{R}^2 = .843,$$
$$(8.936) \quad (15.377)$$

where t statistics are in parentheses. In testing the hypothesis $\beta \neq 1$, the relevant t statistic is -13.776.

TABLE 8.1
Payments Impact on Unskilled Labor, Direct and Indirect, of $1 Purchase of Output from
Industry j, Compared with Direct Value-Added Shares, 1963

Industry	Value-Added Share of Unskilled Labor	Total Payments Impact on Unskilled Labor $(\hat{\theta}_j)$
1. Livestock	.3760	.2908
2. Crops	.3760	.2928
3. Forestry and fishing	.4040	.2355
4. Agricultural services	.4050	.3022
5. Iron mining	.1690	.1129
6. Nonferrous mining	.1680	.1370
7. Coal mining	.2048	.1934
8. Petroleum mining	.1685	.1456
9. Stone and clay mining	.1850	.1689
10. Chemical mining	.1860	.1549
11. New construction	.2440	.2115
12. Maintenance construction	.2440	.2193
13. Ordnance and accessories	.1740	.1742
14. Food	.2111	.2266
15. Tobacco	.1164	.1613
16. Textile mills	.3030	.2353
17. Misc. textiles	.3030	.1921
18. Apparel	.3650	.2858
19. Fabricated textiles	.3650	.2576
20. Wood and products	.3020	.2364
21. Wooden containers	.3000	.2395
22. House furniture	.2750	.2294
23. Office furniture	.2760	.2238
24. Paper and products	.1920	.1643
25. Paper containers	.1930	.1782
26. Printing and publishing	.2176	.1952
27. Basic chemicals	.1330	.1442
28. Synthetics	.1330	.1458
29. Drugs and soaps	.1330	.1605
30. Paints	.1330	.1535
31. Petrol refining	.0665	.1262
32. Rubber products	.2029	.1798
33. Leather tanning	.3170	.2331
34. Shoes	.3200	.2592
35. Glass and products	.1930	.1826
36. Stone and clay	.1930	.1817
37. Iron and steel	.1630	.1485
38. Nonferrous metals	.1630	.1259
39. Metal containers	.2010	.1739
40. Heating	.2020	.1769
41. Stampings, etc.	.2010	.1769
42. Hardware, etc.	.2020	.1760

TABLE 8.1 (continued)

Industry	Value-Added Share of Unskilled Labor	Total Payments Impact on Unskilled Labor (θ_j)
43. Engines and turbines	.1790	.1725
44. Farm machinery	.1790	.1661
45. Construction equipment	.1790	.1717
46. Materials handling equipment	.1790	.1737
47. Metalworking equipment	.1790	.1717
48. Special industrial equipment	.1790	.1674
49. General industrial equipment	.1790	.1719
50. Machine shop production	.1790	.1732
51. Office machinery	.1790	.1750
52. Service industrial machinery	.1800	.1769
53. Electrical apparatus	.2020	.1840
54. Appliances	.2010	.1843
55. Light and wiring equipment	.2010	.1814
56. Communications equipment	.2020	.1899
57. Electronic components	.2010	.1873
58. Batteries, etc.	.2030	.1798
59. Motor vehicles and equipment	.1000	.1417
60. Aircraft and parts	.1750	.1743
61. Trains and ships	.1740	.1725
62. Instruments, etc.	.1650	.1718
63. Photographic apparatus	.1650	.1617
64. Misc. manufactures	.2602	.2036
65. Transportation	.1932	.1810
66. Communications	.1336	.1407
67. Radio and TV broadcasting	.1298	.1715
68. Utilities	.0963	.1405
69. Trade	.2680	.2429
70. Finance and insurance	.0790	.1114
71. Real estate	.0790	.1104
72. Hotels and personnel service	.4070	.3289
73. Business services	.2170	.2012
74. Auto repair	.3118	.2591
75. Amusements	.3220	.2613
76. Medical and education	.2950	.2580
77. Federal government	.2800	.2339
78. State and local government	.2820	.2423
79. Household services	.6374	.6374

Sources and notes: The employment and value-added data are taken from U.S. Department of Commerce (1966, Tables 1.12 and 6.6, pp. 18–21 and 110–113). The data for wages of unskilled labor are the average annual earnings of hired farm labor (Table 6.5, pp. 106–109). The input–output data are the 1963 matrix reported in U.S. Department of Commerce (1969). The consumer expenditure data relate to 1960–1961. These data appear under the title *Survey of Consumer Expenditures and Income, 1960–1961* in various BLS reports (U.S. Department of Labor, 1964). See text for discussion of methods.

PRE-FISC AND POST-FISC: THE ROLE OF GOVERNMENT

The theory of tax and expenditure incidence is sufficiently well developed to have produced frequent attempts to estimate post-fisc distributions—that is, size distributions which appear after government taxation and expenditures have been allocated statistically to pre-fisc nominal income distributions. One of the best of these is a paper by M. Reynolds and Smolensky (1975). Their calculations show that the revenue and expenditure system does indeed reduce inequality significantly, an expected result since "public output is more equally distributed than private output [p. 2]." Indeed, the key to the more equitable 1970 post-fisc distribution is not the tax structure, since it is insufficiently progressive to account for more than a trivial component of the difference in Gini coefficients measuring pre-fisc and post-fisc distributions (M. Reynolds and Smolensky, 1975, p. 13). The lion's share of the difference between pre-fisc and post-fisc Gini coefficients is about equally accounted for by transfer payments and government expenditures.

The weakness in this approach, of course, is its partial-equilibrium nature. Nowhere is there a general-equilibrium calculation that explores the impact of government expenditures on the pre-fisc distribution itself. Surely it seems reasonable to expect that government and private expenditures on goods and services imply very different relative demands for skills, for land, for physical capital, and for the services of the working poor—relatively unskilled individuals with limited asset endowments. Perhaps the correspondence between the income leveling from 1929 to 1948, on the one hand, and the rise in the government-expenditure share in gross national product, on the other, is more than sheer coincidence. One of the present authors (Lindert, 1974), expressed the challenge in the following way:

> If it could be shown that the government's purchase of goods and services create a much greater demand for . . . unskilled labor, than the same amount of displaced private demand, then the rise of government has been a levelling influence on incomes even aside from its effects on . . . aggregate demand, and the progressivity of taxation [p. 55].

While discussing the pretax inequality trends in America since the early 1960s, M. Reynolds and Smolensky (1975) imply the competing hypothesis:

> . . . We do not claim that the 1970 fisc has offset a widening of the distribution of money income since 1961 because *the fisc may have indirectly contributed to the widening* [pp. 21–22, italics ours].

TABLE 8.2
Payments Impact on Unskilled Labor, Direct and Indirect, of $1 Expenditure on Final
Demand, 1963

Final Demand Category (f)	Weighting Scheme	Total Payments Impact on Unskilled Labor $(\hat{\theta}^f)$
Investment Expenditures	SCB (1963)	
Total investment		.1980
Investment, incl. medical and education		.2170
Producer durables		.1786
Construction		.2115
Medical and education		.2580
Consumption Expenditures	BLS (1961)	
Total consumption		.1965
Housing		.1104
Fuel and light		.1405
Autos and appliances		.1497
Other commodities		.1704
Food		.2230
Other services		.2281
Medical and educ. services		.2580
Apparel		.2858
Total consumption (excl. services)		.2001
Government Expenditures	SCB (1963)	
Total federal		.2272
General government		.2864
Government purchases		.1879
Total state and local		.2451
General government		.2817
Government purchases		.2034
Total government		.2359

Sources and notes: The underlying $\hat{\theta}_j$ are for 1963 and are taken from Table 8.1. The final demand weights used to aggregate up to these expenditure categories are from U.S. Department of Commerce (1969), reprinted in *Survey of Current Business* (Nov. 1969, Table 1, p. 35) and abbreviated *SCB* (1963) above; and from U.S. Department of Labor (BLS) (1964), abbreviated BLS (1961) above. The BLS data refer to urban mean family post-tax income.

Table 8.2 allows us to discriminate between these competing hypotheses, at least as they apply to the relative economic position of the working poor.

Table 8.2 underscores the fact that there is far greater variety in unskilled-labor intensities *within* the conventional final demand expenditure categories than *between* them. For the purpose of exploring the impact of shifting final demand mix on the relative economic position of the working poor, $GNP = C + I + G$ simply fails to do the job. Nonetheless, public final demand purchases in 1963 were considerably more intensive in unskilled labor than were private expenditures: the respective values for $\tilde{\theta}^f$ are 0.2359 and 0.1996. The greater unskilled-labor intensity of public expenditures is *not* explained by a different pattern of public purchases from private business, however, since the impact of government purchases is 0.1945, almost identical to the impact of private expenditure. (This statement holds for the "peacetime" conditions of 1963. The full mobilization conditions of the Civil War, World War I and World War II are another matter. More on this below.) The explanation lies instead with "general government activities," among the most unskilled-labor intensive activities in America. It seems plausible to argue that the surge in federal, state, and local government expenditures from 5.0% to 12.1% of national income between 1929 and 1963 must have raised the relative demand for the services of the working poor profoundly. It would appear that *public expenditures have had a pro-poor bias* at the production as well as the consumption level in recent years. As we shall see, there is reason to believe that this pro-poor bias was even stronger prior to World War II, and that we have understated the pro-poor bias even for the 1960s.

A full evaluation of the post-fisc impact on income distribution would, of course, require some judgment regarding *which* private expenditures contract most in response to some specific tax-debt-issue policy. (For historical examples taken from the Civil War and World War I, see Williamson [1974a, 1974b, 1974c].) If aggregate consumption, rather than investment, absorbs the majority of the private expenditure contraction, then the favorable impact on the working poor is somewhat magnified, but not by much. As we shall see below, aggregate investment and consumption have almost identical payments impacts on the working poor, so that it is the public–private expenditure comparison that counts, rather than the aggregate investment–consumption mix. Of course, tax progressivity and incidence may matter. These are analyzed in the next section, where the unskilled-labor intensities of consumption bundles are examined by income class. Similarly, the composition of investment itself may matter, and that too will receive our attention later in this chapter.

ENGEL EFFECTS, REDISTRIBUTION, AND GROWTH

The fashionable claim in the economic development literature is that redistribution from rich to poor is likely to increase the employment of the poor, and thus strengthen the impact of the first-round transfer itself (Morawetz, 1974, pp. 505–506). With very few exceptions, empirical studies from developing countries appear to confirm that the consumption basket of the poor is more intensive in unskilled labor than that of the rich.[3] One obvious explanation for this result is that the poor consume agricultural products intensively. For this reason alone, the consumption expenditures of the rich, who consume relatively small quantities of food, should have a weaker derived demand impact on the low-wage poor. This inference is based on two assumptions: that the rich do not consume other unskilled-labor intensive goods and services with sufficient intensity to offset the impact of their low food share; and that even on the modern mechanized American farm, "labor intensities" are relatively high. Table 8.1 documents that unskilled-labor intensities on the farm are relatively high even in modern America, although we shall show below that this farm–nonfarm factor intensity differential was far higher at the turn of the century than it is today.

When we expand our analysis to include *all* expenditures by the poor, not just food, do their expenditures still have a relatively strong derived demand effect on unskilled labor? The implications are of staggering importance. If the rich consume goods intensive in the services of the working poor, then a redistributive tax–transfer policy may be self-defeating. If, on the other hand, the poor are heavy consumers of their own labor, then redistributive tax–transfer policy will have an egalitarian influence on the pre-fisc distribution itself. That is, the "rise in government" from 1929 to 1948 may have had an egalitarian impact on distribution trends beyond the impact of the private–public expenditure mix discussed above. To the extent that the rise in government was funded by a progressive tax system, the shift to public services *and* the shift away from the consumption expenditures of the rich to those of the poor would both have had an egalitarian influence.

Thus far, we have focused on redistribution by government policy. The issue has obvious twentieth-century relevance, but how about the century prior to 1929, when state expenditures in peacetime were trivial? Even in the absence of overt government policy, Engel effects can have a long-run influence on the derived demand for unskilled labor and thus on distribution trends. Regardless of the endogenous forces generating income growth economy-wide, how do consumption patterns respond to secular growth? The share spent for food declines, of course, thus contributing to the demise of agriculture and in the process diminishing the relative demand for unskilled labor. But surely the influences are more complex. Surely the demand for services and the composition of nonfood commod-

---

[3] True, when capital goods requirements are added to generate the necessary long-run capacity responses, the ranking can be reversed (Morley and Smith, 1973), but it seems more appropriate to treat the capital accumulation issue separately.

ity consumption both matter. The question can therefore be posed with clarity: Does long-run growth in income per capita tend to shift the mix of consumer expenditures to goods and services that are less labor intensive, thus saving on unskilled labor in the aggregate and inducing inequality? Suppose further that secular growth produces inequality, at least initially, for other reasons. Would the distribution of income away from the poor produce a shift in consumption that would induce even further inequality? The old stagnationists drew heavily on the experience of the 1920s and 1930s when developing their models of capitalist growth, distribution, and crisis. Increased inequality and higher profit shares went hand in hand, aggregate consumption suffered, and eventually a crisis in aggregate demand emerged. The modern stagnationists are considerably more sophisticated and appeal primarily to post–World War II Latin America for their evidence.[4] Their sophistication lies in a shift in emphasis from the aggregate demand for labor and overt unemployment to expenditure mix and the derived demand for unskilled labor. For them, once increased inequality emerges it will increase without bounds until checked by violent revolution. The key hypothesis in their models is that the rich consume products intensive in skills and capital: the working poor are caught in an explosive contraction in demands for their services.

Table 8.3 presents the evidence on consumption expenditures by income class. It is *not* true that the poor consume unskilled-labor intensive items more heavily than the rich. On the contrary, the urban rich consume an expenditure bundle *more* unskilled-labor intensive than the urban poor. That is, a dollar's consumption by the urban rich has a more potent payments impact on the working poor than the same dollar spent by the urban poor. This relationship is weaker for rural nonfarm areas, and it disappears entirely for farm families. Nonetheless, for urban households we find the ingredients for a potential paradox: Efforts to redistribute income by transfer payments will be partially thwarted, since the induced change in the economy-wide consumption mix diminishes the relative demand for the services of the working poor. While the mechanism is unlikely to be very strong, we must conclude that *Engel effects have a modest pro-poor bias*, at least for the American economy of the 1960s.[5]

Note that the positive correlation between income levels and unskilled-labor intensities of consumption bundles can be attributed solely to the impact of services. When service expenditures are excluded the correlation disappears entirely. The consumption expenditures listed in Table 8.2 provide some disaggregated data that should be helpful in clarifying these relationships. "Necessities" are a mixed bag. Whereas expenditures for

---

[4] See, for example, the excellent survey by Cline (1975).

[5] Similar findings have been reported by Golladay and Haveman (1976, p. 638).

TABLE 8.3
Payments Impact on Unskilled Labor, Direct and Indirect, of $1 Consumption Expenditure by Region and Income Class, 1961–1963

Income Class	Urban		Rural	
	Excluding Services	Including Services	Nonfarm	Farm
<$1,000	.2029	.1943	.2078	.2121
$1,000–$1,999	.2046	.1940	.2037	.2179
$2,000–$2,999	.2039	.1980	.2003	.2166
$3,000–$3,999	.2009	.1982	.1975	.2140
$4,000–$4,999	.2000	.1972	.1962	.2107
$5,000–$5,999	.2001	.1965	.1959	.2106
$6,000–$7,499	.2008	.1991	.1982	.2091
$7,500–$9,999	.2016	.2015	.1999	.2100
$10,000–$14,999	.2028	.2080	.2043	.2102
$15,000<	.2064	.2218	.2106	.2134
At mean income after taxes	.2001	.1965	.1962	.2107

Sources: The underlying $\hat{\theta}_j$ are for 1963 and are taken from Table 8.1. The consumer expenditure weights are taken from U.S. Department of Labor (BLS) (1964).

housing, fuel, and light all have a very strong anti-poor bias at the production level, food and medical and educational expenditures have a powerful pro-poor bias. Similar anomalies appear for ''luxuries'': Consumer durables have an anti-poor bias, whereas apparel expenditures are very pro-poor on the production side.

CAPITAL ACCUMULATION AND TECHNOLOGICAL PROGRESS

In the 1960s, two-sector growth theories taught us the analytical relevance of comparative factor intensity. Uzawa (1961), for example, found that a sufficient condition for uniqueness of static equilibrium was that the capital goods sector must be more labor intensive than the consumption goods sector. In spite of the empirical work by Gordon (1961) and others, the assumption has always seemed very artificial, especially since skills have rarely been treated adequately either in theory or in empirical application. On these grounds alone it seems relevant to ask whether capital goods are less intensive in the services of the working poor than consumption goods. Or, more generally, are consumer and producer durables less intensive in unskilled labor? Apart from the fact that the empirical evidence brought to bear on the issue was never very convincing, there are other reasons that motivate the inquiry here.

Kendrick (1961, 1973), Carter (1970), and others have documented a high inverse correlation between sectoral price changes and total factor productivity performance. Thus, the output price structure appears to be determined primarily by the wide variance in total factor productivity performance by sector. Nowhere can this be seen more vividly than in the price and output performance of durables and nondurables. Producers have continually raised the share of producer durables in gross fixed capital formation. Consumers have done the same, raising their share of expenditures committed to consumer durables, and this latter force is independent of income effects, since we see it happening at all income levels. Clearly, the relative decline in (quality-adjusted) prices of durable goods encourages accumulation by firms and households economy-wide.

The important point, however, is that the rate of accumulation of durables has not been stable in the twentieth century, nor has the rate of decline in the relative prices of durables, nor for that matter has the relative rate of total factor productivity growth in sectors producing durable goods. Is it sheer coincidence that the episode of income leveling from 1929 to 1948 also exhibits the most sluggish rate of output shift in favor of durables? In 1958 dollars, producer and consumer durables as a share in total private expenditures rose modestly from 16.1% to 19.2% over the nineteen years following 1929. The figure for 1973 was 26.6%, reflecting a near doubling in the annual rate of shift into durables.[6] Here again we have another potential explanation for America's long-term distribution performance which appeals to demand mix. What are facts?

The Uzawa–Gordon premise seems to be unfounded, based upon the 1963 evidence displayed in Table 8.2. The capital goods sector was no more labor intensive than the consumption goods sector, since the difference between 0.1980 and 0.1965 hardly seems significant. The more interesting result, however, lurks just beneath these arbitrary aggregates. Producer and consumer durables were far less unskilled-labor intensive than other investment or consumption expenditures. For example, expenditures on automobiles, appliances, and other durable commodities had almost half the payments impact on the working poor compared with expenditures on apparel and food. Obviously, *any force which favors an economy-wide household shift into consumer durables is strongly anti-poor biased.* Similarly, *any force which favors an investment-mix shift in favor of producer durables is strongly anti-poor biased.* Given what we assume to be very price-elastic demands for durables, then relatively rapid total factor productivity gains in such sectors will inevitably induce inegalitarian trends. Periods of unusual unbalancedness—favoring

---

[6] The data are taken from the *Economic Report of the President* (U.S. Council of Economic Advisers, 1974, Table C-2, p. 250).

durables—in total factor productivity growth will indeed tend to produce inequality, since the working poor will find relative demands for their services declining.

Parameter Stability, Historical Laws, and Nineteenth-Century Inferences

DEMAND, FACTOR INTENSITIES, AND THE EARLY TWENTIETH CENTURY

The relationships between demand and factor intensities uncovered for the 1960s are not peculiar to contemporary America. Most of them were typical of the economy a half century ago, and thus they reappear when 1919 or 1939 data are scrutinized. The comparison is presented in Table 8.4, and sectoral detail can be found in Appendix K.

First, note the extraordinary stability in factor intensity rankings between World War I and the Vietnam decade.[7] Only two expenditure categories change their relative intensity: apparel and construction. The latter is especially noteworthy. Whereas the impact of construction on payments to the working poor was very high in 1963, exceeding that of aggregate consumption, that was not the case in 1919. Over the past five decades, construction has become increasingly unskilled-labor intensive. Since construction was also a larger share in total investment a half century ago, aggregate investment was even less unskilled-labor intensive then, compared to now. Thus, the Uzawa–Gordon premise has even less to support it based on early twentieth-century evidence: Consumption expenditures were far more labor-intensive than capital expenditures in 1919. It might also be noted in passing that this finding suggests confirmation of an inherent instability in the economy of the 1920s: To the extent that greater inequality fostered higher saving and investment shares in GNP, the shifting mix of aggregate demand would have tended to foster even greater inequality, followed by further shifts in demand mix. This inherent "nineteenth-century instability" had disappeared from the American scene by 1939.

Second, producer and consumer durables were even less unskilled-labor intensive in the early twentieth century than in the 1960s. Any shift

---

[7] The "factor intensity reversal" issue has been central to debates in trade theory for some time, especially since Minhas (1962) introduced substitution elasticity (CES) estimates that offered the empirical possibility of reversals across countries and over very long time periods. A recent study of manufacturing across countries suggests that "reversals" are an academic curiosum, a result consistent with our findings from time series in America. See Teitel (1978).

TABLE 8.4
Payments Impact on Unskilled Labor, Direct and Indirect, of $1 Expenditure on Final
Demand, 1919, 1939, and 1963

Final Demand Category (f)	1919	1939	1963
Aggregates			
Consumption I	.2084 (100)	.1764 (100)	.2001 (100)
Consumption II	n.a.	.1411 (80)	.1965 (98)
Investment	.1488 (71)	.1695 (96)	.1980 (99)
Government	n.a.	n.a.	.2392 (120)
Detail			
Housing	0	0	.1104 (55)
Fuel and light	.1479 (71)	.0997 (57)	.1405 (70)
Consumer durables	.1418 (68)	.1288 (73)	.1497 (75)
Misc. consumer goods	.1641 (79)	.1186 (67)	.1704 (85)
Producer durables	.1318 (63)	.1112 (63)	.1786 (89)
Government purchases	n.a.	n.a.	.1943 (97)
Construction	.1653 (79)	.2090 (118)	.2115 (106)
Food	.2443 (117)	.2154 (122)	.2230 (111)
Misc. consumer services	.1993 (96)	.1408 (80)	.2281 (114)
Medical and educational services	n.a.	n.a.	.2580 (129)
General government	n.a.	n.a.	.2840 (142)
Apparel	.1660 (80)	.1776 (101)	.2858 (143)

Sources and notes: For 1963, the data are taken directly from Table 8.2.
For 1939, housing is set equal to zero by assumption. Consumption I refers to commodity purchases, housing, transportation, and communications only, but wholesale and retail markups are accounted for throughout. The underlying $\hat{\theta}_j$ are taken from Appendix K. All consumption expenditure items are weighted at 1935–1936 urban mean family incomes. Producer durables are an unweighted average of the relevant capital goods sectors. Total investment is weighted by the 1939 investment composition.
For 1919, housing is set equal to zero by assumption. Consumption I refers to commodity purchases, housing, transportation, and communications only, but wholesale and retail markups are accounted for throughout. Miscellaneous consumer services refers to transportation and communications. The underlying $\hat{\theta}_j$ are taken from Appendix K. All consumption expenditure items are weighted at 1918–1919 urban workers' mean family income. Producer durables is an unweighted average of the relevant capital goods sectors. Total investment is weighted by 1919 investment composition. Retail and wholesale markups are necessary for 1919 to make input–output and consumer expenditure data consistent. The markups are taken from Barger (1955, Table 26, p. 92).
Figures in parentheses are ratios ($\times$ 100) to Consumption I.

out of nondurables and into durables would have had a far greater labor-saving influence in the 1920s than in the 1960s. Income distribution was thus more sensitive to such changes in output mix during the "durables revolution" than it is now.

Third, we note an important change in the impact of Engel effects. Whereas the 1963 data suggested that Engel effects had a weak pro-poor bias, this was *not* the case prior to World War II. The relationship fails to appear for urban families in the 1930s (Table 8.5, Panel A). Indeed, there is evidence of a weak anti-poor bias, since higher-income brackets ex-hibited slightly lower $\bar{\theta}^f$ than middle- and low-income classes. The anti-poor bias of Engel effects is strongly confirmed for rural nonfarm families and farm families. The evidence for 1919 in Table 8.5 (Panel B) suggests an anti-poor bias even among urban workers. The implication would appear to be that early twentieth-century Engel effects had a modest anti-poor bias, and that nineteenth-century Engel effects had a significant anti-poor bias.

TABLE 8.5

Payments Impact on Unskilled Labor, Direct and Indirect, of $1 Consumption Expenditure: Various Measures

A. By Region and Income Class, 1935–1936

	Urban		Rural	
Income Class	Excluding Services	Including Services	Nonfarm	Farm
< $500	.1852	.1390	.1535	.2106
$500–$749	.1836	.1422	.1550	.2114
$750–$999	.1831	.1422	.1535	.2066
$1,000–$1,249	.1796	.1428	.1523	.1980
$1,250–$1,499	.1795	.1420	.1506	.1951
$1,500–$1,749	.1776	.1419	.1496	.1853
$1,750–$1,999	.1764	.1411	.1480	.1887
$2,000–$2,499	.1753	.1417	.1480	.1817
$2,500–$2,999	.1743	.1406	.1484	.1821
$3,000–$3,999	.1737	.1409	.1489	.1757
$4,000–$4,999	.1724	.1400	.1441	.1641
$5,000–$10,000	.1709	.1376	.1484	.1624
At mean income after taxes	.1764	.1411	.1506	.1980

B. By Urban Workers, 1919

Income Class	Urban Workers
< $900	.2123
$900–$1,199	.2118
$1,200–$1,499	.2096
$1,500–$1,799	.2084
$1,800–$2,099	.2073
$2,100–$2,499	.2062
$2,500 <	.2062
At mean income before taxes	.2084

Sources and notes: The underlying $\hat{\theta}_j$ are for 1939 in Panel A, 1919 in Panel B, and are taken from Appendix K. The consumer expenditure weights in Panel A are taken from U.S. National Resources Planning Board (1941) and in Panel B from U.S. Department of Labor (1924), which is based on a 1918–1919 survey of white urban industrial workingmen's families.

These three conclusions suggest confirmation of the modern stag-nationist thesis based on data drawn from the early twentieth century. This finding is reinforced by the added knowledge that investment—a high-income activity—was far more capital- and skill-intensive then than now. All the ingredients of inherent instability were there, an attractive result given the extensive qualitative literature in which historians have cited inherent structural instability during the 1920s and 1930s. And what is true of instability should also be true of long-term growth.

DEMAND, FACTOR INTENSITIES, AND NINETEENTH-CENTURY GROWTH

Is there any reason to believe that relative factor intensity conditions changed much between 1859 and 1919? Apparently not, at least based on the sole observation available for the nineteenth century, the year 1899. The estimates arrayed in Table 8.6 are derived from William Whitney's re-search, which furnishes the only nineteenth-century input–output data available to compute direct and indirect factor intensity requirements. Not only do the 1899 data supply strong confirmation of the historical stability in factor intensity rankings, but they also suggest that the nineteenth-century American economy had far wider differences in factor intensity by sector and demand "market baskets" than the mid-twentieth century. Tables 8.6 and 8.4 offer a comparison over the six decades between 1899 and 1963. Taking all consumption purchases equal to 100, the unskilled-labor intensity of food expenditures was 180 in 1899 and 111 in 1963; for total investment the figures are 77 in 1899 and 99 in 1963; and for producer durables the figures are 77 in 1899 and 89 in 1963.

The evidence suggests that changes in nineteenth-century demand mix must have had far more potent "composition effects" than identical changes in twentieth-century demand mix. Any force raising income per family economy-wide would have had a tendency to induce inequality simply through Engel effects, since such effects would have served to shift demand mix in a direction which saved on unskilled labor and augmented demand for capital and skills. Any force raising saving and investment shares in GNP (in constant prices) would have induced an even stronger shift toward inequality since the relative unskilled-labor intensity of investment goods production was much less than that of consumption goods production. Any force—such as unbalanced rates of total factor productivity growth—raising expenditure shares on consumer and producer durables would have induced an even stronger shift toward inequality, since the disparity in unskilled-labor intensity was even higher between durable and nondurable goods production. Any force over and above Engel effects causing agriculture to contract as a share in national

TABLE 8.6
Late Nineteenth-Century Payments Impact on Unskilled Labor, Direct and Indirect, by Industry and on Final Demand

Industry	(1) Total Payments Impact on Unskilled Labor	Final Demand Categories (f)	(2) Total Payments Impact on Unskilled Labor
Apparel	.2754		
Shipbuilding	.2119		
Leather and products	.2959	Consumption	.2689 (100)
Processed foods	.3816	Fuel and light	.1134 (42)
Fishing	.5326	Durables	.2130 (79)
Grain mill products	.5084	Food	.4834 (180)
Transport	.1902	Apparel	.2754 (102)
Industry, n.e.c.	.1976	Misc. services	.1360 (51)
Transport equipment	.2342	All nondurables	.2733 (102)
Rubber products	.1446	Investment	.2058 (77)
Textiles	.3367	Durables	.2083 (77)
Machinery	.1938	Construction materials	.2037 (76)
Iron and steel	.1801		
Nonmetal mineral products	.2508		
Lumber and wood products	.2440		
Chemicals	.2511		
Printing and publishing	.1726		
Agriculture and forestry	.6372		
Nonmetallic minerals	.2928		
Petroleum products	.1416		
Nonferrous metals	.1600		
Metal mining	.2095		
Coal products	.2612		
Trade	.1650		
Paper and products	.2592		
Electric power	.1744		
Coal mining	.3269		
Services	.1090		
Petroleum and natural gas	.0998		

Sources and notes: The direct sectoral $\bar{\theta}_j$ underlying Col. (1) are calculated by multiplying 1899 man-year employment estimates (Whitney, n.d., Table V–1, p. 120) times the 1900 hired farm-labor earnings rate (Lebergott, 1964, p. 525), and dividing the result by 1899 dollar output values. The Col. (1) $\hat{\theta}_j$ are then derived by using the 1899 Leontief inverse (Whitney, n.d., Table II–5, p. 28). The estimates in Col. (2) apply 1899 final demand weights to the sectoral $\bar{\theta}_j$. Unfortunately, aggregate consumption does not include housing, and miscellaneous services supply only an incomplete coverage of all services. The figures in parentheses are ratios (× 100) to consumption.

income—such as unbalanced rates of total factor productivity growth—
would have induced the strongest shift toward inequality for the same
reasons. In short, Engel effects, unbalanced total factor productivity
growth favoring the nonfarm and durable goods producing sectors, and
increasing investment shares in GNP should all have served to foster
nineteenth-century labor saving and increasing inequality.

Alternative Measures of the Unskilled-Labor Content of Commodities

DEFINING LOW-WAGE LABOR

Earlier in this chapter we derived the direct and indirect payments
impact on unskilled labor using a set of restrictive assumptions. In particular, all employed man-hours in each sector were assigned an annual
earnings rate for unskilled labor, regardless of occupation mix. The reader
may well object to this procedure, even as an approximation. A counterexample may serve to illustrate the criticism. Two sectors with the
same man-hour input and identical dollar output would yield identical
direct payments impact on the low-wage class, a class we have labeled the
working poor. But suppose one of these sectors used professional and
technical workers very intensively while the other did not. Would we not
overstate the relative payments impact on the working poor for the sector
using high-wage labor intensively? In theory, the answer is surely, Yes. In
fact, paying strict attention to job characteristics and occupation mix does
not matter, except in one important case.

Table 8.7 presents three new measures of sectoral unskilled (low-wage)
labor intensity for 1963. Each of these $\bar{\theta}_j$ uses the BLS occupation–
industry matrix (U.S. Department of Commerce, 1969) and 1970 census
information on wages by occupation (U.S. Department of Labor, 1970).
The procedure requires the allocation of occupations into alternative
definitions of high- and low-wage (unskilled) labor categories. Only low-
wage man-hour inputs are used in the calculation underlying Expression
(8.2). There are three low-wage labor intensities computed in Table 8.7:

Alternative 1 ($\bar{\theta}_j^1$): Unskilled low-wage labor includes operatives,
farm laborers, nonfarm laborers, sales workers, craftsmen and
kindred workers, clerical and kindred workers, service workers,
farmers, and private household workers.

Alternative 2 ($\bar{\theta}_j^2$): Unskilled low-wage labor includes operatives, farm laborers, nonfarm laborers, sales workers in trade, craftsmen and kindred workers, clerical and kindred workers, service workers (except in government jobs), farmers, and private household workers.

Alternative 3 ($\bar{\theta}_j^3$): Unskilled low-wage labor includes operatives, farm laborers, nonfarm laborers, sales workers in trade, craftsmen and kindred workers (except in manufacturing, transport, communications, utilities, and trade), clerical and kindred workers, service workers, farmers, and private household workers.

Regressions calculated for the various pairs of labor intensity measures presented in Table 8.7 suggest some interesting generalizations.[8] First, it is true that our original and restrictive definition of $\bar{\theta}_j$ overstates unskilled-labor intensities throughout the economy. Second, and far more relevant, there is no evidence that unskilled-labor intensity *differentials* are less extensive when either of the three alternative definitions are used. Indeed, there is some evidence that $\bar{\theta}_j$ *understates* the magnitude of unskilled-labor intensity differentials between sectors. It appears that sectors with low man-hour intensities also use high-wage labor in heavier doses than low-wage labor (at least for $\bar{\theta}_j^2$ and $\bar{\theta}_j^3$). Though the correlation is weak, there is some modest confirmation of the "capital–skill complementarity" hypothesis.[9] Thus, all of our earlier conclusions based on final demand calculations would reappear with equal or even greater strength if these alternative measures were used. Nonetheless, we continue to use the original definition of $\bar{\theta}_j$, since only then can we maintain the necessary data comparability for evaluating historical trends in relative unskilled-labor intensity.

---

[8] The following three simple regressions were calculated:

$$\bar{\theta}_j^1 = -.03288 + .99731\ \bar{\theta}_j,\ R^2 = .9423$$
$$(5.60569)\quad (35.45410)$$

$$\bar{\theta}_j^2 = -.03890 + 1.00275\ \bar{\theta}_j,\ R^2 = .9325$$
$$(6.06854)\quad (32.62180)$$

$$\bar{\theta}_j^3 = -.06503 + 1.01992\ \bar{\theta}_j,\ R^2 = .9236,$$
$$(9.32744)\quad (30.50560)$$

where figures in parentheses are t values.

[9] The relevant test is whether in fact the slope coefficients reported in footnote 8 exceed unity. Two of them do, but none of them are significantly different from unity. As we shall see, the support for the "capital–skill complementarity" hypothesis is weakened by the atypical behavior of some key service sectors.

TABLE 8.7
Alternative Measures of Payments Impact on Unskilled Labor, Direct and Indirect, of $1 Purchase of Output from Industry j, 1963

Industry	$\bar{\theta}_j$	$\bar{\theta}_j{}^1$	$\bar{\theta}_j{}^2$	$\bar{\theta}_j{}^3$
1. Livestock	.2908	.2748	.2716	.2644
2. Crops	.2928	.2786	.2750	.2694
3. Forestry and fishing	.2355	.1767	.1743	.1624
4. Agric. services	.3022	.2640	.2602	.2477
5. Iron mining	.1129	.0961	.0929	.0876
6. Nonferrous mining	.1370	.1159	.1136	.1072
7. Coal mining	.1934	.1772	.1752	.1690
8. Petroleum mining	.1456	.1086	.1028	.1000
9. Stone and clay mining	.1689	.1447	.1413	.1336
10. Chemical mining	.1549	.1329	.1310	.1244
11. New construction	.2115	.1767	.1737	.1600
12. Maintenance construction	.2193	.1839	.1814	.1732
13. Ordnance and accessories	.1742	.1267	.1246	.1076
14. Food	.2266	.2032	.1981	.1807
15. Tobacco	.1613	.1447	.1405	.1256
16. Textile mills	.2353	.2115	.2080	.1831
17. Misc. textiles	.1921	.1677	.1638	.1438
18. Apparel	.2858	.2602	.2548	.2309
19. Fabricated textiles	.2576	.2293	.2242	.1985
20. Wood and products	.2364	.2067	.2032	.1722
21. Wooden containers	.2395	.2075	.2051	.1677
22. House furniture	.2294	.2011	.1959	.1526
23. Office furniture	.2238	.1958	.1906	.1449
24. Paper and products	.1643	.1395	.1355	.1108
25. Paper containers	.1782	.1533	.1478	.1213
26. Printing and publishing	.1952	.1552	.1403	.0955
27. Basic chemicals	.1442	.1104	.1061	.0849
28. Synthetics	.1459	.1137	.1102	.0883
29. Drugs and soaps	.1605	.1207	.1127	.0972
30. Paints	.1535	.1195	.1130	.0967
31. Petroleum refining	.1262	.0956	.0909	.0827
32. Rubber products	.1798	.1505	.1467	.1228
33. Leather tanning	.2331	.2118	.2065	.1850
34. Shoes	.2592	.2348	.2292	.1988
35. Glass and products	.1826	.1581	.1546	.1269
36. Stone and clay	.1817	.1529	.1480	.1210
37. Iron and steel	.1485	.1296	.1272	.0937
38. Nonferrous metals	.1259	.1060	.1037	.0821
39. Metal containers	.1739	.1484	.1443	.1113
40. Heating	.1769	.1498	.1462	.1115
41. Stampings, etc.	.1769	.1536	.1502	.1118
42. Hardware, etc.	.1760	.1499	.1462	.1145
43. Engines and turbines	.1725	.1411	.1385	.1059
44. Farm machinery	.1661	.1391	.1358	.1064
45. Construction equipment	.1717	.1428	.1391	.1069

TABLE 8.7 (continued)

Industry	$\bar{\theta}_j$	$\bar{\theta}_j^1$	$\bar{\theta}_j^2$	$\bar{\theta}_j^3$
46. Materials handling equipment	.1737	.1419	.1385	.1072
47. Metalworking equipment	.1717	.1423	.1384	.0960
48. Special industrial equipment	.1674	.1376	.1338	.1016
49. General industrial equipment	.1719	.1416	.1381	.1042
50. Machine shop products	.1732	.1421	.1387	.1039
51. Office machinery	.1750	.1167	.1118	.0896
52. Service industrial machinery	.1769	.1458	.1422	.1105
53. Electrical apparatus	.1840	.1460	.1427	.1188
54. Appliances	.1843	.1537	.1497	.1222
55. Light and wiring equipment	.1814	.1456	.1421	.1188
56. Communication equipment	.1899	.1422	.1396	.1129
57. Electronic components	.1873	.1482	.1448	.1217
58. Batteries, etc.	.1798	.1428	.1400	.1173
59. Motor vehicles and equipment	.1417	.1206	.1182	.0944
60. Aircraft and parts	.1743	.1276	.1254	.0915
61. Trains and ships	.1725	.1455	.1430	.0983
62. Instruments, etc.	.1718	.1342	.1300	.1052
63. Photographic apparatus	.1617	.1250	.1207	.0967
64. Misc. manufactures	.2036	.1711	.1646	.1343
65. Transportation	.1810	.1535	.1497	.1274
66. Communication	.1407	.1176	.1156	.0758
67. Radio and TV broadcasting	.1715	.0934	.0843	.0776
68. Utilities	.1405	.1153	.1068	.0843
69. Trade	.2429	.1884	.1858	.1822
70. Finance and insurance	.1114	.0833	.0710	.0658
71. Real estate	.1104	.0894	.0654	.0631
72. Hotel and personnel service	.3289	.2807	.2756	.2702
73. Business services	.2012	.1292	.1211	.1080
74. Auto repair	.2591	.2227	.2188	.2127
75. Amusements	.2613	.1727	.1647	.1609
76. Medical and education	.2580	.1395	.1359	.1319
77. Federal government	.2339	.1935	.1904	.1828
78. State and local government	.2423	.1945	.1526	.1471
79. Household services	.6374	.6374	.6374	.6374

Sources and notes: See text for alternative measures; $\bar{\theta}_j$ is taken directly from Table 8.1.

THE FACTOR INTENSITY OF HUMAN AND NONHUMAN CAPITAL GOODS PRODUCTION

There is an important exception to the general rule that our restrictive definition of $\bar{\theta}_j$ understates unskilled-labor intensity differentials. Although medical and educational expenditures appear to be highly pro-poor biased when the restrictive $\tilde{\theta}_j$ measures are used, the opposite is true when the alternative measures are utilized. Indeed, an unweighted average of twenty-seven durables-producing sectors (Standard Industrial Classification, 37 through 63) results in a figure of .1392 (using $\bar{\theta}_j^1$), whereas the figure for the medical and education sector is almost exactly the same (.1395). The implications are important. The twentieth century has undergone a pronounced shift in the mode of accumulation (Chap. 3, Table 3.10). Human capital has become the more dominant form of accumulation, and both private and public expenditures on education and medical care have grown at rapid rates in the past half century. The distributional implications of this shifting mode of investment goods production—as opposed to the distribution of the produced human and nonhuman wealth itself—obviously depend on whether these human-capital-creating industries are more or less intensive in the services of the working poor than more conventional capital goods production. The findings in Table 8.7 suggest that the production of conventional durables and human capital have similar and very low unskilled-labor intensities. Whether in the form of durables, skills, or health, capital goods production has a strong anti-poor bias.

9

LABOR SUPPLY GROWTH

The Correlation

Chapter 6 offered good theoretical reasons for suspecting that income inequality should correlate well with labor supply growth. Faster growth of the labor force should raise profit rates and land rents relative to wages, enhancing the relative income position of property owners. Since property is highly concentrated among the rich, faster labor force growth should breed greater income inequality on these grounds alone. Faster growth of the labor force, due either to higher fertility or to a rush of immigration, should also erode equality by imposing skill disadvantages on the marginal entrant to the labor force compared with the average labor force participant which he joins.[1] By cutting the rate of growth of average skills,[2] faster labor force growth in this form tips the balance of labor supply toward lower-paying jobs, depressing the wage rates on common labor relative to the better rates for skilled and professional work. If this expectation is well founded, then higher rates of labor force growth should be correlated with both lower rates of growth in average skills and

---

[1] Clearly, not all kinds of labor force growth contribute to a reduction in the growth of the skills or qualifications of the average member of the labor force. A rise in fertility peculiar to better-off families should feed relatively highly qualified entrants into the labor force a decade or two later. Extra immigration of exceptionally skilled, as in the postwar "brain drain" toward the United States, should also raise rather than lower average skills. But the kinds of increases in fertility and immigration that are most common have the effect of reducing average skills growth.

[2] Here again, as throughout this book, "skills" are those attributes of a jobholder that command higher pay in some base period. Each attribute is weighted by the pay advantage it gives over "common labor" in that base period to derive an overall measure of real skills.

faster rates of increase in wage premia for skilled workers. Let us look first at the correlation between labor force growth and trends in the wage structure, and then investigate what happened to the intervening variable, the rate of growth of skills per man-hour.

Figure 9.1 and Table 9.1 make it clear that periods of rapid labor force growth have tended to coincide with periods of rising wage gaps between nonfarm skilled and unskilled employees. From 1840 to the present, the correlation is remarkably good. Even the slight tendency of 1929–1948 to lie a bit below the "fit line" and for 1948–1966 to lie above it has a fairly easy explanation. As noted also in Chapters 6 and 11, the 1948 wage gap was almost surely depressed a bit by the unanticipated inflation of the 1940s, both during and after World War II, so that some adjustment for this effect would move both the 1929–1948 and 1948–1966 points toward the general pattern. A more serious outlying observation is that for 1820–1840, a period when the wage gap seems to have widened even more than later experience would have suggested. This may result from our wage-gap data base being thinner before 1841, or it may be an artifact of high percentage growth from a low base, an initial state of near-equality between skilled and unskilled wage rates. In any case, even this 1820–1840 pattern fits the general correlation quite well.

Before 1820 American experience probably resembled Point A in Figure 9.1. We have few wage rate series, but we know that such skilled trades as carpenters were paid only a little more than common labor in New England in the eighteenth and nineteenth centuries. The wage premium for skills was thus probably unchanging at low levels. Meanwhile, population growth proceeded at rates like 3% per annum, leaving us around Point A for the entire period from, say, 1700 to 1820.

How can this pre-1820 experience be reconciled with the argument that a significant effect of labor force growth on inequality should produce a good correlation in a diagram like Figure 9.1? Aside from repeating the disclaimer that we mean to look beyond simple correlations, we can offer a good reason why early experience around Point A should lie "off the fit line." Rapid labor force growth before 1840 should have contributed to greater inequality of income and wealth, but not in the form of wider wage rate gaps between the skilled and unskilled. The rapid immigration that accounted for so much of population and labor force growth before 1840 was not of the sort that should have affected the average skill levels of the labor force severely. Aside from the slaves arriving in great numbers in the South, the incoming labor force was not much less skilled than earlier settlers. In this situation, there is no reason to expect rapid labor force growth to raise skill premia (unless the demand for skills was much more price-elastic than the demand for common labor, which seems unlikely).

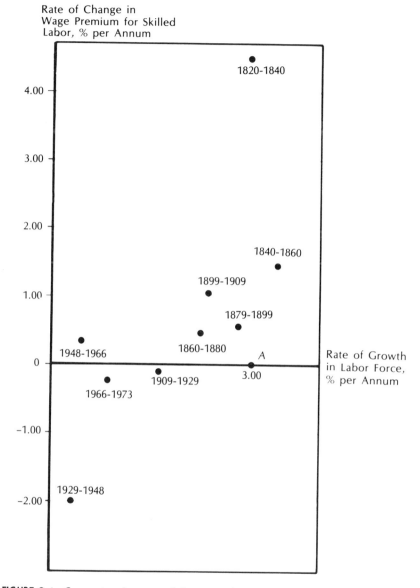

FIGURE 9.1. Comparing the rates of change in the wage premium for skilled labor with rates of growth of the labor force, 1820–1973. From Table 9.1.

TABLE 9.1
Comparing the Rates of Change in the Wage Premium for Skilled Labor with Rates of
Labor Force Growth, 1820–1973 (percentage per annum)

Period	Rate of Labor Force Growth	Rate of Change in the Wage Premium for Skilled Labor
1820–1840	2.95%	4.49%
1840–1860	3.38	1.48
1860–1880	2.24	0.47
1879–1899	2.80	0.59
1899–1909	2.35	1.06
1909–1929	1.62	−0.09
1929–1948	0.32	−1.99
1948–1966	0.45	0.35
1966–1973	0.87	−0.21

Sources and notes: For 1820–1880, the rate of labor force growth is calculated from Lebergott's series on persons gainfully employed (U.S. Department of Commerce, 1973b, Series A107). For 1869–1966, we used the estimates of total man-hours of labor in the national economy from Kendrick (1961, p. 314; 1973, p. 227). The 1973 figure is from the July 1976 *Survey of Current Business*, p. 53.

The rates of change in the skilled-labor wage premium are calculated from Appendix D, Series (5). In each case the terminal years are actually those ending in zero through "1899–1909" (e.g., 1900–1910). For periods within the twentieth century, the years are as stated.

Rather, rapid labor force growth should have raised inequality primarily by raising the return on land and other nonhuman property owned disproportionately by the rich. The impact of rapid immigration on skill premia should therefore have grown over U.S. history, as fresh waves of immigration drew upon lower and lower "qualities" of labor as viewed by the U.S. labor market. As we shall see, it does indeed appear that the negative effect on the growth of skills per person caused by general labor force growth has risen over the past two centuries.

If causal importance is to be attached to this correlation, we must at least support it with another set of correlations. For the labor force growth argument to hold here, it would help greatly if there was evidence confirming that rapid labor force growth contributed to slower growth in average skills. This can be done, though the evidence is sketchier and less direct for the nineteenth century than for the twentieth.

The Growth of Skills in the Nineteenth Century

SCHOOL DAYS

It is not easy to gather information on the skills or "quality" of the nineteenth-century labor force. We have no census series on the educational attainment of the labor force until well into the twentieth century. Yet one clue is offered by enrollment rates and average days of school per year for succeeding generations of children, primarily native-born, after the middle of the nineteenth century. Together these series yield a measure of school days attended per child of school age. This measure can, in turn, be viewed as the contribution these children made to the subsequent growth of average schooling attainment of the labor force.

Table 9.2 documents the growth in school attendance over the 120-year period beginning with 1850. It is clear that school attendance grew more rapidly between 1870 and 1930 than afterwards, at first because of rapid enrollment increases in the 1870s and then eventually because of increases in the number of days in the average school year. This pattern should have raised the schooling attainment of new labor force entrants faster between the late 1870s and the late 1930s than in more recent times. The timing of the faster growth in attendance fails to offer any encouragement to the hypothesis linking wage trends to labor supply growth: It implies that the pay advantage of skilled and more-schooled workers should have declined more between the 1870s and 1930s than afterwards, an event which never occurred.

WAVES OF IMMIGRATION

Another demographic force moved in ways more favorable to the labor supply hypothesis. Immigration involved the arrival of labor force entrants who had to compete disproportionately for lower-paying jobs, since they lacked the market information, training, and language that brought higher pay in the United States. Their numbers and their economic disadvantage varied greatly over the century prior to the immigration restrictions of the 1920s. Figure 9.2 documents U.S. immigration waves both in their volume and character. The gross immigration series may be a fair reflection of the annual contribution of net immigration to the growth of the labor force, since the overstatement stemming from its being a gross series is offset by the understatement resulting from its being a ratio of persons of all ages despite the fact that labor force participants were a higher share among recent immigrants than among the native-born. The period in which new arrivals from abroad had the largest impact on the growth of the labor force was 1846–1855, when the postfamine flood arrived in America. The second greatest wave, as a percentage of the labor force, came between the turn of the century and the First World War.

These two periods of peak influx were also ones in which immigrants seemed to have the lowest skills relative to the indigenous labor force.

TABLE 9.2
Rates of Growth in School Enrollment and Attendance, 1850–1970 *(percentage per annum)*

	Rate of Growth in		
Period	(1) Pupils Enrolled per Child of School Age	(2) Days Attended per Year per Pupil Enrolled	(3) Days Attended per Child of School Age (1) + (2)
1850–1860	0.70%	n.a.	n.a.
1860–1870	−0.44	n.a.	n.a.
1870–1880	1.77	0.34%	2.11%
1880–1890	0.46	0.62	1.08
1890–1900	0.08	1.37	1.45
1900–1910	0.15	1.32	1.47
1910–1920	0.48	0.70	1.18
1920–1930	0.68	1.65	2.33
1930–1940	0.47	0.59	1.06
1940–1950	−0.16	0.39	0.23
1940–1944	−1.39	−0.63	−2.02
1944–1950	0.66	1.09	1.75
1950–1960	0.27	0.14	0.41
1960–1970	0.22	0.23	0.45

Sources and notes: For 1850–1880 Col. (1) is based on ratio of enrollments for all ages to population 5–19. For 1880–1890 Col. (1) is based on ratio of enrollments 5–17, public schools only, to population 5–17. All other figures in Col. (1) are based on ratio of public plus nonpublic school enrollments 5–17 to population 5–17. Cols. (1) and (2) are from U.S. Department of Commerce (1973b, Series B36 and B39); and *Historical Statistics* (1960, pp. 207, 213).

The lower panel of Figure 9.2 illustrates this point in two ways. For the mid-nineteenth-century wave, available data indicate that the share of higher-status occupations among the declared occupations of immigrant members of the labor force hit its all-time low. This was partly because the migrants at mid-century were coming largely from countries where the per capita income was lower than in the United States, as is also shown in Figure 9.2. The flow of immigrants dropped off during the Civil War, and their average preparedness for higher-paying U.S. jobs actually improved. A middling state of affairs continued until 1890, when again the flood began to feature people from the lower-income countries, this time largely from southern and eastern Europe. After World War I, immigrants from much lower-income countries continued to dominate, the main source now shifting toward Latin America. But after 1925 the flows were such a low share of the American labor force that they could hot have had a noticeable effect on average skills growth.

Thus two periods stand out as ones in which heavy immigration should have accelerated the rate of growth of the unskilled labor force: 1846–1855 and 1900–1914. We suspect that this effect was strong enough to

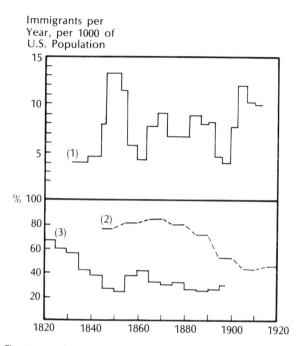

FIGURE 9.2. The size and economic status of immigration flows into the United States, 1820–1920. (1) = yearly gross immigration between business cycle peaks, per 1000 of U.S. population, 1830–1913. From Easterlin (1968, Table B-2). (2) = ratio of average GNP per capita in countries of immigrants' origin to U.S. GNP per capita. From Lindert (1978, Appendix G). The observations plotted refer to shares in U.S. immigration in the second half of each decade (e.g., 1846–1850, 1856–1860). The ratios of GNP per capita to that for the United States are for the preceding U.S. census years (e.g., 1840 for the 1846–1850 immigrants). (3) = share of high-skill and high-status occupations among immigrants declaring their occupations. From *Historical Statistics* (1960, Series C115–C132). The figures refer to average quinquennial shares taken by the categories "professional," "commercial," and "skilled" in total declared occupations. The last observation is 1896–1898, after which a new occupational classification was adopted.

make the average growth of skills per man-hour slower in these periods than the 1.12 percentage rate that we shall find for the period 1909–1973. Since these two periods were also characterized by rapid labor force growth and wage stretching, the evidence suggests confirmation of the hypothesis linking labor force growth to earnings inequality.

A CRUDE AGGREGATE PROXY

School attendance and immigration patterns still fall short of an aggregate measure of the rate of growth of skills. One can compare the impressions gleaned from looking at immigration with those derived by the figures on school attendance of American children, but the net impression can only be very rough. We can, however, get additional clues from a synthetic proxy for aggregate skills growth. The proxy is suggested by the discussion in Appendix J, where two concepts of skills are offered. The second concept can be utilized here. Total compensation of skilled labor can be derived by subtracting total man-hours times the unskilled-labor wage rate (here, the farm rate per hour without board) from total labor compensation including self-employment income. This difference supplies an estimate of the total dollar compensation received by skills. It is the product of the quantity of skills and their price, the latter simply the premium above the wage rate on common labor. If we then divide this compensation by the wage premium on skills, we have a measure of skills defined in the constant-price purchasing power of some base period. We can then compute the growth of this proxy for aggregate skills over time.

We have performed this exercise for the nineteenth and twentieth centuries[3] (Table 9.3). For the antebellum period following 1839/1840 the measure implies that skills per man-hour gainfully employed outside agriculture remained constant. This is not implausible, given the heavy immigrant influx. For the postbellum period from 1869/1870 to 1899/1900, the same measure registers an advance of 0.50% per year. This rate, a little under half the average twentieth-century rate, again seems plausible. Over the long twentieth-century period between 1909 and 1973 the same proxy for skills growth seems to approximate a rate calculated from

---

[3] The calculation of skills growth in Table 9.3 ran as follows: (a) We first defined skills as a factor only employed in the nonagricultural sector, because of the extreme difficulty of inferring returns to skills in agriculture. (b) Total labor compensation outside of agriculture was calculated two ways: For 1839 and 1849, we subtracted Gallman's (1972) estimate of returns to labor in agriculture from his estimate of total labor compensation for the national economy using the interest-rate method (for GNP, Gallman, 1966, p. 26; for the labor share, his calculation in Davis et al., 1972, p. 38). For 1849 through 1909, we used the 1850–1910 estimates of returns to nonagricultural labor in Budd (1960) plus the gross value product of government (King, 1915, p. 138). (c) Nonagricultural man-hours were taken from Kendrick (1961, p. 314) for years from 1869 on; earlier years were covered by splicing Lebergott estimates of the numbers gainfully employed onto the Kendrick man-hours for 1869. (d) The hourly farm wage rate series is a splicing of recent hourly farm wage rates without board; earlier USDA estimates of daily wages without board, spliced at 1929 (Historical Statistics, 1960, Series K181), and Lebergott (1964, pp. 539–540) monthly farm wages with board for the earliest years, spliced at 1869. (e) The product of (c) and (d) here equals the imputed compensation of nonagricultural unskilled labor. (f) The difference between (b) and (e) is the imputed compensation of (nonagricultural) skilled labor. (g) The skilled-labor wage premium for this calculation is the difference between the nonfarm wage rate for skilled labor and the farm wage rate. The ratio of (f) to (g) is the real amount of skills employed in the economy, measured in equivalent hours of the chosen skilled job class to which the wage rate series refers.

TABLE 9.3
Growth Rates in Labor Force "Quality," 1839–1973 *(percentage per annum)*

Period	Denison Index of Skills per Man-Hour	Proxy Index of Skills per Man-Hour outside Agriculture
1839–1859	n.a.	0
1869–1899	n.a.	0.50%
1899–1909	n.a.	−1.17
1909–1914	0.57%	n.a.
1909–1973	1.12	1.30

Sources and notes: The Denison index is taken from Table 9.4. The "Proxy" index is discussed in the text.

Denison: Our skills proxy rose at the rate of 1.30% per man-hour each year, compared with 1.12% using the Denison data. The proxy performs less satisfactorily for subperiods within the twentieth century, however, since it is sensitive to errors in underlying estimates. In particular, the proxy implies that average skills per man-hour gainfully employed outside of agriculture *declined* by 1.17% a year over the decade 1899–1909. This surely overstates the importance of the immigrant influx, and we discard this estimate in favor of Denison's for 1909–1914, a very similar period.

While imperfect, the proxy at least gives plausible growth rates for skills over the two nineteenth-century periods on which we shall focus our attention in the following chapter,[4] 1839/1840–1859/1860 and 1869/1870–

[4] Here we must enter two important technical notes about the specific skills measures discussed here and used in Part Three. First, note that the nineteenth-century skills proxy measures hours of equivalent skill units per man-hour employed (in all occupations) *outside of agriculture*. When measuring the growth of skills throughout the whole economy, we shall add this growth rate for average nonagricultural skills to the growth of man-hours for the whole economy, not just for the nonagricultural sector. This is a realistic concession to the fact that average skill levels are also growing within the large but relatively declining agricultural sector, even though their rewards are hidden within the agricultural incomes of land, capital, and labor. We find it more realistic to assume the same growth in skills per man-hour in all sectors, than to assume zero skills growth and zero skills levels in agriculture and let the rise of the share of nonagriculture in total employment yield an estimate of total skills growth that overstates the rise in the supply of skills that effectively faced nonagricultural employers.

Second, we adjust the Denison (1962, 1974) measure of labor input growth to accord with our use of the second definition of skills spelled out in Appendix J. Our adjustment slightly raises the apparent rate of growth of skills. The subtle distinction is that his approach, like the first measure of skills introduced in Appendix J—but ruled out in Part Three by data constraints—weights each attribute of labor force "quality" by the pay it gets in a base period. Our approach implicitly weights each attribute by the pay *premium* it gets over the farm wage rate in a base period. The underlying definitional algebra yields an adjustment formula. If Denison's measure of the growth rate of total labor input is denoted by $(S\overset{*}{\cdot}L)$

1899/1900. Its behavior in these two periods is consistent with the view that labor supply growth affected skills growth and earnings inequality. Skills growth does seem to have been far lower in the antebellum period of heavy immigration than after the Civil War.

The Growth of Skills in the Twentieth Century

Following 1909, average labor force quality can be gauged with the help of the better estimates supplied by Denison (1962, 1974). Denison developed an index of labor inputs per man-hour by weighting the effects of shifts in age, sex, and schooling on earning capacity. Table 9.4 summarizes Denison's results and compares them with growth rates in the median years of schooling for adults. According to Denison's estimates, the rate of growth of labor force quality peaked in the leveling era 1929–1948. This, of course, fits the argument that the slower labor force growth of this era lies behind the observed equalization of rates of pay. Denison's measure implies that immigration restriction, plus the entrance into the labor force of an interwar cohort of young Americans who had been raised in small families, should have allowed a more rapid growth in the schooling and other qualifications of the labor force. The pre-1950 series on median years of schooling seems to concur, showing an acceleration in the growth of adults' prior schooling even though one might imagine it harder to raise median schooling at higher levels of schooling. The contrast between the 1929–1948 leveling era and what preceded it thus seems to fit the intuition that slower labor supply growth should produce a greater tendency toward equality.

For the postwar period, Denison's series shows slower growth in labor force quality once again, but the rate of growth in median schooling accelerates up to the late 1950s before dropping off. The discrepancy in timing seems to be due to another development captured by Denison's measure. The labor force participation rate for adult women, especially wives, kept rising in the postwar period after a brief initial dip as wartime

---

and his growth rate for man-hours by $\overset{*}{L}$, then the rate of growth of total skills we shall use in Part Three is

$$\overset{*}{S} = (\overset{*}{S} + L) \left[\frac{(\theta_L + \theta_S)}{\theta_S} \right] - \overset{*}{L} \left[\frac{\theta_L}{\theta_S} \right],$$

where θ_L is the share of unskilled-labor compensation in total national product and θ_S is the share of skilled-labor compensation in total national product. For the period 1909–1948, 1929 weights implied the formula $\overset{*}{S} = 1.39(\overset{*}{S} + L) - .39\overset{*}{L}$, while 1963 weights for the period 1948–1973 implied the formula $\overset{*}{S} = 1.47(\overset{*}{S} + L) - .47\overset{*}{L}$.

TABLE 9.4
Growth Rates in Labor Force "Quality" and Schooling, Selected Periods, 1909–1972
(percentage per annum)

Period	Denison's Index of Labor Inputs per Man-Hour	Period	Median Schooling of the Population 25 Years and Older
1909–1919	0.58%	1910–1920	0.12%
1919–1929	0.79	1920–1930	0.24
1929–1948	1.08	1930–1940	0.24
		1940–1950	0.78
1948–1958	0.88	1950–1957	1.87
1958–1965	0.38	1957–1965	1.34
1965–1969	0.58	1965–1972	0.48

Sources and notes: The labor "quality" index is from Denison (1962, p. 85; 1974, Table 4–1). From 1929–1948 on, it refers only to the nonresidential business sector. Denison's index has been criticized, as an overestimate of the rate of growth of labor quality attributable to schooling, by Schwartzman (1968, pp. 508–514). Schwartzman's criticisms, however, do not seem to alter the ranking of different periods according to their rates of growth in labor quality per man-hour.

The series on medium years of schooling is from the U.S. Department of Commerce (1973b, Series B40), reproducing the estimates of Folger and Nam and of the decennial censuses. Other estimates have been offered for 1960 and earlier census years by Gustavus and Nam (1968, pp. 410–421). The Gustavus–Nam revisions lower the median level slightly for 1960 and increasingly for earlier census years. As a result, their revised estimates would raise the rate of growth in median schooling of adults for each decade between 1910 and 1960 and would slightly raise the rate for the early 1960s as well. Their revisions do not cover more recent years, and we have assumed that the recent estimates for 1965–1972 are correct as they stand.

hiring of women dropped off. As Denison notes, new female entrants into the labor force would have had to compete disproportionately for jobs that were on the average already lower-paying, which makes their entry reduce average labor force "quality." Thus the entrance of a new disadvantaged group, now women, offers a minor version of the skill-depressing role played earlier by immigration, and helped bring the income leveling to a stop. Across the late 1960s, this trend continued while the growth in median schooling also decelerated. Together these changes may have helped keep the pay structure of the postwar period stable rather than trending toward equality.

The rates of growth of labor force size and average quality thus join the list of good correlates with trends in pay ratios, along with the degree of technological imbalance, the rate of capital accumulation, and, to a lesser extent, the rate of inflation. We are therefore not in need of good correlates for inequality trends. On the contrary, we have a surplus. The next task is to devise a measure of quantifying their individual causal roles.

Part Three
QUANTITATIVE ACCOUNTING

EXPLAINING THE RISE IN EARNINGS INEQUALITY BEFORE WORLD WAR I

The Task

Earnings inequality seems to be highly correlated with a number of potential explanatory variables. Moving from these simple correlations to a quantification of the sources of earnings inequality requires some explicit modeling. We here exploit one such model to help us decide which of the correlates of earnings inequality have been most important in producing those distribution trends. This and the next chapter quantify the impact of technological change and factor supply growth on wage gap trends for the periods 1839–1909 and 1909–1973. Chapter 12 expands the inquiry by exploring the feedback from inequality to capital accumulation, a force taken to be exogenous here and in Chapter 11.

A traditional rule of thumb is to favor simplicity when choosing among models. Before elaborating a complicated model, it might be wise first to explore how well a naive model could account for the facts, here the observed nineteenth-century trends in the skilled-labor wage ratio, our proxy for overall earnings inequality. Can that inequality experience be captured with a one-sector Cobb-Douglas production function producing gross national product with skilled labor, unskilled labor, and other productive inputs? The prediction of this simple model is unambiguous: Any gap in the percentage growth rates of unskilled- and skilled-labor supplies should produce exactly the same percentage rise in the skilled-labor wage premium. Technological change that saves on unskilled labor can also be quantified in this simple framework as an exogenous shift in factor demand that should serve to augment the wage gap between the skilled and the unskilled.

To explain the uneven rise in skilled-labor wage premia before World

War I with an aggregate Cobb–Douglas production function, we need to show either that the supply of unskilled labor grew faster than skills or that technological change was unskilled labor saving. Table 10.1 illustrates how hard it is to sustain this view based on such a simple model. The supply of skills grew at least as fast as the supply of unskilled labor in the antebellum period. Later in the century skills grew more rapidly, a fact that should have induced a leveling in the earnings structure between the Civil War and World War I. The bias of technological change may be harder to quantify, but at least we can calculate the factor-augmenting biases implied by sectoral differences in productivity growth rates. These show that productivity growth was faster in the sectors using skills more intensively. As far as the naive model goes, this imbalance also should

TABLE 10.1
Comparing Rates of Change in the Nonfarm Skilled-Labor Wage Ratio with Rates of Growth in Skilled and Unskilled Labor, 1839–1909 (percentage per annum)

	1839–1859	1869–1899	1899–1909
(1) Rate of change in the nonfarm wage ratio of skilled to unskilled labor	1.48%	0.30%	1.06%
(2) Growth in unskilled man-hours (total labor force) ($\overset{*}{L}$)	3.38	2.73	2.35
(3) Augmentation in supply of unskilled labor implied by neutral sectoral rates of productivity growth (Π_L)	0.55	1.05	0.77
(4) Growth in skills ($\overset{*}{S}$)	3.38	3.23	2.92
(5) Augmentation in supply of skills implied by neutral sectoral rates of productivity growth (Π_S)	1.05	1.14	1.43
(6) Relative rise in unskilled-labor supply ($\overset{*}{L} + \Pi_L - \overset{*}{S} - \Pi_S$)	−0.50	−0.59	−1.23

Sources and notes: Row (1), rate of change in nonfarm wage ratio, comes from Appendix D, Series (5), for 1840–1860, 1870–1900, 1900–1910.

Row (2), growth in unskilled man-hours, 1869–1909, is from Kendrick (1961, p. 314), which measures growth in man-hours of labor input into the national economy. For 1839–1859 the data are from Lebergott's estimates (*Historical Statistics*, 1975, Part 1, pp. 138–139), which measure the growth in the labor force (including slaves).

Row (3), augmentation in supply of unskilled labor implied by neutral sectoral rates of productivity growth, is from Table 7.9.

Row (4), growth in skills, is taken from Tables 9.3 and 9.4, and footnote 4 to Chapter 9. Note again the weaknesses of this measure, especially for the periods before the turn of the century.

Row (5), augmentation in supply of skills implied by neutral sectoral rates of productivity growth, is from Table 7.9.

have served to depress the wage advantage of skilled laborers, since the naive model implies that skills were "saved" relative to unskilled laborers. Adding up these factor supply growth and factor-saving effects shows that a naive model predicts leveling across the nineteenth century when in fact this simply did not occur. An attempt to rescue the naive, one-sector model by assuming that technological change was strongly unskilled labor saving *within* sectors seems hopeless: The amount of intrasectoral bias required—the difference between Row (1) and Row (6)—exceeds by a large margin any empirical estimate of the extent of labor saving spanning so long a period. In short, a simple, one-sector model cannot explain why and when wage gaps widened. Alas, Occam's razor must be set aside in our search for adequate explanations for American nineteenth-century inequality history.

The Model

The most convenient approach to the determinants of wage gaps is a general-equilibrium model following the suggestions of R. W. Jones (1965). Simple general-equilibrium models offer sufficient promise to justify their assumptions of full employment and competition, at least for present purposes. An expanded general-equilibrium model can accommodate not only skilled and unskilled labor, but other factors as well. We need to add farmland to the model, if for no other reason than to test Frederick Jackson Turner's thesis that expansion in the stock of available land offered opportunities for America's unskilled labor that served to hold up their wage and foster equality. Obviously, we also need to add nonhuman capital, a factor that might have a special relationship to skilled labor. We thus distinguish four factors of production:

Factors:
$(i = J, K, L, S)$

Farmland (J), exclusive of improvements other than initial clearing for cultivation or pasture;

Capital (K), consisting of all nonhuman asset services in the business and government sectors, other than farmland;

Unskilled labor (L), or total man-hours, compensated at the wage rate for unskilled labor; and

Skills (S), or all attributes of labor input generating earnings above the unskilled-labor wage rate in some base period.

The framework also permits us to distinguish among sectors whose different technologies may influence relative factor demands. In order to conserve equations and satisfy data constraints, we shall disaggregate the economy into only three sectors:

Sectors:
($j = A, M, C$)

Agriculture (A), or all gross national product originating in agriculture, forestry, and fisheries;

Industry or manufacturing (M), consisting of all gross national product originating in mining, manufacturing, transportation, communications, and utilities; and

Tertiary activities (C), or all gross national product originating in construction, finance, trade, private services, and government.

Not all factors are used in every sector. The high costs of land conversion make it reasonable to confine farmland to use in the agricultural sector only. We make the opposite assumption about skills: Whereas skilled labor is mobile between the industrial and tertiary sectors, it is not used in agriculture at all. This somewhat uncomfortable assumption is forced on us by the data: returns to skills are extremely difficult to separate from returns to other factors within agriculture. Certainly farmers learned more about local soil and climate conditions, mastered new machinery, and became increasingly educated as time passed. Measuring the impact of those skills on farm income is another matter entirely. Thus, we follow the lead suggested by Gallman, Kendrick, and the Department of Commerce as to how agricultural product was divided between labor, capital, and land, without adding skills. Unskilled labor and capital, on the other hand, are perfectly mobile among all sectors.

The model predicts rates of change in the following nine endogenous variables:

four factor prices

d = the real rental earned on an acre of farmland,
r = the real rental earned on nonhuman capital,
w = the real wage rate earned by unskilled labor, and
q = the real wage rate earned by skilled labor;

two commodity prices

P_M = the price of industrial goods relative to agricultural goods, and
P_C = the price of tertiary goods and services relative to agricultural goods;

three A = the output of the agricultural sector,
sectoral M = the output of the industrial sector, and
outputs C = the output of the tertiary sector.

Agricultural products serve as the *numéraire* ($P_A = 1$). We shall focus primarily on explaining the rate of change in the skilled-labor wage ratio q/w, though it is useful to test the predictions of the model regarding changes in other endogenous variables as well.

The exogenous influences include changes in factor supplies (J, K, L, S), shifts in technological parameters to be defined below (T_j and Π_i), shifts in patterns of product demand (D_M, D_C), and population (Pop).

Under competitive assumptions, price is equated with both average and marginal cost in each sector. The equality of price and average cost yields three *cost equations*:

$$1 \quad = a_{JA}d + a_{KA}r + a_{LA}w \qquad (10.1)$$
$$P_M = \quad\quad a_{KM}r + a_{LM}w + a_{SM}q \qquad (10.2)$$
$$P_C = \quad\quad a_{KC}r + a_{LC}w + a_{SC}q \qquad (10.3)$$

where a_{ij} is a physical input-output ratio (e.g., man-hours per ton). These equations take on an extremely convenient form when they are converted into rate-of-change equations involving factor cost shares. These factor cost shares are defined as

$$\theta_{JA} = a_{JA}d \quad \theta_{KA} = a_{KA}r \quad \theta_{LA} = a_{LA}w$$
$$\theta_{KM} = a_{KM}r/P_M \quad \theta_{LM} = a_{LM}w/P_M \quad \theta_{SM} = a_{SM}q/P_M$$
$$\theta_{KC} = a_{KC}r/P_C \quad \theta_{LC} = a_{LC}w/P_C \quad \theta_{SC} = a_{SC}q/P_C.$$

Factor shares sum to unity in each sector, since costs are assumed to exhaust the value of product.

To arrive at handy linear approximations involving rates of change, we use the asterisk notation for rates of change per annum: $\overset{*}{X} = (dX/dt)/X$. Differentiating the cost equations and converting all variables into rates of change yields

$$0 = \overset{*}{d}\theta_{JA} + \overset{*}{r}\theta_{KA} + \overset{*}{w}\theta_{LA} \qquad + \left[\sum_i \overset{*}{a}_{iA}\theta_{iA} \right] \qquad (10.4)$$

$$\overset{*}{P}_M = \qquad \overset{*}{r}\theta_{KM} + \overset{*}{w}\theta_{LM} + \overset{*}{q}\theta_{SM} \qquad + \left[\sum_i \overset{*}{a}_{iM}\theta_{iM} \right] \qquad (10.5)$$

$$\overset{*}{P}_C = \qquad \overset{*}{r}\theta_{KC} + \overset{*}{w}\theta_{LC} + \overset{*}{q}\theta_{SC} \qquad + \left[\sum \overset{*}{a}_{iC}\theta_{iC} \right] \qquad (10.6)$$

The terms enclosed (by dashed lines) on the right-hand side are weighted sums of increases in physical input–output ratios, where the weights are factor cost shares. These should become more familiar when they are rewritten as *minus* the rate of increase in output–input ratios, weighting all ratios by input cost shares and holding factor prices constant. In other words, each expression enclosed on the right is minus the exogenous rate of total factor productivity growth, or $-\overset{*}{T}_j$. Regrouping so that endogenous variables appear on the left and exogenous variables appear on the right, the cost equations now become

$$\overset{*}{d}\theta_{JA} + \overset{*}{r}\theta_{KA} + \overset{*}{w}\theta_{LA} = \overset{*}{T}_A \tag{10.7}$$

$$\overset{*}{r}\theta_{KM} + \overset{*}{w}\theta_{LM} + \overset{*}{q}\theta_{SM} - \overset{*}{P}_M = \overset{*}{T}_M \tag{10.8}$$

$$\overset{*}{r}\theta_{KC} + \overset{*}{w}\theta_{LC} + \overset{*}{q}\theta_{SC} - \overset{*}{P}_C = \overset{*}{T}_C. \tag{10.9}$$

These are nothing more than *price duals* of total factor productivity growth equations.

Four *full-employment equations* describe the sectoral distribution of each factor by employment:

$$J = a_{JA}A \tag{10.10}$$

$$K = a_{KA}A + a_{KM}M + a_{KC}C \tag{10.11}$$

$$L = a_{LA}A + a_{LM}M + a_{LC}C \tag{10.12}$$

$$S = \phantom{a_{LA}A +} a_{SM}M + a_{SC}C. \tag{10.13}$$

Again, these equations can be converted into more convenient expressions by introducing shares and taking rates of change. The shares in this case are not the factor cost shares within sectors but the proportion of each factor used in a particular sector:

$$\lambda_{JA} = 1$$

$$\lambda_{KA} = a_{KA}A/K \quad \lambda_{KM} = a_{KM}M/K \quad \lambda_{KC} = a_{KC}C/K$$

$$\lambda_{LA} = a_{LA}A/L \quad \lambda_{LM} = a_{LM}M/L \quad \lambda_{LC} = a_{LC}C/L$$

$$\lambda_{SM} = a_{SM}M/S \quad \lambda_{SC} = a_{SC}C/S.$$

The λ_{ij} sum to unity across all sectors for any one factor of production. Taking derivatives of Equations (10.10) through (10.13) and dividing through by total factor supplies, we get

$$\overset{*}{J} = \overset{*}{A} + \overset{*}{a}_{JA} \tag{10.14}$$

$$\overset{*}{K} = \lambda_{KA}\overset{*}{A} + \lambda_{KA}\overset{*}{a}_{KA} + \lambda_{KM}\overset{*}{M} + \lambda_{KM}\overset{*}{a}_{KM} + \lambda_{KC}\overset{*}{C} + \lambda_{KC}\overset{*}{a}_{KC} \tag{10.15}$$

$$\overset{*}{L} = \lambda_{LA}\overset{*}{A} + \lambda_{LA}\overset{*}{a}_{LA} + \lambda_{LM}\overset{*}{M} + \lambda_{LM}\overset{*}{a}_{LM} + \lambda_{LC}\overset{*}{C} + \lambda_{LC}\overset{*}{a}_{LC} \tag{10.16}$$

$$\overset{*}{S} = \phantom{\lambda_{LA}\overset{*}{A} + \lambda_{LA}\overset{*}{a}_{LA} +} \lambda_{SM}\overset{*}{M} + \lambda_{SM}\overset{*}{a}_{SM} + \lambda_{SC}\overset{*}{C} + \lambda_{SC}\overset{*}{a}_{SC}. \tag{10.17}$$

Rates of change in input–output ratios ($\overset{*}{a}_{ij}$) are determined by two forces, one exogenous and the other endogenous:

$$\overset{*}{a}_{ij} = \overset{*}{b}_{ij} + \overset{*}{c}_{ij}.$$

$$\text{(exog-} \quad \text{(induced by shifts in}$$

$$\text{enous)} \quad \text{relative factor prices)}$$

In what follows, we shall collect these exogenous $\overset{*}{b}_{ij}$ terms into summary measures of the factor-augmenting bias resulting from technological change. These factor bias measures, Π_i, quantify the extent to which technological progress "saves" on the use of each factor economy-wide:[1]

$$\Pi_i = \sum_i \lambda_{ij} \overset{*}{b}_{ij}.$$

The endogenous part of each $\overset{*}{a}_{ij}$ is that induced by relative factor prices and changing relative factor scarcity. Each is defined in terms of elasticities of factor substitution and factor price movements:

$$\overset{*}{c}_{ij} = \sum_k \theta_{kj}\sigma^j_{ik} (\overset{*}{v}_k - \overset{*}{v}_i),$$

where $\overset{*}{v}$ refers to the factor price changes $(\overset{*}{d}, \overset{*}{r}, \overset{*}{w}, \overset{*}{q})$.

A key assumption in any such model is the set of values for the elasticities of factor substitution, σ^j_{ik}. A large empirical literature tends to place these elasticities between zero and one. There is also accumulating evidence that argues that capital and skills tend to be less substitutable, and closer to being complements, than either of them is with unskilled labor (Griliches, 1969 and 1970; Fallon and Layard, 1975; Kesselman, Williamson, and Berndt, 1977). We assume this to be the case in the nineteenth century as well as in the twentieth, from which these studies drew their data. Since our focus is on the very long run, we assume relatively high substitution elasticities. Specifically, we shall normally take the elasticity of substitution between capital and skills to be one-half ($\sigma_{KS}^M = \sigma_{KS}^C = 1/2$), while all other elasticities of factor substitution are taken to be unity.[2]

Using these definitions, Equations (10.14) through (10.17) can be restated in terms of growth rates in factor prices, factor supplies, factor bias (Π_i), elasticities of factor substitution, and the factor and sector shares. The resulting equations are long and tedious, and we omit their derivation, giving their final form in Figure 10.1.

[1] The Π_i measures are those already used in Table 7.9 above, where we assumed that each rate of total factor productivity growth in subsectors ranging from three to twelve in number represented the same $\overset{*}{b}_{ij}$ for all factors within that subsector. Thus, while the Π_i used here are related to the $\overset{*}{T}_j$ of the three sectors, the two measures were aggregated from subsector data using different weights (value-added weights versus single-factor-use weights).

[2] In other tests, we used elasticities of factor substitution that were all half of the respective values assumed here. These tests almost invariably yielded poorer predictions than the assumptions favored from the outset of our calculations.

The general-equilibrium model, expressed as a matrix equation (coefficient matrix × endogenous variables = exogenous shift terms):

	$\overset{*}{d}$	$\overset{*}{r}$	$\overset{*}{w}$	$\overset{*}{q}$	$\overset{*}{P}_M$	$\overset{*}{P}_C$	$\overset{*}{A}$	$\overset{*}{M}$	$\overset{*}{C}$		Exogenous Shift Terms
Eq. (10.7)	θ_{JA}	θ_{KA}	θ_{LA}	0	0	0	0	0	0		$\overset{*}{T}_A$
Eq. (10.8)	0	θ_{KM}	θ_{LM}	θ_{SM}	-1	0	0	0	0		$\overset{*}{T}_M$
Eq. (10.9)	0	θ_{KC}	θ_{LC}	θ_{SC}	0	-1	0	0	0		$\overset{*}{T}_C$
Eq. (10.14)	g_{41}	g_{42}	g_{43}	0	0	0	1	0	0	$=$	$\overset{*}{J} + \Pi_J$
Eq. (10.15)	g_{51}	g_{52}	g_{53}	g_{54}	0	0	λ_{KA}	λ_{KM}	λ_{KC}	$\times$	$\overset{*}{K} + \Pi_K$
Eq. (10.16)	g_{61}	g_{62}	g_{63}	g_{64}	0	0	λ_{LA}	λ_{LM}	λ_{LC}		$\overset{*}{L} + \Pi_L$
Eq. (10.17)	0	g_{72}	g_{73}	g_{74}	0	0	0	λ_{SM}	λ_{SC}		$\overset{*}{S} + \Pi_S$
Eq. (10.19)	0	0	0	0	$-\epsilon_M$	$-\epsilon_{MC}$	$-\eta_M\phi_A$	$(1-\eta_M\phi_M)$	$-\eta_M\phi_C$		$\overset{*}{D}_M + (1-\eta_M)\overset{*}{Pop}$
Eq. (10.20)	0	0	0	0	$-\epsilon_{CM}$	$-\epsilon_C$	$-\eta_C\phi_A$	$-\eta_C\phi_M$	$(1-\eta_C\phi_C)$		$\overset{*}{D}_C + (1-\eta_C)\overset{*}{Pop}$

Endogenous Variables: $\overset{*}{d}$, $\overset{*}{r}$, $\overset{*}{w}$, $\overset{*}{q}$, $\overset{*}{P}_M$, $\overset{*}{P}_C$, $\overset{*}{A}$, $\overset{*}{M}$, $\overset{*}{C}$

where $g_{41} = \underbrace{-(\theta_{KA}\sigma_{JK}^A + \theta_{LA}\sigma_{JL}^A)}_{= g_{42}} = g_{43}$

$$g_{52} = \underbrace{-(\lambda_{KA}\theta_{JA}\sigma_{JK}^A + \lambda_{KA}\theta_{LA}\sigma_{KL}^A + \lambda_{KM}\theta_{LM}\sigma_{KL}^M + \lambda_{KC}\theta_{LC}\sigma_{KL}^C + \lambda_{KM}\theta_{SM}\sigma_{KS}^M + \lambda_{KC}\theta_{SC}\sigma_{KS}^C)}_{= g_{51} \quad = g_{53} \quad = g_{54}}$$

$$g_{63} = \underbrace{-(\lambda_{LA}\theta_{JA}\sigma_{JL} + \lambda_{LA}\theta_{KA}\sigma_{KL}^A + \lambda_{LM}\theta_{KM}\sigma_{KL}^M + \lambda_{LC}\theta_{KC}\sigma_{KL}^C + \lambda_{LM}\theta_{SM}\sigma_{LS}^M + \lambda_{LC}\theta_{SC}\sigma_{LS}^C)}_{= g_{61} \quad = g_{62} \quad = g_{64}} \quad \text{and}$$

$$g_{74} = \underbrace{-(\lambda_{SM}\theta_{KM}\sigma_{KS}^M + \lambda_{SC}\theta_{KC}\sigma_{KS}^C + \lambda_{SM}\theta_{LM}\sigma_{LS}^M + \lambda_{SC}\theta_{LC}\sigma_{LS}^C)}_{= g_{72} \quad = g_{73}}$$

FIGURE 10.1. The general-equilibrium model in rate-of-change form.

Product demands are endogenous. Each sectoral demand equation takes the form

$$Q_j = D_j(Y/Pop)^{\eta_j}P_j{}^{\epsilon_j}P_k{}^{\epsilon_{jk}}(Pop)^{\epsilon_{jPop}}, \qquad (10.18)$$

where again all prices are relative to those of agriculture, and D_j is an exogenous demand shift term; Y is gross national product;[3] Pop is total population; η_j is the income elasticity of demand for j; ϵ_j and ϵ_{jk} are, respectively, the own-price and cross-price elasticities of demand for j; and ϵ_{jPop} is the elasticity of demand for j with respect to population size, given prices, and income per capita.

In what follows we shall assume that the population-size elasticities are all unity. We shall also assume that demand patterns are independent of the income distribution (i.e., that output demands are independent of factor prices and factor supplies). This latter assumption may appear to have the effect of dampening our predictions of movements in the skilled-labor wage premium, since it does not allow increasing inequality to shift demand away from unskilled-labor-intensive agriculture, thus fostering further inequality. Yet the results of Chapter 8 suggest that the demand-independence-of-inequality assumption bears close conformity with twentieth-century facts, at least as it applies to consumption expenditures by income class.

Converting the demand equations into rate-of-change form, setting $\epsilon_{jPop} = 1$, and rearranging to put exogenous variables on the right-hand side yields

$$(1 - \eta_M\phi_M)\overset{*}{M} - \eta_M\phi_A\overset{*}{A} - \epsilon_M\overset{*}{P_M}$$
$$- \epsilon_{MC}\overset{*}{P_C} - \eta_M\phi_C\overset{*}{C} = \overset{*}{D_M} + (1 - \eta_M)\overset{*}{Pop}, \qquad (10.19)$$

and

$$(1 - \eta_C\phi_C)\overset{*}{C} - \eta_C\phi_A\overset{*}{A} - \epsilon_{CM}\overset{*}{P_M}$$
$$- \eta_C\phi_M\overset{*}{M} - \epsilon_C\overset{*}{P_C} = \overset{*}{D_C} + (1 - \eta_C)\overset{*}{Pop}, \qquad (10.20)$$

where the ϕ_j are initial final demand or sectoral output shares in GNP. The

---

[3] The expression for gross national product deflated by the agricultural *numéraire* price is $Y_A = A + P_M M + P_C C$. The national income concept more relevant for demand is gross national product deflated by a general consumer price index. We simplify slightly by assuming that foreign trade is initially in balance for each of the three sectors, so that the shares of the sectors in domestic absorption equal their shares in domestic production, defined as ϕ_i. Then $Y = Y_A$ divided by the GNP deflator $= (A + P_M M + P_C C)/(\phi_A + \phi_M P_M + \phi_C P_C)$. The rate of change in constant price gross national product is therefore

$$\overset{*}{Y} = \phi_A \overset{*}{A} + \phi_M(\overset{*}{P_M} + \overset{*}{M}) + \phi_C(\overset{*}{P_C} + \overset{*}{C}) - \phi_M\overset{*}{P_M} - \phi_C\overset{*}{P_C}$$
$$= \phi_A\overset{*}{A} + \phi_M\overset{*}{M} + \phi_C\overset{*}{C}.$$

This is the rate-of-change expression for the income term that is fed into Equations (10.19) and (10.20).

national budget constraint and these two demand equations make the demand equation for agriculture products redundant. It should be noted, however, that the budget constraint implicitly assumes that the nation's trade with the rest of the world is balanced, with no net international transfers or capital flows. The responsiveness of international trade flows in the three sectors to prices and domestic income is implicit in the assumed (relatively high) demand elasticities.

Finally, we shall assume the following income, own-price and cross-price elasticities:

$$\begin{array}{lll} & & \eta_M \quad \eta_C \\ & \text{with 1850 parameters} & 1.60 \quad 1.00 \\ \text{income elasticities} & & \\ & \text{with 1900 parameters} & 1.35 \quad 1.00 \end{array}$$

$$\text{own-price elasticities} \quad \begin{array}{l} \epsilon_M = -1.30 \\ \epsilon_C = -1.00 \end{array}$$

$$\text{cross-price elasticities} \quad \epsilon_{MC} = \epsilon_{CM} = 0.50.$$

The income elasticities have been chosen so as to be consistent with an income elasticity of demand for agricultural product of 0.50 for 1850 and 0.40 for 1900, values broadly consistent with a number of empirical studies.

Our system consists of nine rate-of-change equations—Equations (10.7) through (10.9), (10.14) through (10.17) after the substitutions explained in the text, and (10.19) and (10.20)—containing nine endogenous variables: the three output growth rates $\overset{*}{A}$, $\overset{*}{M}$, and $\overset{*}{C}$; the four factor price changes $\overset{*}{d}$, $\overset{*}{r}$, $\overset{*}{w}$, and $\overset{*}{q}$; and two product price changes $\overset{*}{P}_M$ and $\overset{*}{P}_C$. The exogenous variables are the rates of sectoral total factor productivity growth ($\overset{*}{T}_j$), the rates of factor-augmenting technological bias (Π_i), the factor supply growth rates, the population growth rate, and the demand shift terms.

The entire system of equations is summarized in Figure 10.1. Numerical values for elasticity parameters combined with observed initial conditions of factor and sector shares yield causal statements regarding the impact of each exogenous variable's measured historical growth rate on each endogenous variable's temporal behavior. Aggregating over each exogenous variable's impact yields overall model predictions about how factor prices, product prices, and outputs should have moved over time. Not all exogenous variables are easy to quantify, however. In what follows we first examine the predictions generated by the growth in quantifiable exogenous variables, and then ask what other forces might account for any residual growth in the endogenous variables of interest. Factor supply expansion, sectoral total factor productivity growth, and a technical adjustment for a demand effect of population growth[4] are easy to quantify. We may also wish to add separate conjectures about the possible magnitudes of product demand shifts ($\overset{*}{D}_M$, $\overset{*}{D}_C$), factor-saving biases *within* sectors, and the relevance of inflation and institutional changes. Some of the endogenous variables are also hard to quantify. In particular, we lack firm estimates of the rental on capital services before 1929, and sectoral relative product prices are also often difficult to measure. Other endogenous variables are more easily quantified. For example, our model accounts quite well for observed movements in aggregate GNP, sector outputs, and the real wage of unskilled labor. These side-results reinforce the credibility of the model's predictions on pay-ratio and inequality trends.

Explaining Trends in Wage Gaps before 1910

PERIODS AND PARAMETERS

If the general-equilibrium model is to be used to advantage, it should be applied over long periods, since the longer the time period the less objectionable are assumptions about full employment, competition, and equilibrium. One must also select periods for which data are available. For the years prior to World War I, this means leaning heavily on decennial census dates. If we are to have even rough estimates of factor supply, output growth, and total factor productivity growth by sector, our choice of periods is further restricted. Such documentation is unavailable for the years prior to 1839, a date almost halfway through the antebellum rise in the wage advantage of skilled labor. The Civil War decade must also be excluded, since the available estimates often are either antebellum or date

---

[4] This technical adjustment is the sum of two effects of population growth on demand. The first is tied to the growth of the labor force in a way that is of minor interest only. In relating product demands to income per man-hour of labor force, we tied them to a ratio of an endogenous variable (national income) to an exogenous variable (labor force size). The model has already incorporated the growth of total income into the demand equations, but this leaves a demographic term on the right-hand sides of Equations (10.19) and (10.20). To the extent that this demographic term reflects labor force growth, or $\overset{*}{L}$, it could just as easily have been added to the factor supply effects of $\overset{*}{L}$. The second effect is tied to the rise in dependents per man-hour of labor supply, or $\overset{*}{Pop} - \overset{*}{L}$, a rise that is equivalent to a reduction in income levels per man-hour.

The coefficient for the demand effects of population growth shown in text tables below has been calculated by the sum ($\overset{*}{D}_M$ coefficient) $(1 - \eta_M) + (\overset{*}{D}_C$ coefficient) $(1 - \eta_C)$, an expression that can be derived from Equations (10.19) and (10.20).

TABLE 10.2
Factor Proportions in Three Sectors of the U.S. Economy, 1850 and 1900

	Share of Factor *i* employed in Sector *j* (λ_{ij})					Share of Compensation for Factor *i* in Income Originating in Sector *j* (θ_{ij})				
					1850					
	i =						*i =*			
	J	*K*	*L*	*S*	All factors (ϕ_j)		*J*	*K*	*L*	*S*
A	1.0000	.1656	.5951	0	.4022	*A*	.1430	.1110	.7460	0	1.0000
j= M	0	.5241	.1871	.2095	.2710	*M*	0	.5216	.3479	.1305	1.0000
C	0	.3103	.2178	.7905	.3268	*C*	0	.2560	.3360	.4080	1.0000
	1.0000	1.0000	1.0000	1.0000	1.0000		.0575	.2697	.5041	.1687	1.0000

from 1869. This constraint is especially severe for estimates of sectoral total factor productivity growth.

Given these constraints, we shall focus on three periods: the last two antebellum decades, 1839–1859; the late nineteenth century, 1869–1899; and the start of the twentieth century, 1899–1909.[5] These were episodes of rising wage gaps, although the rise was far more dramatic in the first and third periods than in the late nineteenth century (Table 10.1). It would have been desirable to break the postbellum era at 1889 rather than at 1899 in order to give each later period a twenty-year span, but this was prevented by difficulties of calculating skills and total factor productivity growth.

To estimate the impact of any exogenous variable, the model needs to be equipped with factor- and sector-share parameters from benchmark dates. We have selected mid-century and turn-of-the-century benchmarks, 1850 and 1900,[6] in order to make best use of key data supplied by Gallman and others. Table 10.2 documents the sectoral patterns of factor use at these dates. There is a clear relationship between mobile factors and sectors for both years: unskilled labor tends to be concentrated relatively intensively in agriculture, capital in industry, and skills in the tertiary sector.[7] The contrast between the industrial and tertiary sectors is

---

[5] Before 1929, census ''dating'' actually refers variously to the census year and the year before. Thus in what follows we are actually examining the periods 1839/1840–1859/1860, 1869/1870–1899/1900, and 1899/1900–1909/1910 for exogenous variables, and 1840–1860, 1870–1900, and 1900–1910 for the wage gap trends.

[6] Strictly, these dates are 1849/1850 and 1899/1900.

[7] That is, $\lambda_{LA} > \lambda_{KA} > \lambda_{SA}$, $\lambda_{KM} > \lambda_{SM} > \lambda_{LM}$, and $\lambda_{SC} > \lambda_{KC} > \lambda_{LC}$.

TABLE 10.2 (continued)

	Share of Factor i employed in Sector j (λ_{ij})						Share of Compensation for Factor i in Income Originating in Sector j (θ_{ij})				
					1900						
			$i =$						$i =$		
	J	K	L	S	All factors (ϕ_j)		J	K	L	S	
A	1.0000	.0755	.3762	0	.2172	A	.1580	.1320	.7100	0	1.0000
$j= M$	0	.5002	.2807	.3811	.3721	M	0	.5104	.3092	.1804	1.0000
C	0	.4243	.3431	.6189	.4107	C	0	.3922	.3424	.2654	1.0000
	1.0000	1.0000	1.0000	1.0000	1.0000		.0343	.3797	.4099	.1761	1.0000

Sources and notes: All estimates are rougher and cruder than the twentieth-century counterparts presented in Chapter 11.

We began by accepting the Gallman (1966, p. 26) estimate of gross national product of $2.32 billion for 1849/1850, and the Kendrick (1961, p. 296) estimate of gross national product, commerce concept, of $18.68 billion for 1900.

The total income originating in agriculture was estimated not by the (more appropriate) value-added measure, but as gross farm output minus interest paid to nonfarmers, since we were constrained to follow Gallman's (1972, p. 205) use of this latter measure in dividing total farm sector incomes among the factors of production. Note that agriculture here means the farm sector, whereas it will refer to all production originating in agriculture, forestry, and fisheries in Chapter 11.

The next task was to estimate the income originating in the industrial sector consisting of mining, manufacturing, transportation, communications, and utilities. For mining and manufacturing we used the 1849 and 1899 value-added estimates reported by Gallman (1960, p. 43). For transportation, communications, and utilities, we had to resort, with misgivings, to the early estimates of W. I. King (1915, pp. 260–263). King again is the source for the calculation of the share of capital (property) in the industrial sector's value added, with capital here including returns to self-employment.

Employee compensation in the industrial sector is split between returns to skilled and unskilled labor by using the farm wage rate and man-hours in industry. The hourly farm wage rate is derived from splicing antebellum Lebergott daily wages without board and postbellum USDA daily wages without board onto the more recent USDA hourly rate without board that commences with 1929. Total man-hours in industry were derived by splicing Lebergott (1966, p. 118) estimates of persons gainfully employed in the mid-nineteenth century onto the Kendrick (1961, p. 314) estimates of sectoral man-hours from 1869 onwards. The product of the farm wage rate and man-hours is used as a measure of unskilled-labor compensation following the reasoning contained in Appendix J. The remainder of employee compensation in industry is the return to skills in that sector.

The value added in the tertiary (residual) sector is derived by subtracting value added in agriculture and industry from gross national product. Dividing this value-added into separate factor returns is not an easy task, given the data at hand. We calculated total nonagricultural labor compensation using different sources for the two dates. For 1850 we subtracted the Gallman estimate of agricultural labor incomes from the Davis et al. (1972) estimate of all labor incomes (as a share of the Gallman gross national product), which implicitly includes returns to self-employment as labor incomes. For 1900 our estimate of nonagricultural labor income was the sum of the Budd (1960, Tables 1, 2) nonagricultural labor income, including income from private self-employment, plus King's (1915, p. 138) figure for the value of government product (unlike King, we did not deduct property income in the government sector). We then subtracted industrial labor incomes from total nonagricultural labor incomes to get total labor compensation in the tertiary sector. The returns to unskilled labor in the tertiary sector were calculated by using the same sources and procedures as described for unskilled industrial labor above.

Our procedure can be no better than the underlying source estimates. One particular error is likely to have crept in: Discrepancies in the treatment of nonagricultural self-employment incomes are likely to have labeled some industrial skilled-labor incomes as capital, and to have labeled some tertiary returns to capital as returns to skills. We thus suspect that our estimates have overstated the skill-intensity for the tertiary sector and understated it for industry.

perhaps a bit overdrawn here, since we have used a procedure that probably gives the former a little too much capital at the expense of skills and the latter a little too much skilled labor at the expense of capital (as explained in the notes to Table 10.2). The contrast nonetheless appears valid, and the tertiary sector—with its teachers, lawyers, merchants, doctors, ministers, and government officials—appears to have been the most skill intensive.

THE ANTEBELLUM WIDENING

Equipped with its full set of parameters, the general-equilibrium model can "predict" a large part of the observed widening of the wage gap between skilled and unskilled workers before World War I. Let us look first at the last two antebellum decades, during which the wage advantage of skilled workers rose at the rate of 1.48% per annum. The model's predictions are shown in Table 10.3.

Both technological and factor supply changes contributed to the antebellum rise in wage inequality. The fact that technological progress was slower in labor-intensive agriculture than elsewhere seems to account for a widening of the gap by 0.26 per year, when all the various effects of differential productivity growth on relative factor demands have been taken into account. This confirms the intuition developed in Chapter 7, where we noted the correlation between periods in which productivity growth in agriculture lagged behind and periods in which the pay advantage of skills increased. But the details of the nonagricultural technological pattern offer some surprises. The coefficient on productivity growth in the industrial sector ($\hat{T}_M$) is close to zero and slightly negative,[8] contrary to Chapter 7's focus on industry as a sector whose productivity growth would favor skills. The reason appears to be that skills were no greater a share of income in the industrial sector than they were in the economy as

---

[8] The unit effects of $\hat{T}_A$, $\hat{T}_M$, and $\hat{T}_C$ on wage inequality are closer to zero than their reported coefficients imply. One must remember that any unit change in a sector productivity growth rate also affects the measures of factor bias, since each $\Pi_i = \Sigma_i \lambda_{ij} \hat{T}_j$. When the unit impact of each $\hat{T}_j$ is adjusted for these side-effects, the unit impacts of sectoral productivity growth rates turn out to be

	1850	*1900*
adjusted coefficient for $\hat{T}_A$	−0.1441	−0.4540
adjusted coefficient for $\hat{T}_M$	−0.0064	0.2592
adjusted coefficient for $\hat{T}_C$	0.3446	0.3428

In each case, the sign is the same as that shown for the direct coefficient in Table 10.3 or 10.4, but the absolute value is lower.

TABLE 10.3

Accounting for Changes in the Skilled-Labor Wage Premium ($*q - *w$), 1839–1909, Using 1850 Factor and Sector Shares (percentage per annum)

Exogenous Shift Term	Coefficient for ($*q - *w$)	1839–1859 Shift	1839–1859 Effect	1869–1899 Shift	1869–1899 Effect	1899–1909 Shift	1899–1909 Effect	Average, 3 Periods Shift	Average, 3 Periods Effect
$*T_A$	−0.7611	0%	0%	0.79%	−0.61%	−0.24%	0.18%	0.36%	−0.28%
$*T_M$	−0.1087	2.00	−0.22	1.70	−0.18	0.98	−0.11	1.68	−0.18
$*T_C$	0.8758	0.80	0.70	0.80	0.70	1.70	1.49	0.95	0.83
Π_J	−0.0215	0	0	0.79	−0.02	−0.24	0.01	0.36	−0.02
Π_K	0.2568	1.30	0.33	1.25	0.32	1.19	0.31	1.26	0.32
Π_L	1.0015	0.55	0.55	1.05	1.05	0.77	0.77	0.84	0.84
Π_S	−1.0487	1.05	−1.10	1.14	−1.20	1.43	−1.50	1.16	−1.22
All "technology" (total factor productivity growth) effects			0.26		0.06		1.15		0.31
$*J$	−0.0215	3.32	−0.07	2.44	−0.05	0.47	−0.01	2.41	−0.05
$*K$	0.2568	6.57	1.69	5.20	1.34	3.84	0.99	5.43	1.40
$*L$	1.0015	3.38	3.39	2.73	2.73	2.35	2.35	2.88	2.89
$*S$	−1.0487	3.38	−3.54	3.23	−3.39	2.92	−3.06	3.23	−3.39
All factor supply effects			1.47		0.63		0.27		0.85
Demand adjustment for population growth	3.09		−0.58	2.19	−0.41	1.92	−0.36	2.45	−0.46
Predicted			1.15		0.28		1.06		0.70
Actual			1.48		0.30		1.06		0.82

Note: All three-period averages are calculated across rows, and some totals differ from column sums owing to rounding.

a whole in 1850. This combined with our elasticity assumptions prevents any large net effect of industrial productivity growth on the antebellum advantage of skilled workers, though a role for antebellum industrial progress reappears when we examine its effects on capital accumulation in Chapter 12. As the estimates now stand, however, technological imbalance contributed to the antebellum rise in wage inequality primarily because the rate of technological progress was even lower in the agricultural sector than the estimated rate for the tertiary sector.

Factor supply growth played a greater role in accounting for the antebellum wage stretching than did the pattern of technological progress. An outstanding fact about the two decades before the Civil War was the extraordinarily high rate of capital accumulation. Taken as an exogenous force, this alone would explain the observed movement in wage rate inequality. The story of why wage rates became more unequal before the Civil War would have to include the tendency of rapid mechanization to shift labor demand toward more skilled groups, despite the attempts of several authors to mount an argument that mechanization in such industries as textiles had an overall effect of reducing relative demand for skills. If capital accumulation thus emerges as a central proximate explanation for the rise of wage inequality, more attention should be paid to the determinants of the high rate of accumulation and the acceleration of this trend over the early nineteenth century. We return to this task in Chapter 12.

Other factor supplies appear to have had less potent effects when 1839–1859 is compared with growth experience in the pre-1839 period. The model tells us that the rapid expansion of farmland had no significant role in leveling wage rates, even though the model has assumed that expanding the farm sector would draw off only unskilled, and not skilled, labor.[9] The growth of skills and of unskilled labor actually had a combined negative net effect, since the inegalitarian consequences that followed from the slightly rising labor supply growth between the pre-1839 and post-1839 periods was more than offset by the matching growth of skills and the tendency of the rapid population growth to shift demand back

[9] The 1850 model implies that expanding the supply of farmland by even 1% per annum would have had only a trivial tendency (0.0163% a year) to raise the wage rate for common labor relative to the return on capital. The only noteworthy effect of expanding the supply of farmland, according to the model, is to depress the rents earned on that land itself. This result is not surprising, since the present 1850 model has assumed a Cobb–Douglas production function within the agricultural sector. Alternative models with elasticities of substitution of one-half within agriculture imply that expanding the supply of farmland does improve the position of unskilled labor relative to skills and capital, but still only slightly so. The Turner thesis has only a marginal role to play in accounting for American inequality trends.

toward skills-sparing agriculture. A more positive role for labor supply reappears to some extent, however, when its possible influence on capital accumulation is considered in Chapter 12.

The influences captured by the 1850 model account for over three-quarters of the observed wage stretching (1.15% out of 1.48%). This is a noteworthy performance, in view of the low quality of the underlying data fed into the model and the wage gap series it attempts to explain.

THE LATE NINETEENTH CENTURY

To analyze the last three decades of the nineteenth century, we should use parameter values drawn from the post–Civil War period. Given the estimates of factor and sector shares for 1850 and 1900, one should consult both models for insights into this period of substantial change. Table 10.4 and Figure 10.2 give the 1900-based results that are to be compared with those based on 1850 parameters. While the 1850-based predictions fit neatly the late-nineteenth-century experience—indeed, they fit neatly into American experience until World War II—the 1900-based predictions seriously overestimate the extent of wage gap widening in the late nineteenth century. Such inaccuracy is not surprising given the quality of the underlying data, but both models agree on the contrast between the late nineteenth century and the two mid-century decades. Both supply approximately the same explanations for the deceleration in the wage advantage of the more skilled.

All of the forces mentioned in connection with the antebellum episode played a part in keeping the wage inequality from worsening as fast after the Civil War as before. The pattern of technological progress became more balanced. The estimates of Gallman and Kendrick show that agricultural productivity growth advanced in this period, erasing any clear bias toward the use of skills over common labor. Capital accumulation also slowed down, again reducing the tendency of factor demand to shift toward skills. The trend toward wage inequality was also retarded because the labor force and population were growing at a slower rate. The growth of skills slowed down much less than the growth of the labor force and population, tipping the scales more toward an abundance of skills and helping to check a continuation of wage stretching. The contrast between the two nineteenth-century periods thus assigns important roles to three forces: a shift toward more balanced productivity growth, slower capital accumulation, and a further rise in skills per man-hour.

The importance of exogenous technology and factor supply "shocks" in producing a retardation in late-nineteenth-century inequality trends cannot be overdrawn. Indeed, it should be pointed out that inequality in

TABLE 10.4

Accounting for Changes in the Skilled-Labor Wage Premium $(q^* - w^*)$, 1839–1909, Using 1900 Factor and Sector Shares (percentage per annum)

Exogenous Shift Term	Coefficient for $(q^* - w^*)$	1839–1859		1869–1899		1899–1909		Average, 3 Periods	
		Shift	Effect	Shift	Effect	Shift	Effect	Shift	Effect
$\dot{T}_A$	−0.7557	0%	0%	0.79%	−0.60%	−0.24%	0.18%	0.36%	−0.27%
$\dot{T}_M$	0.2070	2.00	0.41	1.70	0.35	0.98	0.20	1.68	0.35
$\dot{T}_C$	0.5451	0.80	0.44	0.80	0.44	1.70	0.93	0.95	0.52
Π_J	−0.0677	0	0	0.79	−0.05	−0.24	0.02	0.36	−0.02
Π_K	2.5190	1.30	0.67	1.25	0.65	1.19	0.62	1.26	0.65
Π_L	0.8776	0.55	0.48	1.05	0.92	0.77	0.68	0.84	0.73
Π_S	−1.1691	1.05	−1.23	1.14	−1.33	1.43	−1.67	1.16	−1.35
All "technology" (total factor productivity growth) effects			0.77		0.38		0.96		0.61
$\dot{J}$	−0.0677	3.32	−0.22	2.44	−0.17	0.47	−0.03	2.41	−0.16
$\dot{K}$	0.5190	6.57	3.41	5.20	2.70	3.84	1.99	5.43	2.82
$\dot{L}$	0.8776	3.38	2.97	2.73	2.40	2.35	2.06	2.88	2.53
$\dot{S}$	−1.1691	3.38	−3.95	3.23	−3.78	2.92	−3.41	3.23	−3.69
All factor supply effects			2.21		1.15		0.61		1.32
Demand adjustment for population growth		3.09	−0.49	2.19	−0.35	1.92	−0.30	2.45	−0.39
Predicted $(q^* - w^*)$			2.49		1.18		1.27		1.63
Actual $(q^* - w^*)$			1.48		0.30		1.06		0.82

Note: All three-period averages are calculated across rows, and some totals differ from column sums owing to rounding.

Rate of Increase in
Wage Premium for Skilled
Labor, % per Annum

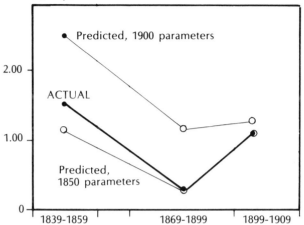

FIGURE 10.2. Predicted and actual changes in the wage premium for skilled labor, 1839–1909.

the American economy became *increasingly sensitive* to those forces as the century progressed. That is, the exogenous forces which prevailed 1839–1859 would have produced a far more drastic inequality trend based on the 1900 structure of the economy than based on its 1850 structure (+1.15 in Table 10.3 versus +2.49 in Table 10.4). Similarly, the impact of exogenous forces in producing relative inequality quiescence 1869–1899 would have been far more pronounced based on the 1900 structure of the economy than based on its 1850 structure (+0.28 in Table 10.3 versus +1.18 in Table 10.4). It appears, therefore, that nineteenth-century American inequality was becoming increasingly sensitive to exogenous shocks, owing to the combined forces of changing sectoral factor intensity differentials and the sheer relative size of sectors. Thus, as the economy entered the twentieth century it was ripe for further dramatic inequality change even if the extraordinary antebellum exogenous forces had failed to reappear with quite the same strength.

THE START OF THE TWENTIETH CENTURY

The final prewar period of our pre–World War I wage structure analysis is the first decade of the present century. Ten years may well be too short a time for testing the explanatory power of a long-run general-equilibrium model. As it happens, however, the model seems to explain what happened rather well.

The reappearance of a strong trend toward earnings inequality seems to have a clearer explanation than the previous, late-nineteenth-century deceleration of the inequality trend. Changes in factor supply growth rates cannot explain why the skilled began once again to pull ahead of the unskilled in the first decade of this century.[10] The capital stock grew more slowly than before the turn of the century, providing less support for skills. The rate of labor force growth also tapered off, matched by deceleration in skills and population. While the high tide of immigration of low-skilled workers from southern and eastern Europe may have accelerated labor quantity growth and decelerated labor "quality" growth, as hypothesized in Chapter 9, these labor supply forces were apparently offset by acceleration in indigenous skills growth. The farmland frontier began to close up sharply in this period, but the model again assigns almost no importance to this change in explaining wage inequality trends. What we know about factor supply growth turns out to play a minor role in explaining the resurgence of wage rate inequality at the start of this century.

The model clearly points to changes in the pattern of technological progress as the explanation of the resurgence. Agricultural total factor productivity actually declined, according to the Kendrick estimates, a development that should have undercut the growth in demand for common labor. Kendrick's figures further imply faster productivity growth in the rest of the economy, with productivity growth in the tertiary sector now hitting its fastest rate ever. The model tells (Table 10.4) that this acceleration of productivity in the skill-intensive tertiary sector explains why teachers, mechanics, carpenters, and other skilled groups enjoyed rising wage advantages in the first decade of this century.

Although the model's stress on technological imbalance corresponds with one of our intuitions about the early twentieth century, we must note that the locus of this imbalance may be misrepresented by the available estimates. Kendrick's figure of 1.7% per annum as the growth rate for the tertiary sector is well above his figure for the national economy over the same decade (1.1%). It is hard to see where the rapid productivity growth should have occurred within the tertiary sector consisting of construction, trade, finance, real estate, insurance, private services, and government. Perhaps the estimated tertiary productivity growth should be scaled down considerably, thereby cutting the predicted wage inequality trend.

---

[10] The period in which the pay advantage of skilled workers is rising is, more precisely, 1888–1914, 1892–1914, or 1896–1914, depending on which local trough one chooses as a starting point.

At the same time, two other aspects of productivity imbalance in the first decade of this century would tend to raise its importance. First, there is a noticeable correlation between skill-intensity and productivity growth rates across subsectors within industry. Productivity advanced relatively slowly in the less skill-intensive mining and manufacturing sectors, but rose rapidly in new skill-intensive fields such as telephones, electric utilities, and natural gas (Kendrick, 1961, pp. 136, 137). Had the data permitted a more disaggregated model capable of giving this point its due, technological progress would probably have had about as much influence as it is now given in Tables 10.3 and 10.4. Second, it must be remembered that faster technological progress in capital-intensive and capital-producing industries, as apparently happened then, is likely to induce extra capital formation. Some of the skills-favoring effect of capital formation in this period (and probably also in the nineteenth century) should be chalked up to technological imbalance.

For the entire period before World War I, then, the model seems quite capable of explaining why wage stretching occurred. Relative to a pre-1839 world of comparable growth in labor supply and skills, the leading explanatory factors were capital accumulation and technological imbalance, especially the former. The labor supply story sketched in Chapter 9 seems to have played a minor role. The labor supply role becomes greater when the pre–World War I period is contrasted with subsequent twentieth-century experience, and both labor supply and technological imbalance figure importantly when the determinants of capital accumulation are examined in Chapter 12.

11

EXPLAINING TWENTIETH-CENTURY
DISTRIBUTION TRENDS

Twentieth-century distribution experience, like that of the last century, can be better understood with the aid of a macroeconomic model. Yet the trends requiring explanation are somewhat different from those analyzed in Chapter 10.

The Task

The main distributional event in this century was, of course, the "income revolution" documented in Part One. We now know that the decline in aggregate income inequality in the second quarter of this century was due in large part to a compression in pay rates. The earnings of janitors, domestic servants, farmhands, and other low-skilled groups advanced relative to the earnings enjoyed by skilled workers and professionals. The central task is not only to explain why this happened, but also to explain why the leveling was restricted to the period between 1929 and mid-century.

The difficulty of the task is evident once we have repeated an exercise performed in Chapter 10 for the nineteenth century. Consider a simple aggregate explanation of the income leveling. Suppose we tried to account for the decline in the pretax earnings advantage of the more skilled by appeal solely to the relative expansion in skilled- and unskilled-labor supplies. Table 11.1 shows that (technologically augmented) skilled-labor supplies have grown more rapidly than unskilled-labor supplies since 1909, the first date for which we have Denison's direct measure of labor force quality. Other things equal, this faster growth in skills should have depressed the relative pay of skilled workers and professionals especially

TABLE 11.1
Comparing Rates of Change in the Nonfarm Skilled-Labor Wage Ratio with Rates of Growth in Skilled and Unskilled Labor, 1909–1973 *(percentage per annum)*

	1909–1929	1929–1948	1948–1966	1966–1973
(1) Rate of change in the nonfarm wage ratio of skilled to unskilled labor	−0.09%	−1.99%	+0.38%	−0.21%
(2) Growth in unskilled man-hours (total labor force) ($\overset{*}{L}$)	1.62	0.32	0.45	0.87
(3) Augmentation in supply of unskilled labor implied by neutral sectoral rates of productivity growth (Π_L)	1.06	2.01	1.36	1.48
(4) Growth in hours of skills ($\overset{*}{S}$)	2.58	1.82	1.43	1.75
(5) Augmentation in supply of skills implied by neutral sectoral rates of productivity growth (Π_S)	1.32	2.01	1.47	1.59
(6) Relative rise in augmented unskilled-labor supply ($\overset{*}{L} + \Pi_L - \overset{*}{S} - \Pi_S$)	−1.22	−1.50	−1.09	−0.99

Sources and notes: Row (1), for 1909–1966, the occupational ratios used are those from Series (5) and (6) in Appendix D, with one adjustment. We found that the lone NICB observation for 1948 seems to understate the decline in the pay advantage of skills since the last prewar NICB observation, that for 1939. The NICB 1948 ratio is based on rates of pay that are implausibly higher than unskilled labor's wage rate (for custodians) and, especially, the skilled-labor wage rates of mechanics, electricians, and carpenters in six major cities in 1950/1951. Furthermore, the lone 1948 figure is a poor reflection of what happened to a broader fixed-employment-weighted measure of the pay advantage of all professionals and skilled workers. This can be seen by contrasting the NICB rate of decline in the skill premium of only −0.76% per annum for 1929–1948 with the following rates of change in the percentage pay premia over the wages of 2000 hours of unskilled labor between 1929 and 1948:

	(percentage per annum)
Wage rate premia of skilled workers (1929–1950/1951)	−1.99%
Median 12-month salary, engineers (1929–1946)	−3.43
Median 9-month salary, associate professors	−3.28
Average 9-month salary, college teachers	−5.20
Average annual net income, nonsalaried lawyers	−3.36
Average annual net income, nonsalaried dentists	−2.65
Average annual net income, nonsalaried physicians	−0.06

In view of these ratios, the 1929–1950/1951 drop in the skilled-labor wage premium of 1.99% per annum seems a better reflection of the overall trend in pay differentials than the lesser drop implied by the 1929 and 1948 NICB figures (*Historical Statistics,* 1975, Part 1, pp. 175, 176; Appendix D).

For the period 1966–1973, the simple wage premia for skilled labor estimated earlier in Chapter 4 from BLS occupational wage survey data seem inadequate for the task. This is partly because this series had a local peak around 1973, from which it had dropped considerably by 1975, but a more serious problem is in the periods 1929–1948 and 1966–1973. Yet this simple two-factor reasoning fails to explain why the pay ratio was steady or rising for the two decades before 1929 and after 1948. It also fails to explain why the earnings structure has not compressed nearly so dramatically in the period 1966–1973 as in the period 1929–1948, since both periods saw comparable rates of growth in skills per man-hour. A more complicated model is needed to account for the behavior of pay ratios since 1909.

New Parameters

The same basic model that illuminated prewar trends also helps out with more recent trends, once it is outfitted with more up-to-date assumptions and parameters. First, as a convenience, we drop farmland from the model, aggregating its returns and its growth into the capital category. This is justified by the fact that even in the nineteenth century, when unimproved farmland was still growing at a considerable rate, its rate of growth failed to have a significant impact on wage inequality outside of agriculture. By dropping farmland we save an equation and an endogenous variable.

Second, our assumptions about demand elasticities need to be altered from those used for the prewar era. The continuing decline of the agricultural sector means that lower income elasticities and lower (absolute) price elasticities have to be assumed for the industrial and tertiary sectors, which now add up to almost the entire economy. At the same time, T. W. Schultz and others have noted an apparent decline in the underlying income elasticity of demand for foodstuffs over time, a trend that must be

---

that by the 1970s the skilled group, consisting of mechanics, electricians, and carpenters, is at best a dim reflection of the large numbers of white-collar professionals. A better measure is possible, thanks to the work of Sheldon Danziger and Robert Plotnick (1977) using computer tapes of the 1965 and 1974 Current Population Surveys of consumer income. Danziger and Plotnick held constant the weights of a dozen demographic groups, in order to keep shifts between these groups (defined by age and sex of household head and household type) from affecting the measure of income inequality. From the underlying distributions generously supplied by Sheldon Danziger, we have computed the percentage change in the pay advantage of the fourth quintile over the second, roughly the skilled and professionals over the working unskilled. This rate of change is the -0.21% shown here.

Row (2), growth in man-hours of the civilian labor force of the national economy, is from Kendrick (1961, p. 314 for 1909–1948; 1973, p. 227 for 1948–1966) and the July 1976 *Survey of Current Business* (p. 53, for 1973).

Rows (3) and (5) are from Table 7.9.

Row (4), growth in total skills in the nonresidential sector, is from Denison (1974, p. 32). The "1966–1973" figure is for 1966–1969 only. As explained in footnote 4 to Chapter 9, we have transformed Denison's measure slightly to make it consistent with the way in which skills have been measured throughout most of this book.

TABLE 11.2
Factor Proportions in Three Sectors of the U.S. Economy, 1929, 1963, and 1976

Share of Factor i Employed in Sector j (λ_{ij})				Share of Compensation for Factor i in Income Originating in Sector j (θ_{ij})			
			1929				
$i =$				$i =$			
K	L	S	All factors (ϕ_j)	K	L	S	
A	.2684	.2260	0	.1202	A	.5977	.4023	0	1.0000
$j = M$	.3575	.3194	.3751	.3584	M	.2669	.1906	.5425	1.0000
C	.3741	.4546	.6249	.5214	C	.1920	.1866	.6214	1.0000
	1.0000	1.0000	1.0000	1.0000		.2676	.2140	.5184	1.0000

			1963				
$i =$				$i =$			
K	L	S	All factors (ϕ_j)	K	L	S	
A	.0932	.0807	0	.0388	A	.4980	.5020	0	1.0000
$j = M$	.3978	.2806	.3718	.3551	M	.2324	.1909	.5767	1.0000
C	.5090	.6387	.6282	.6061	C	.1742	.2546	.5712	1.0000
	1.0000	1.0000	1.0000	1.0000		.2075	.2416	.5509	1.0000

reflected in elasticities of demand for industrial and tertiary products. These considerations lead to the following assumed elasticities:[1] cross-price elasticities are everywhere $\epsilon_{MC} = \epsilon_{CM} = 0.5$ and

	Income Elasticities		Own-Price Elasticities	
	η_M	η_C	ϵ_M	ϵ_C
with 1929 parameters	1.30	1.00	-1.30	-1.00
with 1963 parameters	1.03	1.03	-1.25	-0.30
with 1976 parameters	1.02	1.02	-1.25	-0.25

We retain the three-sector division of the economy, although slight changes in sectoral definitions have been introduced. With the better twentieth-century data base, we can scan across a dozen major sectors of

---

[1] While "reasonable stylized facts," these assumptions are arbitrary. They also imply "reasonable" elasticities for the agricultural sector. For example, the reported income elasticities were selected to imply $\eta_A = 0.20$ for all dates—a reasonable value, to judge from the extensive literature on consumer demand testing Engel's Law.

TABLE 11.2 (continued)

	Share of Factor i Employed in Sector j (λ_{ij})				Share of Compensation for Factor i in Income Originating in Sector j (θ_{ij})			
	$i =$			*1976*	$i =$			
	K	L	S	All factors (ϕ_j)	K	L	S	
A	.0667	.0476	0	.0294	.4258	.5742	0	1.0000
$j = M$	.3838	.2532	.3425	.3186	.2266	.2823	.4911	1.0000
C	.5495	.6992	.6575	.6520	.1585	.3808	.4607	1.0000
	1.0000	1.0000	1.0000	1.0000	.1881	.3551	.4568	1.0000

Sources and notes: The factor and sector shares were computed from matrices of the dollar values of gross product originating and of factor compensations within each sector. First, unskilled-labor compensation was estimated by multiplying total employment by the wage rate for farm labor. The remainder of total labor compensation, sometimes including imputations for the self-employed (see below), was attributed to skills. Property compensation, or the return to conventional capital, was treated as a residual.

For 1929 (Kuznets, 1941), income originating is net of capital consumption allowances. Labor compensation consists of employee compensation only. For further details, see Williamson (1974e, Table A-2).

For 1963 the main source is U.S. Department of Commerce (1966). In this case it was possible to use man-hours rather than persons as part of the measure of labor inputs. The work year for farm operators and workers was assumed to average 2250 hours (Denison, 1974, p. 182, and various issues of the *Survey of Current Business*). For nonfarm sectors the work year was estimated using figures from Kendrick (1974, p. 227 and appendices) and various issues of the *Survey of Current Business*. With man-hours estimated, total labor compensation per man-hour was calculated for each sector. This rate of pay was then applied to all persons engaged in production; thus attributing unskilled and skilled labor to the self-employed in the same proportions as characterized employees in the same sector. This procedure was repeated for each of the twelve sectors which aggregate into the three used in our model.

For 1976 the source is *Survey of Current Business* (July 1977). The procedure is the same as for 1963, described above.

the economy looking for clusters of sectors with similar factor proportions. The national income and product accounts show that the transportation sector has emerged with a much lower capital-intensity than have other industrial sectors. Thus we now define the industrial (M) sector as consisting of mining, manufacturing, communications, and utilities. The tertiary (C) sector includes construction, transportation, trade, finance,[2] private services, and government.

It is wise to use parameters that are as contemporary as possible with the events one is trying to explain. Table 11.2 reveals a subtle and

---

[2] In all that follows finance has been included in the tertiary (C) sector despite its having factor proportions more like those of the M sector. This decision was necessitated by the fact that total factor productivity is very hard to measure for finance, but it is likely to have proceeded at rates characteristic of the tertiary sector. We felt it safer to calculate rates of total factor productivity growth that lumped finance into the residual category, even at the cost of slightly blurring the intersectoral contrast in factor proportions.

important evolution in factor proportions across the twentieth century. In 1929 the tertiary sector still maintained its high skill-intensity, in contrast to the relatively heavier reliance on both capital and unskilled labor in agriculture and industry. After World War II the picture is different: It is now the industrial sector that has the highest ratio of skilled to unskilled labor. As we shall see, this alters the likely effects of the expansion of productivity or demand in different sectors on the relative pay positions of skilled and unskilled labor, tying the advantage of skilled workers more to the relative expansion of industry than to tertiary activities.

Explaining Twentieth-Century Trends in Pay Ratios

To repeat, a general-equilibrium model is most likely to be relevant if physical output and relative price behavior are examined over long periods. Within this century, there have been three periods of about twenty years each over which we can examine movements in the wage premium for skilled labor ($\overset{*}{q} - \overset{*}{w}$) between initial and final years of nearly full employment. The first stretches from the census of 1909 to the census of 1929, on the eve of the great crash. The second extends from 1929 across the abyss of depression and war to the first postwar peak of 1948. The final period extends from 1948 to 1966, when the resumption of full employment was just beginning to yield to the Vietnam wave of inflation. The years since 1966 have been complicated by inflation, rising unemployment, and a bout of wage and price controls under Nixon. For our purposes, the best terminal year is 1973, when unemployment was lower than it was about to become in the wake of the victory of the Organization of Petroleum Exporting Countries (OPEC). These periods, three long and one short, suffice to reveal the explanatory power of the model just presented.

BEFORE THE CRASH, 1909–1929

The two decades ending in the Wall Street crash were tumultuous enough to distress farmers and fool a large number of investors. The main disruption, of course, was World War I. Yet by 1929 prices had been stable and employment fairly full for some time—and the ratio of skilled-labor wage rates to unskilled had returned to its prewar level.

The model presented here explains this stability in pay ratios easily enough. To understand the period 1909–1929 it helps to use the model with the most contemporary parameters, the 1929 model, whose results are shown in Table 11.3 and Figure 11.1. The predicted and actual pay

TABLE 11.3

Accounting for Changes in the Skilled-Labor Wage Premium ($\overset{*}{q} - \overset{*}{w}$), 1909–1973, Using 1929 Factor and Sector Shares (percentage per annum)

Exogenous Shift Term	Coefficient for ($\overset{*}{q} - \overset{*}{w}$)	1909–1973		1909–1929		1929–1966		1929–1948		1948–1966		1966–1973	
		Shift	Effect	Shift	Effect	Shift	Effect	Shift	Effect	Shift	Effect	Shift	Effect
$\overset{*}{T}_A$	−0.7446	1.13%	−0.84%	0.02%	−0.01%	1.78%	−1.33%	2.06%	−1.53%	1.44%	−1.07%	1.02%	−0.76%
$\overset{*}{T}_M$	0.2558	2.13	0.54	2.44	0.62	1.88	0.48	1.45	0.37	2.35	0.60	2.51	0.64
$\overset{*}{T}_C$	0.4888	1.09	0.53	0.84	0.41	1.19	0.58	1.58	0.77	0.77	0.38	1.29	0.63
Π_K	−0.1564	1.52	−0.24	1.26	−0.20	1.70	−0.27	2.25	−0.35	1.12	−0.18	1.28	−0.20
Π_L	0.9020	1.47	1.33	1.06	0.96	1.69	1.52	2.01	1.81	1.36	1.23	1.48	1.33
Π_S	−0.6026	1.60	−0.96	1.32	−0.80	1.75	−1.05	2.01	−1.21	1.47	−0.89	1.59	−0.96
All "technology" (total factor productivity growth) effects			0.36		0.98		−0.04		−0.14		0.07		0.68
$\overset{*}{K}$	−0.1564	2.42	−0.38	3.16	−0.49	1.92	−0.30	0.93	−0.15	2.98	−0.47	2.92	−0.46
$\overset{*}{L}$	0.9020	0.82	0.74	1.62	1.46	0.39	0.35	0.32	0.29	0.45	0.41	0.87	0.78
$\overset{*}{S}$	−0.6026	1.94	−1.17	2.58	−1.55	1.63	−0.98	1.82	−1.10	1.43	−0.86	1.75[a]	−1.05
All factor supply effects			−0.80		−0.58		−0.94		−0.96		−0.92		−0.73
Demand adjustment of population growth	−0.1430	1.32	−0.18	1.50	−0.21	1.28	−0.18	0.96	−0.14	1.63	−0.23	0.98	−0.14
Predicted ($\overset{*}{q} - \overset{*}{w}$)			−0.62		0.19		−1.16		−1.24		−1.08		−0.19
Actual ($\overset{*}{q} - \overset{*}{w}$)			−0.54		−0.09		−0.85		−1.99		0.35		−0.21

Note: Figures for 1909–1973 and 1929–1966 are weighted row averages, and totals may not equal column sums owing to rounding.

[a] 1966–1969 nonresidential sector only.

Rate of Change in Wage Premium
for Skilled Labor, % per Annum

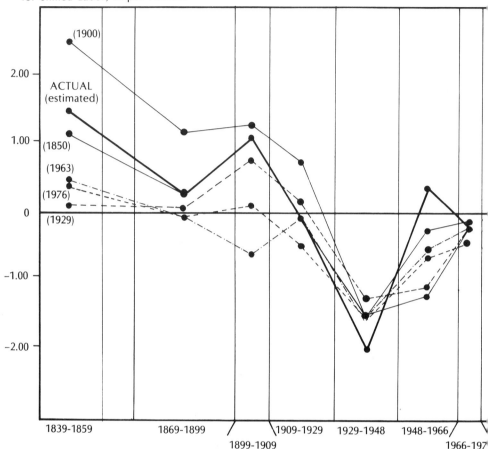

FIGURE 11.1. Actual (estimated) and predicted (based on parameters from various dates) changes in the wage premium for skilled labor since 1839.

ratio trends nearly coincide, and the model offers an explanation for their relative stability. In spite of the rapid growth in immigrant-augmented unskilled labor, stressed in the conventional literature, the pay advantage of the skilled would have *declined* if only factor supplies had mattered. The relatively fast growth of skills compared with conventional capital and unskilled labor would have served to depress skill premia by 0.58% a year between 1909 and 1929. This tendency toward leveling in pay ratios also received strong reinforcement from the demand effects of population growth. Why, then, does the "income revolution" fail to occur until after

1929? The answer appears to lie with unbalanced technological progress before 1929. Sectoral technological progress was such as to raise the skilled-labor wage premium by 0.98% a year. This upward pressure on pay ratios resulted from the fact that technological progress was comparatively rapid in the industrial (M) sector, raising the relative demand for more skilled labor both through this sector's high skill-intensity and through the tendency of the accompanying income growth to favor demand for capital- and skill-intensive nonfarm products. The pre-1929 stability in pay ratios, and in other measures of income inequality, no longer seems puzzling. Furthermore, exogenous shifts in demand and nonneutral technical progress within sectors are not required to rationalize any residual in pay ratio movements, since the model appears to predict historical trends quite accurately without appeal to such nonquantifiable exogenous influences.

THE LEVELING AND ITS END, 1929–1966

The leveling that occurred between 1929 and mid-century was not undone across the postwar era. The observed movements and those predicted by the model seem to match for the whole period 1929–1966. The observed net decline in the wage premium for skilled labor was 0.85% per year. Tables 11.3 and 11.4 show that the model predicts a decline of 1.16% per year with the 1929 parameters, and a decline of 1.03% per year with 1963 parameters.

The models depart from the observed movements, however, when it comes to the division of this overall historic change into the periods before and after 1948. Although the model *does* predict the massive leveling after 1929, it underpredicts the extent of the leveling before 1948. The model makes the opposite error for the postwar period, predicting a slow further decline in earnings dispersion when the wage rate ratios seem to have shown a slow rise between 1948 and 1966. This pattern of offsetting errors may have a straightforward explanation. In 1948, pay ratios were depressed by short-run inflation more than had been predicted by long-run demand and supply considerations, in clear contrast to the price stability of the late 1920s and the mid-1960s. The early postwar inflation may therefore have had some of the effect usually attributed to unanticipated inflation, allowing the shorter-contract wage rates for unskilled labor to jump faster than the more institutionalized wage and salary rates for the better-paid. Of course, it might also be argued that the rise in government served to shift demand in a direction that favored the unskilled. We shall argue below that this influence could not have been great, however. A stronger argument can be made that the sharp post-1929

TABLE 11.4

Accounting for Changes in the Skilled-Labor Wage Premium ($\overset{*}{q} - \overset{*}{w}$), 1909–1973, Using 1963 Factor and Sector Shares (percentage per annum)

Exogenous Shift Term	Coefficient for ($\overset{*}{q} - \overset{*}{w}$)	1909–1973 Shift	1909–1973 Effect	1909–1929 Shift	1909–1929 Effect	1929–1966 Shift	1929–1966 Effect	1929–1948 Shift	1929–1948 Effect	1948–1966 Shift	1948–1966 Effect	1966–1973 Shift	1966–1973 Effect
$\overset{*}{T_A}$	−0.3544	1.13%	−0.40%	0.02%	−0.01%	1.78%	−0.63%	2.06%	−0.73%	1.44%	−0.51%	1.02%	−0.36%
$\overset{*}{T_M}$	0.3904	2.13	0.83	2.44	0.95	1.88	0.73	1.45	0.57	2.35	0.92	2.51	0.98
$\overset{*}{T_C}$	−0.0358	1.09	−0.04	0.84	−0.03	1.19	−0.04	1.58	−0.06	0.77	−0.03	1.29	−0.05
Π_K	0.0360	1.52	0.05	1.26	0.05	1.70	0.06	2.25	0.08	1.12	0.04	1.28	0.05
Π_L	0.9479	1.47	1.39	1.06	1.00	1.69	1.60	2.01	1.91	1.36	1.29	1.48	1.40
Π_S	−0.9240	1.60	−1.48	1.32	−1.22	1.75	−1.62	2.01	−1.86	1.47	−1.36	1.59	−1.47
All "technology" (total factor productivity growth) effects			0.36		0.74		0.12		−0.09		0.35		0.55
$\overset{*}{K}$	0.0360	2.42	0.09	3.16	0.11	1.92	0.07	0.93	0.03	2.98	0.11	2.92	0.11
$\overset{*}{L}$	−0.9479	0.82	0.78	1.62	1.54	0.39	0.37	0.32	0.30	0.45	0.43	0.87	0.82
$\overset{*}{S}$	−0.9240	1.94	−1.79	2.58	−2.38	1.63	−1.51	1.82	−1.68	1.43	−1.32	1.75[a]	−1.62
All factor supply effects			−0.92		−0.73		−1.07		−1.35		−0.78		−0.69
Demand adjustment for population growth	−0.0599	1.32	−0.08	1.50	−0.09	1.28	−0.08	0.96	−0.06	1.63	−0.10	0.98	−0.06
Predicted ($\overset{*}{q} - \overset{*}{w}$)			−0.64		−0.08		−1.03		−1.50		−0.53		−0.20
Actual ($\overset{*}{q} - \overset{*}{w}$)			−0.54		−0.09		−0.85		−1.99		0.35		−0.21

Note: Figures for 1909–1973 and 1929–1966 are weighted row averages, and totals may not equal column sums owing to rounding.

[a] 1966–1969 nonresidential sector only.

deceleration in capital stock growth caused an accommodating short-run relative contraction in capital goods production and thus, based on the factor intensities reported in Chapter 8, a relative contraction in skill demands. Thus, we interpret the sharp reduction in occupational wage gaps to 1948 as the result of both long-run and short-run forces, the former more important than the latter. If we are right, the *predicted* changes for 1929–1948 and 1948–1966 themselves show roughly how pay relationships would have evolved over the entire period 1929–1966 had not postwar price acceleration made the leveling go further and stop sooner than it would have under price stability.

The model (using either 1929 or 1963 parameters) supplies detailed explanations for the leveling to have started after 1929, and for its cessation at or after mid-century. The leveling era ushered in a pattern of technological change and factor supply growth that had not been experienced for at least a century. No longer was technological advance biased in favor of the more skill- and capital-using industries. Thanks in large part to the revolutionary switch to hybrid seed varieties, increased use of synthetic fertilizers, and mechanization, total factor productivity improved as rapidly (or more rapidly) in agriculture as in the rest of the economy. Service activities underwent an acceleration in total factor productivity as well. The results in Tables 11.3 and 11.4 make it clear that this epochal shift alone accounted for about half of the observed shift toward a more egalitarian earnings trend from the period 1909–1929 to 1929–1948. It would be hard to explain the onset of the leveling without some reference to this change in the pattern of productivity growth.

Demographic changes also accounted for something like 30% of the observed shift toward leveling, as one can confirm by examining the entries for labor supply, skills supply, and population growth for 1909–1929 and 1929–1948. The leveling took place when it did partly because Americans were having fewer babies per family, because they slammed the door on most would-be immigrants, and because their mode of accumulation shifted from physical capital to human capital. The model's accounting thus agrees with our speculation (Chap. 9) that causation lay behind the correlation between changes in skill premia and changes in labor force growth. This interpretation hinges on our belief that faster growth of man-hours means slower growth of skills per man-hour. If it did not, then the reduction in the rate of growth of the labor force ($\overset{*}{L}$) would be matched by an equal reduction in the rate of growth of skills ($\overset{*}{S}$), leaving virtually no net impact on ratios of skilled to unskilled wages. Yet we feel that a drop in $\overset{*}{L}$ due to declining fertility a generation earlier or due to contemporaneous cuts in immigration from poorer countries diminished $\overset{*}{S}$ far less, leaving a sizable net leveling effect in labor markets.

It is also interesting to note that the significant swings in the rate of capital accumulation are given much less importance here than in the nineteenth century. The present models assign to capital accumulation coefficients that are near zero or, in the case of the 1929 model, a bit negative. The reason for this appears to lie in the evolution of factor proportions in different sectors. If our estimates are correct, the nineteenth-century association of capital with skills in the more modern sectors has broken up in this century. According to Table 11.2 above, capital had, by 1929, shifted away from its earlier degree of concentration in the skill-intensive tertiary sector, in part because the capital-intensity of agriculture began to approach that of the economy as a whole. This tendency has continued, though the decline in agriculture's share of the national economy has reduced the importance of its factor proportions. The upshot is that since World War I a shift in the rate of capital accumulation no longer implies a rise in the supply of a cooperating factor concentrated in skill-intensive sectors. Capital growth now has a weaker tendency to favor the relative pay position of skilled workers.

When it comes to explaining why the leveling stopped at or after mid-century, a slight shift in emphasis is required. The growth of the labor force remained slow, giving little direct insight into why the leveling stopped. More important was the deceleration in the growth of skills and the impressive acceleration in the growth of capital. Denison's measure of skills grew more slowly between 1948 and 1966 than it had earlier, primarily because of changes in the age–sex composition of the labor force (Denison, 1974, pp. 32–35). Women in the 35–64 age bracket were the most conspicuously rising labor force group, one tending to compete mainly for jobs a little below the median or mean among employees in all sectors. Although the slow and steady postwar influx of wives was no match for the earlier surges of immigrants from southern and eastern Europe, they did depress the growth of average skills, sustaining the pay advantage of the already higher-paid (male) groups.

At the same time, an imbalance in productivity growth reappeared. The industrial sector once more emerged as the locus of fastest productivity improvement, outpacing such unskilled-labor-intensive areas as agriculture (according to the USDA estimates) and private services. The effect of this change depends on the parameters used, but its role is best described as small but noticeable in either Table 11.3 or Table 11.4.

Our accounting thus far has made little reference to exogenous shifts in product demand that might be unrelated to the issue of investment and capital accumulation discussed above. This is a potentially important omission, since the period 1929–1966 witnessed a rise in government from a negligible share of national product to the dominant consumer, directly purchasing nearly a quarter of the national product by the 1960s. Could it be that the rise in government spending generated a relative expansion in unskilled-labor demands before 1948 while favoring the purchase of skill-intensive services thereafter?

If the rise of government played such a role, it did so only in indirect ways. To the extent that government spending propped up aggregate demand and created jobs, it helped the relative position of the lower-paid groups by raising their relative market wage rates as well as by creating jobs for some of them. Alternatively, one might stress the positive effect of more generous payments to the unemployed on the wage rates of the unskilled, though this argument is compromised by the fact that these payments rose in generosity as much after the leveling stopped as during the leveling era itself.

The factor content of government purchases was explored in Chapter 8. There we found that the government bought a slightly more unskilled-labor-using bundle of final products than did the private economy, although this result was sensitive to the measure of skills used. By itself, this finding might suggest that the rise of government was a force pulling up the unskilled *both* in 1929–1948 *and* in 1948–1966. If one could establish that the government shifted its purchases toward greater skill-intensity after 1948, lining professional pockets with aerospace and education dollars while cutting back on soldiers and mail carriers, one could create a new controversial explanation of the end of the leveling.

The evidence now available does not encourage this view. As we noted briefly in Chapter 8, government demand in 1963 was *not* noticeably more skill-intensive and unskilled-labor-sparing than the general economy or than earlier bundles of government purchases. If the rise of government had a net effect on relative factor demands, the main effect was a modest shift in demand toward all kinds of labor at the expense of capital, both before and after mid-century. For this reason, we continue to stress factor supply growth and unbalanced improvement in total factor productivity as the more basic determinants of pay-ratio trends in this century.

Recent Experience and Prospects

This chapter offers some strong suggestions about future trends in pay ratios. Tables 11.4 and 11.5 show that whether we use 1963 or 1976 parameters, we get predictions very near the actual change 1966–1973. The models find this period similar to the period 1948–1966 and continue to find cause for a slight net leveling of the wage structure. At the same time, the models offer several good reasons for expecting a further level-

TABLE 11.5

Accounting for changes in the Skilled-Labor Wage Premium ($\overset{*}{q} - \overset{*}{w}$), 1909–1973, Using 1976 Factor and Sector Shares (percentage per annum)

Exogenous Shift Term	Coefficient for ($\overset{*}{q} - \overset{*}{w}$)	1909–1973		1909–1929		1929–1966		1929–1948		1948–1966		1966–1973	
		Shift	Effect	Shift	Effect	Shift	Effect	Shift	Effect	Shift	Effect	Shift	Effect
$\overset{*}{T}_A$	0.2004	1.13%	−0.23%	0.02%	0%	1.78%	−0.36%	2.06%	−0.41%	1.44%	−0.29%	1.02%	−0.20%
$\overset{*}{T}_M$	0.2410	2.13	0.51	2.44	0.59	1.88	0.45	1.45	0.35	2.35	0.57	2.51	0.60
$\overset{*}{T}_C$	−0.0405	1.09	−0.04	0.84	−0.03	1.19	−0.05	1.58	−0.06	0.77	−0.03	1.29	−0.05
Π_K	0.1085	1.52	0.16	1.26	0.14	1.70	0.18	2.25	0.24	1.12	0.12	1.28	0.14
Π_L	0.9545	1.47	1.40	1.06	1.01	1.69	1.61	2.01	1.92	1.36	1.30	1.48	1.41
Π_S	−1.0280	1.60	−1.64	1.32	−1.36	1.75	−1.80	2.01	−2.07	1.47	−1.51	1.59	−1.63
All "technology" (total factor productivity growth) effects			0.17		0.35		0.07		−0.03		0.16		0.27
$\overset{*}{K}$	0.1085	2.42	0.26	3.16	0.34	1.92	0.21	0.93	0.10	2.98	0.32	2.92	0.32
$\overset{*}{L}$	0.9545	0.82	0.78	1.62	1.55	0.39	0.37	0.32	0.29	0.45	0.43	0.87	0.83
$\overset{*}{S}$	−1.0280	1.94	−1.99	2.58	−2.65	1.63	−1.68	1.82	−1.87	1.43	−1.47	1.75[a]	−1.80
All factor supply effects			−0.95		−0.76		−1.11		−1.48		−0.72		−0.65
Demand adjustment for population growth	−0.0351	1.32	−0.05	1.50	−0.05	1.28	−0.04	0.96	−0.03	1.63	−0.06	0.98	−0.03
Predicted ($\overset{*}{q} - \overset{*}{w}$)			−0.82		−0.46		−1.09		−1.54		−0.62		−0.41
Actual ($\overset{*}{q} - \overset{*}{w}$)			−0.54		−0.09		−0.85		−1.99		0.35		−0.21

Note: Figures for 1909–1973 and 1929–1966 are weighted row averages, and totals may not equal column sums owing to rounding.

[a] 1966–1969 nonresidential sector only.

ing in pretax pay rates over the remainder of this century. This expectation emerges from themes already introduced: demographic trends, convergence in the structure of the economy, and convergence in sectoral productivity growth rates.

There has been a slow but noticeable tendency for sectoral factor proportions to converge since the nineteenth century. Agriculture in particular has approached economy-wide factor proportions ever since 1899, when such calculations first became possible. Statements about factor proportions in agriculture are hazardous, of course, in view of the problems associated with decomposing farm income into returns to labor, skills, capital, and land. Yet there is good evidence that the capital share in agriculture has overtaken and slightly surpassed its share in the whole national economy. The share of unskilled labor in agriculture also seems to have declined toward the national average. This convergence implies that Engel's Law and unbalanced productivity growth would continue to induce agriculture to decline relative to other sectors. The decline, however, would no longer have any effect on relative demands for different factors. This inference is reinforced by a more obvious development: Agriculture now accounts for less than 3% of national income, so that forces influencing its future expansion cannot much affect economy-wide factor demands. Yet the convergence in factor proportions has not been restricted to agriculture. Indeed, the convergence has been sufficiently pronounced that—at least according to the 1976 model—we have almost reached a situation in which one could reason correctly from a single-sector view of the economy. In a one-product economy, the mere fact that skills per man-hour in the labor force continue to rise is almost sufficient to yield the prediction of further declines in the ratio of the wage rates of skilled to unskilled labor.

Demographic trends should also favor the pay position of the less skilled. Between 1948 and 1966, the rise in the labor force participation of women 30–64 slightly upheld the advantage of the higher-paid groups by adding more competition in lower-paid job markets. Since the mid-1960s, however, the continued rise of female labor force participation has been linked to the "baby bust," and the latter will have a stronger ultimate effect on equalizing pay ratios. The rate of growth of the labor force is already dropping off, and as the labor force stagnates and ages, the relative supply of unskilled labor will continue to taper off. This should depress skill premia. There will be some offset, of course, since declining skill premia will themselves cause fewer people to seek higher education.[3]

---

[3] We see no clear strong effect from another possible shift in labor force participation. The rate of labor force growth would rise should the age of retirement now start to increase. The extra elderly workers, however, are unlikely to be "low-wage" employees, given their

Yet the direction of the effect of slower labor force growth is clear enough.

There is another, more tentative reason to expect more leveling in the late twentieth century than was true in the postwar period up to 1973. It is, of course, extremely hazardous to try to forecast rates or patterns of productivity improvement. We have one important guide, however. The OPEC victory affects the United States economy in a way that is similar to a decline in total factor productivity in the energy-intensive sectors of the economy. The energy-intensive sectors also tend to be more skill- and capital-intensive (Berndt and Wood, 1975; Hillman and Bullard, 1978). This being the case, continued fuel and resource scarcity should tend to depress the relative pay position of more skilled members of the labor force.

We find ourselves adopting a somewhat unconventional view of America's past and future inequality. The usual temptations are to debate the lessons of a "growth–equity trade-off," to debate the "inevitable" trends of capitalism, or to point out how social attitudes about relations between class and pay evolve. It seems to us that a more direct route to understanding the determinants of trends in pay ratios and inequality is to explore the demographic and technological trends that accompany economic development.

---

greater prior work experience and their self-employment potential with the help of personal savings. Later retirement should therefore have no clear effect on the ratio of skilled to unskilled wage rates.

12

INEQUALITY AND ACCUMULATION: A NINETEENTH-CENTURY GROWTH–EQUITY CONFLICT?

The Problem

As we have seen in Chapters 10 and 11, capital accumulation appears to have played an important role in contributing to wage inequality movements, especially in the first part of the nineteenth century. Yet, capital accumulation may in fact simply serve as a proxy for other, more fundamental technological and labor force influences. Indeed, of all the factors that seemed to be important in accounting for wage inequality movements, our inclusion of capital accumulation in the list of influential *exogenous* variables seems most objectionable. After all, the rate of capital accumulation is most certainly influenced by other determinants of inequality, and it may well be affected by inequality itself. Only when we have taken a more careful look at the possible determinants of capital accumulation can we be confident that a complete accounting of inequality trends has been offered.

This chapter attempts to unravel the complex relationship between inequality and accumulation in the nineteenth century. The problem is approached in a slightly altered form, however, so that comparisons with past literature are more transparent. Rather than focus directly on the rate of capital stock growth, we shall examine instead the share of investment or saving in national product. Although the rate of capital stock growth and the investment share in income are hardly monotonically related,[1] they are, nonetheless, intimately related, and it is the investment share which has attracted attention in the literature.

Nineteenth-century American growth experience would appear to sup-

---

[1] That is, $\overset{*}{K} = (I/Y)(Y/K) - \delta$ where I is gross investment and δ the depreciation rate.

TABLE 12.1
Wealth per Capita and Capital per Worker Growth Rates, 1685–1966 (percentage per annum)

Period	(1) Private Physical Wealth per Capita (1967 dollars)	(2) Depreciable Capital per Laborer (1860 dollars)	(3) Reproducible Capital per Man-Hour (1840, 1860 dollars)
1685–1805	0.23%	n.a.	n.a.
1800–1835	n.a.	n.a.	0.77%
1805–1850	1.60	n.a.	n.a.
1835–1850	n.a.	n.a.	1.60
1840–1850	n.a.	2.17%	n.a.
1855–1871	n.a.	n.a.	2.85
1850–1900	1.90	2.63	n.a.
1900–1958	n.a.	1.00	n.a.
1900–1966	1.20	n.a.	n.a.

Sources and notes: Col. (1) is based primarily on two sources. For 1774–1966, we use A. H. Jones's (1970, Table 53, p. 135) "variant I" estimates. These are economy-wide estimates, including land and structures, excluding cash, servants, and slaves. For 1685–1774, we use Menard's (1976, Table 3, p. 124) eclectic estimates for Maryland and New England, applying population weights to derive an aggregate. The weights are taken from *Historical Statistics* (1975, Part 2, p. 1168). Col. (2) is taken directly from Davis et al. (1972, Table 2.9, p. 34) and excludes land. Col. (3) is derived from Abramovitz and David (1973, Table 2, p. 431), net stock including land improvements.

ply abundant evidence of the correlation between accumulation and inequality. Table 12.1 shows that the rate of accumulation accelerated across the nineteenth century. Prior to 1805, the rates of nonhuman wealth accumulation were very modest, at around 0.23% per annum in per capita terms. The pace quickened up to 1835, but the biggest leap took place between 1835 and the end of the Civil War decade. The trend acceleration continued, but at retarding rates, until the turn of the century, after which the pace slowed down to a modest level not unlike the first three decades of the nineteenth century. Associated with this accumulation was rise in current price gross saving rates.[2] By the early 1840s, the saving share in gross national product was already 16%, but it surged to 28% by the end of the century. The rise was even greater in constant prices, since the relative price of investment goods declined over the nineteenth century (Table 12.2). Thus, whether measured in terms of gross domestic investment or gross domestic savings, capital formation shares in constant

[2] Temin (1971), Davis and Gallman (1973), and one of the present authors (Williamson 1974b, pp. 104–112, and 1974c) first brought attention to this problem, but the approach taken here, as well as the focus on the "growth–equity trade-off," is sharply different from theirs. A recent paper by David (1977) adds another voice to the dialogue. Indeed, the discussion contained in this chapter owes much to David's formulation of the problem. A more compressed version of this chapter appeared as Williamson (1979).

TABLE 12.2
Gross and Net Real Investment Shares, 1817–1897

Period and Mid-Point	Gross Investment Share (in percentages)		(3) D/Y	Net Investment Share (in percentages)		Relative Price of Investment Goods (6) Gallman (1860 = 100)
	(1) Gallman	(2) Gallman–Davis–David		(4) Gallman	(5) Gallman–Davis–David	
1800–1835 (1817)		11%	3.06%		7.9%	
1834–1843 (1839)	10%		4.06	5.9%		107.7
1839–1848 (1844)	11		4.49	6.5		107.0
1844–1853 (1849)	13		5.11	7.9		103.4
1849–1858 (1854)	15		5.77	9.2		95.0
(1859)						98.0
1869–1878 (1874)	23		9.32	13.7		82.3
1874–1883 (1879)	21		10.13	10.9		81.3
1879–1888 (1884)	23		10.94	12.1		84.6
1884–1893 (1889)	27		11.75	15.3		82.4
1889–1898 (1894)	28		12.54	15.5		77.0
1890–1905 (1897)		28	13.03		15.0	73.3

Sources and notes: Constant 1860 prices are used. Cols. (1) and (2) refer to the U.S. gross domestic investment share in gross domestic product. Concepts include value added by home manufacturers and the value of farm improvements made with farm materials (Gallman, 1966, Table 3, Col. (3), p. 11; and David, 1977, Table 4, p. 196). The share of depreciation in gross domestic product, D/Y, is derived from $(D/Y = \delta v)$ linear interpolations on v (the capital–output ratio) and δ (the depreciation rate), which David supplies for 1800–1835, 1835–1855, 1855–1890, and 1890–1905.

Col. (6) is based on Gallman's implicit price deflators for gross investment in manufactured durables and new construction (1966, Table A–3, p. 34), and for gross national product (Table A–1, p. 26). The observation for 1897 refers to 1894–1903.

257

prices rose by about 12 percentage points from the 1840s to the 1870s. Between 1839 and the turn of century, the rise was even more pronounced, about 18 percentage points, but it seems apparent that most of the drama was centered on the shorter period from the 1830s to the 1870s. In net terms, the rise was almost 10 percentage points, from 6% in 1839 to 15% in 1897.

The period of rising rates of capital formation nearly coincides with the era of wage stretching and surging wealth inequality. As we have seen in Part One, wages and wealth within regions became increasingly more unequal between the 1820s and the early 1860s and stayed very unequal until World War I. Income gaps between regions widened dramatically in the 1860s, and again remained high until World War I.

The timing is sufficiently close to suggest that nineteenth-century America offers a classic example where inequality and accumulation rates rose together. A venerable tradition in economic theory appeals to this correlation to justify the conclusion that the *increasing* investment requirements of early capitalist development can only be satisfied by the surplus generated by *higher* inequality. Indeed, such correlations from other countries and other times have suggested to many observers the presence of a "growth–equity conflict." That is, higher inequality begat increased capital formation. Without the former, so the argument goes, the latter would never have followed, nor would modern economic growth have attained the impressive rates now recorded in our history books. This chapter will argue that such causal inferences are not only empirically unfounded, but probably wrong. If so, then the contemporary policy implications are embarrassingly obvious: the vast majority of historical analysts have written their histories of early capitalist systems assuming the presence of growth–equity conflicts when in fact such conflicts never really existed. Increasing inequality was never a necessary condition for accelerating accumulation in nineteenth-century America.

In this chapter we present the theoretical framework that implements this controversial conclusion. The model is then utilized to estimate the sources of rising capital formation shares in nineteenth-century America. The theme—the nonexistence of growth–equity conflicts in history—is resumed in a concluding section. Spurious correlation has been the villain of the piece far too long; the time has come to cast him out.

The Relative Price of Capital Goods and Unbalanced Total Factor Productivity Growth

The data document a greater rise in economy-wide investment shares when constant price series are used in place of current prices. The explanation is apparent when the relevant nineteenth-century price data are given even the most cursory look. Gallman's implicit price deflators in Table 12.2 record a decline in the relative price of investment goods from an index of 108 in 1839 to 82 in 1869–1878, while relative stability is the rule after the 1870s. To be more precise, the relative price of investment goods declined by 31% between the 1840s and 1899–1908. A roughly comparable pattern emerges when a similar index is constructed for textiles (Williamson, 1974b, pp. 106–109). Thus, whether examined at the industry or national level, the average relative price of capital goods in the 1870s was far below that of the 1840s.

The decline in the price of investment goods was especially dramatic for equipment, which plunged from the late 1840s to the 1870s. Equipment prices kept falling up to 1879–1888, and it was only an offsetting rise in construction costs that produced stability in the relative price of all capital goods after the 1870s (Williamson, 1974b, p. 107). Given these price trends, it comes as no surprise that the constant-price share of producer durables investment in gross domestic capital formation rose from 22% in 1854 to 45% in 1879–1888. It also seems evident that the direction of causation went from relative price change to investment-mix change, since the relative price of investment goods declined in spite of the enormous increase in capital formation rates and the abrupt shift in composition toward producer durables. Indeed, it might be argued that the relative price of equipment would have declined at a far more dramatic rate in the antebellum period if an apparently very elastic demand for producer durables had not held that relative price up.

We have made much of these relative price trends for two reasons. First, they contrast sharply with R. A. Gordon's (1961) influential paper which documented a long-term secular rise in the relative price of capital goods dating from the 1870s, although he emphasized the upward surge from the turn of the century.[3] The sharp decline in nineteenth-century

---

[3] Kuznets noted the same phenomenon in *Capital in the American Economy* (1961), but Gordon's paper received more attention. In reference to twentieth-century trends, Kuznets said: "... the price trend in capital formation ... shows a somewhat greater long-term rise than that in national product as a whole [p. 94]."

Based on implicit price deflators (1929 prices: *Historical Statistics*, 1975, F71–105), the ratio of the gross public and private capital formation price deflator to that of gross national product is as follows through the 1920s:

1897–1901	94.1
1907–1911	93.8
1922–1926	99.5

For the more recent period, the ratio of the gross private domestic investment price deflator to that of gross national product (1958 prices) is as follows:

capital goods prices is thus even more remarkable when viewed in terms of twentieth-century experience. But there is a second reason for stressing these price trends: The sharp price decline offers one hypothesis capable of explaining the rise in nineteenth-century "conventional" saving rates. The decline may best be explained by one or a combination of two effects:[4] (*a*) a relatively dramatic downward shift in the cost function in the capital goods sector due to technological discovery; (*b*) the imposition of war tariffs, which tended to raise the relative price of manufactured consumer goods compared to capital goods. Both of these effects would induce a decline in the relative price of producer durables, although the second of the two would take hold only after the Civil War had raised the duties on consumer goods (later reinforced by the post-1875 protectionist drift), and the 1873–1896 deflation made the specific and mixed duties add increasing percentages to the relative prices of manufactured consumer goods. The first of these forces was probably more fundamental.

Figure 12.1 should help clarify these technology-induced price effects emanating from the capital goods sector. The left-hand panel describes an asset market where capital is initially fixed in supply, at K_0^*, and demand has its normal inverse relation to price, P_K. The market is assumed to be in equilibrium at K_0^* and $P_{K,0}^*$. At this point, new capital goods are produced at a rate sufficient only to replace depreciated assets (i.e., net investment is zero). The capital goods sector is described in the right-hand panel. Now, let the supply function in the capital goods sector shift outward owing to relatively rapid growth of total factor productivity there. The system would now be in disequilibrium and we would observe the following: The relative price of capital goods would decline over time; the "heavy industry" (producer durables) sector would enjoy relative expansion; the rate of capital accumulation would be high; and investment shares would be unusually large, especially in constant prices. If the supply curve in the investment goods sector continued to shift to the right, the process might go on for some time. Obviously, the asset demand function could at the same time shift upwards (to, say, D_1), either owing to

| 1929 | 79.2 | 1957 | 101.2 |
| 1948 | 95.7 | 1969 | 98.1 |

No doubt more careful attention to quality improvement would erase a portion of the upward drift in the prices of capital goods since the late nineteenth century, but the sharp contrast with the first three-quarters of the nineteenth century remains.

[4] Williamson (1974b, pp. 106–107). As we shall see below, these relative price trends account for a good portion of the American nineteenth-century rise in accumulation rates. Recent work on Japan since the late Meiji suggests similar forces at work there (DeBever and Williamson, 1976; and Williamson and DeBever, 1978).

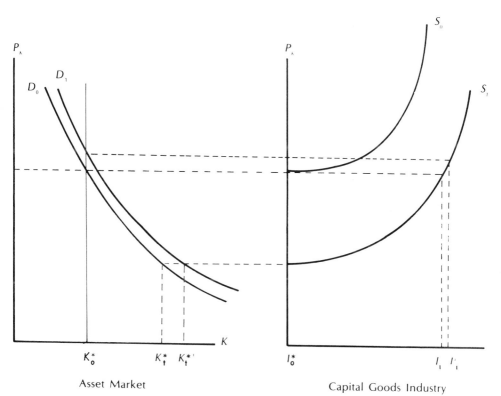

Asset Market   Capital Goods Industry

FIGURE 12.1. Some effects of improved supply of capital goods.

an exogenous rise in saving rates or a rise in profit rates on machines, or both. These additional forces will be examined shortly, but we note that the narrative is, for the most part, reinforced.[5]

Conventional neoclassical growth theory yields an explicit prediction regarding an economy's behavior in response to episodic changes in the prices of capital goods. The equilibrium capital–labor and capital–output ratios rise. Other things being equal, the rate of capital stock growth declines from the initial high levels to a rate asymptotically approaching the rate of labor force growth. As a result, the rate of real output growth

---

[5] If D_t shifted outward, the relative price of capital goods would first rise before undergoing its long-term secular fall. The relative stability of the prices of capital goods through the 1840s (and the short-run rise in the relative price of producer durables: see David, 1977, p. 209) would seem to be consistent with an early nineteenth-century rise in D_t which paralleled the rate of supply shift through total factor productivity growth. Obviously, the cost reductions in the capital goods sector may have been induced either by technological discovery or by economies of scale.

per worker must decline over time. Perhaps even more pertinent to our search for explanations of the nineteenth-century saving behavior, conventional growth theory would also predict a lower net rate of return to capital.

If the net rate of return to capital should decline over time in response to technology-induced cost improvements in the investment goods sector, what about returns to equity capital and real interest rates? Following the initial shock, the rate of return to equity capital should rise to high levels. Economic intuition should suggest that result, but a little formalism may help that intuition along. Let r be the net rental rate on capital, $P = (P_K/P_Y)$ be the price of capital goods relative to GNP, and i be the real interest rate. In equilibrium, $r = Pi$, where i incorporates expected price inflation. When that equilibrium is disturbed by falling capital goods prices, interest rates (the nominal cost of funds) should initially rise. This is so because holding the capital–labor ratio, and thus r, constant in the short run, yields $dr = Pdi + idP = 0$ or $di/i = -dP/P$. Indeed, to maintain short-run equilibrium prior to an accumulation response, interest rates must rise at a rate equal to the percentage by which the relative prices of capital goods decline. At the same net rental rate on capital, we would observe more saving to the extent that saving is responsive to interest rates and returns to equity capital.

There is abundant evidence to support the prediction of rising interest rates following a precipitous decline in P. Consider two "blue chip" bonds. The average yield (adjusted for expected price inflation) on federal bonds between 1845 and 1861 was 3.91%, while the comparable figure for 1867–1878 was 8.85%. New England municipal bonds exhibit a similar increase: from 4.08% to 9.82%. Those who hold to the plausible view that aggregate saving is positively influenced by the real rate of return will welcome this evidence.[6] The rise in real interest rates between the 1840s and the 1870s is certainly consistent with the observed discontinuity in the saving rate. Clearly, we must add the interest-rate hypothesis to our list of potential explanations for the episodic rise in nineteenth-century saving rates.

Recall, however, the long-run predictions of conventional growth theory *after* the initial shock from the declining relative price of capital goods, when rising capital formation shares begin to have their impact on the net rental rate on capital itself. With the subsequent capital accumulation, the net rate of return declines, as do interest rates. Indeed, the

---

[6] For an excellent review of the historical evidence on the interest (or rate of return) elastic saving hypothesis, see Edelstein (1977). We shall rely on some of Edelstein's econometric results below.

decline in both nominal and effective interest rates from the 1870s to the turn of the century is well known. The important issue, then, is what happened to the net rate of return from early in the century to late. David (1977, p. 207) supplies an estimate: The average real net profit rate on conventional reproducible assets fell from 10.5% in the 1800–1835 period to 6.6% around the turn of the century.

We thus have the following nineteenth-century events to explain: a rise in the net real share of saving in real gross product from 6% or 8% to 15%, a fall in the relative price of investment goods by 31%, and a fall in the net rate of return from 10.5% to 6.6%. A number of hypotheses have emerged from the discussion which in concert might account for the events enumerated. The next section will attempt to introduce those hypotheses into a consistent formal framework. Not only do we hope to isolate the causes of the nineteenth-century rise in accumulation rates, but we hope to supply estimates of the role of trending inequality in accounting for the rise in saving rates. If the role can be shown to be minor, then we will have undermined empirical support for a growth–equity conflict in America. We will also supply evidence along the way for an alternative endogenous explanation of accumulation which, while supporting the correlation between inequality trends and rising accumulation rates, will appeal to other forces driving both variables.

Modeling Nineteenth-Century Accumulation

Models of saving and accumulation can be classified according to three attributes.[7] First, is saving viewed as an "active" constraint on accumulation or does it passively respond to investment demand? Second, if saving is viewed as an active constraint, how elastic is aggregate saving to rates of return, if at all? Third, does the supply of investment goods play an active and systematic role as an additional influence on the rate of physical accumulation? While the literature often takes an extreme position on each of these attributes, Figure 12.2 offers a more eclectic view which, we believe, is more consistent with nineteenth-century trends.

The saving rate, (I/Y), is written on the horizontal axis, where it is to be understood that *net* real saving (or investment) ratios are being measured. The rise from A to E roughly corresponds to the near doubling in the net real savings rate in America, from 6% or 8% in the 1830s to 15% at the

---

[7] Although the paper is now some 25 years old, we have still found Abramovitz's (1952) taxonomy very useful in sorting out the sources of accumulation in nineteenth-century America.

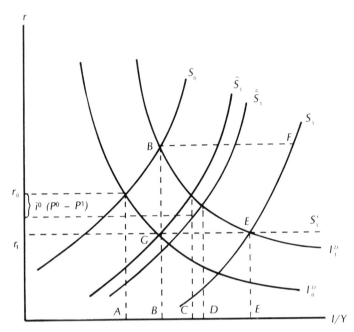

FIGURE 12.2. Nineteenth-century shifts in investment and saving behavior.

turn of the century. The decline in the net rate of return on reproducible capital, from r_0 to r_1, roughly corresponds to the observed fall from 10.5% to 6.6% over the same time period documented by David. We allow some positive slope to the saving function so that a rise in net rates of return induces additional investment. The elasticity is kept small intentionally, since there is little econometric evidence supporting the alternative, elastic view.[8]

Suppose the investment demand function shifts to the right in response to two basic forces. First, the rate of labor force growth rises. Chapter 9 documented exactly this kind of quickening in the first two-thirds of the nineteenth century. According to Lebergott (1966, Table 1, p. 118) the total labor force grew at 2.67% per annum between 1800 and 1830. The

[8] Contemporary evidence abounds, although the earlier econometric results suffered from at least three flaws. First, the simultaneous-equations bias ensured an understatement of the estimated elasticity. Second, the independent variable most often used was the interest rate in money markets rather than rates of return to equity. Third, Edelstein's results suggest that nineteenth-century elasticities were far higher than those for the twentieth century. See Edelstein (1977); C. Wright (1967); and Leff and Sato (1975). For an excellent survey of the more recent research on the interest elasticity hypothesis, see von Furstenberg and Malkiel (1977, pp. 840–842), where relatively high positive elasticities are reported.

rate accelerated in the middle third of the century: the per annum rate was 3.3% between 1830 and 1860. The acceleration is even more striking for the free labor force, which rose from 2.2% to 3.6% per annum between the same two periods. There is reason to believe, therefore, that this trend acceleration fostered a rise in accumulation rates during the first half of the century by shifting investment demand to the right, by raising the net rate of return, and by inducing increased net saving rates. Labor force growth will not, however, help explain the continued shift in investment demand later in the century, since, as is well known, labor force growth rates declined after the Civil War.

Second, the investment demand function may shift to the right in response to an *increased* rate of laborsaving (capital-using) technical change. Chapter 6 documented a number of forces that would yield this result, some appealing to labor saving within industries, and some appealing to forces that shifted the output mix in a direction which favored skills and machines. Chapters 7 and 10 stressed one force in particular: Unbalanced rates of growth of nineteenth-century total factor productivity seemed to favor those sectors utilizing capital and skills most intensively and unskilled labor least intensively. This form of unbalanced technological progress unleashed two forces: (*a*) It tended to foster inequality trends; and (*b*) it raised the aggregate demand for investment goods as those sectors using machines (and skills) intensively expanded. We shall be far more precise in identifying the shift in I^D below, but for the moment note the predictions of Figure 12.2. First, saving rates rise in response to the rise in investment demand. The investment ratio increases from A to B. Second, the saving function shifts to the right in response to three forces: (*a*) the rise in inequality induced by laborsaving technical change and rapid growth of the unskilled-labor force, both exogenous forces; (*b*) an exogenous shift in the saving function due to changes in attitudes toward thrift and/or improvements in savings mobilization; and (*c*) the shift in the saving function in response to declining relative price of capital goods. We shall have more to say about these three forces below, but they all in combination should contribute to a shift from B to F. Successful accumulation should drive down the net rate of return over the century, thus cutting the saving ratio back from F to E. It should be stressed that the rise in inequality is reinforced by two additional forces. Since production of producer durables is itself capital- and skill-intensive (Chap. 8), the rise in the investment share implies further unskilled-labor saving and inequality. In addition, the accumulation of machines induces a rising demand for skills, if skills and machines are complements in production, and thus skill premia, wage differentials, and earnings inequality are given an added boost.

It should be noted, incidentally, that a perfectly elastic saving schedule cannot be defended by an appeal to nineteenth-century capital flows from abroad. Such an argument is cast by reference to $\hat{S}_1'$ and S_1 in Figure 12.2. The saving function S_1' would represent the function aggregated to include the postulated elastic supply of finance from Europe. This characterization would attribute a significant portion of domestic investment ratios, $(E - B)$ to be precise, to foreign capital. More important, it would attribute *all* of the increase in net investment shares above B to foreign capital as domestic investment requirements rose over time from I_0^D to I_1^D. There is no evidence to support such an interpretation. Except for some brief critical episodes in the first half of the nineteenth century, foreign investment was always a small share of total domestic investment in America, never exceeding 5% after the 1830s. Furthermore, the share declines over time (Gallman, 1966, pp. 14–15). Indeed, to use foreign capital to defend the elastic saving specification would place far more weight on the efficient operation of international capital markets than the historical evidence can support (Edelstein, 1974).

Let us now elaborate the narrative suggested by Figure 12.2. The model accounts for the following six forces:

1. Technical progress with a capital-deepening (laborsaving) bias
2. An acceleration in the rate of labor force growth for the first two-thirds of the century
3. Inelastic (but not completely) saving response to rates of return
4. A distributive impact on saving
5. A role for the decline in the relative price of capital goods, the phenomenon stressed earlier in this chapter
6. And a role for exogenous savings mobilization and changing attitudes towards thrift.

Figure 12.2 will be given empirical content in the next section; here we shall deal with its qualitative predictions. Following David's (1977) modern restatement of an older tradition, "the investment demand schedule was not elastic" and "therefore must have shifted to the right as a consequence of conventional capital-deepening bias in the progress of Invention during the nineteenth century [p. 207]." We certainly have no argument with this general view, although our rationalization of the unskilled-labor-saving bias is quite different from his, to judge from a comparison between his 1975 book, *Technical Choice, Innovation, and Economic Growth,* and the arguments presented here in Chapter 7. We attribute a large share of the *increased rate* of labor saving after 1820 to two sources: a shift to capital- and skill-intensive sectors in response to a higher rate of total factor productivity there in general, and the shift within the nonfarm commodity-producing sector to the production of investment goods—in particular, producer durables—for the same reason. In addition, some of the shift in the investment demand function must also be assigned to the acceleration in labor force growth rates. A key point of departure, however, is this: If unskilled-labor saving plays a role in shifting I^D to the right, it must also do the same for the saving schedule. Surely the inequality induced by labor saving must have had some positive impact on saving. The question is, How much?

We can perform a simple calculation on the *maximum* potential impact of distribution on saving. We emphasize the word "maximum." We wish to err on the high side in the calculation, since if even then distribution is shown to have had a minor impact on aggregate saving we shall have presented the strongest case against the "growth–equity conflict" position. Assume that *all* saving in reproducible assets (we ignore human capital formation here) has its source in nonlabor income. This is no more than the extreme classical Cambridge postulate which plays such an important role in contemporary growth-and-development models, as well as in Simon Kuznets's search for capital accumulation theories.[9] We have estimated trends in unskilled labor's share in national income over the

---

[9] *Capital in the American Economy* (1961). Kuznets would reject our Marxian, or modern Cambridge, assumption as far too extreme, although he looks with favor on the view that inequality may foster rising net saving rates economy-wide. Kuznets's empirical translation of the Marx–Ricardo–Robinson saving postulate can best be stated in his own words:

> We might divide the whole body of personal savers into two groups: the overwhelming majority—say, the lower 95 percent classified by their relatively permanent income position—who perhaps account for 80 percent of income and 50 percent of total personal net savings; and the top 5 percent who account for the other 50 percent of total personal savings. A countrywide (net) savings-income rate of 10 percent under these conditions implies a savings-income ratio of about 6 percent . . . for the lower 95 percent, and of 25 percent . . . for the top 5 percent. The figures are illustrative, intended only to suggest the broad lines of the dichotomy [p. 100].

While the figures may have been used only to "illustrate" the impact of changing distribution on saving, the example has been repeated often enough to have gained the status of "fact." Some empirical confirmation of the postulate on contemporary data drawn from the Third World can be found in Houthakker (1965) and Williamson (1968), although there has been further confirmation in studies done since the mid-1960s.

In short, the assumptions used in the text must indeed be viewed as an *upper bound* on the impact of changing distribution on changing net saving rates in nineteenth-century America. This must be so, even if we recognize that the distribution of human and nonhuman property income itself became more unequal concomitant with the shift of income away from unskilled labor. After all, Kelley's (1972) analysis of urban workers for the late nineteenth century has shown that saving rates out of average urban workers' incomes were indeed far in excess of zero, negating the extreme characterization of saving as undertaken only by the capitalist class, which is implied by our experiment.

nineteenth century. Labor's share (θ_L) declined by approximately 11 percentage points over the half century following 1839–1840. The vast majority of the decline took place by the 1880s. Indeed, the share fell by almost 16 percentage points up to 1879–1888. Let the constant net saving rate out of property (human and nonhuman) income be denoted by s_p, the initial aggregate saving ratio by s_0, and the predicted 1890 aggregate saving ratio by $\hat{s}_1$. Holding the rate of return constant, and equating average and marginal propensities to save, the primitive classical saving model would then predict the following:

$$s_0 = \theta_L(s_L) + \theta_K(s_p) = .296(s_p) = .08$$
$$\therefore s_p = (.08)(.296)^{-1} \simeq .27$$
$$\hat{s}_1 = .593(0) + .407(.27) \simeq .11.$$

We would therefore estimate distribution at *maximum* to have raised aggregate net saving rates from .08 to .11 from the 1830s to the 1890s, *ceteris paribus*. It is an upper-bound statement about the *shift* in the saving function, not a statement about equilibrium values. Alternatively, we note that the rise in equilibrium net investment ratios was more or less complete by 1869–1878, as was the inequality surge. Nonetheless, the calculations over the longer period will serve well enough for the moment. Later in this chapter we will decompose the nineteenth century into shorter "episodic" parts. Now if the observed change in distribution was explained entirely by a laborsaving bias, the above calculation would indeed supply an upper-bound estimate of the "induced-distribution" shift in the aggregate saving function. To some readers the calculation may appear to understate the distribution influence, since the initial inequality bias is offset in Figure 12.2 by conventional accumulation, the subsequent decline in r from high disequilibrium levels, and the offsetting decline in θ_K, which would inevitably follow. Indeed, this tale is consistent with the inequality facts which show the surge in inequality arrested by the end of the 1870s and a very modest drift toward equality thereafter up to the turn of the century. It will be understood, therefore, that $\hat{s}_1$ refers to the *net* inequality trends which accumulate to the end of the disequilibrium period.

We are now equipped to decompose qualitatively the sources of rising nineteenth-century saving rates depicted in Figure 12.2. Biased technological progress and labor force growth induce an increase in net saving ratios equal to $(D - A)$. This in turn is composed of three parts:

1. *Impact of investment demand on saving.* Laborsaving technological change and acceleration in labor force growth shift the investment demand function to the right. If the saving function is held fixed, the net

investment ratio would rise to B if some saving elasticity with respect to r is granted.

2. *Induced distribution impact on saving.* The same laborsaving technological progress tends to induce increased inequality and thus causes the saving function to shift to the right to $\hat{S}_1$. An additional increase in the investment ratio is forthcoming, $(C - B)$. This must be viewed as an endogenous saving response to the same technological forces that are driving I^D. As we have argued above, the inequality effect may in addition be reinforced by the rise in the production of investment goods and by capital–skill complementary forces.

3. *Increased saving induced by declining prices of capital goods.* Technological change was also biased in favor of the capital goods sector. This lowered the relative price of capital goods and thus raised the level of saving forthcoming at any given r. The induced saving response amounts to $(D - C)$.[10]

The remaining shift in saving, $(E - D)$, is the residual exogenous shift due to financial intermediation, mobilization, government debt–tax policy, external capital flows, and changing attitudes towards thrift, as well as errors in measurement.

Why Nineteenth-Century Net Investment Rates Rose: The Long View

We require only two parameters to impart empirical content to Figure 12.2, the saving and investment elasticities with respect to r. If we assume constant elasticities over relevant ranges for both functions, then we have (where I^D, S, T, Z are now written as *shares* in Y):

$$
\begin{array}{ll}
\textit{In Absolutes} & \textit{In Rates of Change} \\
I^D = Tr^\epsilon & \overset{*}{I}{}^D = \overset{*}{T} + \epsilon \overset{*}{r} \\
S = Zr^\eta & \overset{*}{S} = \overset{*}{Z} + \eta \overset{*}{r} \\
S = I^D & \overset{*}{I}{}^D = \overset{*}{S}
\end{array}
$$

---

[10] The mechanism which translate the decline in the relative price of investment goods into a saving response requires some amplification. Although, as already mentioned, this sharp decline has been appreciated for some time now, David (1977, p. 208) has recently made the link more explicit. In equilibrium $r = Pi$, so that $(r_0 - r_1) = P_1(i_0 - i_1) + i_0(P_0 - P_1)$. It is the second term on the right-hand side of this expression, $i_0(P_0 - P_1)$, which motivates the saving response to declining relative capital goods prices. In effect, the same saving would be forthcoming at $r_0 - i_0(P_0 - P_1)$ as would be forthcoming at r_0 prior to the decline in capital goods prices. This induced effect is translated in Figure 12.2 into a shift in the saving function from $\hat{S}_1$ to $\hat{S}_1$, thus fostering a rise in the investment ratio equal to $(D - C)$.

It can be shown that $\epsilon = -\sigma$, where σ is the elasticity of substitution in a CES production function.[11] Twentieth-century econometric evidence supports the assertion $0 < \sigma \leq 1$, and to be consistent with the assumptions underlying the analysis in Chapter 10, we shall focus most of our attention on the case $\epsilon = -0.5$. Similarly, we insist that saving exhibit a fairly inelastic response to rates of return, so that our experiments are restricted to cases where $0 < \eta \leq 1$. Based on the contemporary econometric estimates in general, and those applied to the Goldsmith data 1897–1949 in particular,[12] to explore cases where $\eta > 1$ may amount to an irrelevant exercise. Do we have any additional information about the magnitude of the "interest" elasticity of saving? A recent econometric study of the United Kingdom offers some guidelines (Edelstein, 1977). Under various models of saving behavior, the long-run elasticities range between 0.11, 0.37, 0.60, and 0.70 for the period 1870–1965 as a whole. For the period 1870–1913, however, Edelstein finds η approximately equal to unity. The (admittedly limited) evidence suggests the nineteenth-century interest elasticities were higher than twentieth-century elasticities and

---

[11] David's (1977) elegant statement is useful at this point. Let the economy be characterized by the following CES production function:

$$Y = [\alpha(E_L L)^{1-1/\sigma} + \beta(E_K K)^{1-1/\sigma}]^{[\sigma(1-\theta_R)/(\sigma-1)]}(E_R R)^{\theta_R},$$

where the E_j refer to levels of factor augmentation through technical progress; L, K, and R refer respectively to unskilled labor, capital, and land; σ is the elasticity of substitution between K and L; and the θ_j are factor shares. If we focus on long-run equilibrium, then the ratio of net investment to output, I^D, can be written as $I^D = v(r)G$, where v is the capital–output ratio and G is a constant. Influences on G can be seen in the expression

$$G = (\overset{*}{L} + \overset{*}{E}_L)[\theta_L/(1 - \theta_K)] + \overset{*}{R}[\theta_R/(1 - \theta_K)].$$

The capital–output ratio is related to the rental rate on capital by $v = Br^{-\sigma}$. Thus,

$$I^D = B(r^{-\sigma})G$$

and so $\epsilon = -\sigma$.

[12] The reference is to Colin Wright's estimates of positive, but "low," interest elasticity of saving using Raymond Goldsmith's data for the United States, 1897–1949. C. Wright (1967, p. 854) found saving elasticities ranging between 0.19 and 0.24. The more recent U.S. estimates reported in von Furstenberg and Malkiel (1977, pp. 840–842) are higher and range between 0.3 and 1.76. For those who view even this accumulating evidence with suspicion, recall that this chapter deals with aggregate saving behavior, not just household saving behavior. There is reason to believe, of course, that firm reinvestment rates are far more sensitive to rates of return than household saving rates. It may also be argued that the interest rate elasticity may have been higher in the nineteenth century than in the twentieth. Both of these presumptions have been confirmed by the research reported by Edelstein on England (1977). Indeed, Edelstein (p. 292) estimates an interest rate elasticity of unity in the pre–World War I era. The estimated rate drifts downward to zero in the post–World War II era.

thus we initially set $\eta = 1.0$, although we shall explore the implications of lower values as well.

We have the following data on (assumed) equilibrium values between the 1830s and the turn of the century:

$$\overset{*}{r} = \frac{.066 - .105}{.105} = -.371$$

$$\overset{*}{I}{}^{D}(\equiv\overset{*}{S}) = \frac{.15 - .08}{.08} = +.875.$$

We can also solve for the shift in the investment demand and saving "supply" schedules:

$$\overset{*}{T} = \overset{*}{I}{}^{D} - \epsilon\overset{*}{r} = +.6895,$$

and

$$\overset{*}{Z} = \overset{*}{S} - \eta\overset{*}{r} = +1.2460.$$

In summary, for what we shall label Case 1A, we have

$$
\begin{array}{ll}
\overset{*}{r} = -.371 & \overset{*}{T} = +.6895 \\
\overset{*}{I}{}^{D} = +.875 & \eta = +1.0 \\
\overset{*}{Z} = +1.246 & \epsilon = -0.5.
\end{array}
$$

We can now decompose the rising net saving into its four components. *First,* there is the impact of investment demand shifts $(B - A)$ in Figure 12.2:

$$\overset{*}{S} = \eta \; \frac{-\overset{*}{T}}{\epsilon - \eta} = +.4597$$

$S(\equiv I)$ rises from .08 to .1168, or $(B - A) = .0368$.

Second, there is the (maximum) induced impact on saving due to distribution effects alone, $\overset{*}{Z}_D$:

$$\overset{*}{Z}_D = \frac{.11 - .08}{.08} = +.375$$

$$\overset{*}{S} = \frac{\epsilon\overset{*}{Z}_D}{\epsilon - \eta} = +.125.$$

$S(\equiv I)$ rises from .1168 to .1314, or $(C - B) = .0146$.

Third, the impact of declining capital goods prices $(D - C)$ can be easily determined when we recall $(P_1 - P_0) = (.69 - 1.00) = -.31$. Thus, $\overset{*}{r}{}' =$

$-.31$ from the decline in capital goods prices. It follows that its impact is $\overset{*}{I}{}^D = \epsilon\overset{*}{r}{}' = +.155$.

$S(\equiv I)$ rises from .1314 at C to .1518 at D, or $(D - C) = .0204$.

Fourth, the residual is $-.0018$. A summary appears in Table 12.3.

What do we conclude from this experiment? Case 1A in Table 12.3 suggests that the vast majority of rising saving rates in nineteenth-century America were induced by technology or labor force growth. If the residual can be attributed to exogenous savings mobilization rather than errors in measurement, then its impact appears to have been trivial and negative, a result in sharp contrast with conventional histories' emphasis on the improved operation of financial markets during nineteenth-century American development.[13] That the "mobilization effect" is negative may encourage some to reject the experiment as implausible. We hasten to remind the reader of two facts which can readily account for the negative residual: First, the distribution experiment is an *upper bound* (a maximum value for $\overset{*}{Z}_D$ is assumed), and thus the residual saving mobilization component is a lower bound. Second, recall that the foreign investment share in American gross domestic capital formation *fell* over the nineteenth century. Foreign investment never did augment domestic savings by more than 5% or so in the most buoyant antebellum years, but the share declined over time so that by the turn of the century America became a net capital exporter. Thus, the negative residual in Case 1A may simply reflect the drift towards self-financing over the nineteenth century. In any case, the *maximum* impact of changing inequality on rising saving rates is also quite modest, only one-fifth of the total increase. In contrast, labor saving and labor force growth combined to account for more than half of the observed rise in net saving rates, while the technology-induced decline in the relative price of capital goods accounted for almost a third. The experiment suggests only the weakest support for a nineteenth-century growth–equity conflict, certainly much too weak to warrant the attention lavished on it in the historical and development literature.

Cases 1B, 1C, and 1D offer some alternative experiments for various "reasonable" values of ϵ and η. How robust are the results of Case 1A? In no case does the (*upper-bound*) impact of distribution on saving ratios exceed one-quarter of the total increase in saving ratios over the nineteenth century. Once again, although the inequality trends were quite pronounced after the 1830s, they appear to have made a relatively minor

---

[13] The literature is very extensive. See, for example, Davis and Gallman (1973) and the effort by Williamson (1974b, Chap. 6) to introduce interregional saving mobilization into a general-equilibrium model of the late nineteenth century.

TABLE 12.3

Estimating the Sources of Rising Nineteenth-Century Net Investment Rates: The Long View

Sources of Increase in Net Saving Ratio	Case 1A ($\epsilon = -.5$; $\eta = 1.0$)	Case 1B ($\epsilon = -.3$; $\eta = 1.0$)	Case 1C ($\epsilon = -.7$; $\eta = 1.0$)	Case 1D ($\epsilon = -.5$; $\eta = .5$)	Case 2 ($\epsilon = -.5$; $\eta = 0$)	Case 3 ($\epsilon = -.5$; $\eta = \infty$)
Total increase in net saving ratio	.0700	.0700	.0700	.0700	.0700	.0700
Induced by technology and labor force	.0718	.0708	.0828	.0676	.0471	.0762
Investment demand ($B - A$)	.0368	.0470	.0359	.0276	0	.0552
Distribution ($C - B$)	.0146	.0110	.0179	.0202	.0300	0
Decline in prices of capital goods ($D - C$)	.0204	.0128	.0290	.0198	.0171	.0210
Residual impact ($E - D$)	−.0018	−.0008	−.0128	.0024	.0229	−.0062

Source: See text.

contribution to the total rise in net saving ratios over the nineteenth century. In every case, at least 95% of the observed rise in saving rates can be attributed to the combined influences of the three effects induced by technology and growth in the labor force. Exogenous savings mobilization (if it can be equated with the residual), so important in qualitative historical accounts, never plays a significant role in any experiment.

Table 12.3 presents two additional cases which we view to be less attractive interpretations of nineteenth-century America. Case 2 allows the saving function to be completely inelastic with respect to r. In our opinion, this case is wide of reality, not only because we believe that nineteenth-century firms did respond positively to rising net returns on equity, but also because the assumption predicts a rise in r in response to shifts in I^D which cannot be established by fact. That is, the initial impact of the distribution and mobilization forces on saving rates would have served to raise the rate of return from 10.5% to almost 25%![14] Although the inelastic saving specification seems unrealistic to us, even here distribution changes account for only 40% of the total increase in net saving ratios. The key difference between Case 2 and Case 1A is that the impact of laborsaving investment demand is zero, and exogenous savings mobilization usurps its role completely. Case 3 assumes a perfectly elastic saving function with respect to r. Here, of course, distribution has no impact at all.

Why Nineteenth-Century Net Investment Rates Rose: Shorter-Run Episodic Phases

Gallman's net investment share series in Table 12.2 supplies evidence on episodic phases of saving rate experience. The net investment rate in America did not drift upwards smoothly across the nineteenth century, but rather surged upwards in two apparently quite distinct phases. Between c. 1839 and c. 1854, it rose by 3.3 percentage points or by 0.22% per annum. Between c. 1854 and c. 1871, it rose by 4.5 percentage points or by 0.26% per annum. During the late nineteenth century the rise was more modest, 1.3 percentage points, or 0.06% per annum. Were the sources of the rise more or less the same in each of these three episodes? More to the point of this chapter, did the antebellum surge in inequality account for far more of the rise in net investment rates prior to the Civil War? We have already shown that inequality trends are unlikely to account for a very

---

[14] The calculation is straightforward: $\overset{*}{r} = \overset{*}{I}(\eta - \epsilon)^{-1} = +1.379$, so r would have risen by 14.5 percentage points, that is, from 10.5 to 25%.

large share of the quickening in accumulation rates across the nineteenth century as a whole. Were they a far more critical influence in the first half of the century? Can a stronger argument be made for the growth–equity conflict early in America's modern economic growth?

Using the assumptions and methodology of Case 1A in the previous section, there is no reason why we cannot decompose the sources of rising net investment rates in each of these three nineteenth-century episodes. All we require are the estimates of r in Table 12.4. The results of the numerical experiment are reported in Table 12.5. They are enlightening, to say the least.

The sources of the rise in Gallman's net investment rate for the six decades as a whole (1839–1897) are more or less the same as those previously calculated in Table 12.3 on slightly different data and for a somewhat longer period. Once again, "savings mobilization" (more precisely, the residual) plays a trivial role, accounting for only a very small share of the total increase. Furthermore, the combined influence of rising investment demand and declining relative capital goods prices accounts for the lion's share of the increase, 6.9 of the 9.1 percentage points. Rising inequality fails to play a very important role, 1.6 of the 9.1 percentage points, even though we continue to adopt the "classical saving assumption" which maximizes the potential impact of distribution. On the other hand, rising inequality does appear to play a more important role in accounting for rising saving rates during the antebellum period when

TABLE 12.4
Implied Net Rates of Return on Reproducible Capital Stock, c. 1817–c. 1897

Year or Period	θ_K	v	δ	$\hat{r}$
1800–1835 (c. 1817)	.23	1.80	.0170	.1108
(1835)	(.25)	(1.90)	(.0195)	(.1121)
1835–1855	.27	2.19	.0209	.1024
(1855)	(.32)	(2.48)	(.0238)	(.1052)
1855–1871	.34	2.80	.0261	.0953
(1871)	(.34)	(3.11)	(.0284)	(.0809)
1871–1890	.35	3.31	.0312	.0745
1890–1905 (c. 1897)	.37	3.62	.0360	.0662

Sources and notes: The θ_K and v figures in parentheses are linear interpolations, except for the 1855 estimate of θ_K. Almost all of the rise in θ_K between 1835–1855 and 1855–1871 seems to have been centered on the 1845–1855 period. The 1855 estimate of θ_K is adjusted accordingly.
The real net profit on the reproducible capital stock can be written as $r = (\theta_K/v - \delta)$, where θ_K, the "conventional" reproducible capital share, is taken from Abramovitz and David (1973, Table 2, p. 431). The capital–output ratio, v, is taken, for 1800–1835 and 1890–1905, from David (1977, Table 4, p. 196). Intervening dates are derived from capital stock and output growth rates in Abramovitz and David (1973, Table 2, p. 431). The depreciation rate on reproducible capital, δ, is from David (1977, Table 4, p. 196).

TABLE 12.5

Estimating the Sources of Rising Nineteenth-Century Net Investment Rates: Shorter-Run Episodic Phases

Case 1A Decomposition ($\epsilon = -.5; \eta = 1.0$)	(1) c. 1839–c. 1854	(2) c. 1854–c. 1871	Episodes (3) c. 1871–c. 1897	(4) c. 1839–c. 1897
Total Increase in net saving ratio	+.0330	+.0450	+.0130	+.0910
Induced by technology and labor force	+.0363	+.0283	+.0088	+.0857
Investment demand	+.0206	+.0229	+.0004	+.0525
Changing rate of labor force growth	+.0074	−.0201	+.0159	−.0029
Technology changes	+.0132	+.0430	−.0155	+.0554
Decline in prices of capital goods	+.0047	+.0077	+.0060	+.0169
Distribution	+.0110	−.0023	+.0024	+.0163
Residual impact	−.0033	+.0167	+.0042	+.0053

Sources and notes: See text. Cols. (1), (2), and (3) should add to Col. (4) only in the first line of the table. In effect, a Laspeyres weighting scheme is used throughout in the decomposition analysis. Thus, Col. (4) need not correspond to the sum of the other three columns along any line. In fact, aggregating across lines yields the following:

Induced by Technology and Labor Force	+.0734
Investment Demand	+.0439
Capital Goods Prices	+.0184
Distribution	+.0111
Residual	+.0176
Total	+.0910

inequality was on an especially steep trend. Even here, however, a shifting distribution *at a maximum* accounts for only a third of the rise in net savings ratios (1.1 of the 3.3 percentage points). For the period 1839–1871 as a whole, increasing inequality accounts at maximum for only a tenth of the rise in net investment shares (0.87 of the 7.8 percentage points). While some readers may wish to debate our interpretation, it seems to us that rising inequality was hardly the main source of rising accumulation rates even very early in American modern economic growth, when inequality was sharply on the rise.

Note, however, the changing sources of rising net real investment rates from period to period. The residual mobilization impact was apparently fairly important, although still not the dominant influence, between the 1850s and the 1870s. This result is certainly comforting to one of the present authors who recently argued (Williamson, 1974b, 1974c) that the Civil War was indeed a watershed in accumulation performance. A portion of these relatively strong ''mobilization'' forces may be attributable to an accumulation response to war destruction and emancipation in the South, a portion to federal debt management in the North and ''catching up'' after the war, and a portion to those financial intermediation developments which play such a dominant role in our conventional histories. The important insight which our experiment offers is that these mobilization effects were limited to the c. 1854–c. 1871 period alone: they play no significant role elsewhere in the nineteenth century. Our second finding is that the declining relative price of capital goods had a consistent positive impact throughout, although its contribution is more impressive after the 1850s than before. Nonetheless, it still accounted for a seventh of the rise in net investment shares between 1839 and 1854. (The comparable figures for 1854–1871 and 1871–1897 are, respectively, one-sixth and one-half.) Finally, the investment demand impact associated with labor-saving technical change and rising labor force growth is most pronounced in the antebellum period, accounting for six-tenths of the total increase. This last result is consistent with the findings of both Chapters 7 and 10: the rate of economy-wide labor saving induced by changes in output mix was most dramatic prior to the Civil War; the unbalanced rate of total factor productivity growth was also most pronounced up to 1860; and the rate of labor force growth reached its zenith between 1830 and 1860. Nevertheless, the investment demand impact is still striking during the 1854–1871 episode, accounting for half of the total increase in the net investment share. It is insignificant for the remainder of the nineteenth century, when rates of total factor productivity and output growth were relatively balanced. Technological quiescence was consistent with inequality quiescence, and with relatively stable net investment shares.

It might be worthwhile to report one additional calculation. Economic intuition tells us that episodes of accelerating rates of labor force growth should have raised investment requirements and thus the net investment share, especially to the extent that investment was highly "population sensitive" in the nineteenth-century economy (e.g., residential construction, transportation, and other forms of social overhead investment). Indeed, it can be shown formally that the shift in the investment demand schedule, $\overset{*}{T}$, can be decomposed into two parts, $\overset{*}{T}_L$, the impact of rates of change in labor force growth, and a residual, presumably due to technological (and land-expansion) forces. The labor force impact on investment demand is written as[15]

$$\overset{*}{T}_L = d\overset{*}{L}/\overset{*}{L} + d[\theta_L/(1 - \theta_K)]/[\theta_L/(1 - \theta_K)].$$

Since labor force growth rates accelerated between the early and late antebellum periods, a positive contribution to investment demand from this source between c. 1839 and c. 1854 is to be expected. A tentative estimate is offered in Table 12.5: the acceleration in labor force growth rates served to raise net investment shares by 0.74 percentage points, or a little less than one-third of the total increase attributable to investment

[15] In terms of the notation in the text

$$\overset{*}{I}^D = \overset{*}{T} + \epsilon\overset{*}{r}$$

where (see footnote 11)

$$T = B(G) = B[\overset{*}{L}(\theta_L)/(1 - \theta_K) + \overset{*}{R}(\theta_R)/(1 - \theta_K) + \overset{*}{E}_L(\theta_L)/(1 - \theta_K)];$$

B is a constant, the θ are factor shares economy-wide, $\overset{*}{L}$ and $\overset{*}{R}$ refer, respectively, to labor force and land stock growth, and $\overset{*}{E}_L$ denotes the rate of labor augmentation through technological change. Our interest here is in the impact of changing labor force growth on investment demand, and this component can be written as

$$T_L = B[\overset{*}{L}(\theta_L)/(1 - \theta_K)].$$

It follows that

$$\overset{*}{T}_L = d\overset{*}{L}/\overset{*}{L} + d[\theta_L/(1 - \theta_K)]/[\theta_L/(1 - \theta_K)].$$

Stanley Lebergott (1966, Table 1, p. 118) offers the following estimates of $\overset{*}{L}$: 1800–1840 (c. 1839), 2.77; 1840–1860 (c. 1854), 3.43; 1860–1880 (c. 1871), 2.27; and 1880–1900 (c. 1897), 2.60. These plus the θ estimates supplied by Abramovitz and David (1973, Table 2, p. 431), and by Table 12.4 above, yield the following approximations

	c. 1839–54	c. 1854–71	c. 1871–97	c. 1839–97
$d\overset{*}{L}/\overset{*}{L}$	+.238	−.338	+.145	−.061
$d[\theta_L/(1 - \theta_K)]/[\theta_L/(1 - \theta_K)]$	−.050	+.011	+.029	−.012
$\overset{*}{T}_L$	+.188	−.327	+.174	−.073

These estimates of $\overset{*}{T}_L$ are utilized in Table 12.5.

demand shifts and a little more than one-fifth of the total increase in net investment rates in the antebellum period. The share attributable to this source is even greater following the 1870s (c. 1871–c. 1897). But for the nineteenth century as a whole, labor force growth does not appear to account for any of the rise in the net investment ratio. The reason is obvious: The rate of labor force growth in fact *declined* from 2.77% per annum between 1800 and 1840, to 2.60% per annum between 1880 and 1900. In short, labor force expansion helps account for a modest portion of the expansion in savings rates during the first half of the nineteenth century but fails to account for any of the rise over the century as a whole.

The Gordian Knot Untied

This chapter has shown that nineteenth-century America replicates the inequality and accumulation experience typical of most "successful" contemporary Third World economies.[16] The time-series evidence confirms a high positive correlation between inequality, capital formation shares, and accumulation performance. The correlation is certainly close enough to have suggested support for the classic view of capitalist development where growth and equity are in conflict. Indeed, the conflict was sufficiently obvious to nineteenth-century economists that their models of development were all built on the premise that accumulation rates could only be increased with shifts in income toward property income recipients. That premise gained some support with early econometric work on the saving function. A revisionist literature has accumulated since then, however, which tends to deflate the influence of distribution on saving performance. Yet, even William Cline's (1972) oft-cited book fails to offer a true alternative to the classic model, since it only confronts the impact of inequality on saving, ignoring the explanation of inequality itself. The advantage of the classical model is that distribution and accumulation are *both* endogenous variables. Perhaps this explains why the Ricardian–Marxian systems are just as central to modern growth and distribution theory today as they were a century ago. Sir W. Arthur Lewis's (1954) model of surplus labor still reigns supreme as the central thesis underlying contemporary models of Third World development,

---

[16] As Gustav Ranis (1977) has recently reminded us, there are some significant exceptions to "the old chestnut of an unequal distribution of income required to generate high savings rates [p. 265]." There are three well-documented cases which offer the simultaneous experience of high saving rates and relative equality, all from Asia: Japan, Korea, and Taiwan.

and it is even used to explain post–World War II growth in Europe (Kindleberger, 1967). Modern dualistic models of development are applied systematically everywhere in the developing Third World, and even play a central role in accounting for Japan's leap to modern economic growth. The theoretical tradition is alive, of that there is no doubt, and it is in large part based on correlations like those uncovered by American growth, inequality, and accumulation experience.

This chapter has shown the growth-equity-conflict inference to be suspect in the American nineteenth-century case.[17] One would be hard pressed to find a more relevant and important example of the "identification problem," or a stronger argument for the more extensive use of general-equilibrium models in history. We have shown that increased inequality was unlikely to have accounted for a significant portion of increased saving rates, and foreign capital never offered an easy means of accelerating accumulation performance either. Inequality may have been a by-product of modern economic growth, but modern economic growth was *not* dependent upon increased inequality in any important way.

Although it does not appear that increasing inequality was an important determinant of rising investment shares across nineteenth-century America, Chapter 10 informs us that the rate of capital stock growth was a critical force in producing wage inequality. Indeed, the *direct* impact of unbalanced total factor productivity growth in the antebellum period was apparently dwarfed by the impact of capital accumulation. The present chapter implies that the conclusion is misleading, since the *indirect* effect of unbalanced total factor productivity growth, through capital formation and then on inequality, was an additional potent influence. We estimate that more than half of the antebellum rise in capital accumulation rates may have been due to these *indirect* effects of unbalanced total factor productivity growth. Similarly, perhaps a quarter was due to the *indirect* effect of labor force growth. It appears, therefore, that Chapter 10 has understated the role of labor force growth and technological forces in accounting for inequality trends in nineteenth-century America. The contrast with the twentieth century, where capital accumulation seems to have contributed little to wage inequality trends compared with labor force and technological forces (Chap. 11), is more apparent than real.

---

[17] The Japanese case from Meiji to Taisho is also being reappraised, with similar results. See Kelley and Williamson (1974); DeBever and Williamson (1976); and Williamson and DeBever (1978).

13

THE SOURCES OF INEQUALITY

Three Centuries of American Inequality

American inequality trends confirm the Kuznets hypothesis. Income and wealth inequality did rise sharply with the onset of modern economic growth in the early nineteenth century. Long-term trends toward equality only appear with the advent of mature capitalist development in the twentieth century. In the interim, America generated seven decades of extensive inequality not unlike that experienced in Europe or in much of the contemporary Third World. Thus, in spite of abundant land, alleged equality of opportunity, democratic institutions, and a nineteenth-century reputation as an ideal "poor man's country," America did not avoid the economic inequality commonly believed to be associated with capitalist development.

Data on wages and salaries permit a tentative dating of the nineteenth-century rise in inequality. Between 1816 and 1856 the nominal pay advantage of such skilled groups as engineers, teachers, carpenters, and mechanics rose dramatically over common labor. The advantages thus gained were maintained and even reinforced through 1916; a slight decline in late nineteenth-century pay ratios was followed by another abrupt rise between the 1890s and 1914, the latter surge appearing in the dispersion of high income as well as pay ratios among wage and salary earners. The initial wage structure around 1816 was sufficiently narrow to suggest that there could hardly have been any earlier widening, although there are no reliable colonial wage series to confirm that assertion.

The inequality of personal wealth also seems to have widened dramatically sometime before the Civil War. This widening was first suggested by the marked contrast between the size distribution of wealth found for 1774 by A. H. Jones (1978) and that documented for 1860 by Soltow (1975). The same marked upward drift shows up in regional wealth inequality measures for Massachusetts, for Butler County, Ohio, for Brooklyn and New York City, and for southern slave ownership, although these local trends should be weighted and combined with new data from other regions before they can be accepted as additional evidence of national trends during the century between the Revolutionary and Civil wars.

The measured rise in wealth concentration between 1774 and 1860 apparently occurred sometime after about 1820, to judge from these admittedly meager but additional scraps of local and regional data. If further research confirms this timing, then it appears that the era of rising wealth concentration was also one of wage stretching and increased earnings inequality, in sharp contrast to the egalitarian tones traditionally used to paint the intervening Jacksonian era. Distribution theory is not sufficiently advanced to have predicted this coincidence between wealth and wage inequality trends. Once evident, however, the coincidence suggests that what was happening to the structure of wages was also happening to the overall distribution of income, if we make the plausible assumption that wealth concentration reflects the concentration of contemporaneous incomes from property. Only if the estimates themselves are in error, or if the well-known twentieth-century positive correlation between household wage and property income failed to hold for the nineteenth century, would it be an error to infer rising inequality in the national size distribution of income from the available nineteenth-century wealth and earnings data.

Debate continues over wealth inequality trends in the colonial era. The importance of this debate is magnified by the fact that we have no other measures of material inequality for the colonial era, though future research may yield fresh time series on wage rates, commercial profits, land rents, tax assessments, and the shares of households excused from local taxes by reason of indigence. We have tentatively concluded that wealth holding among free households did not become more concentrated between the mid-seventeenth century and the Revolution for the thirteen colonies as a whole, though it may have done so for individual areas. The absence of a clear colony-wide trend toward concentration seems due in part to the settlement process. The settlement process set in motion two equalizing forces. First, it raised the share of the population residing at the more egalitarian frontier, reducing the relative importance of the more inegalitarian settlements on the seaboard. Second, wealth accumulation rates were apparently more rapid in frontier settlements, thus reducing the gap between settled and frontier regions. If further research confirms this view of pre-Revolutionary trends, it will further highlight the importance of the period from 1820 to 1860 in dating the shift to more concentrated wealth in America.

The movements in nineteenth-century regional income inequality do not parallel wage or wealth inequality trends within regions. Easterlin's estimates show that regional inequality of nominal income per capita (or per worker) was steady between 1840 and 1860, widening dramatically only between 1860 and 1880. The fact that regional inequality was closely tied to a widening of the North–South gap points to the Civil War as the main source of regional disparities. It should be noted, however, that this interregional inequality, once established, followed the intraregional measures along a high inequality plateau, sharply declining only following the 1920s.

We have made an effort to anticipate the criticism that these aggregate trends may have been created by shifts in age composition or by differences in class and regional cost-of-living trends. Yet, changes in the adult age distribution played no significant role in accounting for the measured rise in wealth inequality between Independence and the twentieth century. Furthermore, Chapter 5 revealed the surprisingly consistent result that trends (not levels) in nominal occupational or regional inequality actually understate real inequality trends after deflation by appropriate class or regional cost-of-living indices.

Much more evidence could be gathered on the course of inequality before World War I. To whet revisionist appetites, we shall focus on the kind of new information which would have the best chance of overthrowing the conclusions reached in Part One of this book. New occupational wage series could be pulled together from company records and combined with local cost-of-living indices. Such series might overturn our belief in an antebellum surge in wage inequality in any of several ways. It might turn out that we have relied too heavily on intraregional and nonfarm wage series. Wage rates in other regions or in agriculture might prove on closer examination to have moved in such a fashion as to reduce inequality before the Civil War. (The trick in this case is to use truly local cost-of-living indices.) Or perhaps a careful check will show that the skilled and unskilled job definitions changed in such a way as to widen the percentile rank gap between skilled and unskilled before 1860, making wage stretching an artifact of changing job status. Or perhaps the antebellum surge documented here is based on a few unrepresentative cases. On this issue and others, new wage series could shed considerable light.

There are hundreds of thousands of probate documents awaiting scholars seeking a fuller view of wealth at death for all periods in American history. As we noted in Chapter 3, these have hardly been tapped for the long period between Independence and World War I, and even colonial wealth research could yield a richer harvest if more data were gathered. In particular, new nineteenth-century data could possibly revise the trends we have sketched. It may be that the rise of wealth concentration between 1774 and 1860 was a mirage due to defects either in the Jones or in the Soltow estimates. Alternatively, we may have fallen victims of a fallacy of composition invited by the fragmented local returns for the intervening dates between 1774 and 1860. Aside from the issue of aggregate wealth concentration, the same records could be applied to a study of the relative wealth position of women or of blacks after 1865.

The exploration of distribution trends can be pushed in new directions as well. One could gather profit rates for a wider range of industrial enterprises, land rents and values, poor relief rolls, and local tax records. One could also explore the distribution of life expectancy across income and wealth classes, to see if the gap in life expectancy between the better-paid and worse-paid widened or narrowed across the nineteenth century (we fear the former).

For the present, however, we think there is sufficient evidence to support the belief in a rise in wage and wealth inequality which occurred most markedly in the four decades leading up to the Civil War. There apparently was a Kuznetsian Fall from Grace as America embarked on the path of modern economic growth.

In the twentieth century, the structure of income and wealth apparently did become more equal, as Kuznets initially estimated. We have cross-checked his trends in top income recipient shares in several ways. The most important of these checks is supplied by occupational wage data. These come from truly separate sources and are independent of federal tax-return data. If wage and salary gaps failed to move in harmony with the share of top recipients in reported income, then either the tax-return data would have been in error, or the wage series would have been in error, or group shifts would have accounted for the discrepancy, or some combination of these explanations would have held. Yet Chapter 4 documented a striking parallelism between the income inequality series and the occupational pay ratio series. Both reveal a brief but sharp leveling during World War I, a resumption of the prewar inequalities across the 1920s, a pronounced leveling between 1929 and mid-century, and rough stability in the post–World War II era. It looks as though income distribution trends were influenced by true changes in the inequality of rewards in the marketplace for skills.

This view of twentieth-century inequality is reinforced by additional evidence. The 1929–1948 leveling and the postwar stability remain in clear view even after adjusting for shifts in age structure and differences in cost-of-living trends for different groups and regions. The move toward greater equality in the second quarter of this century was evident across the full range of the income spectrum: The bottom gained on the middle, and the middle gained on the top. And the leveling in *pre*-fisc inequality was as great as all the income equalization directly achieved by progressive tax and transfer policies by 1950.

Within the twentieth century, as within the nineteenth, there is a suggestive coincidence between the timing of the income-inequality and wealth-inequality trends. Even with adjustments for population coverage and experiments quantifying the effects of changes in age structure, wealth inequality dropped between 1929 and mid-century, as argued earlier by Lampman. Wealth inequality has shown no clear trend since, though the absence of an independent survey of private wealth since 1962 is the most serious gap in the twentieth-century data base on income and wealth distribution.

The greatest prize for a revisionist attacking this characterization of twentieth-century distribution trends is to show that the leveling never occurred. Such a stunning revision would have to rest on fresh evidence that the income and wealth data are all just an increasingly biased lie. Charges made with only moderate effect by Perlo (1954) would have to be greatly strengthened. What is needed is a demonstration that the income and wealth of the rich, but not of the poor, have become increasingly hidden over time, through such devices as hidden fringes, expense-account living, or outright lying to both survey researchers and tax collectors. The demonstration will not be easy, in part because the rise in underreporting among the rich may have been far less in percentage terms than that for such modest-income recipients as farmers or employees with fringe benefits.

For the present, we maintain the belief that the twentieth-century leveling, like the rise in inequality almost a century earlier, was real and of sufficient magnitude to require explanation.

The Sources of Inequality

Explaining the observed movements in wage inequality, or income inequality more generally, is not a trivial exercise. The observed movements do not correlate in any obvious way with single explanatory variables that occur readily to intuition. Leveling and inflation are not highly correlated, though an unexpected rise in the rate of inflation probably did have a leveling effect in some short-run episodes. Unionization or the rise of government cannot explain the timing of the nineteenth-century inequality trends, and there are good reasons to doubt their role even during the 1929–1948 leveling, as noted in Chapters 6 and 8.

We have argued in Parts Two and Three that trends in factor demands and supplies unrelated to such institutions as government or unions offer more promise for explaining why some periods saw widening income gaps, others saw narrowing gaps, and still others brought no change at all. Part Two suggested this by noting that inequality seemed to correlate well with movements in labor supply, imbalance in technological progress between sectors, and capital accumulation. Since each of these correlated well with inequality movements, an explicit quantitative model had to be used to disentangle their empirical relevance.

The models used in Part Three have, we feel, identified the major roles played by technological progress, labor supplies, and capital accumulation in making pay ratios widen, then remain wide, then narrow, and then stabilize again over a period spanning more than a century and a half. Quantifying these roles required the use of a general-equilibrium model in Chapters 10 and 11 and an equilibrium model of capital formation in Chapter 12.

The apparent surge in wage inequality before the Civil War seems to have been due primarily to extraordinary rates of capital accumulation (6.57% per annum between 1839 and 1859). Rapid accumulation favored skilled and high-wage workers in two ways. First, capital can substitute for unskilled labor more readily than for skilled labor, which is needed as a complement to machinery. This meant that a greater proportion of unskilled labor than skilled labor was replaced by mechanization, at least at the macro level. Second, the accumulation helped raise income per capita, and this rise, through Engel's Law, caused agriculture to contract as a share of national income, a process which released more unskilled than skilled labor. Technological change was also unbalanced and favored the expansion of the more skill-using sectors, but the models used in Chapter 10 assign to this factor less importance than capital accumulation in the antebellum era.

If this interpretation is accepted, the next task is to explain the high and rising rate of antebellum capital accumulation. After all, it may have been due to the high and rising levels of income inequality that characterized the antebellum economy. Chapter 12 considers this possibility and places limits on the role which inequality might have played in explaining why the last two antebellum decades brought such rapid capital accumulation. When the role of inequality is given an upper-bound value, the lion's share of the high rate of accumulation still remains unexplained. Although various forces could have contributed to the rapid accumulation, most of it appears to be explained by the sectoral imbalance in antebellum technological progress, a force which ironically played only a secondary role in our direct accounting for inequality trends in Chapter 10. The fact that total factor productivity growth was most rapid in the industrial sector seems to have raised the rate of accumulation in two ways. First, it was particularly rapid in those sectors supplying producers' equipment. This served to cut the supply price of producer durables, making it possible with the same income (in units of consumer goods) to purchase more equipment relative to other commodities. Second, total factor productivity growth was also biased toward those sectors using relatively large doses of capital (and, to a lesser extent, skills) as a factor of production. As these sectors expanded, this served to raise the demand for capital and skills nationwide, checking part of the decline in the relative price of capital goods, further raising capital accumulation, and further buoying up the wages of skilled labor. It thus appears that the explanation of the antebellum rise in wage inequality owes quite a bit to technological imbalance, much of this influence being transmitted through the rate of capital accumulation.

In the late nineteenth and early twentieth centuries, pay ratios followed a path requiring a more eclectic explanation than the simple contrast between rapid antebellum industrialization and the slow growth and relative quiescence of the eighteenth century. In the late nineteenth century, capital accumulation was a bit less rapid, and productivity growth a bit less unbalanced among sectors, than in the antebellum period. These changes explain about half of the observed shift from sharply rising to relatively stable pay ratios in the nonfarm sector. Another important role was assumed by demographic changes. To judge from some very tentative estimates, skills per man-hour grew significantly in the late nineteenth century after having remained stable in the last two antebellum decades. The apparent cause of this acceleration was the decline in the share of the labor force consisting of unskilled immigrants from lower-income countries. Whereas the mid-century flood of Irish and Germans was apparently sufficient to keep the average skill level from rising despite improved literacy among free native workers, immigration late in the century was a smaller share of labor force growth and came in larger proportion from Great Britain. The resulting rise in the growth of skills helped prevent a continuation of the more rapid antebellum widening of the gap between the wages of skilled and unskilled labor.

The first decade of this century brought a resumption in wage stretching. The framework used in Chapter 10 can account for most of the observed change. This time, however, the rising trend owed nothing to capital accumulation or to demographic shifts. Capital accumulation continued to decelerate, a drift that should have induced a narrowing in pay gaps. The growth of skills per member of the labor force (or per man-hour, the measure actually used here) did not change greatly, as best we can judge from shaky numbers. Rather the explanation for the return to widening gaps seems to rest on a resumption of more unbalanced technological progress. Early in this century, overall productivity progress in agriculture may have stopped or even declined, according to the Kendrick estimates. The locus of the fastest productivity advance was in the skill-intensive sectors: telephones, electric utilities, natural gas, and possibly some of the service industries. With agricultural progress slow and skill-intensive progress rapid, common labor found food prices rising almost as fast as their nominal earnings, while skilled groups had more substantial improvements in real income.

Across the 1910s and 1920s, the wage structure first compressed and then widened again, leaving no net change in wage inequality. Our model offers two interesting perspectives on this net stability. First, the failure of the 1899–1909 wage widening to continue seems to be due in part to the changing structure of the economy. For example, while the rate of capital accumulation changed little over the first three decades of this century, prewar parameters were such as to make capital accumulation one force contributing to wage inequality, yet 1929 parameters greatly diminish capital accumulation's role. The reason is the *sectoral convergence pattern* noted in Chapter 11. Across World War I and the 1920s, sectors became more similar in capital intensity. Agriculture became much more capital-intensive, whether or not one includes returns to farmland in the definition of capital compensation. Industry, meanwhile, moved away from capital intensity, shifting toward greater reliance on skills. As a result, after 1909, rapid capital accumulation had come to mean accumulation of a factor widely spread across all sectors rather than one concentrated in relatively skill-intensive sectors. Identifying this sectoral convergence pattern is an important step toward understanding structural changes in the twentieth-century economy. Identifying its changing importance for income distribution is one of the fruits of using the general-equilibrium model: here the model is directing our attention to a change that common sense could not have seen until the model had been employed.

Second, if the only kind of growth from 1909 to 1929 had been growth in factor supplies, the era of income leveling would have been ushered in two decades earlier. This would have happened, says the model, because immigration and fertility were making smaller contributions to labor force growth, especially during World War I and after the immigration restrictions took effect in 1924–1925. These demographic changes meant slower labor force growth and faster growth in skills per person, which acted to depress the pay advantage of the more skilled. But in fact there was no net decline in skill premia, since the 1920s undid the momentary inflation-related compression of the pay structure during World War I. The model offers an explanation which will sit well with most historians of the Roaring Twenties: The era 1909–1929 was again one of very unbalanced technological progress, with productivity advancing faster in automobiles, tires, consumer appliances, petrochemicals, and electric utilities than in the rest of the economy. The locus of faster total factor productivity growth was close enough to the locus of skill intensity to create disproportionately heavy demands for skills. This offset the leveling effect of demographic forces, making the model predict the stability that actually occurred.

The leveling that finally came after 1929 is now readily explained. It was completed by 1948 rather than later, in part because the inflation of the 1940s raised wage rates for the unskilled faster than the stickier rates for skilled and professional labor. By the 1960s, however, the actual net leveling of the wage structure was no greater than that predicted by the model. The arrival of the leveling era was largely the result of both technological and demographic forces. Total factor productivity growth was more evenly balanced among sectors than in any other era since 1840, accelerating in agriculture and some services. The switch to balanced productivity growth after 1929 eliminated a key source of rising wage inequality that had been at work almost without cessation since 1820. This change seems to have accounted for about half of the observed wage leveling between 1929 and 1948. Another 30% of the observed wage leveling is explained by demographic forces: By having fewer babies and by shutting out would-be immigrants from the Old World, Americans helped themselves achieve more equal pay between 1929 and the postwar era.

The model used in Chapter 11 also predicted that the leveling of wage and salary rates should have continued in the postwar era, but at a rate slower than the "income revolution" of 1929–1948. The rate of leveling should have been slower since recent female entrants (with lower prior experience and fewer advantages) rose as a share of the labor force fast enough to hold down the relative growth of average "skills." To a lesser extent, the model also predicted less leveling for the postwar years because sectoral productivity growth imbalances seem to have reappeared.

There are, it seems, three good reasons for expecting continued downward pressure on the pay advantages of the more skilled: Labor force growth will drop off and remain low throughout the 1980s; more balanced patterns of productivity growth are likely to be forthcoming in the wake of the jump in the relative price of the fuels; and the pattern of factor proportions has converged among sectors in a fashion that makes further leveling likely as average skill levels grow.

These causal explanations are advanced on the basis of the general-equilibrium modeling in Part Three. But we should emphasize what we have *not* shown. The coincidence between inequality facts and the model's predictions does *not* mean that our assumptions are correct. It does *not* imply that we believe perfect competition and full employment best characterize the American economy. Our analysis does *not* mean that no other forces affected inequality trends, even when the model's predictions and the inequality facts coincide. What we can assert is (*a*) that the model has expanded our perspective by suggesting plausible interpretations that appeal to economic intuition once suggested; and (*b*) that the model has given the best available quantification of the influence of *those exogenous forces it considered*. If readers will grant that we have achieved this much, then we know where to look next in any further attempts to search for the sources of changing inequality in the long run.

Growth, Accumulation, and Equality

American experience now offers a clearer perspective on the alleged growth–equity trade-off. As we noted earlier in this book, it has frequently been argued that to achieve faster growth a nation must accumulate more rapidly, and that redistributive policies which favor the rich (who save) are regrettably necessary if growth is to be promoted. We now see several reasons for doubting this argument. First, it lacks the look of raw correlation that was supposed to be its opening wedge. The periods of high (or rising) inequality and high (or rising) investment shares in the United States were periods in which national income per capita grew no faster than the twentieth-century era of leveling and slower accumulation. Growth in income per capita has been remarkably stable across periods bounded by full-employment years, ever since 1839. If one is still inclined to argue that high or rising inequality raised the growth rate in income per capita, one must be prepared to introduce fresh evidence that other forces just happened to offset this tendency at the right times.

The main reason why the growth–inequality correlation is missing from American experience is that when inequality and accumulation were declining, technological progress was rapid. In particular, a central theme emerging from this study is the way in which the twentieth century, with slower factor growth but faster productivity growth, serves as an instructive counterexample to the nineteenth. The link between income inequality and the rate of growth is very tenuous and pliable. It depends critically on the *source* of both the inequality and the growth. In the nineteenth-century, unbalanced productivity growth, rapid growth in the labor supply, and slow skills growth per man-hour combined to yield considerable growth in income per capita based largely on capital accumulation. It also produced inequality. In the twentieth century, more balanced (and generally faster) productivity growth, slower labor force growth, and faster growth in skills per man-hour brought about the same growth rates with income equalization.

American experience thus supports part of the position taken by World Bank economists (Chenery et al., 1974). As we noted in Chapter 1, this group has stressed the need to expand our perspective on the policy options dealing with both growth and inequality. Their central message is that policy can serve both the growth and the equality goals by encouraging those kinds of investments that enhance the value of poor people's human and nonhuman assets, possibly in combination with direct redistribution of land and income.

American experience can speak to the question, What policies foster growth with redistribution? It cannot yet resolve the debate over the efficiency and growth effects of direct redistribution from rich to poor, partly because such redistribution is of recent vintage only. But the full range of experience since 1840 underlines the point that whatever raises agricultural productivity, be it government encouragement or private initiative, has a much different impact on the overall distribution of earnings and income than the same amount of productivity improvement in industry. This was evident from the role of sectoral productivity differences in both the nineteenth and the twentieth centuries. If there is no *a priori* reason to assume that government tax incentives to investment, or government enterprise investment, or government infrastructure investment, is inherently more productive if made in industry than in agriculture, then it is proper and essential to include the income-distributive effects of the investment choice in policy debate.

Finally, American experience also underlines the potential importance of government demographic policies on income distribution. The clear link between labor force quantity and skill growth on the one hand and inequality trends on the other argues that policies restricting fertility and immigration are important instruments to cushion the impact of rapid population growth on inequality early in the demographic transition.

These are the sorts of conclusions that emerge when income distribution trends are related to the changing patterns of productivity and population growth that have accompanied the development process in the American past. As we see it, these are the key forces driving Kuznets's inverted-U relating inequality to economic development.

Appendices

TRENDS IN COLONIAL
WEALTH INEQUALITY *(percentages of wealth held by top wealth holders)*

New England Colonies

Connecticut: Probate Wealth

Period	(1a) Top 10% Hartford (Personal)	(1b) Top 10% Hartford (Total)	(2a) Top 30% Hartford (Personal)	(2b) Top 30% Hartford (Total)	(3) Top 10% Hartford (Real)
1650–1669	45.5%	47.8%	75.0%	76.2%	53.0%
1670–1679	43.0	54.1	68.0	76.7	55.0
1680–1684 ⎱ 1685–1689 ⎰	47.0	56.4	73.0	81.6	60.0 48.0
1690–1694 ⎱ 1695–1699 ⎰	43.0	52.1	71.0	74.9	40.0 36.0
1700–1709	46.0	40.3	72.0	69.4	36.0
1710–1714	45.0	45.6	70.0	70.8	41.0
1715–1719	43.5	45.0	66.5	71.4	47.0
1720–1724	45.5		71.0		38.0
1725–1729	42.5		65.0		37.0
1730–1734	48.0		70.0		47.0
1735–1739	33.0		62.0		42.0
1740–1744	44.0		68.0		48.0
1745–1749	43.0		70.0		53.5
1750–1754	39.0		65.0		49.0
1755–1759	34.0		68.0		50.0
1760–1764	47.0		70.0		54.0
1765–1769	48.5		69.5		42.5
1770–1774	45.0		71.0		49.4

Connecticut and New Hampshire: Unadjusted Probate Wealth

		Connecticut: Top 30%		(7)
	(4)	(5) Middle-Sized	(6) Small	Portsmouth, New Hampshire
Period	Hartford	Towns	Towns	Top 30%
1700–1720	74.03%	50.12%		65.5%
1720–1740	73.02	63.95		75.3
1740–1760	77.27	69.05	60.83%	79.7
1760–1776	73.94	69.07	67.50	79.1

Massachusetts: Boston and Suffolk County, Probate Wealth

	(8) Top 10%		(9) Top 10%
Period	Boston	Period	Boston
1650–1664	60.0%		
1665–1674	64.0		
1685–1694	46.0	1684–1699	41.2%
1695–1704	50.0		
1705–1714	56.0	1700–1715	54.5
1715–1719	54.0		
		1716–1725	61.7
		1726–1735	65.6
		1736–1745	58.6
1750–1754	53.0	1746–1755	55.2
		1756–1765	67.5
1760–1769	53.0	1766–1775	61.1
1782–1788	56.0		

	(10) Top 10% Suffolk		(11) Top 30%
Period	County	Period	Boston
1695–1697	40.6%		
1705–1706	50.2	1700–1720	84.25%
1715–1717	36.4		
1726–1727	50.8		
1735–1737	38.7	1720–1740	82.45
1746–1747	50.9		
1755–1757	55.7	1740–1760	87.94
1766–1767	48.6		
1777–1778	41.4	1760–1776	85.30

Massachusetts: Boston, Tax Lists

	Boston: Top 10%	
Year	(12) Unadjusted	(13) Adjusted
1681		42.30%
1687	46.60%	
1771	63.60	47.50
1790	64.70	

Massachusetts: Rural Areas, Probate Wealth

Period	(14) Top 30% Rural Suffolk	(15) Top 30% Worcester	(16) Top 10% Essex
1635–1660			36.0%
1661–1681			49.0
1700–1720	62.52%		
1720–1740	58.01	60.24%	
1740–1760	67.57	64.42	
1760–1776	68.05	68.06	

Period	(17) Top 10% Rural Suffolk	(18) Top 10% Hampshire	(19) Top 10% Worcester
1650–1664	37.0%		
1665–1674	37.0	30.0%	
1685–1694	34.0	37.0	
1695–1704	36.0	35.0	
1705–1714	33.0	38.0	
1715–1719	31.0	52.0	
1750–1754	31.0	41.0	
1760–1769	38.0		39.0%
1782–1788	42.4		43.0

Massachusetts: Rural Areas, Tax Lists

	Hingham	
Year	(20) Top 10%	(21) Top 30%
1754	37.44%	72.90%
1765	40.09	72.40
1772	39.93	71.43
1779	46.52	77.58
1790	44.66	74.53

Middle Colonies

New York and Pennsylvania: Tax Lists

	(22)	Philadelphia		(25)
Year	Top 10% Chester, Pa.	(23) Top 10%	(24) Top 4%	Top 10% New York City
1693	23.8%	46.0%	32.8%	
1695				44.5%
1715	25.9			
1730	28.6			43.7
1748	28.7			
1756		46.6	34.0	
1760	29.9			
1767		65.7	49.5	
1772		71.2	54.7	
1774		72.3	55.5	
1782	33.6			
1789				45.0

Maryland and Pennsylvania: Probate Wealth

Period	(26) Top 10% Maryland	(27) Top 10% Maryland (Adjusted)	Period	(28) Top 10% Philadelphia	Period	(29) Top 20% Chester County
1675–1679	49.5%					
1680–1684	51.0					
1685–1689	53.0					
1690–1694	55.0		1684–1699	36.4%		
1695–1699	53.0					
1700–1704	54.7	67.2%				
1705–1709		57.7	1700–1715	41.3		
1710–1714		66.2				
1715–1719		65.5	1716–1725	46.8	1714–1731	46.41%
			1726–1735	53.6		
			1736–1745	51.3	1734–1745	53.02
1750–1754		65.8	1746–1755	70.1		
			1756–1765	60.3	1750–1770	52.53
			1766–1775	69.9		
1782–1788		60.0			1775–1790	60.49

Sources and notes: Cols. (1a), (1b), (2a), (2b), and (3): Professor Jackson T. Main has kindly supplied us with these data underlying his (1976) article on Connecticut wealth. The estate inventory data, which cover the great majority of adult male decedents before mid-eighteenth century, have been age-adjusted to estimate the distributions of personal estate, real estate, and total estate among living adult males whose estates were likely to be inventoried at death.

Cols. (4), (5), (6), and (7): Unadjusted probate wealth, sampled counties, is from Daniels (1973–1974, Tables 3 and 4, pp. 131–132). The middle-sized Connecticut towns are Danbury, Waterbury, and Windham. The small Connecticut towns are the "frontier settlements" Canaan, Kent, Salisbury, and Sharon, all of which are in Litchfield County.

Col. (8): Wealth inventories of adult male decedents, total estate values, are from G. Main (1976, Table IV).

Col. (9): Unadjusted inventoried personal wealth (excluding real estate) is from Nash (1976b, Table 3, p. 9).

Col. (10): Suffolk County includes Boston. Inventoried total wealth, unadjusted, is from Warden (1976, Table 2, p. 599).

Col. (11): Unadjusted probate wealth, total estate value, is from Daniels (1973–1974, Table 2, p. 129).

Cols. (12) and (13): Taxable wealth from Boston tax lists is augmented to include adult males without wealth. The 1687 and 1771 figures in Col. (12) are from Henretta (1965, Tables I and II, p. 185); the 1790 entry is from Kulikoff (1971, Table 2B, p. 381). Gerard Warden has warned that one takes great risks in trying to infer the level and trend of wealth inequality from Boston's tax assessments. Undervaluation ratios varied greatly over time and across assets, and many assets escaped assessment altogether. His adjustments (Warden, 1976, p. 595) for these valuation and coverage problems are presented in Col. (13).

Cols. (14) and (15): Unadjusted probate wealth, total estate values, is from Daniels (1973–1974, Table 2, p. 129). Rural Suffolk refers to Suffolk County excluding Boston, whereas Worcester refers to the county including the city.

Col. (16): Unadjusted total estate values are from Koch (1969, pp. 57–59), as cited in G. Main (1976, Table I).

Cols. (17), (18), and (19): County data from Suffolk excludes Boston. Total estate values among adult male decedents are reported in G. Main (1976, Table IV).

Cols. (20) and (21): Taxable wealth, adult males, is from Hingham, Massachusetts, tax lists, adjusted to include males without property, from D. S. Smith (1973, Table III-1, p. 90). Smith also reports top wealth shares for 1647, 1680, and 1711, but these observations are unsuited for time-series analysis. For justification of their exclusion, see D. S. Smith (1973, Appendix Tables III–1 and III–2) and Warden (1976, p. 595).

Col. (22): Taxable wealth among taxpayers, unadjusted for the propertyless, is from Lemon and Nash (1968, Table I, p. 11). Lemon and Nash also report an observation for 1800–1802, but since it includes Delaware County as well, we exclude it from the time series.

Cols. (23) and (24): Taxable wealth among taxpayers is unadjusted for the propertyless. Except for 1772, all observations are from Nash (1976b, Table 1, p. 6 and Table 2, p. 7). The 1772 figure is from Nash (1976b, Table 2, p. 11). Tax assessment data are beset with problems, and Philadelphia is no exception. For example, Nash (1976b, p. 8) noted that the 1756 records omitted all those in the lowest wealth class who, nevertheless, would have paid the head tax "ordinarily." It is not clear whether the same is true of 1693. Furthermore, since the minimum assessment was set at £8 in 1756, £2 in 1767, and £1 in 1774, there is an upward bias imparted to the inequality trends over time.

Col. (25): Taxable wealth among taxpayers is unadjusted for the propertyless. The figure for 1730 is from Nash (1976b, Table 1). The entries for 1695 and 1789 are from G. Main (1976, Table I).

Cols. (26) and (27): "Maryland" is actually a pooling of six counties: Anne Arundel, Baltimore, Calvert, Charles, Kent, and Somerset. The 1675–1754 observations are based on inventoried adult male wealth, personal estate only. The 1782–1784 observation is of questionable comparability, since it is based on taxable wealth (real and personal) distribution among taxpayers. Both cols. are taken from G. Main (1976, Tables A–1, and IV). Col. (27) reports inventoried adult male personal estates, adjusted for underreporting. Main also reports the unadjusted top 10% for 1705–1754, but since the adjustments are so large, no purpose would be served in reporting the erroneous figures beyond 1704. She does not attempt to adjust the pre-1700 series.

Col. (28): Inventoried personal wealth is from Nash (1976b, Table 3, p. 9).

Col. (29): Chester County, Pennsylvania, inventoried wealth, excluding land, is from Ball (1976, Table 7, p. 637).

UNDERLYING DATA FOR ANALYSIS OF COLONIAL WEALTH DECOMPOSITION

The following summary table displays average wealth benchmarks for colonial Boston and New England:

Area	Year or Period	Wealth (*pounds*)	Population	Wealth per Capita ($\overline{W}$) (*pounds*)
Boston (*B*)	1687	£331,820	5,925	£56.00
	1771	815,136	16,540	49.28
New England (*NE*)	1680–1689	2,346,858	67,376	34.83
	1774	22,322,880	606,596	36.80
Non-Boston (*NB*)	1680–1689	2,015,038	61,451	32.79
	1771–1774	21,507,744	590,056	36.45

W_B/W_{NE} = 1.608 in 1680s; 1.339 in 1770s.

W_{NB}/W_{NE} = .941 in 1680s; .990 in 1770s.

Boston's share of = .088 in 1680s; .027 in 1770s.
population

Sources and notes: The Boston wealth estimates are based on taxable wealth adjusted by Warden (1976, pp. 588–589) for both undervaluation and incomplete lists. New England wealth estimates are based on probate samples. The 1680–1689 figure is taken from Anderson (1975, Table 9, p. 169), and the 1774 figure is from A. H. Jones (1972, Table 1, p. 102). All population estimates are taken from the same sources except the Boston estimate for 1687. Using Shattuck's data, Warden reports the following per annum Boston averages: 1692–1699, 6600; and 1700–1709, 7378. Applying the growth rate between 1692–1699 and 1700–1709 backwards to 1687 yields a Boston population estimate of 5925. Average wealth benchmarks per capita for Philadelphia and the middle colonies in 1774 are Philadelphia, £525; middle colonies, £377; and Non-Philadelphia, £371. All of these are calculated from A. H. Jones (1971, Tables 13 and 17), based on net worth rather than physical wealth, and adjusted to all living potential wealth holders.

TOP WEALTH-HOLDER SHARES IN THE NORTHEAST, 1760-1891

(1) Top decile shares of net worth among all decedents, Massachusetts, 1829/1831–1889/1891

1829–1831:	71.3–73.1%
1859–1861:	80.4
1879–1881:	87.2
1889–1891:	82.5–83.4

(3) Top decile shares of total wealth inventoried at death, among adult males, Boston, 1760–1891

1760–1769:	53.0%
1782–1788:	56.0
1829–1831:	83.0
1859–1861:	93.8
1879–1881:	83.9
1889–1891:	85.8

(5) Top decile shares of total taxable wealth, among property taxpayers plus adult males with zero property, Hingham, Massachusetts, 1765–1880

1765:	40.1%
1772:	39.9
1779:	46.5
1790:	44.7
1800:	41.9
1810:	39.1
1820:	46.2
1830:	47.0
1840:	51.4
1850:	56.7
1860:	58.8
1880:	57.5

(2) Top decile shares of taxable wealth among taxpayers, Boston, 1771–1845

1771:	63.5%
1790:	64.7
1820:	50.3
1830:	66.2
1845:	72.9

(4) Top decile shares of total wealth inventoried at death, among adult males of rural Suffolk County, Massachusetts, 1763/1769–1889/1891

1763–1769:	38.0%
1783–1788:	42.4
1829–1831:	59.5
1859–1861:	72.9
1889–1891:	80.8

(6) The share of estimated nonbusiness wealth held by the top 4% of "population," New York City, 1828–1845

1828:	49%
1845:	66

(7) The share of estimated nonbusiness wealth held by the top 1% of "population," of Brooklyn, 1810–1841

1810:	22%
1841:	42

Sources and notes: (1) Massachusetts, 1829–1891: The shares of total estimated wealth held by the richest decile of the adult males dying in Massachusetts are given in the periods 1829–1831, 1859–1861, 1879–1881, and 1889–1891. The values held at death show greater inequality than would the values held by living adult males at any point in time. The primary data on the values of probated estates are from Massachusetts Bureau of Statistics of Labor (1895). The figures for the later three periods were adjusted for estimated deaths of males without wealth and for assumed distributions of wealth among uninventoried estates by King (1915, Tables IX and X and accompanying text). A careful scrutiny of King's estimates revealed the specific assumptions he made. These assumptions were not given any careful justification but do not seem implausible. King's assumptions were also applied to the 1829–1831 distribution of probated wealth. For 1829–1831 it was assumed that the total number of adult male deaths was in the same ratio to the adult male population of Massachusetts as in 1859–1861, an assumption based on a reading of Vinovskis (1972).

(2) Boston Taxpayers, 1771–1845: The eighteenth-century estimates are from Kulikoff (1971, Table II) and Henretta (1965, Tables I and II, p. 185). The estimates for 1820, 1830, 1845 were taken from G. Main (1976, Table II). She has reworked the data originally published in Pessen (1973, pp. 38–40) and in Shattuck (1846, p. 95).

(3) Boston Inventoried Estates, 1760–1891: This is the top decile of total wealth inventoried at time of death of adult males. See discussion in (1) above. The figures for 1760–1788 are taken from G. Main (1976, Table IV). Those for 1829–1891 are "adjusted" and taken from the same source, Table VI.

(4) Rural Suffolk County, Massachusetts, 1763–1891: This is the top decile of total wealth inventoried at time of death of adult males (G. Main, 1976, Table IX).

(5) Hingham, Massachusetts, 1765–1880: The share of total taxable wealth held by the top decile in Hingham, property taxpayers plus adult males with zero property, is from D. S. Smith (1973, Table III–1 and Appendix Table III–2).

(6) New York City, 1828–1845 and (7) Brooklyn, 1810–1841: The estimates for both cities are taken from Pessen (1973, Tables 3–1, 3–2, 3–3, and 3–4, pp. 33–37). For New York City, Pessen supplies the share of noncorporate wealth among "the population" held by the top 4%. The data for Brooklyn refer to the top 1%, whose share rose from 22% to 42% between 1810 and 1841.

OCCUPATIONAL PAY RATIOS IN THE NONFARM UNITED STATES SINCE COLONIAL TIMES, 1771–1972

(1) Carpenters, Mass., Daily Wages

1771–1780	1.388	1831–1840	1.606
1781–1790	1.259	1841–1850	1.608
1791–1800	1.181	1851–1860	2.082
1801–1810	1.334	1861–1880	1.635
1811–1820	1.242	1881–1883	1.840
1821–1830	1.244		

(2) Public School Teachers, (2a) urban and (2b) rural (1915 = 1.000)

	(2a) Urban	(2b) Rural		(2a) Urban	(2b) Rural
1841	.461	.434	1866	.530	.569
1842	.462	.442	1867	.605	.566
1843	.459	.459	1868	.638	.593
1844	.466	.446	1869	.650	.589
1845	.448	.455	1870	.710	.675
1846	.435	.464	1871	.714	.755
1847	.425	.462	1872	.698	.745
1848	.433	.458	1873	.706	.704
1849	.466	.459	1874	.744	.732
1850	.460	.480	1875	.779	.743
1851	.479	.446	1876	.788	.853
1852	.495	.465	1877	.801	.808
1853	.517	.477	1878	.779	.915
1854	.513	.498	1879	.727	.926
1855	.547	.525	1880	.749	.886
1856	.535	.535	1881	.733	.853
1857	.562	.538	1882	.704	.740
1858	.600	.585	1883	.693	.729
1859	.572	.533	1884	.689	.745
1860	.564	.537	1885	.720	.846
1861	.544	.602	1886	.713	.843
1862	.526	.564	1887	.699	.754
1863	.482	.494	1888	.686	.812
1864	.489	.498	1889	.687	.835
1865	.486	.513	1890	.694	.874

(3) Artisans to Laborers

1841	1.704	1858	1.698	1875	1.837
1842	1.714	1859	1.670	1876	1.887
1843	1.683	1860	1.629	1877	1.930
1844	1.693	1861	1.641	1878	1.924
1845	1.683	1862	1.619	1879	1.890
1846	1.727	1863	1.556	1880	1.906
1847	1.701	1864	1.586	1881	1.872
1848	1.659	1865	1.667	1882	1.812
1849	1.718	1866	1.652	1883	1.789
1850	1.667	1867	1.728	1884	1.780
1851	1.656	1868	1.791	1885	1.807
1852	1.652	1869	1.813	1886	1.831
1853	1.668	1870	1.810	1887	1.795
1854	1.686	1871	1.786	1888	1.766
1855	1.710	1872	1.807	1889	1.766
1856	1.673	1873	1.775	1890	1.773
1857	1.703	1874	1.804		

(4) Engineers to Common Laborers, U.S.

1851	1.41	1861	1.81	1871	1.68
1852	1.53	1862	1.80	1872	1.72
1853	1.50	1863	1.67	1873	1.75
1854	1.50	1864	1.58	1874	1.79
1855	1.48	1865	1.65	1875	1.81
1856	1.62	1866	1.61	1876	1.86
1857	1.63	1867	1.61	1877	1.87
1858	1.60	1868	1.62	1878	1.90
1859	1.74	1869	1.61	1879	1.88
1860	1.73	1870	1.67	1880	1.85

(5) *Urban Skilled Workers*

1816	1.094	1858	1.630	1900	1.825
1817	1.176	1859	1.668	1901	1.829
1818	1.149	1860	1.668	1902	1.809
1819	1.218	1861	1.668	1903	1.826
1820	1.207	1862	1.758	1904	1.878
1821	1.278	1863	1.676	1905	1.857
1822	1.280	1864	1.677	1906	1.846
1823	1.271	1865	1.652	1907	1.849
1824	1.278	1866	1.684	1908	1.879
1825	1.287	1867	1.749	1909	1.909
1826	1.341	1868	1.753	1910	1.919
1827	1.355	1869	1.744	1911	1.949
1828	1.381	1870	1.754	1912	1.960
1829	1.368	1871	1.761	1913	1.960
1830	1.346	1872	1.774	1914	1.989
1831	1.361	1873	1.812	1915	1.989
1832	1.376	1874	1.810	1916	1.989
1833	1.392	1875	1.796	1917	1.876
1834	1.407	1876	1.762	1918	1.764
1835	1.422	1877	1.740	1919	1.722
1836	1.437	1878	1.745	1920	1.806
1837	1.452	1879	1.697	1921	1.904
1838	1.468	1880	1.734	1922	1.943
1839	1.483	1881	1.736	1923	1.917
1840	1.498	1882	1.741	1924	1.933
1841	1.498	1883	1.747	1925	1.952
1842	1.498	1884	1.747	1926	1.953
1843	1.498	1885	1.703	1927	1.922
1844	1.511	1886	1.726	1928	1.919
1845	1.537	1887	1.705	1929	1.893
1846	1.564	1888	1.697	1930	1.922
1847	1.784	1889	1.700	1931	1.903
1848	1.773	1890	1.702	1932	1.951
1849	1.673	1891	1.732	1933	1.912
1850	1.736	1892	1.706	1934	1.865
1851	1.762	1893	1.717	1935	1.880
1852	1.738	1894	1.735	1936	1.917
1853	1.735	1895	1.718	1937	1.893
1854	1.769	1896	1.717	1938	1.901
1855	1.781	1897	1.797	1939	1.888
1856	1.836	1898	1.801		
1857	1.679	1899	1.825	1948	1.773

(6) Skilled Workers

1950/1951	1.580	1965/1966	1.611
1955/1956	1.556	1970/1971	1.646
1960/1961	1.603	1972/1973	1.673

(7) Skilled Workers in Manufacturing

1907	2.05	1945–1947	1.55
1918–1919	1.75	1952–1953	1.37
1931–1932	1.80	1955–1956	1.38
1937–1940	1.65		

(8) Public School Teachers

Year	Value	Year	Value	Year	Value	Year	Value
1841	.812	1867	1.065	1893	1.293	1922	1.622
1842	.813	1868	1.123	1894	1.323	1924	1.456
1843	.808	1869	1.144	1895	1.341	1926	1.473
1844	.820	1870	1.250	1896	1.355	1928	1.510
1845	.789	1871	1.257	1897	1.349	1930	1.548
1846	.766	1872	1.229	1898	1.356	1932	1.862
1847	.748	1873	1.243	1899	1.409	1934	1.343
1848	.762	1874	1.310	1900	1.421	1936	1.332
1849	.820	1875	1.371	1901	1.407	1938	1.213
1850	.810	1876	1.387	1902	1.444	1940	1.213
1851	.843	1877	1.410	1903	1.409	1942	1.004
1852	.871	1878	1.371	1904	1.455	1944	.993
1853	.910	1879	1.280	1905	1.470	1946	1.001
1854	.903	1880	1.319	1906	1.500	1948	1.090
1855	.963	1881	1.290	1907	1.494	1950	1.096
1856	.942	1882	1.239	1908	1.460	1952	1.119
1857	.989	1883	1.220	1909	1.550	1954	1.136
1858	1.056	1884	1.213	1910	1.553	1956	1.167
1859	1.007	1885	1.268	1911	1.596	1958	1.172
1860	.993	1886	1.255	1912	1.638	1960	1.222
1861	.958	1887	1.231	1913	1.573	1962	1.256
1862	.926	1888	1.208	1914	1.576	1964	1.290
1863	.849	1889	1.209	1915	1.539	1966	1.338
1864	.861	1890	1.222	1916	1.470	1968	1.343
1865	.856	1891	1.233	1918	.906	1970	1.305
1866	.933	1892	1.268	1920	.984	1972	1.301

(9) Methodist Ministers, Mass. and N.Y.

1860	4.513	1882	4.861	1904	4.747
1862	4.114	1884	4.936	1906	4.580
1864	3.370	1886	5.021	1908	4.226
1866	3.696	1888	5.147	1910	4.458
1868	4.321	1890	5.163	1912	4.428
1870	4.340	1892	5.458	1914	4.147
1872	5.032	1894	5.665	1916	3.743
1874	5.105	1896	5.387	1918	2.114
1876	5.233	1898	5.284	1920	1.903
1878	5.684	1900	5.137	1922	2.932
1880	5.163	1902	5.094	1924	2.829

(10) Associate Professors

1908	4.522	1928	3.479	1953	2.025
1909	4.691	1929	3.456	1954	n.a.
1910	4.798	1930	3.499	1955	1.952
1911	5.011	1931	3.715	1956	n.a.
1912	4.867	1932	4.224	1957	1.808
1913	4.552	1933	n.a.	1958	1.838
1914	4.586	1934	n.a.	1959	1.951
1915	4.441	1935	2.932	1960	1.996
1916	4.050	1936	2.976	1961	1.943
1917	3.387	1937	2.758	1962	1.964
1918	2.362	1938	2.721	1963	2.012
1919	2.128	1939	n.a.	1964	2.053
1920	2.313	1940	2.678	1965	2.091
1921	3.140	1941	n.a.	1966	2.155
1922	3.740	1942	2.150	1967	2.196
1923	3.441			1968	2.191
1924	3.367	1948	2.178	1969	2.158
1925	n.a.			1970	2.047
1926	3.427	1951	2.104	1971	2.053
1927	3.394	1952	n.a.	1972	1.928

(11) Physicians

1929	5.374	1941	3.700	1955	5.412
1930	5.094	1942	4.356		
1931	4.541	1943	4.900	1959	6.341
1932	3.973	1944	5.494		
1933	3.676	1945	5.984	1962	6.364
1934	3.530	1946	5.026	1963	6.397
1935	3.732	1947	4.676	1964	6.968
1936	4.196	1948	4.616	1965	6.879
1937	3.759	1949	n.a.	1966	7.368
1938	3.492	1950	5.178	1967	7.580
1939	3.560	1951	5.373	1968	7.655
1940	3.634			1969	7.699

(12) *Skilled Workers in Manufacturing*

1903	2.05	1956	1.42

(13) *Skilled Workers in Building Trades*

1907	1.85	1923	1.80	1939	1.70
1908	1.88	1924	1.80	1940	1.69
1909	1.91	1925	1.81	1941	1.67
1910	1.92	1926	1.77	1942	1.60
1911	1.95	1927	1.80	1943	1.59
1912	1.97	1928	1.79	1944	1.58
1913	1.97	1929	1.79	1945	1.54
1914	1.99	1930	1.77·	1946	1.47
1915	1.99	1931	1.79	1947	1.43
1916	1.99	1932	1.79	1948	1.40
1917	1.91	1933	1.82	1949	1.41
1918	1.83	1934	1.78	1950	1.39
1919	1.80	1935	1.79	1951	1.38
1920	1.66	1936	1.75	1952	1.38
1921	1.68	1937	1.72		
1922	1.74	1938	1.70		

(14) *Skilled Workers in Building Trades*

1947	1.557	1956	1.406	1965	1.311
1948	1.510	1957	1.384	1966	1.316
1949	1.510	1958	1.388	1967	1.329
1950	1.485	1959	1.354	1968	1.341
1951	1.486	1960	1.340	1969	1.356
1952	1.500	1961	1.314	1970	1.272
1953	1.477	1962	1.324	1971	1.341
1954	1.459	1963	1.322	1972	1.354
1955	1.431	1964	1.312		

Sources and notes: (1) Carpenters: This is the ratio of carpenters' to common day laborers' daily wage rates (without board). For 1621–1641 the figures given in *Historical Statistics* (1960, Series Z324 and Z329) are the legal maximum rates reported for Virginia (1621), Massachusetts (1633), New Haven (1640), and New Haven (1641). The ratios ranged from 1.25 to 1.33. For 1771–1780 through 1881–1883, reported in table, the ratio is the Massachusetts average given in Massachusetts Bureau of Labor Statistics (1885).

(2) Public School Teachers: Data are taken from Lindert (1974, Table 2, p. 23).

Urban Variant: For 1841–1890, the teachers' pay series is based on the average weekly salary for male public elementary and secondary school teachers in 21 cities given in Burgess (1920, pp. 32–33). The unskilled-labor wage rate used as the denominator in the urban variant, 1841–1920, is Burgess's series for "laborers" (p. 71).

Rural Variant: The teachers' pay series is based on the average weekly salary for rural male teachers in public elementary and secondary schools in 20 counties in 10 states given in

Burgess (1920, pp. 32–33). The unskilled-labor wage rate is the index of wage rates for Vermont male farmhands given in T. M. Adams (1944, pp. 87–89).

(3) Artisans vs. Laborers: Data are from Burgess (1920, Table 8). His artisans were blacksmiths, carpenters, machinists, painters, and printers. Apparently Burgess spliced together various series taken from the U.S. Department of Labor, reports of the Massachusetts Bureau of Labor Statistics, the *Weeks Report* and the *Aldrich Report*.

(4) Engineers vs. Common Laborers, U.S.: The ratio of daily wages, engineers to common laborers, based on payroll data in the *Weeks Report*, drawn from manufacturing, mining, and mechanical firms, is from Coelho and Shepherd (1976, Tables 6 and 7, pp. 218–219).

(5) Urban Skilled Workers, 1816–1939, 1948: This is a spliced series of ratios of skilled to unskilled workers' wage rates in manufacturing and the building trades, for 1816–1939 and 1948. The ratios are calculated from daily wage rates up to 1890, and from weekly rates thereafter. Though a wide variety of sources was used, two main primary sources were the *Aldrich Report* of 1891 and the series constructed from BLS wage surveys by the National Industrial Conference Board. A detailed discussion of the series is given in Williamson (1975).

(6) Skilled Workers 1950/1951–1972/1973: This is the average ratio of skilled to unskilled hourly wage rates, where the wage rate for skilled labor is a weighted average of the rates for mechanics, electricians, and carpenters in six cities (Boston, New York, Atlanta, Chicago, Denver, and San Francisco–Oakland) and the wage rate for unskilled labor is that for janitors and custodians in the same cities. The employment weights used are those for the skilled categories in the six cities in the 1960 census. The series was calculated from the BLS occupational wage surveys of metropolitan areas.

(7) Skilled Workers in Manufacturing: The ratio of hourly skilled-labor to hourly unskilled-labor wage rates in several manufacturing industries in several cities is from Ober (1948, p. 130) and Miller (1966, p. 79).

(8) Public School Teachers, 1841–1972: This ratio is of school teachers' pay per 180 days to the wages received by industrial unskilled laborers per 2000 hours. From 1890 through 1972, this ratio is calculated by dividing the annual rate of pay for primary and secondary public school teachers first by the number of days in the school year and then by 2000 times the hourly unskilled wage rate in industry. For 1841–1890, see Series (2) above. The unskilled hourly wage rate was computed as follows: (*a*) 1950/1951–1972/1973: the average hourly wage of unskilled custodial and maintenance workers in all industries, six cities (Boston, New York, Atlanta, Chicago, Denver, San Francisco–Oakland), using 1960 census employment weights, from BLS occupational wage surveys; (*b*) 1914, 1920–1948: the NICB series for males in 25 industries, cited in *Historical Statistics* (1960, Series D663); (*c*) 1915–1919: interpolated from the NICB series, using the Douglas data on weekly earnings, cited in Williamson (1975) divided by the all-manufacturing average daily hours given by E. B. Jones (1963) and the *Aldrich Report*, and adjusted so as to equal the NICB figure in dollars per hour for 1914.

(9) Methodist Ministers, 1860–1924: The average annual pay of Methodist ministers in the New England and New York conferences is divided by 2000 times the unskilled-labor hourly wage series described for Series (5) above. The New England Conference data covered "the eastern part of New York, exclusive of Long Island and part of New York City." The figures plotted here are the simple average of the annual cash salaries in these two conferences, times 1.25 to adjust for the estimated rental value of the parsonage, divided by 2000 hours times the hourly wage rate for unskilled labor. The series on ministers' pay is from Thorndike and Woodyard (1927).

(10) Associate Professors, 1908–1972: The median salaries of associate professors in large

public universities, 9-month basis, are divided by 2000 hours times the unskilled-labor hourly wage rate series described for Series (5) above. The pay series for associate professors is from Peterson and Fitzharris (1974, Appendix Table 4). Peterson and Fitzharris used data from Stigler (1950) for 1908–1942; and the *Bulletin* of the American Association of University Professors, for 1948–1972.

(11) Physicians, 1929–1969: The average annual income of self-employed physicians is divided by 2000 hours of pay for unskilled workers, as described for Series (5) above. The concept of physicians' incomes differs among the three series used for different subperiods. For 1929–1951, the figure refers to the mean net income of independent physicians, given by Stigler (1956, Table 5). For 1955–1966, the figure refers to the median income of self-employed physicians, multiplied by 1.02145 (the ratio of mean to median incomes in 1951), as reported by Rayack (1971, Table 2). For 1966–1969, the figure refers to the median income of self-employed physicians under 65, estimated by the U.S. Department of Health, Education, and Welfare, again multiplied by 1.02145. For 1966–1969, the figures tended to run about 13–15% above those reported by the IRS and about 10% above those reported by the American Medical Association. Figures for the period from 1969 on refer to the incomes of unincorporated physicians only, though a rapidly rising share of physicians, presumably those with higher incomes, became incorporated.

(12) Skilled Workers in Manufacturing: Keat (1960) gives these 1903 and 1956 benchmark skilled-labor wage ratios averaged over a wide range of manufacturing industries. Additional annual series on dispersion of wage rates for many manufacturing industries can be found in Rees and Hamilton (1971, p. 486). The Rees–Hamilton index plummets from 1941 to 1947, then rises somewhat across the 1950s and remains steady across the 1960s.

(13) and (14) Skilled Workers in Building Trades: These data are from Ober (1948, p. 130), Douty (1953, pp. 61–76) and, for 1947–1972, U.S. Department of Labor (1973, p. 218). The series is the average ratio of hourly wage rates relative to journeymen, helpers, and laborers in the building trades, averaged over a number of cities.

E

NOMINAL WAGE GAPS, URBAN VS. FARM, NEW ENGLAND, 1751–1900

(1) Massachusetts, Urban over Farm Nominal Daily Wages: "Decade Average"			
1751–1760	.932	1811–1820	1.164
1761–1770	.985	1821–1830	.991
1771–1780	1.194	1831–1840	.997
1781–1790	1.081	1841–1850	.897
1791–1800	1.306	1851–1860	.965
1801–1810	1.049	1861–1880	1.130
		1881–1883	.956

(2) Massachusetts, Urban over Farm Nominal Daily Wages: "Annual"			
1820–1830	1.033	1845	1.050
1835	.830	1860	1.070

(3) Vermont, Urban over Farm Nominal Daily Wages			
1835–1839	1.344	1870–1874	1.286
1840–1844	1.244	1875–1879	1.468
1845–1849	1.340	1880–1884	1.280
1850–1854	1.260	1885–1889	1.326
1855–1859	1.118	1890–1894	1.498
1860–1864	1.084	1895–1899	1.664
1865–1869	1.060		

Sources and notes: (1) and (2), Massachusetts: Both are taken from C. D. Wright (1889, Part IV, pp. 317–318, 323–325, and 434–435). In Series (2), medium was used when high, medium, and low rates were reported; when high and low were reported, an average was used.

(3), Vermont: The nominal daily wage for farm labor is taken from T. M. Adams (1944, Table 47, pp. 97–98). The urban nominal daily wage is a product of the hourly rates reported in Appendix G and average hours per day in industry. The average hours are from the *Aldrich Report* (Table 44, p. 179) except for 1835–1839 = 11.4 and 1892–1900 = 10.0.

TIME SERIES ON INCOME INEQUALITY IN THE UNITED STATES

(1) *Share of Income Received by Top 60% of Households (OBE–Goldsmith)*

1929–1935	87.5%		1951	83.7%
1936	86.7		1954	84.1
1941	86.4		1956	83.9
1944	84.2		1959	84.5
1947	84.0		1962	84.5
1950	84.3			

(2) *Share of Income Received by Top 5% of Recipients (Kuznets–Economic Variant)*

1919	26.10%	1929	31.88%	1938	27.80%
1920	25.76	1930	30.69	1939	27.77
1921	31.70	1931	31.96	1940	26.83
1922	30.39	1932	32.12	1941	25.67
1923	28.08	1933	30.83	1942	22.47
1924	29.06	1934	29.13	1943	20.86
1925	30.24	1935	28.77	1944	18.68
1926	30.21	1936	29.26	1945	19.27
1927	31.19	1937	28.51	1946	19.96
1928	32.06				

(3) *Share of Income Received by Top 5% of Recipients (OBE–Goldsmith)*

1929–1935	30.0%		1951	20.7%
1936	26.5		1954	20.3
1941	24.0		1956	20.2
1944	20.7		1959	20.2
1947	20.9		1962	19.6
1950	21.4			

(4) Share of Income Received by Top 5% of Recipients, Social Security Population (Brittain)

1951	21.15%	1961	20.50%
1952	20.52	1962	20.51
1953	20.03	1963	20.58
1954	20.54	1964	20.21
1955	19.51	1965	20.32
1956	20.74	1966	21.52
1957	20.36	1967	21.73
1958	20.63	1968	21.34
1959	20.70	1969	21.07
1960	20.80		

(5) Share of Income Received by Top 1% (Kuznets–Basic Variant)

1913	14.98%	1925	13.73%	1937	13.00%
1914	13.07	1926	13.93	1938	11.53
1915	14.32	1927	14.39	1939	11.80
1916	15.58	1928	14.94	1940	11.89
1917	14.16	1929	14.50	1941	11.39
1918	12.69	1930	13.82	1942	10.06
1919	12.84	1931	13.29	1943	9.38
1920	12.34	1932	12.90	1944	8.58
1921	13.50	1933	12.14	1945	8.81
1922	13.38	1934	12.03	1946	8.98
1923	12.28	1935	12.07	1947	8.49
1924	12.91	1936	13.37	1948	8.38

(6) Coefficient of Inequality (Inverse Pareto Slope) among Richest Taxpayers (Tucker–Soltow)

1866	0.71%	1916	0.75%	1927	0.66%
1867	0.69	1917	0.68	1928	0.70
1868	0.71	1918	0.61	1929	0.70
1869	0.71	1919	0.58	1930	0.62
1870	0.67	1920	0.55	1931	0.585
1871	0.71	1921	0.53	1932	0.57
		1922	0.58	1933	0.565
1894	0.61	1923	0.58	1934	0.57
		1924	0.60	1935–1936	0.56
1913	0.64	1925	0.65		
1914	0.65	1926	0.645	1965	0.47
1915	0.71				

(7) *Variance in the Log of Personal Income (Chiswick and Mincer)*

	(7a) Males 25–64	(7b) Males 35–44
1949	.6533	.6229
1950	.6341	.5477
1953	.5844	.5231
1960	.6635	.5886
1965	.6282	.5629
1969	.5813	.5231

(8) *Two Measures of Regional Inequality of Income*

(8a) Entropy: Nine Regions		(8b) Weighted Coefficient of Variation: States	
1880	.0912	1880	.355
1900	.0724	1900	.322
1920	.0469	1910	.324
1930	.0590	1919	.276
1940	.0546	1920	.331
1950	.0137	1921	.373
1960	.0140	1929	.369
1965	.0098	1948	.214
1970	.0067		

Sources and notes: (1) Share of Income Received by Top 60% of Households, 1929–1962: The OBE–Goldsmith estimates extended to 1962, as given in Budd (1967, p. xiii). The OBE–Goldsmith estimates are a hybrid of different sets of primary data. For 1929 they mixed tax returns with an independent Brookings Institution estimate of the entire income distribution. For 1935/1936 and 1941, they adjusted the results of two household surveys. For later years the results of the Census Bureau's Current Population Surveys were adjusted to the OBE–Goldsmith definitions of income and recipient unit.

(2) Share of National Income Received by Top 5%, 1919–1946: Kuznets's (1953, p. 635) economic variant measures income in a way corresponding more closely with the concept of income before taxes and transfers used here, for reasons given in his introduction. Unlike other main series on aggregate inequality, Kuznets's are based on a ranking of taxpaying units by income *per person.*

(3) Share of Income Received by Top 5%, 1929–1962: This is from OBE–Goldsmith, the same as (1) above.

(4) Share of Income Received by Top 5%, 1951–1969: This was estimated by Brittain (1972, p. 107), from unpublished data supplied by the Social Security Administration. The "income" in this case is earnings before payroll taxes, and the recipient unit is the earning individual rather than the family or household. Brittain's numbers show degrees of inequality very close to other main series because the reduction in inequality implicit in his use of data on earnings rather than total income roughly offsets the greater inequality implied by his exclusion of transfer payments and perhaps also by his use of data on earnings of individuals of all ages rather than on households.

(5) Share of National Income Received by Top 1%, 1913–1948: Kuznets's basic variant has

the same source as (2) above. He used the basic variant in order to cover the extra years (1913–1918, 1947, 1948) for which he could not estimate the economic variant.

(6) Coefficient of Inequality among Richest Taxpayers, 1866–1871, 1894, 1913–1935/1936, 1965: This is from Tucker (1938, pp. 547–587) and Soltow (1969, Table 2). The coefficient is the inverse Pareto slope, which measures the percentage by which income must rise to cut by 1% the proportion of the population having incomes above this income in the year in question. Soltow gives this inverse Pareto slope, while Tucker gives its reciprocal.

(7) Variance in the Log of Personal Income, Males, 25–64 and 35–44, 1949–1969: This is from Chiswick and Mincer (1972, p. S60). For alternative series, see T. P. Schultz (1971).

(8a) Entropy Measure of Inequality, 1880–1970: This is from Lindert (1974, Table 1, p. 9). It is based on nine census regions using Theil's formula

$$H_G = \sum_{g=1}^{G} Y_g \ln(Y_G/N_G),$$

where Y_g is the gth region's share of national personal income before taxes and N_g is the region's share of national population.

(8b) Weighted Coefficient of Variation, 1880–1948: Except for 1910, the regional inequality series is based on estimates by Easterlin (1960) and Hanna (1959) as reported in Williamson (1965, Table 4, p. 25). The weighted coefficient of variation uses state per capita income estimates weighted by state population. The 1910 estimate is from Lindert (1978, Table G–3), who constructed regional income estimates for 36 states in 1910 by interpolating on census production data between 1900 and 1920.

G

THE PRICE OF "RAW" LABOR: WAGES OF EMPLOYED URBAN UNSKILLED WORKERS, 1820–1948 *(1860 = 100)*

| | (1) *1820–1889* | | | | | | | |
Year	Nominal	Real	Year	Nominal	Real	Year	Nominal	Real
1820	77.7	61.9	1844	80.6	100.0	1867	156.3	89.2
1821	66.4	55.2	1845	82.5	100.2	1868	156.5	89.3
1822	65.4	51.7	1846	88.3	107.8	1869	164.8	100.8
1823	64.5	51.9	1847	88.3	88.6	1870	169.7	106.5
1824	64.8	56.9	1848	86.4	94.4	1871	161.1	103.4
1825	65.5	56.6	1849	90.3	98.2	1872	161.1	103.5
1826	65.5	58.2	1850	88.3	98.9	1873	160.2	105.2
1827	65.5	57.5	1851	86.9	97.4	1874	159.2	108.2
1828	65.5	57.6	1852	88.3	89.8	1875	156.3	110.6
1829	65.5	57.8	1853	92.2	90.7	1876	155.4	115.0
1830	72.8	67.4	1854	99.0	83.5	1877	133.3	100.2
1831	65.5	59.0	1855	97.1	76.9	1878	126.6	102.3
1832	75.2	68.6	1856	99.0	83.5	1879	126.6	107.0
1833	79.7	72.3	1857	98.1	78.0	1880	127.5	106.3
1834	80.1	76.9	1858	98.1	96.7	1881	134.3	108.1
1835	91.0	77.6	1859	98.1	95.6	1882	147.7	115.3
1836	94.8	69.6	1860	100.0	100.0	1883	149.6	123.9
1837	96.3	69.8	1861	102.3	100.0	1884	149.6	133.8
1838	89.2	67.0	1862	104.4	94.1	1885	148.6	136.7
1839	95.7	72.7	1863	117.1	89.4	1886	147.7	134.4
1840	92.2	84.4	1864	137.1	77.5	1887	147.7	134.2
1841	88.3	89.8	1865	152.4	81.8	1888	146.7	129.1
1842	83.5	94.5	1866	157.4	84.5	1889	145.8	127.8
1843	76.7	92.3						

	(2) *1890–1948*		
Year	Real	Year	Real
1890	130.2	1920	179.9
1891	131.9	1921	158.5
1892	131.7	1922	157.6
1893	131.7	1923	174.1
1894	136.0	1924	177.9
1895	141.0	1925	174.1
1896	142.7	1926	178.8
1897	144.4	1927	184.7
1898	144.5	1928	189.6
1899	144.5	1929	192.1
1900	144.7	1930	178.4
1901	146.5	1931	173.1
1902	146.7	1932	145.4
1903	146.8	1933	159.6
1904	148.7	1934	171.1
1905	152.1	1935	185.3
1906	152.2	1936	199.6
1907	150.5	1937	216.1
1908	152.2	1938	203.6
1909	157.3	1939	228.2
1910	152.2	1940	236.7
1911	150.7	1941	265.6
1912	150.7	1942	285.9
1913	155.4	1943	312.6
1914	153.9	1944	327.5
1915	157.0	1945	320.1
1916	152.5	1946	294.7
1917	151.7	1947	295.9
1918	173.4	1948	293.2
1919	168.7		

Sources and notes: The nominal wage series links the urban common-labor series found in the following sources: 1820–1834, T. M. Adams (1944); 1835–1839, Layer (1955); 1840–1869, revisions of Abbott (1905); 1870–1890, U.S. Department of Labor (1898); 1891–1926, Douglas (1930); 1927–1948, National Industrial Conference Board (1950). Each of these series is for employed workers only. The deflators are for unskilled workers in northeastern cities: for 1844–1948, see text Tables 5.2 and 5.4 to 5.9; for 1820–1843, see Williamson (1976a, Table 2).

FARM PRICES (USDA) RELATIVE TO URBAN PRICES (BLS) OF FIVE COMMODITIES, 1914–1948 *(1914 = 100)*

Year	Food	Clothing	Fuel and Light	Furnishings	Miscellaneous
1914	100.0	100.0	100.0	100.0	100.0
1915	102.9	101.7	102.0	95.9	98.8
1916	94.6	105.2	100.7	93.2	98.2
1917	98.4	108.1	108.2	96.5	90.2
1918	92.7	117.9	92.0	89.6	97.8
1919	100.2	127.8	97.0	85.4	88.9
1920	116.2	103.9	96.3	100.5	83.1
1921	96.7	113.8	82.0	108.4	81.0
1922	92.2	112.2	81.8	95.8	74.6
1923	94.7	113.6	79.9	92.3	76.4
1924	94.1	107.5	81.1	93.3	79.4
1925	91.7	107.2	71.1	93.6	80.7
1926	90.8	106.6	75.5	94.6	80.5
1927	92.6	106.8	76.2	93.7	76.3
1928	94.4	104.0	75.7	96.3	74.9
1929	89.2	104.9	76.2	95.9	75.5
1930	86.8	108.7	75.3	94.5	71.6
1931	84.6	115.8	70.8	91.6	67.8
1932	82.2	127.8	68.6	88.2	68.9
1933	91.2	121.5	69.1	89.6	71.7
1934	93.8	115.2	71.8	89.0	76.3
1935	95.5	119.9	72.3	88.4	76.1
1936	94.7	120.9	72.0	86.4	76.8
1937	93.4	122.0	73.3	80.9	76.6
1938	90.7	125.6	73.5	78.7	77.8
1939	93.1	126.7	73.5	77.4	77.4
1940	91.7	127.0	73.6	76.2	77.1
1941	91.6	120.3	74.8	75.9	78.9

Year	Food	Clothing	Fuel and Light	Furnishings	Miscellaneous
1942	92.2	115.2	74.9	76.4	81.1
1943	94.9	105.9	75.6	82.0	82.2
1944	98.0	100.8	75.8	82.1	82.8
1945	97.8	97.5	77.2	82.1	81.3
1946	98.5	94.7	81.8	83.1	77.5
1947	96.9	96.1	88.6	82.4	79.6
1948	93.9	96.8	83.4	80.1	82.3

Sources: The farm prices are taken from U.S. Department of Agriculture (1962: food and tobacco, p. 6; clothing, p. 24; household operations, p. 39; household furnishings, p. 44; and autos and auto services, p. 72). The urban price indices are taken from *Statistical Abstract of the United States* (1951, pp. 282–283), where the five commodity groups are food, apparel, fuel and light, furnishings, and miscellaneous.

"KOFFSKY-ADJUSTED" REGIONAL COST-OF-LIVING RELATIVES, 1840-1970
(New England = 100)

Region	1840	1880	1900	1920	1929	1950	1970
New England	100.0	100.0	100.0	100.0	100.0	100.0	100.0
ME	97.0	95.2	96.3	99.2	97.2	95.9	96.7
NH	96.7	97.1	98.2	99,6	96.7	94.5	94.3
VT	95.1	92.1	94.7	98.6	93.5	94.5	94.3
MASS	104.4	103.1	101.5	100.2	103.0	104.1	104.9
RI	104.6	103.3	101.8	100.2	97.8	104.1	104.9
CONN	99.8	100.5	100.3	100.0	101.2	102.7	103.3
Mid Atlantic	98.5	95.7	99.1	101.3	101.3	100.0	98.4
NY	98.6	95.6	99.1	101.4	101.1	105.5	105.7
NJ	99.2	97.8	100.2	101.5	102.0	106.8	106.6
PA	98.7	95.9	99.3	101.3	101.8	97.3	95.1
DEL	96.7	92.1	96.2	100.7	99.1	94.5	91.8
MD	96.9	92.6	94.8	100.9	100.1	94.5	91.8
East North Central	80.2	82.5	88.0	96.1	99.0	100.0	95.9
OHIO	80.8	83.3	88.9	96.3	98.6	98.6	94.3
IND	79.4	81.0	86.7	95.7	90.6	98.6	94.3
IL	79.4	82.4	88.9	96.4	101.6	101.4	97.5
MICH	79.1	82.9	87.6	96.1	101.3	98.6	95.1
WIS	82.4	82.1	87.0	95.5	101.2	102.7	96.7
West North Central	100.8	93.4	93.0	98.8	92.7	95.9	94.3
MIN	—	94.0	94.0	99.0	102.6	102.7	100.0
IOWA	100.9	92.9	92.8	98.7	86.6	100.0	97.5
MO	100.6	94.1	93.8	99.1	96.7	97.3	95.1
DAKS	—	95.3	90.7	97.5	90.3	90.4	89.3
NEB	—	92.5	92.1	98.4	91.2	90.4	89.3
KAN	—	92.1	92.1	98.6	83.2	95.9	94.3
South Atlantic	123.3	100.4	95.7	99.5	91.6	95.9	91.0
VA	125.3	102.6	96.9	100.2	93.1	102.7	98.4
WV	—	102.5	98.0	100.8	89.9	97.3	93.4
NC	122.3	99.6	95.1	99.1	87.7	94.5	90.2

Region	1840	1880	1900	1920	1929	1950	1970
SC	122.1	99.1	94.6	98.5	84.3	94.5	90.2
GA	121.7	99.6	94.9	99.0	90.8	91.8	87.7
FLA	123.9	101.4	97.4	100.6	91.7	90.4	86.9
East South Central	83.5	80.6	90.6	97.2	84.0	94.5	88.5
KY	84.4	81.9	91.5	97.6	88.3	98.6	91.8
TENN	83.4	81.0	91.1	97.5	86.7	93.2	86.9
ALA	82.9	80.0	90.5	97.1	81.7	91.8	87.7
MISS	82.6	79.4	89.3	96.3	78.2	91.8	87.7
West South Central	92.1	81.9	87.3	94.6	86.1	91.8	87.7
ARK	90.4	80.8	87.0	93.7	79.2	91.8	87.7
LA	92.6	82.7	88.0	95.0	89.9	91.8	87.7
TEX & OK	—	81.9	87.1	94.7	86.1	91.8	86.9
Mountain				117.6	94.0	98.6	95.1
MONT				117.3	93.5	98.6	95.1
IDA				116.9	92.7	98.6	95.1
WYO				117.7	94.2	98.6	95.1
COLO				118.1	92.9	98.6	95.1
NM				116.8	93.8	98.6	95.1
ARIZ				118.1	96.8	98.6	95.1
UTAH				117.9	93.2	98.6	95.1
NEV				118.3	93.9	98.6	95.1
Pacific				103.1	97.7	100.0	97.5
WASH				103.1	94.1	101.4	98.4
ORE				102.7	92.4	101.4	98.4
CAL				103.1	103.7	95.9	95.9

Sources and notes: The table lists the region and state cost-of-living relatives used for the regional inequality computations in the text. The data are expressed in terms of New England = 100 throughout. Thus, they are useful only for relative deviations in cost of living across space, not time.

Basic sources are Koffsky (1949), Coelho and Shepherd (1974), Stecker (1937), and U.S. Department of Labor (1970 and 1971).

For 1950–1970, data were taken directly from U.S. Department of Labor (1970, Table 139, p. 326); and (1971, Table 118, pp. 270–273). Both years refer to an "intermediate budget," 4-person family, using (primarily) metropolitan areas. The regional figures are unweighted averages of the states themselves.

For 1840–1929, the procedure was to first collect estimates of urban price indices by state. These urban price indices were then adjusted to include the impact of cost-of-living differentials between urban and farm areas. We refer to this adjustment procedure as the "Koffsky adjustment." Using 1935/1936 budget weights and 1941 prices, Nathan Koffsky (1949) estimated that the urban cost of living, C_J, was higher than the farm cost of living, C_{JF}, by 27% when farm weights were used, and by 14% when city weights were used. In both cases, the budgets of the "lowest significant income levels" were used. In Chapter 5, we estimated that the ratios of these two costs of living were almost exactly the same in 1929 and 1941. Thus, we assume that the Koffsky differential was the same in 1929. Using the cost-of-living trends in Table 5.12, we have estimated the Koffsky differential for the following years:

	Farm Weights	City Weights	$(Z - 1)$ Unweighted Average
1891–1892	31.9%	18.3%	25.1%
1900	24.0	11.3	17.7
1919–1921	12.2	0.8	6.5
1929	27.0	14.0	20.5
1948	11.9	0.5	6.2

The state cost-of-living index, $\hat{C}_j$, is estimated by the expression

$$\hat{C}_j = C_j [1 + (Z^{-1} - 1)\alpha_j^R]$$

where α_j^R is a weight, the share of agricultural labor force in the total labor force of the given state j, and Z is the percentage by which C_j exceeds C_{jF}. Thus, the Koffsky adjustment supplies a means by which the state urban cost-of-living indices can be blown up to state coverage.

For the 1840 and 1880 calculations, we assume that the 1891–1892 unweighted average differential (approximated at 25%) applies. For the remaining years prior to 1950, we use the unweighted averages as indicated above. No "Koffsky adjustments" were made in the 1950 and 1970 state price indices reported by the Department of Labor since the Koffsky differentials are apparently quite small and, of course, the farm labor force was a very small share of total labor force in both years and in all states.

The urban state relative prices, 1840–1929, were derived from the sources above, with some adjustments. First, the 1840 relative prices are in fact for 1851. Second, Coelho and Shepherd (1974, Table 4, p. 571) were unable to directly observe price data for the West South Central region at all over their period (1851–1880), and only over 1866–1880 for the South Atlantic. We have estimated the missing values by interpolation. In effect, we have assumed that the cost-of-living ratio between the South Atlantic and the East South Central for 1866–1869 holds for the antebellum period as well; and that the ratio of the West South Central to the East South Central for 1867 and 1869 (see Coelho and Shepherd, p. 572, n. 36) holds for the antebellum period as well. Third, 1880, 1900, and 1920 use Lindert (1978, Table G-1, p. 383). Fourth, the 1929 period figure is actually the 1935 estimate supplied by Stecker (1937, Tables 3 and 6, pp. 8, 162–163).

J

TWO MEASURES OF SKILLS

Human earnings now account for more than three-quarters of national income. A central task in understanding income inequality is thus to explain why some people work for higher hourly rates than others. Controversy surrounds the issue of earnings inequality, and particularly the role played by attributes often called skills. Human-capital theorists argue that people get paid what their skills deserve. Critics reply that earnings inequality reflects artificial restrictions to higher-paying positions, not skills as such. A related critique is that the process of capitalist growth, while creating higher rates of pay, does not raise skills but rather lowers skills, as when factory textiles replaced the more "skilled" artisans.

Given our focus on earnings inequality and the nature of the data available to us, there is only one operational concept of skills we can use: Skills are those attributes that give a worker higher pay than common labor. These attributes can range from good grooming ιo membership in a restrictive professional association, to education, age, or luck. For present purposes the important thing is to try to develop an aggregate measure of skills that is either available or in use, and to measure its average rate of pay.

First Measure: Skilled Jobs Are Entirely Skilled

One way to define skills and their compensation is to divide the total supply or employment of labor into two groups, those receiving high and those receiving low rates of pay. The number of man-hours supplied by the former is a measure of total input of skills, while the man-hours of the latter measure total input of unskilled labor. The division is arbitrary, of course, but is reasonable as long as it cuts at a single point in the earnings ranks. One might, for example, decide that unskilled labor consists of janitors, custodians, materials movers, farm workers, gas station attendants, domestic servants, and a few other groups, with all others being thrown into the skilled class. This measure probably corresponds to the usual conception of how skilled and unskilled labor would be differentiated.

In practice, this first measure requires detailed information on the breakdown of man-hours by occupation, so that we can know how many hours there were of skilled and unskilled labor. This requirement is rarely met. Often it is easier to know total man-hours, the total value of labor compensation, including imputed labor earnings from self-employment where possible, and the rates of pay for a representative range of skilled and unskilled labor than it is to know how many man-hours were worked in each occupation. This is the situation we face, and it makes it more convenient to resort to another measure.

Second Measure: Skilled Jobs are Partly Unskilled

If we take the view that skills are advantages commanding pay above that of common labor, then it is reasonable to say that anybody's labor is unskilled up to the point of his or her earning an income equal to that of a full-time unskilled worker, but this labor is skilled to the extent that it earns anything more. The greater the percentage pay advantage a given occupation has over common labor in some base period, the greater the share of its earnings that is a return to skilled labor. Or, in metaphor, the second measure views farmhands as having no skills, while mechanics are skilled from the shoulders up, lawyers from the knees up, and physicians from the ankles up. On this convention, the relevant skilled-labor wage premium is just that, a gap or markup, not the ratio of skilled-labor to unskilled-labor wage rates. This second measure is used in Chapter 7 and in most of what follows.

Using either measure, one can infer trends in skills growth from movements in relative wage rates or vice versa. National income can be viewed as divided into returns to common labor, skilled labor, and property as follows:

$$P_Y Y = rK + \bar{w}L = rK + wL + qsL,$$

where

$P_Y Y$ = the nominal value of national income,
r = the rent earned on capital services,

K = the flow of capital services,
$\bar{w}$ = the overall average wage rate,
w = the wage rate for common labor,
L = the total man-hours of all kinds of labor,
q = the wage rate for skilled labor, and
s = the average units of skills per man-hour, where the unit of skills is defined as that set of attributes which commands the pay advantage, $q - w$, over common labor.

This breakdown defines s as the skilled part of skilled-job attributes if we are using the second measure, or as the share of all man-hours performed by skilled occupations if we are using the first.

To reveal trends in skills growth from aggregate data, one can focus on the total wage bill. Subtracting out the product of total man-hours and the wage rate for the unskilled (wL), one gets the total returns to skills (qsL). Dividing this by total man-hours yields returns to skills per man-hour in the base period (qs). The growth in this nominal return over time is the result of two rates of change, the change in the unit pay premium on skills ($\overset{*}{q}$) and the change in average skills per man-hour ($\overset{*}{s}$). If we think we have good measures of $\overset{*}{s}$, we can subtract this rate of growth from that of the total skills compensation ($\overset{*}{qs} = \overset{*}{q} + \overset{*}{s}$) to get a measure of the rate of growth in the skilled-labor wage premium ($\overset{*}{q}$). Or, if we have more faith in the wage rate data, we can subtract $\overset{*}{q}$ from ($\overset{*}{q} + \overset{*}{s}$) to reveal the rate of growth of skills per man-hour. For the nineteenth century, it was necessary to resort to this latter procedure to estimate the skills growth that feeds into the calculations of total factor productivity in this chapter, and into the discussion of American nineteenth-century skills growth in Chapters 9 and 10.

RETURN TO UNSKILLED LABOR FROM INDUSTRIES, 1919 AND 1939

(1) *Payments Impact on Unskilled Labor, Direct and Indirect, of $1 Purchase of Output from Industry j, 1919*

Industry	Value-Added Share of Unskilled Labor	$\bar{\theta}_j$
1. Agriculture	.3617	.3444
2. Flour, etc.	.2912	.2772
3. Canning, etc.	.2912	.2046
4. Bakery products	.2912	.1745
5. Sugar, etc.	.2912	.1046
6. Beverages	.2912	.1310
7. Tobacco	.2912	.1418
8. Meat packing	.2912	.2804
9. Butter and cheese	.2912	.2794
10. Other food manufacturing	.2912	.1066
11. Iron mining	.2008	.1355
12. Blast furnaces	.2481	.1527
13. Steel and rolling mills	.2481	.1799
14. Other iron and steel	.2481	.1432
15. Automobiles	.2481	.1453
16. Nonferrous metals	.2008	.1803
17. Smelting and refining	.2481	.1386
18. Brass, etc. manufacturing	.2481	.1068
19. Nonmetal minerals	.2556	.1631
20. Petroleum and natural gas	.2481	.1217
21. Refined petroleum	.2556	.1252
22. Coal	.3261	.2434
23. Coke	.3261	.2183

(1) *Continued*

Industry	Value-Added Share of Unskilled Labor	$\bar{\theta}_j$
24. Manufactured gas	.2905	.1575
25. Electric utilities	.1576	.1246
26. Chemicals	.2356	.1116
27. Lumber products	.3299	.1939
28. Other wood products	.3299	.2183
29. Pulp and paper	.2811	.1180
30. Other paper products	.2811	.1512
31. Printing and publishing	.2967	.1617
32. Yarn and cloth	.2870	.1954
33. Clothing	.2870	.1664
34. Other textiles	.2870	.1634
35. Leather tanning	.2870	.1441
36. Leather shoes	.2870	.1670
37. Other leather products	.2870	.1566
38. Rubber products	.2556	.1261
39. Industries, n.e.c.	.2556	.1386
40. Construction	.2454	.1653
41. Transportation	.2482	.1993

(2) *Payments Impact on Unskilled Labor, Direct and Indirect, of $1 Purchase of Output from Industry j, 1939*

Industry	Value-Added Share of Unskilled Labor	$\hat{\theta}_j$
1. Agricultural and fishing	.4990	.2857
2. Food processing	.1829	.1559
3. Ferrous metals	.1610	.0969
4. Iron and steel foundry	.1840	.1157
5. Shipbuilding	.1840	.1359
6. Agricultural machinery	.1600	.1054
7. Engines and turbines	.1640	.0975
8. Motor vehicles	.1432	.1302
9. Aircraft	.1840	.1219
10. Transportation equipment	.1688	.0947
11. Industrial and heating equipment	.1610	.0954
12. Machine tools	.1610	.1009
13. Merchandising and services machines	.1620	.1168
14. Electrical equipment	.1683	.1125
15. Iron and steel products	.1910	.1080
16. Nonferrous metals	.1758	.0849
17. Nonmetallic minerals	.1930	.1134
18. Petroleum refining	.1210	.1037
19. Coal and coke	.1821	.1357
20. Gas and electrical power	.0918	.0837

(2) *Continued*

Industry	Value-Added Share of Unskilled Labor	$\bar{\theta}_j$
21. Communications	.1428	.1221
22. Chemicals	.1255	.1031
23. Lumber	.3174	.1660
24. Furniture	.2777	.1538
25. Pulp and paper	.2055	.1129
26. Printing and publishing	.1764	.1213
27. Textile production	.3477	.1575
28. Apparel	.3193	.1820
29. Leather	.3127	.1574
30. Rubber	.1888	.1028
31. Other manufactured goods	.2115	.1261
32. Construction	.2881	.2090
33. Misc. transportation	.2029	.1464
34. Transoceanic transportation	.1836	.0417
35. Steam railroads	.1475	.1342
36. Trade	.2407	.1574
37. Business and personnel service	.1850	.1325
38. Eating places	.3750	.1915

Sources and notes: In examining historical trends relating to who purchases low-wage labor, we use input–output data from three points in time: 1919, 1939, and 1963 (1963 data are in text Table 8.1). Before any operations were carried out, we reclassified the sectoral cost share data and the consumer expenditures to align them with the input–output sectoral breakdown. Especially for the earlier years, this procedure was extensive and often quite arbitrary. In addition, the 1919 calculations required the application of retail and wholesale markups to reconcile the expenditure and input–output data. The markups were taken from Barger (1955, Table 26, p. 92). Finally, although it is the wages share of unskilled labor in total costs which is relevant to the text calculations, we found it useful to take an intermediate step and compute the wage share of unskilled labor in value added.

(1) The employment and value-added ("national income originating") data are taken from Kuznets (1941, Tables 59 and 63, pp. 326 and 334). The 1919 wage for unskilled labor is the average annual earnings of hired farm labor. It is taken from Lebergott (1964, Table A.18, p. 525). The consumer expenditure data are based on the 1918–1919 white family urban industrial worker sample in U.S. Department of Labor (BLS), *Cost of Living in the United States* (1924). The input–output data are the 1919 matrix reported by Leontief (1951, Table 5). See discussion in text, Chapter 8.

(2) The employment and value-added data are taken from U.S. Department of Commerce (1966, Tables 1.12 and 6.6, pp. 18–21 and 110–113). The 1939 wage for unskilled labor is the average annual earnings of hired farm labor (Table 6.5, pp. 106–109). The consumer expenditure data are taken from U.S. National Resources Planning Board (1941), and relate to the years 1935–1936. The input–output data are the 1939 matrix reported in Leontief (1951, Table 24). See discussion in text, Chapter 8.

REFERENCES

Abbott, E. 1905. *The wages of unskilled labor in the United States, 1850–1900.* Chicago: University of Chicago Press.

Abramovitz, M. A. 1952. Economics of growth. In B. F. Haley (Ed.), *A survey of contemporary economics.* Homewood, Ill.: Irwin.

Abramovitz, M. A., and David, P. A. 1973. Reinterpreting economic growth: Parables and realities. *American Economic Review, 58,* 428–439.

Adams, D. R. 1968. Wage rates in the early national period: Philadelphia, 1785–1830. *Journal of Economic History, 28,* 404–426.

Adams, T. M. 1944. *Prices paid by Vermont farmers.* Bulletin 507, Burlington, Vt.: Vermont Agricultural Experiment Station.

Ahluwalia, M. 1976. Inequality, poverty and development. *Journal of Development Economics, 3,* 307–342.

Aldrich, M. 1971. Earnings of American civil engineers, 1820–1859. *Journal of Economic History, 31,* 407–419.

American Association of University Professors. 1948–1972. *Bulletin* (various issues).

Ames, E., and Rosenberg, N. 1968. The Enfield Arsenal in theory and history. *Economic Journal, 78,* 827–842.

Anderson, T. L. 1975. Wealth estimates for the New England colonies, 1650–1709. *Explorations in Economic History, 12,* 151–176.

Anderson, T. L. 1979. Economic growth in colonial New England: "Statistical renaissance." *Journal of Economic History, 39,* 243–258.

Anderson, T. L., and Thomas, R. P. 1978. Economic growth in the seventeenth century Chesapeake. *Explorations in Economic History, 15,* 368–387.

Asher, E. 1972. Industrial efficiency and biased technical change in American and British manufacturing: The case of textiles in the nineteenth century. *Journal of Economic History, 32,* 431–442.

Ashton, T. S. 1954. The treatment of capitalism by historians. In F. A. Hayek (Ed.), *Capitalism and the historian.* London: Routledge and Kegan Paul, Ltd.

Atkinson, A. B. 1970. On the measurement of inequality. *Journal of Economic Theory, 2,* 244–263.

Atkinson, A. B., and Harrison, A. J. Forthcoming. *The distribution of personal wealth in Britain.* Cambridge: At the University Press.

Ball, D. E. 1976. Dynamics of population and wealth in eighteenth-century Chester County, Pennsylvania. *Journal of Interdisciplinary History*, 6, 621–644.

Ball, D. E. and Walton, G. M. 1976. Agricultural productivity change in eighteenth-century Pennsylvania. *Journal of Economic History*, 36, 102–117.

Baran, P., and Sweezy, P. 1966. *Monopoly capital: An essay on the American economic and social order.* New York: Monthly Review Press.

Barger, H. 1955. *Distribution's place in the American economy since 1869.* New York: National Bureau of Economic Research.

Barro, R. J. 1977. Social Security and private saving—evidence from the U.S. time series. Mimeo. Department of Economics, University of Rochester.

Baumol, W. 1967. Macroeconomics of unbalanced growth: The anatomy of urban crisis. *American Economic Review*, 57, 415–426.

Berndt, E. R., and Christensen, L. R. 1973. Testing for the existence of a consistent aggregate index of labor inputs. Social Science Research Institute Workshop Paper 7317, Madison, Wis.

Berndt, E. R., and Wood, D. O. 1975. Technology, prices, and the derived demand for energy. *Review of Economics and Statistics*, 57, 259–268.

Blank, D. M., and Stigler, G. 1957. *The demand and supply of scientific personnel.* Princeton, N.J.: Princeton University Press.

Brady, D. S. 1964. Relative prices in the nineteenth century. *Journal of Economic History*, 24, 145–203.

Brady, D. S. 1972. Consumption and the style of life. In L. E. Davis et al., *American economic growth: An economist's history of the United States.* New York: Harper and Row.

Bridenbaugh, C. 1955. *Cities in revolt: Urban life in America, 1743–1776.* New York: A. Knopf.

Brito, D. C., and Williamson, J. G. 1973. Skilled labor and nineteenth-century Anglo-American managerial behavior. *Explorations in Economic History*, 10, 235–252.

Brittain, J. A. 1972. *The payroll tax for Social Security.* Washington, D.C.: Brookings Institution.

Bronfenbrenner, M. 1971. *Income distribution theory.* Chicago: Aldine.

Bronfenbrenner, M. 1978. Review of *Distribution of Personal Wealth in Britain* by A. B. Atkinson and A. J. Harrison. *Journal of Economic Literature*, 16, 1460–1462.

Brown, M. 1966. *On the theory and measurement of technological change.* Cambridge: At the University Press.

Budd, E. C. 1960. Factor shares, 1850–1910. In *Trends in the American economy in the nineteenth century.* Studies in Income and Wealth, Vol. 24. New York: National Bureau of Economic Research.

Budd, E. C. 1967. *Inequality and poverty.* New York: Norton.

Budd, E. C. 1970. Postwar changes in the size distribution of income in the U.S. *American Economic Review*, 60, 247–260.

Burgess, W. R. 1920. *Trends in school costs.* New York: Russell Sage Foundation.

Burns, A. F. 1954. *The frontiers of economic knowledge.* Princeton, N.J.: Princeton University Press.

Carter, A. P. 1970. *Structural change in the American economy.* Cambridge, Mass.: Harvard University Press.

Chenery, H. B. 1960. Patterns of industrial growth. *American Economic Review*, 50, 624–654.

Chenery, H. B., et al. 1974. *Redistribution with growth.* London: Oxford University Press.

Chiswick, B. R. 1974. *Income inequality.* New York: National Bureau of Economic Research.

Chiswick, B. R., and Mincer, J. 1972. Time-series changes in personal income inequality in the United States from 1939, with projections to 1985. *Journal of Political Economy, 80,* Part 2, 534–566.

Christoffel, T., et al. 1970. *Up against the American myth.* New York: Holt, Rinehart, and Winston.

Clark, C. 1957. *Conditions of economic progress.* 3rd ed. New York: Macmillan.

Clemens, P. G. 1974. From tobacco to grain: Economic development on Maryland's Eastern Shore, 1660–1750. Unpublished Ph.D. dissertation, Department of History, University of Wisconsin, Madison.

Cline, W. R. 1972. *Potential effects of income redistribution on economic growth.* New York: Praeger Publishers.

Cline, W. R. 1975. Distribution and development: A survey of literature. *Journal of Development Economics, 1,* 359–400.

Coelho, P., and Ghali, M. 1971. The end of the North–South wage differential. *American Economic Review, 61,* 932–937.

Coelho, P., and Shepherd, J. 1974. Differences in regional prices: The United States, 1851–1880. *Journal of Economic History, 34,* 551–591.

Coehlo, P., and Shepherd, J. 1976. Regional differences in real wages: The United States, 1851–1880. *Explorations in Economic History, 13,* 203–230.

Coen, R. M. 1973. Labor force and unemployment in the 1920s and 1930s: A re-examination based on postwar experience. *Review of Economics and Statistics, 55,* 46–55.

Crotty, J. R., and Rapping, L. A. 1975. The 1975 report of the President's Council of Economic Advisers: A radical critique. *American Economic Review, 65,* 791–811.

Daniels, B. 1973–1974. Long run trends of wealth distribution in 18th century New England. *Explorations in Economic History, 11,* 123–136.

Danziger, S., Haveman, R., and Smolensky, E. 1976. The measurement and trend of inequality: A basic revision: Comment. Institute for Research on Poverty Discussion Paper 335–76. University of Wisconsin, Madison.

Danziger, S., and Plotnick, R. 1975. Demographic change, government transfers, and the distribution of income. Institute for Research on Poverty Discussion Paper 274–75. University of Wisconsin, Madison.

David, P. A. 1967. The growth of real product in the United States before 1840: New evidence, controlled conjectures. *Journal of Economic History, 27,* 151–197.

David, P. A. 1970. Learning by doing and tariff protection: A reconsideration of the case of the ante-bellum United States cotton textile industry. *Journal of Economic History, 30,* 521–601.

David, P. A. 1975. *Technical choice, innovation, and economic growth.* Cambridge: At the University Press.

David, P. A. 1976. Invention and accumulation in America's economic growth: A nineteenth century parable. Center for Research in Economic Growth Memorandum 199. Stanford University, Stanford, Calif.

David, P. A. 1977. Invention and accumulation in America's economic growth: A nineteenth century parable. *Journal of Monetary Economics,* Supplement, 6, 179–228.

David, P. A., and van de Klundert, T. 1965. Biased efficiency growth and capital–labor substitution in the U.S., 1899–1960. *American Economic Review, 55,* 357–394.

Davis, L. E., et al. 1972. *American economic growth: An economist's history of the United States.* New York: Harper and Row.

Davis, L. E., and Gallman, R. E. 1973. The share of savings and investment in gross national product during the 19th century in the U.S.A. In F. C. Lane (Ed.), *Fourth International Conference of Economic History.* Paris: Mouton.

DeBever, L., and Williamson, J. G. 1976. Accumulation and the state: Population control, militarism and myths in Japanese history. Mimeo. National Bureau of Economic Research, Stanford, Calif.

DeCanio, J., and Mokyr, J. 1977. Inflation and the wage lag during the American Civil War. *Explorations in Economic History, 14,* 311–336.

Denison, E. F. 1962. *The sources of economic growth in the United States.* New York: Committee for Economic Development.

Denison, E. F. 1967. *Why growth rates differ: Postwar experiences in nine western countries.* Washington, D.C.: The Brookings Institution.

Denison, E. F. 1974. *Accounting for United States economic growth, 1929–1969.* Washington, D.C.: The Brookings Institution.

Diamond, P. A., and McFadden, D. 1965. Identification of the elasticity of substitution and the bias of technical change: An impossibility theorem. Working Paper No. 62, University of California, Berkeley. March. Mimeo.

Douglas, P. 1930. *Real wages in the United States: 1891–1926.* Boston: Houghton Mifflin.

Douty, H. M. 1953. Union impact on wage structure. *Proceedings of the Sixth Annual Meeting of the Industrial Relations Research Association,* pp. 61–76.

Drucker, P. F. 1976. Pension fund socialism. *Public Interest,* No. 42, pp. 1–14.

Easterlin, R. A. 1960. Inter-regional differences in per capita income, population, and total income, 1840–1950. In *Trends in the American economy in the nineteenth century.* Studies in Income and Wealth, Vol. 24. Princeton, N.J.: Princeton University Press.

Edelstein, M. 1974. The determinants of U.K. investment abroad, 1870–1913: The U.S. case. *Journal of Economic History, 34,* 980–1007.

Edelstein, M. 1977. U.K. savings in the age of high imperialism and after. *American Economic Review, 67,* 288–294.

Engerman, S. L. 1966. The economic impact of the Civil War. *Explorations in Economic History, 3,* 178–183.

Engerman, S. L. 1971. Some economic factors in Southern backwardness in the nineteenth century. In J. F. Kain and J. R. Meyer (Eds.), *Essays in regional economics.* Cambridge, Mass.: Harvard University Press.

Evans, R. 1971. *The labor economies of Japan and the United States.* New York: Praeger.

Fallon, P. R., and Layard, P. R. G. 1975. Capital–skill complementarity, income distribution, and output accounting. *Journal of Political Economy, 83,* 279–302.

Fei, J. C. H., and Ranis, G. 1964. *Development of the labor surplus economy: Theory and policy.* Homewood, Ill.: Irwin.

Fei, J. C. H., and Ranis, G. 1966. Agrarianism, dualism, and economic development. In I. Adelman and E. Thorbecke (Eds.), *The theory and design of economic development.* Baltimore: Johns Hopkins Press.

Feldstein, M. 1974. Social Security, induced retirement, and aggregate capital accumulation. *Journal of Political Economy, 82,* 905–926.

Feldstein, M. 1976. Social Security and the distribution of wealth. *Journal of the American Statistical Association, 71,* 800–807.

Fishlow, A. 1966. Productivity and technological change in the railroad sector, 1840–1910. In *Output, employment and productivity in the United States after 1800.* Studies in Income and Wealth, Vol. 30. New York: National Bureau of Economic Research.

Fishlow, A. 1973. Comparative consumption patterns, the extent of the market, and alternative development strategies. In E. B. Ayal (Ed.), *Micro aspects of development.* New York: Praeger.

Fogel, R. W., and Engerman, S. L. 1969. A model for the explanation of industrial expansion during the nineteenth century: With an application to the American iron industry. *Journal of Political Economy, 77,* 306–328.

Fogel, R. W., and Engerman, S. L. 1971. *The reinterpretation of American economic history.* New York: Harper and Row.

Fogel, R. W., and Engerman, S. L. 1974. *Time on the cross: The economics of American Negro slavery.* Boston: Little Brown.

Gallman, R. E. 1960. Commodity output, 1839–1899. In *Trends in the American economy in the nineteenth century.* Studies in Income and Wealth, Vol. 24. New York: National Bureau of Economic Research.

Gallman, R. E. 1966. Gross national product in the United States, 1834–1909. In *Output, employment, and productivity in the United States after 1800.* New York: National Bureau of Economic Research.

Gallman, R. E. 1969. Trends in the size distribution of wealth in the nineteenth century: Some speculations. In L. Soltow (Ed.), *Six papers on the size distribution of wealth and income.* New York: National Bureau of Economic Research.

Gallman, R. E. 1972. Changes in total U.S. agricultural factor productivity in the nineteenth century. In D. P. Kelsey (Ed.), *Farming in the new nation: Interpreting American agriculture 1790–1840.* Washington, D.C.: Agricultural History Society.

Gallman, R. E. 1974. Equality in America at the time of Tocqueville. Unpublished. Department of Economics, University of North Carolina, Chapel Hill.

Gallman, R. E. 1975. The agricultural sector and the pace of economic growth: U.S. experience in the nineteenth century. In D. C. Klingaman and R. Vedder (Eds.), *Essays in nineteenth century economic history: The old Northwest.* Athens: Ohio University Press.

Garrett, P. W. 1920. Government control over prices. Washington, D.C.: U.S. Government Printing Office.

Gastwirth, J. L. 1972. The estimation of the Lorenz Curve and Gini Index. *Review of Economics and Statistics, 54,* 306–316.

Gilbert, M. 1958. *Comparative national products and price levels.* Paris: Organization for European Economic Cooperation.

Gilbert, M., and Kravis, I. B. 1954. *An international comparison of national products and the purchasing power of currencies.* Paris: Organization for European Economic Cooperation.

Goldsmith, R. W. 1962. *The national wealth of the United States in the postwar period.* Princeton, N.J.: Princeton University Press.

Goldsmith, S. F. 1951. Appraisal of basic data available for constructing income size distributions. *Studies in income and wealth,* Vol. 13. New York: National Bureau of Economic Research.

Goldsmith, S. F. 1958. The relation of census income distribution statistics to other income data. In George Garvey (Ed.), *An appraisal of the 1950 census income data.* Studies in Income and Wealth, Vol. 23. New York: National Bureau of Economic Research.

Goldsmith, S. F. 1967. Changes in the size distribution of income. In E. C. Budd (Ed.), *Inequality and poverty.* New York: Harper and Row.

Golladay, F., and Haveman, R. 1976. Regional and distributional effects of a negative income tax. *American Economic Review, 66,* 629–641.

Gordon, R. A. 1961. Differential changes in the prices of consumers' and capital goods. *American Economic Review, 51,* 937–957.

Gordon, R. J. 1971. Measurement bias in price indexes for capital goods. *Review of Income and Wealth,* Series 16, pp. 121–173.

Griliches, Z. 1969. Capital–skill complementary. *Review of Economics and Statistics, 51,* 465–468.

Griliches, Z. 1970. Notes on the role of education in production functions and growth accounting. In W. L. Hansen (Ed.), *Education, income, and human capital.* New York: National Bureau of Economic Research.

Griliches, Z. 1971. Introduction: Hedonic price indexes revisited. In Z. Griliches (Ed.), *Price indexes and quality change*. Cambridge, Mass.: Harvard University Press.

Gustavus, S. O., and Nam, C. B. 1968. Estimates of the "true" educational distribution of the adult population of the United States from 1910 to 1960. *Demography, 5,* 410–421.

Habakkuk, H. J. 1962. *American and British technology in the nineteenth century*. Cambridge: At the University Press.

Hammett, T. M. 1976. Two mobs of Jacksonian Boston: Ideology and interest. *Journal of American History, 62,* 845–868.

Hanna, F. A. 1959. *State income differentials, 1919–1954*. Durham, N.C.: Duke University Press.

Hartley, W. B. 1969. Estimation of the incidence of poverty in the United States, 1870 to 1914. Unpublished Ph.D. dissertation. Department of Economics, University of Wisconsin, Madison.

Hartwell, R. M., and Engerman, S. 1975. Models of immiseration: The theoretical basis of pessimism. In A. J. Taylor (Ed.), *The standard of living in Britain in the Industrial Revolution*. London: Methuen.

Heilbroner, R. 1974. The clouded crystal ball. *American Economic Review, 59,* 121–124.

Henle, P. 1972. Exploring the distribution of earned income. *Monthly Labor Review, 95* (December), 16–27.

Henretta, J. A. 1965. Economic development and social structure in revolutionary Boston. *William and Mary Quarterly, 22,* 75–92.

Hicks, J. R. 1932. *The theory of wages*. London: Macmillan.

Hildebrand, G. H., and Delahanty, G. E. 1966. Wage levels and differentials. In R. A. Gordon and M. S. Gordon (Eds.), *Prosperity and unemployment*. New York: John Wiley and Sons.

Hillman, A. L., and Bullard, C. W. 1978. Energy, the Heckscher–Ohlin Theorem, and U.S. international trade. *American Economic Review, 68,* 96–106.

Historical statistics of the United States, colonial times to 1957. 1960. Washington, D.C.: U.S. Government Printing Office.

Historical statistics of the United States, colonial times to 1970. 1975. Parts 1 and 2. Washington, D.C.: U.S. Government Printing Office.

Hollister, R., and Palmer, J. 1969. The impact of inflation on the poor. Institute for Research on Poverty Discussion Paper 40–69. University of Wisconsin, Madison.

Holmes, G. K. 1893. The concentration of wealth. *Political Science Quarterly, 8,* 589–600.

Holt, C. F. 1977. Who benefitted from the prosperity of the twenties? *Explorations in Economic History, 14,* 277–289.

Houthakker, H. S. 1957. An international comparison of household expenditure patterns, commemorating the centenary of Engel's Law. *Econometrica, 25,* 532–551.

Houthakker, H. S. 1965. On some determinants of saving in developed and underdeveloped countries. In E. A. G. Robinson (Ed.), *Problems in economic development*. New York: Macmillan.

Jones, A. H. 1970. Wealth estimates for the American Middle Colonies, 1774. *Economic Development and Cultural Change, 18,* Part 2 (entire issue).

Jones, A. H. 1971. Wealth distribution in the American Middle Colonies in the third quarter of the eighteenth century. Paper read to the Organization of American Historians, New Orleans, April 17.

Jones, A. H. 1972. Wealth estimates for the New England colonies about 1770. *Journal of Economic History, 32,* 98–127.

Jones, A. H. 1978. *American colonial wealth: Documents and methods*. New York: Arno Press.

Jones, A. H. Forthcoming. *Wealth of the colonies on the eve of the American Revolution.* New York: Columbia University Press.

Jones, E. B. 1963. New estimates of hours of work per week and hourly earnings. *Review of Economics and Statistics, 45,* 374–385.

Jones, R. W. 1965. The structure of simple general equilibrium models. *Journal of Political Economy, 73,* 557–572.

Jorgenson, D. W. 1961. The development of a dual economy. *Economic Journal, 71,* 309–334.

Katona, G. 1971. *1970 Survey of consumer finances.* Ann Arbor: University of Michigan Press.

Keat, P. 1960. Longrun changes in occupational wage structure, 1900–1956. *Journal of Political Economy, 68,* 584–600.

Keller, R. 1973. Factor income distribution in the United States during the 1920's: A reexamination of fact and theory. *Journal of Economic History, 33,* 252–273.

Kelley, A. C. 1972. Demographic changes and American economic development: Past, present and future. In E. R. Morss and R. H. Reed (Eds.), *Economic aspects of population change,* The Commission on Population Growth and the American Future, Research Reports, Vol. 2. Washington, D.C.: U.S. Government Printing Office.

Kelley, A. C., and Williamson, J. G. 1974. *Lessons from Japanese development: An analytical economic history.* Chicago: University of Chicago Press.

Kelley, A. C., Williamson, J. G., and Cheetham, R. J. 1972. *Dualistic economic development: Theory and history.* Chicago: University of Chicago Press.

Kendrick, J. W. 1961. *Productivity trends in the United States.* New York: National Bureau of Economic Research.

Kendrick, J. W. 1973. *Postwar productivity trends in the United States, 1948–1969.* New York: National Bureau of Economic Research.

Kendrick, J. W. 1976. *The formation and stocks of total capital.* New York: National Bureau of Economic Research.

Kesselman, J. R., Williamson, S. H., and Berndt, E. R. 1977. Tax credits for employment rather than investment. *American Economic Review, 67,* 330–349.

Kindleberger, C. P. 1967. *Europe's postwar growth: The role of labor supply.* Cambridge, Mass.: Harvard University Press.

King, W. I. 1915. *The wealth and income of the people of the United States.* New York: Macmillan.

King, W. I. 1927. Wealth distribution in the continental United States at the close of 1921. *Journal of the American Statistical Association, 22,* 135–153.

King, W. I. 1930. *The national income and its purchasing power.* New York: National Bureau of Economic Research.

Koch, D. W. 1969. Income distribution and political structure in seventeenth century Salem, Massachusetts. *Institute Historical Collections, 105,* 50–71.

Koffsky, N. 1949. Farm and urban purchasing power. In *Studies in Income and Wealth,* Vol. 11. New York: National Bureau of Economic Research.

Kolko, G. 1962. *Wealth and power in America.* New York: Praeger.

Kolodrubetz, W. W. 1975. Employee benefit plans, 1973. *Social Security Bulletin, 38* (May), 22–29.

Kravis, I. B. 1962. *The structure of income.* Philadelphia: University of Pennsylvania Press.

Kulikoff, A. 1971. The progress of inequality in revolutionary Boston. *William and Mary Quarterly, 28,* 375–412.

Kulikoff, A. 1979. The economic growth of the eighteenth-century Chesapeake colonies. *Journal of Economic History, 39,* 275–288.

Kuznets, S. 1941. *National income and its composition, 1919–1938*. New York: National Bureau of Economic Research.

Kuznets, S. 1953. *Shares of upper income groups in income and savings*. New York: National Bureau of Economic Research.

Kuznets, S. 1955. Economic growth and income inequality. (Presidential address.) *American Economic Review, 45*, 1–28.

Kuznets, S. 1961. *Capital in the American economy: Its formation and financing since 1870.* Princeton, N.J.: Princeton University Press.

Kuznets, S. 1966. *Modern economic growth*. New Haven, Conn.: Yale University Press.

Kuznets, S. 1970. *Economic growth and structure*. New Haven, Conn.: Yale University Press.

Kuznets, S. 1974. Income-related differences in natural increase: Bearing on growth and distribution of income. In P. A. David and M. W. Reder (Eds.), *Nations and households in economic growth: Essays in honor of Moses Abramovitz*. New York: Academic Press.

Lampman, R. J. 1959. Changes in the share of wealth held by top wealth-holders, 1922–1956. *Review of Economics and Statistics, 41*, 379–392.

Lampman, R. J. 1962. *The share of top wealth-holders in national wealth, 1922–1956*. Princeton, N.J.: Princeton University Press.

Layer, R. G. 1955. *Earnings of cotton mill operatives, 1825–1914*. Cambridge, Mass.: Harvard University Press.

Leamer, E. E., and Stern, R. M. 1970. *Quantitative international economics*. Boston: Allyn and Bacon.

Lebergott, S. 1964. *Manpower in economic growth*. New York: McGraw-Hill.

Lebergott, S. 1966. Labor force and employment, 1800–1960. In *Output, employment, and productivity in the United States after 1800*. New York: National Bureau of Economic Research.

Lebergott, S. 1976a. Are the rich getting richer? Trends in U.S. wealth concentration. *Journal of Economic History, 36*, 147–162.

Lebergott, S. 1976b. *The American economy: Income, wealth and want*. Princeton, N.J.: Princeton University Press.

Leff, N., and Sato, K. 1975. A simultaneous equations model of savings in developing countries. *Journal of Political Economy, 83*, 1217–1228.

Lemon, J. T., and Nash, G. B. 1968. The distribution of wealth in eighteenth century America: A century of changes in Chester County, Pennsylvania, 1693–1802. *Journal of Social History, 2*, 1–24.

Leontief, W. 1951. *The structure of the American economy, 1919–1939*. New York: Oxford University Press.

Leven, M., Moulton, H. G., and Warburton, C. 1934. *America's capacity to consume.* Washington, D.C.: The Brookings Institution.

Lewis, H. G. 1961. *The effects of unions on industrial wage differentials*. New York: National Bureau of Economic Research.

Lewis, H. G. 1963. Unionism and relative wages in the United States. Chicago: University of Chicago Press.

Lewis, W. A. 1954. Development with unlimited supplies of labour. *Manchester School of Economics and Social Studies, 20* (May), 139–192.

Lillard, L. A. 1977. Inequality: Earnings vs. human wealth. *American Economic Review, 67*, 42–53.

Lindert, P. H. 1974. Fertility and the macroeconomics of inequality. Institute for Research on Poverty Discussion Paper 219–74. University of Wisconsin, Madison.

Lindert, P. H. 1978. *Fertility and scarcity in America*. Princeton, N.J.: Princeton University Press.

Lindert, P. H., and Williamson, J. G. 1976. Three centuries of American inequality. In P. Uselding (Ed.), *Research in economic history*, Vol. 1. Greenwich, Conn.: Johnson Associates.

Lockridge, K. A. 1970. *A New England town the first hundred years: Dedham, Massachusetts, 1636–1736*. New York: Norton.

Lockridge, K. A. 1972. Land, population and the evolution of New England society, 1630–1790. In S. N. Katz (Ed.), *Colonial America: Essays in politics and social development*. Boston: Little, Brown.

Lydall, H., and Lansing, J. B. 1959. A comparison of distribution of personal income and wealth in the United States and Great Britain. *American Economic Review, 49*, 43–67.

Maddison, A. 1971. *Class structure and economic growth: India and Pakistan since the Moghuls*. London: Allen and Unwin.

Main, G. 1976. Inequality in early America: The evidence of probate records from Massachusetts and Maryland. Paper presented to Cliometrics Conference, Madison, Wisconsin, April 22–24.

Main, J. T. 1965. *The social structure of revolutionary America*. Princeton, N.J.: Princeton University Press.

Main, J. T. 1971. Trends in wealth concentration before 1860. *Journal of Economic History, 31*, 445–447.

Main, J. T. 1976. The distribution of property in colonial Connecticut. In James Kirby (Ed.), *The human dimensions of nation making*. Madison, Wis.: The State Historical Society.

Mak, J., and Walton, G. 1972. Steamboats and the great productivity surge in river transportation. *Journal of Economic History, 32*, 619–640.

Mak, J., and Walton, G. 1973. The persistence of old technologies: The case of flatboats. *Journal of Economic History, 33*, 444–451.

Massachusetts Bureau of Statistics of Labor. 1885. *Sixteenth annual report of the Commissioner of Labor*. Massachusetts Public Document 15, Vol. 3. Boston: Wright and Potter.

Massachusetts Bureau of Statistics of Labor. 1895. *Twenty-fifth annual report of the Commissioner of Labor*. Massachusetts Public Document 15, Vol. 11. Boston: Wright and Potter.

Menard, R. R. 1973. Farm prices of Maryland tobacco, 1659–1710. *Maryland Historical Magazine, 68*, 80–85.

Menard, R. R. 1976. Comment on paper by Ball and Walton. *Journal of Economic History, 36*, 118–125.

Menard, R. R., Harris, P. M. G., and Carr, L. G. 1974. Opportunity and inequality: The distribution of wealth on the lower Western Shore of Maryland, 1638–1705, *Maryland Historical Magazine, 69*, 169–184.

Mendershausen, H. 1956. The pattern of estate tax wealth. In R. W. Goldsmith et al., *A study of saving in the United States*, Vol. 3. Princeton, N.J.: Princeton University Press.

Mereness, N. D. (Ed.) 1916. *Travels in the American colonies*. New York: Macmillan.

Merwin, C. L. 1939. American studies of the distribution of wealth and income by size. In *Studies in Income and Wealth*, Vol. 3. New York: National Bureau of Economic Research.

Metcalf, C. E. 1972. *An econometric model of the income distribution*. Chicago: Markham.

Mikesell, R. F., and Zinser, J. E. 1973. The nature of the savings function in developing countries: A survey of the theoretical and empirical literature. *Journal of Economic Literature, 11*, 1–26.

Miller, H. P. 1966. *Income distribution in the United States*. Washington, D.C.: U.S. Government Printing Office.

Minami, R. 1973. *The turning point in economic development: Japan's experience*. Tokyo: Kinokuniya Bookstore.

Mincer, J. 1974. *Schooling experience and earnings.* New York: National Bureau of Economic Research.

Minhas, B. S. 1962. The Homohypallagic Production Function, factor-intensity reversals, and the Heckscher-Ohlin Theorem. *Journal of Political Economy, 70,* 138–156.

Mitchell, W. C. 1903. *A history of the greenbacks.* Chicago: University of Chicago Press.

Mitchell, W. C. 1908. *Gold, prices, and wages under the greenback standard.* Berkeley: University of California Press.

Mitchell, W. C., King, W. I., Macauley, F. R., and Knauth, O. W. 1921. *Income in the United States: Its amount and distribution, 1909–1919,* Vol. 1. New York: Harcourt, Brace.

Monthly Labor Review. Monthly. U.S. Department of Labor. Washington, D.C.: U.S. Government Printing Office.

Morawetz, D. 1974. Employment implications of industrialization in developing countries: A survey. *Economic Journal, 84,* 491–542.

Morishima, M., and Saito, M. 1968. An economic test of Hick's Theory of Biased Induced Inventions. In J. Wolfe (Ed.), *Value, capital and growth.* Chicago: Aldine.

Morley, S. A., and Smith, G. 1973. The effect of changes in the distribution of income on labor, foreign investment and growth in Brazil. In A. Stepan (Ed.), *Authoritarian Brazil.* New Haven, Conn.: Yale University Press.

Munnell, A. H. 1976. Private pensions and saving: New evidence. *Journal of Political Economy, 84,* 1013–1032.

Nash, G. B. 1976a. Urban wealth and poverty in pre-revolutionary America. *Journal of Interdisciplinary History, 6,* 545–584.

Nash, G. B. 1976b. Poverty and poor relief in pre-revolutionary Philadelphia. *William and Mary Quarterly, 33,* 3–30.

National Industrial Conference Board. 1939. *Studies in enterprise and social progress.* New York: NICB.

National Industrial Conference Board. 1950. *The economic almanac for 1950.* New York: NICB.

Nelson, R. R., and Winter, G. 1975. Growth theory from an evolutionary perspective: The differential productivity puzzle. *American Economic Review, 65,* 338–344.

Newell, W. H. 1977. The wealth of testators and its distribution: Butler County, Ohio, 1803–65. Paper presented to the National Bureau of Economic Research, Conference on Research in Income and Wealth, "Modelling the distribution and intergenerational transmission of wealth," Williamsburg, Va., December 8–9.

Nickless, P. J. 1979. A new look at productivity in the New England cotton textile industry, 1830–1860. *Journal of Economic History, 39,* 889–910.

North, D. C. 1968. Sources of productivity growth in ocean shipping, 1600–1850. *Journal of Political Economy, 76,* 953–970.

Ober, H. 1948. Occupational wage differentials, 1907–1947. *Monthly Labor Review, 67* (August), 127–134.

Orcutt, G. H. 1950. Measurement of price elasticities in international trade. *Review of Economics and Statistics, 32,* 117–132.

Ornati, O. 1966. *Poverty amid affluence.* New York: The Twentieth Century Fund.

Ozanne, R. 1962. *Wages in practice and theory: McCormick and International Harvester, 1860–1960.* Madison, Wis.: University of Wisconsin Press.

Paglin, M. 1975. The measurement and trend of inequality: A basic revision. *American Economic Review, 65,* 598–609.

Paukert, F. 1973. Income distribution at different levels of development: A survey of evidence. *International Labour Review, 108,* 97–125.

Perlo, V. 1954. *The income "revolution."* New York: International Publishers.

Pessen, E. 1973. *Riches, class, and power before the Civil War.* Lexington, Mass.: D. C. Heath.

Peterson, W. L., and Fitzharris, J. C. 1974. The organization and productivity of the federal-state research system in the United States. University of Minnesota, Department of Agricultural and Applied Economics, Staff Paper P74–23, October.

Phelps-Brown, E. H. 1968. *A century of pay.* London: Macmillan.

Pomfret, R. 1976. The mechanization of reaping in nineteenth-century Ontario: A case study of the pace and causes of the diffusion of embodied technical change. *Journal of Economic History, 36,* 399–415.

Projector, D. S., and Weiss, G. A. 1966. *Survey of financial characteristics of consumers.* Washington, D.C.: Federal Reserve Board.

Ranis, G. 1977. Development theory at three-quarters century. In M. Nash (Ed.), *Essays in economic development and cultural change.* Chicago: University of Chicago Press.

Ransom, R. L., and Sutch, R. 1977. *One kind of freedom: The economic consequences of emancipation.* Cambridge: At the University Press.

Rayack, E. 1971. The physicians' service industry. In W. F. Adams (Ed.), *The structure of American industry.* 4th ed. New York: Macmillan.

Rees, A. 1961. *Real wages in manufacturing, 1890–1914.* New York: National Bureau of Economic Research.

Rees, A., and Hamilton, M. T. 1971. Changes in wage dispersion. In J. F. Burton et al. (Eds.), *Readings in labor market analysis.* New York: Holt, Rinehart and Winston.

Reynolds, L. G., and Taft, C. H. 1956. *The evolution of wage structure.* New Haven, Conn.: Yale University Press.

Reynolds, M., and Smolensky, E. 1975. Post-fisc distribution of income: 1950, 1961, and 1970. Institute for Research on Poverty Discussion Paper 270–75. University of Wisconsin, Madison.

Rivlin, A. 1975. Income distribution—Can economists help? *American Economic Review, 65,* 1–15.

Robinson, S. 1976. A note on the U hypothesis relating income inequality and economic development. *American Economic Review, 66,* 437–440.

Rosenberg, N. 1967. Anglo-American wage differences in the 1820s. *Journal of Economic History, 27,* 221–229.

Schultz, T. P. 1971. Long term change in personal income distribution: Theoretical approaches, evidence and explanations. Mimeo. The Rand Corporation, Santa Monica, Calif.

Schultz, T. W. 1961. Education and economic growth. In N. B. Henry (Ed.), *Social forces influencing American education.* Chicago: University of Chicago Press.

Schultz, T. W. 1963. *The economic value of education.* New York: Columbia University Press.

Schwartzman, D. 1968. The contribution of education to the quality of labor, 1929–1963. *American Economic Review, 58,* 508–514.

Shattuck, L. 1846. *Report to the committee of the city council appointed to obtain the census of Boston for the year 1845.* Reprint. New York: Arno Press, 1976.

Shepherd, J. F., and Walton, G. M. 1972. *Shipping, maritime trade and the economic development of colonial North America.* New York and London: Cambridge University Press.

Smith, B. G. 1977. Death and life in a colonial immigrant city: A demographic analysis of Philadelphia. *Journal of Economic History, 37,* 863–889.

Smith, D. S. 1973. Population, family, and society in Hingham, Massachusetts, 1635–1880.

Unpublished Ph.D. dissertation. Department of History, University of California, Berkeley.

Smith, D. S. 1975. Underregistration and bias in probate records: An analysis of data from eighteenth-century Hingham, Massachusetts. *William and Mary Quarterly, 32,* 100–110.

Smith, J. D. 1974. The concentration of personal wealth in America, 1969. *The Review of Income and Wealth,* Series 20, pp. 143–180.

Smith, J. D., and Franklin, S. D. 1974. The concentration of personal wealth, 1922–1969. *American Economic Review, 64,* 162–167.

Smith, W. B. 1963. Wage rates on the Erie Canal, 1828–1881. *Journal of Economic History, 23,* 298–311.

Soltow, L. 1969. Evidence on income inequality in the United States, 1866–1965. *Journal of Economic History, 29,* 279–286.

Soltow, L. 1971a. Economic inequality in the United States in the period from 1790 to 1860. *Journal of Economic History, 31,* 822–839.

Soltow, L. 1971b. *Patterns of wealthholding in Wisconsin since 1850.* Madison, Wis.: University of Wisconsin Press.

Soltow, L. 1975. *Men and wealth in the United States, 1850–1870.* New Haven, Conn.: Yale University Press.

Spahr, C. B. 1896. *An essay on the present distribution of wealth in the United States.* New York: Thomas Crowell.

Star, S. 1974. Accounting for the growth of output. *American Economic Review, 64,* 123–135.

Statistical abstract of the United States. Annual. Washington, D.C.: U.S. Government Printing Office.

Stecker, M. L. 1937. *Intercity differences in cost of living in March 1935, 59 cities.* Works Progress Administration, Division of Social Research, Research Monograph XII. Washington, D.C.: U.S. Government Printing Office.

Stigler, G. 1950. *Employment and compensation in education.* New York: National Bureau of Economic Research.

Stigler, G. 1956. *Trends in employment in the service industries.* Princeton, N.J.: Princeton University Press.

Survey of Current Business. Various issues. U.S. Department of Commerce (Bureau of Economic Analysis). Washington, D.C.: U.S. Government Printing Office.

Taussig, F. W. 1927. *International trade.* New York: Macmillan.

Teitel, S. 1978. The Strong Factor-Intensity Assumption: Some empirical evidence. *Economic Development and Cultural Change, 26,* 327–339.

Temin, P. 1964. *Iron and steel in nineteenth-century America: An economic enquiry.* Cambridge, Mass.: MIT Press.

Temin, P. 1971. General-equilibrium models in economic history. *Journal of Economic History, 31,* 251–264.

Theil, H. 1967. *Economics and information theory.* Chicago: Rand McNally.

Thomas, R. P., and Anderson, T. 1973. White population, labor force, and the extensive growth of the New England economy in the seventeenth century. *Journal of Economic History, 33,* 634–667.

Thorndike, E. L., and Woodyard, E. 1927. The effect of violent price-fluctuations upon the salaries of clergymen. *Journal of the American Statistical Association, 22,* 66–74.

Tocqueville, A. de. 1839. *Democracy in America.* Reprint. New York: A. A. Knopf, 1963.

Todaro, M. P. 1969. A model of labor migration and urban unemployment in less developed countries. *American Economic Review, 59,* 138–148.

Tucker, R. S. 1938. The distribution of income among income taxpayers in the United States, 1863–1935. *Quarterly Journal of Economics, 52,* 547–587.

U.S. Commissioner of Labor. 1904. *Eighteenth annual report*. Washington, D.C.: U.S. Government Printing Office.

U.S. Congress. 1926. 69th Congress, 1st Session, Senate Document 126, *National wealth and income*. Washington, D.C.: U.S. Government Printing Office.

U.S. Council of Economic Advisers. 1969. *Economic report of the president*. Washington, D.C.: U.S. Government Printing Office.

U.S. Council of Economic Advisers. 1974. *Economic report of the president*. Washington, D.C.: U.S. Government Printing Office.

U.S. Department of Agriculture (Statistical Reporting Service). 1962. *Prices paid by farmers for commodities and services, United States 1910–1960*. Statistical Bulletin 319. Washington, D.C.: U.S. Government Printing Office.

U.S. Department of Agriculture (Statistical Reporting Service). 1970. *Major Statistical Series of the USDA*, Vol. 2, *Agricultural production and efficiency*. USDA Agricultural Handbook No. 365. Washington, D.C.: U.S. Government Printing Office.

U.S. Department of Agriculture (Economic Research Service). 1973. *Farm real estate historical series data: 1850–1970*. Washington, D.C.: U.S. Government Printing Office.

U.S. Department of Commerce (Bureau of the Census). 1918. *19th annual report of mortality statistics*. Washington, D.C.: U.S. Government Printing Office.

U.S. Department of Commerce (Bureau of the Census). 1921. *22nd annual report of mortality statistics*. Washington, D.C.: U.S. Government Printing Office.

U.S. Department of Commerce (Bureau of the Census). 1923. *24th annual report of mortality statistics*. Washington, D.C.: U.S. Government Printing Office.

U.S. Department of Commerce (Office of Business Economics). 1966. *National income and product accounts of the U.S., 1929–1965*. Supplement to *Survey of Current Business*. Washington, D.C.: U.S. Government Printing Office.

U.S. Department of Commerce (Office of Business Economics). 1969. *Input–output structure of the U.S. economy: 1963*. Reprinted in *Survey of Current Business*, November.

U.S. Department of Commerce. 1973a. Money income in 1972 of families and persons in the United States. *Current Population Reports*, Series P–60, No. 90. Washington, D.C.: U.S. Government Printing Office.

U.S. Department of Commerce (Bureau of Economic Analysis). 1973b. *Long Term Economic Growth, 1860–1970*. Washington, D.C.: U.S. Government Printing Office.

U.S. Department of Commerce (Office of Business Economics). Various Issues. *Survey of Current Business*. Washington, D.C.: U.S. Government Printing Office.

U.S. Department of Labor (Bureau of Labor Statistics). 1898. *Wages in the United States and Europe, 1870 to 1898*. Bulletin 18. Washington, D.C.: U.S. Government Printing Office.

U.S. Department of Labor (Bureau of Labor Statistics). 1924. *Cost of living in the United States*. Bulletin 357. Washington, D.C.: U.S. Government Printing Office.

U.S. Department of Labor (Bureau of Labor Statistics). 1929. *History of wages in the United States from colonial times to 1928*. Bulletin 604. Washington, D.C.: U.S. Government Printing Office.

U.S. Department of Labor (Bureau of Labor Statistics). 1964. *Consumer expenditures and income, 1960–1961*. Report 237–38, Supplement 3, Part A. Washington, D.C.: U.S. Government Printing Office.

U.S. Department of Labor (Bureau of Labor Statistics). 1970. *Handbook of labor statistics, 1970*. Washington, D.C.: U.S. Government Printing Office.

U.S. Department of Labor (Bureau of Labor Statistics). 1971. *Handbook of labor statistics, 1971*. Washington, D.C.: U.S. Government Printing Office.

U.S. Department of Labor (Bureau of Labor Statistics). 1973. *Handbook of labor statistics, 1973*. Washington, D.C.: U.S. Government Printing Office.

U.S. Department of the Treasury (Internal Revenue Service). 1967. *Statistics of income, 1962. Supplemental report: Personal wealth estimated from estate tax returns.* Washington, D.C.: U.S. Government Printing Office.

U.S. Department of the Treasury (Internal Revenue Service). 1973. *Statistics of income, 1969. Supplemental report: Personal wealth estimated from estate tax returns.* Washington, D.C.: U.S. Government Printing Office.

U.S. Department of the Treasury (Internal Revenue Service). 1976. *Statistics of income, 1972. Supplemental report: Personal wealth estimated from estate tax returns.* Washington, D.C.: U.S. Government Printing Office.

U.S. National Resources Planning Board. 1941. *Consumer income and expenditures: Family expenditure in the U.S.* Washington, D.C.: U.S. Government Printing Office.

Uselding, P. 1972. Technical progress at the Springfield Armory, 1820–1850. *Explorations in Economic History, 9,* 291–316.

Uselding, P. 1975. Wage and consumption levels in England and on the Continent in the 1830's. *Journal of European Economic History, 4,* 501–513.

Uzawa, H. 1961. On a two-sector model of economic growth. *Review of Economic Studies, 29,* 40–47.

Vinovskis, M. A. 1972. Mortality rates and trends in Massachusetts before 1860. *Journal of Economic History, 32,* 202–213.

von Furstenberg, G. M., and Malkiel, B. G. 1977. The government and capital formation: A survey of recent issues. *Journal of Economic Literature, 15,* 835–878.

Warden, G. B. 1976. Inequality and instability in eighteenth-century Boston: A reappraisal. *Journal of Interdisciplinary History, 6,* 585–620.

Weinstein, M. M., and Smolensky, E. 1976. Poverty. Institute for Research on Poverty, notes and comments, University of Wisconsin, Madison.

Wells, R. 1975. *The population of the British colonies in America before 1776.* Princeton, N.J.: Princeton University Press.

Whitney, W. G. n.d. The structure of the American economy in the late nineteenth century. Department of Economics Discussion Paper 80. University of Pennsylvania, Philadelphia.

Williamson, J. G. 1964. *American growth and the balance of payments, 1820–1913: A study of the long swing.* Chapel Hill: University of North Carolina Press.

Williamson, J. G. 1965. Regional inequality and the process of national development. *Economic Development and Cultural Change, 13,* Part 2 (entire issue).

Williamson, J. G. 1967. Consumer behavior in the nineteenth century: Carroll D. Wright's Massachusetts workers in 1875. *Explorations in Entrepreneurial History, 4,* 98–135.

Williamson, J. G. 1968. Personal saving in developing nations. *Economic Record, 44,* 194–210.

Williamson, J. G. 1971. Capital accumulation, labor-saving and labor absorption once more. *Quarterly Journal of Economics, 85,* 40–65.

Williamson, J. G. 1974a. Demand and the distribution of income: America, 1913–1929. Paper presented to the Sixth International Congress on Economic History, Copenhagen, Denmark, August 19–23.

Williamson, J. G. 1974b. *Late nineteenth-century American development.* Cambridge: At the University Press.

Williamson, J. G. 1974c. Watersheds and turning points: Conjectures on the long term impact of Civil War financing. *Journal of Economic History, 34,* 636–661.

Williamson, J. G. 1974d. Migration to the New World: Long term influence and impact. *Explorations in Economic History, 11,* 357–390.

Williamson, J. G. 1974e. War, immigration and technology: American distribution experience, 1913–1929. Graduate Program in Economic History Paper EH 74–24. University of Wisconsin, Madison.

Williamson, J. G. 1975. The relative costs of American men, skills, and machines: A long view. Institute for Research on Poverty Discussion Paper 289–75. University of Wisconsin, Madison.

Williamson, J. G. 1976a. American prices and urban inequality since 1820. *Journal of Economic History, 36,* 303–333.

Williamson, J. G. 1976b. The sources of American inequality, 1896–1948. *The Review of Economics and Statistics, 58,* 387–397.

Williamson, J. G. 1976c. Who buys the services of the working poor? Institute for Research on Poverty Discussion Paper 334–76. University of Wisconsin, Madison.

Williamson, J. G. 1977a. Strategic wage goods, prices and inequality. *American Economic Review, 67,* 29–41.

Williamson, J. G. 1977b. Unbalanced growth, inequality and regional development: Some lessons from American history. Paper presented to the symposium "A national policy toward regional change: Alternatives to confrontations," Austin, Texas, September 24–27.

Williamson, J. G. 1979. Inequality, accumulation, and technological imbalance: A growth–equity conflict in American history? *Economic Development and Cultural Change, 27,* 231–254.

Williamson, J. G. Forthcoming. Greasing the wheels of sputtering export engines: Midwestern grains and American growth. In R. Caves, D. North, and J. Price (Eds.), *Exports and economic growth.* Princeton, N.J.: Princeton University Press.

Williamson, J. G., and DeBever, L. J. 1978. Saving, accumulation and modern economic growth: The contemporary relevance of Japanese history. *Journal of Japanese Studies, 4,* 125–167.

Williamson, J. G., and Lindert, P. H. 1977. Long term trends in American wealth inequality. Paper presented to the National Bureau of Economic Research Conference on Research in Income and Wealth, "Modelling the distribution and intergenerational transmission of wealth," Williamsburg, Va., December 8–9.

Wright, C. 1967. Some evidence on the interest elasticity of consumption. *American Economic Review, 57,* 850–855.

Wright, C. D. 1889. *Comparative wages, prices, and cost of living.* Boston: Wright and Potter.

Wright, G. 1970. Economic democracy and the concentration of agricultural wealth in the Cotton South, 1850–1860. *Agricultural History, 44,* 63–93.

Wright, G. 1978. *The political economy of the Cotton South: Households, markets and wealth.* New York: W. W. Norton.

Zabler, J. F. 1972. Further evidence on American wage differentials, 1800–1830. *Explorations in Economic History, 10,* 109–117.

Zevin, R. B. 1971. The growth of cotton textile production after 1815. In R. Fogel and S. Engerman (Eds.), *The reinterpretation of American economic history.* New York: Harper and Row.

INDEX

A

Abramovitz, M. A., 136n, 137, 156n, 157, 163, 169, 278n
Adams, T. M., 120
Age distribution
  income distribution and, 85, 93
  wealth and, 42, 52–53, 57–58, 283
Aggregate consumption, 188, 193
Aggregate investment, 188, 193
Aggregate labor saving, 155–163, 179
Aggregate saving, income inequality and, 150, 268
Agricultural sector, 241, 243, 244, 249, 253
Agriculture, *see also* Farm cost of living; Farm income; Farm labor
  changes in, and Engel's Law, 141–143
  factor productivity growth in, 169–170, 172, 173, 230, 236, 288
  in income distribution, 241
  technological advances in, 249
  technological bias and, 145, 146
Ahluwalia, M., 7
Aid to Dependent Children, 93
Aldrich, M., 70n
Aldrich Report, 70, 105
Allen, Z., 67, 71
American colonies
  age and wealth in, 25–29
  age distribution in, 27–30
  as egalitarian democracy, 9–10
  emigration from Europe to, 29–30
  frontier, *see* Frontier
  growth of towns and cities, 29–30
  northern, 30–31
  population trends in, 22–24
  revisionist interpretations of, 10, 14
  southern, 31
  wealth inequality in, *see* Wealth inequality in American colonies
American Revolution, 10
Anderson, T., 28n
Anti-poor bias, 191, 192, 194–195
Asher, E., 156n, 157
Ashton, T. S., 97, 103
Atkinson, A. B., 4, 80
Atkinson's inequality index, 113–118
Automobiles, on farms, 121n

B

Ball, D. E., 24, 25n, 169n
Baran, P., 139
Barro, R. J., 62
Berndt, E. R., 149, 223, 254
Blank, D. M., 86n
Bonds, interest rates on, 262–263
Boston, 46
  colonial, 9, 10, 23
  immigration to, 29–30
  wealth inequality in colonial period, 15–19, 21–23, 296, 297, 301, 303–304
Brady, D. S., 100
Bridenbaugh, C., 10
Brissot de Warville, J. P., 9

Britain, *see* United Kingdom
Bronfenbrenner, M., 87, 91n
Brooklyn, N.Y., 46, 282, 303
Brown, M., 144, 156–157
Budd, E. C., 84, 92n, 210n
Bullard, C. W., 254
Bureau of Labor Statistics, 91, 92
Burns, A. F., 33, 83
Butler County, Ohio, 46, 282

C

Canada, regional inequality in, 74–75
Capital accumulation
  earnings inequality and, 250, 255–280,
    286–287
  foreign capital in U.S., 266, 272
  income inequality and, 149–151
  investment share in national product,
    255–258
  Kuznets's interpretation of theories,
    267n
  rising investment rates and, 269–280
  rising rates of, 258–259
  technological progress and, 191–193,
    260, 265–267, 269, 277, 280
Capital goods, 110, 138, 151, 180, 189n
  consumption goods compared with,
    191–193
  human and nonhuman, 201–202
  prices of, 260–262, 269, 277
  prices of, and total factor productivity
    growth, 258–263
Capital-intensive sectors
  investment in, 196, 250, 266
  productivity growth in, 168, 237, 288
Capitalism, income inequality and, 83
Capital–labor ratio, 156, 158, 261, 262
Capital–output ratio, 261
Capital stock, rates of return on, 275
Carr, L. G., 20
Carter, A. P., 180, 183, 191
Census Bureau, 3, 92
Cheetham, R. J., 71, 124n, 145, 169n
Chenery, H. B., 8, 291
Chester County, Pa., wealth inequality in
    colonial period, 16, 18, 24
China, People's Republic of, 8

Chiswick, B. R., 82, 92n, 115, 181
Christensen, L. R., 149
Christoffel, T., 89
Cities
  immigration to, 124
  income inequality in, *see* Urban income
    inequality
  migration from farms to, 124
Cities, in American colonies, 10, 11, 24
  age distribution and growth of, 29–30
  de-urbanization of, 24
  migration to, 29–30
Civil War
  cost of living in, 108, 112
  economic consequences of, 79, 81, 82,
    277, 283
  end of, 75
  government expenditures in, 188
  prices in, 108, 109, 260
  wages in, 108n
  wealth inequality in North and South,
    33, 283
Cline, W. R., 8, 138, 190n, 279
Clothing, prices of, 99n, 104, 109, 112
Cobb–Douglas production function, 217,
    218
Coefficient of inequality, Tucker–Soltow,
    77, 79
Coefficient of variation, 113, 129
  weighted, 74, 79
Coelho, P., 71n, 105, 124n, 127
Coen, R. M., 80n
Colonial America, *see* American colonies;
    Wealth inequality in American
    colonies
Commodities
  farm prices and urban prices of,
    321–325
  luxuries and necessities, 99–100, 102,
    103
  in World War I, 110
Commodity demand, 179
Connecticut (colony)
  age and wealth in, 26
  wealth inequality in, 14–16, 20–21, 295,
    296
Construction industry, 193
Consumer goods, 103, 105, 112–113
  capital goods compared with, 191–193
  durable, 99, 109, 110, 112, 118–119,
    191–194

Consumer units, 54
Consumption
  aggregate, 188, 193
  expenditures, 187, 190–191, 193,
    195–197
  by rich, 189–191
  by working poor, 189–191
Cost of living
  1855–1880, 105, 107
  1890–1914, 106
  estimates by socioeconomic classes,
    98n, 99–100, 102–119
  on farm, see Farm cost of living
  of high-income families, 98–102, 110,
    112, 114–115, 120, 121
  inflation and, see Inflation, and cost of
    living
  leveling in, 113, 115, 116, 121
  in 1920s, 110–112, 114–115
  occupational pay ratios and, 102, 105
  of poor, 97–103, 105, 110
  regional differences in, 127–130,
    323–325
  urban, 125–126, 182, see also Urban
    poor
  in World War I, 109–110
Cost-of-living deflators, 124, 127
Cost-of-living indices, 127–130
  Koffsky-adjusted, 127–128, 323–325
  urban, 128
Cotton mills, wages in, 70
Cotton production, 43, 44
Cotton textiles, productivity growth, 170
Crotty, J. R., 179n

D

Daniels, B., 20, 21
Danziger, S., 92n, 93n, 241n
David, P. A., 144, 156, 157, 162, 163, 169,
    256n, 261n, 264, 266, 269n, 270n,
    278n
Davis, L. E., 149, 256n, 272n
DeBever, L., 260n, 280n
DeCanio, J., 136
Decomposition-of-variance approach, in
    study of American colonies, 22, 24,
    301

Deflation, of relative income shares,
    1917–1948, 112–113
Delahanty, G. E., 140
Demand, see also Factor demand
  factor intensities and, 193–198
  final demand expenditure, 182–183,
    187–188, 194, 197
Demand elasticity, 241, 243
Demand shifts, 250–251
Denison, E. F., 59, 60, 168, 210, 212, 213,
    239, 241n, 250
Department of Agriculture, 120
Department of Commerce, 198, 220
Department of Labor, 198
Diamond, P. A., 157n
Douglas, P., 98n, 125
Drucker, P. F., 61n
Durable goods, see Consumer goods, du-
    rable; Producer durables

E

Earnings inequality, 281–291
  before World War I, 217–237, 283
  capital accumulation and, 250, 255–280,
    286–287
  future trends and prospects, 251–254
  inflation and, 136–138, 285, 288–289
  models, 219–227, 241–253
  occupational pay ratios and, 218–219,
    239–241, 244–251, 284, 287
  technological progress and, 217, 218,
    230, 237, 247, 249, 286–289
  twentieth-century distribution trends,
    239–254
Easterlin, R. A., 73, 283
Edelstein, M., 262n, 264n, 266, 270
Engel effects, 179, 188–191, 194–196, 198
Engel's Law, 141–143, 243n, 253, 286
Engerman, S. L., 73, 130, 162, 170
Equality of opportunity, 34
Erie Canal, wages of laborers, 70
Estate-multiplier method, 12, 36, 49, 53
Estate tax, 47, 49, 53–55
  avoidance of, 55, 57
Evans, R., 140
Expenditures
  anti-poor bias, 191, 192, 194–195
  consumption, see Consumption

government, *see* Government
  expenditures
pro-poor bias, 188, 190, 191
taxes and, 186
of working poor, 189–191

F

Factor demand, 146, 179–180, 286
  unbalanced growth and, 161, 168
Factor intensity
  of capital goods and consumption
    goods, 191–193
  demand and, 193–198
  of human and nonhuman capital goods,
    201–202
  in nineteenth century, 196–198
  reversal, 193n
Factor–price ratios, 156, 157n, 158–159
Factor productivity, *see also* Productivity
    growth; Unbalanced productivity
    growth
  relative capital bias, 174, 175
  relative skills bias, 174–176
  total factor productivity growth,
    168–171, 173, 227, 229, 232, 236, 249,
    258–263, 265, 277, 280
Factor-saving bias, 159, 160, 223, 227
Factor–share ratios, 156n–157n, 158
Factor supply, 146–147, 159
  earnings inequality and, 219–237, 253,
    286
  elasticities in, 223, 225, 226
Factor–use ratios, 156, 157n, 158–159
Fallacy of composition, 11, 21
Fallon, P. R., 149, 223
Family size, income inequality and,
    147–148
Farm cost of living, 105n, 119–126, 182
  absolute and relative, 122–123
  1910–1929, 120–121
  urban costs compared with, 121, 126
  wage gaps and, 121, 124–125
Farm income, 119–126
  farm–nonfarm inequality, 77, 120–127
Farm labor, 120, 148
  Engel's Law and, 141–143
  labor intensities, 189
  skills increasing, 220

unskilled, 162, 189
  wages compared with urban labor,
    71–74, 85–86, 94, 124–126, 315
  in World War I, 81
Farm prices and urban prices of commod-
    ities, 321–325
Farm products, consumption by working
    poor, 189
Farms, migration to cities from, 124, 142
Federal Reserve Board surveys, 3, 37,
    53–55, 57, 89
Federal Trade Commission survey of in-
    come and wealth, 1912–1923, 48–51
Fei, J. C. H., 149
Feldstein, M., 61
Fertility
  labor supply and, 146–149, 203n
  reduction in, 147–148, 249, 288, 289
Fogel, R. W., 73, 170
Food, share of income spent on, and En-
    gel's Law, 141–143
Food prices, 103, 105, 108–119
  on farms and in cities, 121
France
  regional inequality, 74
  wealth concentration, 33, 52
Franklin, S. D., 53–55, 56n, 57, 61
Frontier
  equality and, 10–11, 52
  immigration from Europe to, 30
  wealth inequality and, 22, 30–31, 282

G

Gallman, R. E., 25n, 39, 43, 44n, 48, 51n,
    52–53, 161, 165, 170, 210n, 220, 229,
    233, 256n, 259, 266, 272n, 274, 275
Garrett, P. W., 110
Gastwirth, J. L., 92n
General-equilibrium theory, 136, 138,
    146–147, 161, 179
Ghali, M., 124n
Gini coefficient, 36, 37, 42, 49, 51n, 59,
    84n, 113, 114, 186
Goldberg, Victor, 48–49n
Goldsmith, R. W., 270
Goldsmith, S. F., 83, 87
Golladay, F., 190n
Gordon, Lord Adam, 9

Gordon, R. A., 191–193, 259
Gordon, R. J., 103n
Government
  in industrial growth, 138, 291
  rise and growth of influence, 152
Government expenditures
  earnings inequality and, 251
  in income distribution, 186–188
  pro-poor bias, 188
Great Depression, income inequality in, 75, 77, 83–84, 86
Greenback movement, 108
Griliches, Z., 149, 223
Growth–equality trade-off, 7–8, 256n, 258, 267, 272, 275, 280, 290–291

H

Habakkuk, H. J., 67, 155–156
Hampshire County, Mass., 17
Harris, P. M. G., 20
Hartford, Conn.
  age and wealth in colonial period, 26
  wealth inequality in colonial period, 15, 20–21, 295, 296
Hartley, W. B., 131–132
Hartwell, R. N., 130
Haveman, R., 93n, 190n
Heilbroner, R., 89
Henle, P., 92n, 93
Henretta, J. A., 10, 14
Hildebrand, G. H., 140
Hillman, A. L., 254
Hingham, Mass., 46
  wealth inequality in colonial period, 17
Hollister, R., 113
Holmes, G. K., 47, 48
Households, estimates of wealth, 54–57
Houthakker, H. S., 267n
Human capital
  distribution of, 58–60
  estimate of, 181–182
  nonhuman capital and, 201–202

I

Immigration
  to American colonies, 29–30
  to cities, 124
  fertility rates and labor supply, 146–148, 203n

inequality and, 34, 42, 53
  labor supply growth and, 203n, 206–209, 236, 246, 249, 287, 289
  of skilled persons, 203n
Income, nominal, and cost of living, 127, 129–130
Income distribution
  age distribution and, 85, 93
  post-fisc, 65, 85, 92, 186–188
  pre-fisc, 5, 84–85, 89, 92–93, 186, 189, 285
  redistribution from rich to poor, 188–191, 291
  twentieth-century trends, 239–254
Income elasticity, 241, 243
Income inequality, 3–7, 281–291, *see also* Earnings inequality; Wealth inequality
  age distribution and, 85
  Atkinson's index of, 113–118
  capital accumulation and, 149–151
  capitalism and, 83
  from Civil War to Great Depression, 75–82
  concepts and explanations of, 65, 135–136
  consumption expenditures and, 189–191
  deflation of relative income shares, 1917–1948, 112–113
  distributional stability since World War II, 92–94
  economic growth and, 95
  factor intensity relationships, 179–202
  on farms, *see* Farm income
  fertility rates and, 146–149
  inflation and, 136–138, 285, 288–289
  labor saving and unbalanced growth, 155–177
  labor supply growth and, 203–213
  leveling, *see* Leveling in income inequality
  in lower- and middle-income groups, 80–82, 84
  measurement of, 65–67
  "no-change" view of, 89–92
  population shifts and, 66
  prices and, 97–98, 103–105, 108, 113–119
  real wages and, 130–132
  regional differences, 72–75, 77, 79, 84, 127–130, 283
  sources of, 285–290

tax avoidance and, 87–88
taxes and, 93
technological bias and, 143–146
time series, 315–318
twentieth-century distribution trends,
    239–254
unbalanced growth and, 155–177
unions and, 139–140
urban, 103, 105, 113–118
wealth inequality and, 12, 49–51, 95
Income revolution, 1929–1951, 82–87, 92,
    239, 246–247
Income tax
    avoidance or concealment, 87–88
    federal, 4, 75, 77
    income inequality and, 79, 82–83
    state, before 1913, 4
Indiana, real estate, 51n
Industrial elite, rise of, 37, 39
Industrial growth
    early modern, 161–165, 171–172
    government policy and, 138, 291
    late nineteenth century, 165–167,
        172–173
    unbalanced, see Unbalanced output
        growth; Unbalanced productivity
        growth
Industrial sector, 241, 243, 244, 247, 250
Inequality, see Earnings inequality; In-
    come inequality; Wealth inequality
Inequality index, Atkinson's, 113–118
Inflation
    demand-pull, 137–138
    income inequality and, 136–138, 285,
        288–289
    in 1970s, 137
    pay ratios and, 136–137, 247
    wage-lag theory and, 136–137
    wages affected by, 82, 136–137, 204
    in wartime, 137
    after World War II, 244, 247, 249
Inflation, and cost of living
    on farms, 120, 121
    in nineteenth century, 108–109
    occupational pay ratios and, 136–137
    in urban families, 118
    in World War I, 110, 112
    since World War II, 113
Inheritance, in distribution of wealth, 35n
Interest rates, capital accumulation and,
    262–263

Internal Revenue Service, Statistics of In-
    come, 92
Inverse Pareto slope, 77n, 80n
Investment
    aggregate, 188, 193
    capital formation and, 258–259
    rising rates, in nineteenth century,
        269–280
Investment demand, and saving, 268–269,
    277, 278
Investment demand function, 264–266, 277
Investment goods, prices of, 256–259
Investment–saving ratio, 265, 268
Investment share in national product,
    255–258

J

Japan, economic growth, 280
Jones, A. H., 4, 12–14, 24n, 36, 39n,
    40–41, 43, 282, 284
Jones, R. W., 219

K

Katona, G., 92n
Keller, R., 139, 145, 146
Kelley, A. C., 71, 124n, 145, 146, 168,
    169n, 172, 191, 210n, 220, 233, 236,
    237, 241n, 288
Kesselman, J. R., 223
Kindleberger, C. P., 149, 280
King, W. I., 48n, 49–51, 52n, 90–91, 98n,
    165, 210n
Koffsky, N., 121
Koffsky-adjusted cost-of-living indices,
    127–128, 323–325
Kolko, G., 83, 87, 89–91
Korean War, 82, 84, 139
Kravis, I. B., 91
Kulikoff, A., 9, 10, 53
Kuznets, S., 3, 5, 7, 22n, 33, 34, 82, 83,
    85, 87–89, 95, 111, 141–142, 147, 165,
    259n, 267, 281, 284
Kuznets inverted-U (Kuznets curve), 63,
    67, 142, 291
Kuznets's basic variant (Topper), 80–81n

L

Labor, *see also* Farm labor; Pay ratios,
    occupational; Unemployment; Wages
  capital per worker and wealth per cap-
    ita, 256
  share in national income, 267–268
  technological bias and, 143–145
  in World War I, 81, 82, 150, 167
Labor, skilled, measurement of, 327–329
Labor, skilled and unskilled
  earnings, 281–282
  earnings distribution in twentieth cen-
    tury, 239–241, 244–254
  earnings inequality before World War I,
    217–219, 229–237
  in unions, 139–140
  wages, *see* Wages
Labor, unskilled
  consumption expenditures, 190–191,
    194–197
  expenditures, government and private,
    186–189
  factor intensity, 193
  on farms, *see* Farm labor
  labor intensity, 189, 193, 198–199
  labor saving and, 162–166, 168,
    173–175, 177
  low-wage, 198–199
  measurement of raw labor intensity,
    180–183
  payments impact on, 184–185, 187, 191,
    194, 195–198, 200–201
  return to unskilled labor from indus-
    tries, 1919 and 1939, 331–334
  wages of urban workers, 1820–1948,
    319–320
Labor–capital ratio, *see* Capital–labor
    ratio
Labor force, *see* Labor supply
Labor intensity
  direct, 183
  raw, measurement of, 180–183
  unskilled labor, 189, 193, 198–199
Labor saving
  aggregate, 155–163, 179
  econometric studies, 144–146, 156–160
  rates of, 144–146
  shift from, to labor using, 161

technological progress and capital accu-
    mulation, 265–267, 269, 277
  unbalanced output growth and, 160–168
  unbalanced productivity growth and,
    168–177
Laborsaving bias, 156–157
Laborsaving forces, macro, 144
Labor supply
  capital accumulation and, 150, 286
  earnings inequality and, 236, 239–241,
    286
  education of labor force, 206–208, 212,
    213
  fertility rates and, 146–149, 203n, 249,
    253
  government action affecting, 152, 251
  immigration and, *see* Immigration
  women in labor force, 212–213, 250, 253
Labor supply growth, 203–213
  changes in, 249–251, 253–254, 278, 279
  in nineteenth century, 264–267, 272,
    277, 280
  skills in, 203–206, 209–213
  wages and, 203–206
Labor unions, wages and, 139–140
Labor using, shift from labor saving to,
    161
Lampman, R. J., 3, 5, 12, 19, 48, 52n, 53,
    55, 61, 285
Land, supply of, 140–141
Land prices, and wages in colonial period,
    21n
Lansing, J. B., 53
Layard, P. R. G., 149, 223
Layer, R. G., 70
Leamer, E. E., 159
Lebergott, S., 50, 80n, 82, 210n, 264,
    278n
Leff, N., 264n
Lemon, J. T., 14, 24
Leveling in income inequality, 53–62,
    82–92, 113, 115, 116, 120, 121, 239,
    246, 247, 249, 250, 254, 284–285, 289
Lewis, H. G., 139
Lewis, W. A., 149, 279
Lillard, L. A., 59
Lindert, P. H., 21, 22n, 24n, 41, 42,
    49–51, 58, 79n, 94n, 147, 149, 186
Living standards, absolute and relative,
    130–132

Lockridge, K. A., 10
Lydall, H., 53

M

Macro distribution performance, 146
Macroeconomic effects on population and
    labor supply, 148
Macro laborsaving forces, 144
Maddison, A., 7–8
Main, G., 12–14, 18–20, 24, 40
Main, J. T., 4, 10, 11n, 12, 13, 20, 21n,
    25n, 28–29n, 39
Malkiel, B. G., 264n, 270n
Market failure, labor markets and, 124
Marx, K. (Marxist economics), 155, 267n,
    279
Maryland (colony)
    age and wealth in, 26
    wealth inequality in, 14, 16–21, 24, 301
Massachusetts, 51n
    state income tax, 4
    wages, 1771–1870, 68–72
    wages of urban workers, 105, 108
    wealth inequality in colonial period,
        14–19, 21, 282, 296–298, 303–304
McCormick Works, 139
McFadden, D., 157n
Menard, R. R., 20, 169n
Mendershausen, H., 12, 55
Mereness, N. D., 9
Mergers, 139
Metcalf, G. E., 147
Middle colonies, *see also* Maryland; New
    Jersey; New York; Pennsylvania
    age and wealth in, 26–30
    de-urbanization, 24
    population trends, 23–24
    wealth inequality, 14, 17–21, 24–25
Military forces, pay rates, 86
Minami, R., 149
Mincer, J., 82, 92n, 115, 181
Minhas, B. S., 193n
Minimum wage legislation, 140
Mitchell, W. C., 90n, 136
"Mitchell's Paradox" of falling real
    wages,108n
Mobilization effect in saving, 272, 275,
    277
Mokyr, J., 136

Morawetz, D., 138, 145, 161, 188
Morishima, M., 144, 145, 157, 160, 161n,
    163
Morishima–Saito index of U.S. labor sav-
    ing, 1901–1955, 158
Morley, S. A., 189n
Munnell, A. H., 61

N

Nash, G. B., 9, 10, 12, 14, 24, 29
National Industrial Conference Board, 86,
    90–91
Newell, W. H., 46
New England
    wage gaps, nominal, urban vs. farm,
        1751–1900, 313
    wages, 1760–1889, 71, 72, 204
New England colonies
    age and wealth in, 26
    population trends in, 22–23
    wealth inequality in, 14–24, 295–304
New Hampshire (colony), 28
New Jersey (colony), 28
New York
    in colonial period, 28, 298, 303
    wages in nineteenth century, 70
New York City, 46, 282
    population in colonial period, 23, 24
    wealth inequality in colonial period, 14,
        15, 17
Nixon, R. M., 244
Nonhuman wealth, 35n, 58, 60, 256
North (northern states)
    income inequality, 72–75, 84
    wage differentials, 71–73
    wealth inequality in Civil War, 33

O

OBE–Goldsmith data series, 84n, 89
Opportunity, equality of, 34
Orcutt, G. H., 159
Organization of Petroleum Exporting
    Countries (OPEC), 244, 254
Ornati, O., 132
Output growth
    early modern, 161–165
    late nineteenth century, 165–167

twentieth century, 167–168
unbalanced, 160–168
Output mix, 161, 163, 165, 167, 179
    labor intensity and, 180, 183–185
    technological bias and, 145

P

Paglin, M., 58, 93n
Pakistan, five-year plan, 7
Palmer, J., 113
Pareto slope, inverse, 77n, 80n
Paukert, F., 7
Pay, see Wages
Pay ratios, occupational, 80–82, 85–86, 94
    cost of living and, 102, 105
    earnings inequality and, 218–219,
        239–241, 244–251, 284, 287
    future trends and prospects of, 251–254
    inflation and, 136–137
    Massachusetts, 1771–1870, 68–69
    nonfarm, 1771–1972, 305–312
    nonfarm, since 1830, 78, 79
    twentieth-century trends of, 244–251
    unions and, 140
Pennsylvania
    iron-producing firms in 1840s, 70
    wealth inequality in colonial period, 14,
        16, 298, 299
Pensions, 61–62
Perlo, V., 83, 87, 89, 285
Pessen, E., 39
Phelps-Brown, E. H., 67
Philadelphia
    colonial, 9, 10
    immigration to, 29–30
    population in colonial period, 23, 24, 29
    wealth inequality in colonial period,
        14–16, 18, 21, 24, 29, 298
Plotnick, R., 93n, 241n
Poor, see Poverty; Urban poor; Working
    poor
Population growth, demand effect of, 227n
Population shifts
    income distribution and, 249–250
    income inequality and, 93
Portable personal property, 19
Portsmouth, N.H., wealth inequality in
    colonial period, 16, 296

Post-fisc income distribution, 65, 85, 92,
    186–188
Poverty
    absolute, 131–132
    cost of living and, 97–103, 105, 110
    incidence of, 131–132
Pre-fisc income distribution, 5, 84–85, 89,
    92–93, 186, 189, 285
Price controls, in World War I, 110
Price elasticity, 241, 243
Prices
    of capital goods, 258–262, 269, 277
    of consumer and producer durables,
        191–193
    farm and urban purchasing power,
        121
    farm prices and urban prices of com-
        modities, 321–327
    of food, 103, 105, 108–119, 121
    income inequality and, 97–98, 103–105,
        108, 113–119
    of investment goods, 256–259
    leveling, see Leveling in income
        equality
    of producer durables in capital forma-
        tion, 259, 260
    regional income and cost-of-living in-
        dices, 127–130
    urban income and, 98–119
    urban inequality and, 113–118
    wages and, 100, 102, 103, 105, 108–111
    in World War I, 109–110, 112
    since World War II, 113
Probate recods, 11–13, 21, 36, 40, 41,
    47–51, 52n
Producer durables, 138, 193–194, 265, 267,
    287
    constant-price share in capital forma-
        tion, 259, 260
Productivity, in manufacturing and agri-
    culture, 146, 230, 288
Productivity growth
    in capital-intensive sectors, 168, 237,
        288
    earnings inequality and, 227, 229, 232,
        236, 237, 249, 250, 253, 287–289
    estimates of, 168–173
    sectoral, 169, 171–175, 177, 291
    total factor, 168–171, 173, 227, 229, 232,
        236, 249, 258–263, 265, 277, 280,
        287–289

unbalanced, *see* Unbalanced productivity growth
Projector, D. S., 53, 57, 59, 61
Prussia, wealth concentration in, 33, 52

R

Ranis, G., 149, 279n
Ransom, R. L., 74
Rapping, L. A., 179n
Real estate, 40, 51n
  in colonial period, 12, 13, 19, 21n
  1850–1860, 43
Redistribution of income, from rich to poor, 188–191, 291
Rees, A., 98n, 105
Regional differences
  in cost of living, 127–130, 323–325
  in income inequality, 72–75, 77, 79, 84, 127–130, 283
Relative capital bias, 174, 175
Reynolds, L. G., 124n
Ricardo, D., 267n, 279
Rivlin, A., 93
Robinson, S., 22n, 142
Rosenberg, N., 67
Rural income, *see* Farm income

S

Saito, M., 144, 145, 157, 160, 161n, 163
Sato, K., 264n
Saving
  aggregate, income inequality and, 150, 268
  investment demand and, 268–269
  mobilization effect, 272, 275, 277
  nineteenth-century rates, 268–269, 272, 274
  private, pension and social security plans affecting, 62
Saving–investment ratio, 265, 268
Savings, share in gross national product, 256
Schools
  crowding of, 147–148
  education of labor force in, 206–208, 212, 213
Schultz, T. P., 85, 93n, 115
Schultz, T. W., 59, 60, 241

Services, expenditures for, 100, 110
Sheperd, J. F., 71n, 105, 124n, 127, 169
Skill, measurement of, 329–331
Skill-intensive sectors
  investment in, 196, 266
  productivity growth in, 168, 237, 288
Slave ownership, 35, 43–44, 282
Slaves, 204
  in colonial period, 19, 28, 31
  emancipation, 33, 47, 62
  in population, and wealth inequality, 37, 38
Smith, B. G., 29
Smith, D. S., 13, 40
Smith, G., 189n
Smith, J. D., 53–55, 56n, 57, 61
Smith, W. B., 70n
Smolensky, E., 84n, 92n–94n, 186
Social mobility, 34
Social security, 60–62, 93
Social Security Administration, 92
Social security taxes, 61
Soltow, L., 4, 11n, 25, 36, 39–44, 47, 51n, 77, 80, 280, 284
South
  before Civil War, 43–45
  in Civil War, 33
  since Civil War, 47–48
  in colonial period, 31
  income inequality, 73–75, 84
  slaves in, *see* Slaves
Soviet Union, first five-year plan, 8
Stagnationists, 190, 196
Stalin, J., 8
Standards of living, absolute and relative, 130–132
Stern, R. M., 159
Stigler, G., 86n
Substitution elasticity, 193n
Suffolk County, Mass., wealth inequality
  in colonial period, 16–19, 21, 296, 297
Survey of Consumer Finances, 92
Survey Research Center, 89
Sutch, R., 74
Sweezy, P., 139

T

Taft, C. H., 124n
Tariff, 138, 260

Taussig, P. W., 67n
Taxes, 46, *see also* Estate tax; Income
    tax
  expenditures and, 186
  redistributive tax–transfer policy, 189
Teachers, pay ratio compared with un-
    skilled labor, 68, 69, 82, 94, 136–137
Technological bias, 143–146
  labor saving and, 155–156
  sectoral differences in, 145–146
Technological progress
  capital accumulation and, 191–193,
    260–261, 265–267, 269, 272, 277, 280
  earnings inequality and, 217, 218, 230,
    237, 247, 249, 286–289
  unbalanced, 173–177, 289
Teitel, S., 193n
Temin, P., 138, 256n
Tertiary sector, 241, 243, 244
Theil, H., 53, 79n, 142
Third World, economic growth of, 8, 279,
    280
Thomas, R. P., 28n
Tice, H. S., 57
Time-series evidence, 43, 46–51, 68–70,
    315–318
Tobacco prices and exports, 20
Tocqueville, A. de, 9, 37, 39, 52
Todaro, M. P., 71
Topper (Kuznets's basic variant), 80–81n
Total personal wealth, 35, 57–60
Transfer payments, 92, 93
Transportation, factor productivity in,
    170, 171
Tucker–Soltow coefficient of inequality,
    77, 79
Tucker–Soltow inverse Pareto slope, 77n,
    80n
Turner, F. J., 219
Two-sector growth theories, 191

U

Unbalanced output growth, 160–168
Unbalanced productivity growth, 168–177
  factor biases in, 174–177
  technological imbalance and pay gaps,
    173–177
Unemployment
  in first half of twentieth century, 5–6
  of skilled and unskilled labor, 82

Unions, wages and, 139–140
United Kingdom
  wages, 67, 71
  wealth concentration, 33, 52–53
Urban income inequality, 103, 105
  prices and, 113–118
  strategic commodities, inflation, and in-
    equality, 118
Urbanization
  in colonial period, 29–30
  labor markets and wage gaps in, 124
  in nineteenth century, 42–43, 165
Urban poor
  cost of living, 98–103, 105, 110, 121,
    125–126
  farm families compared with, 119–121
Uselding, P., 67n, 171n
Uzawa, H., 191–193

V

van de Klundert, T., 144, 156, 157n
Vermont, 71
Vietnam War, 82, 137
von Furstenberg, G. M., 264n, 270n

W

Wage gaps, 284, 286–288
  farm cost of living and, 121, 124–125
  labor force growth and, 204
  nominal, urban vs. farm, New England,
    313
  before World War I, 219, 227–237
Wage goods, 100, 103, 105, 117–119, 127
Wage inequality, *see* Earnings inequality
Wages
  in Civil War, 108n
  1816–1880, 67–75
  inflation and, 82, 136–137, 204
  labor supply and inequality of, 147–149
  labor supply growth and, 203–206
  minimum wage legislation, 140
  occupational pay ratios, *see* Pay ratios,
    occupational
  prices and, 100, 102, 103, 105, 108–111
  real, and inequality, 130–132
  regional differences, 71–75
  of skilled and unskilled labor, 67–71,

80n, 81, 82, 85–86, 94, 105–108,
110–111, 162n, 163, 164, 203–206,
217–219, 230–237, 239–240
skilled-wage premium, 108, 204–206
technological bias and, 143–146
unbalanced output growth and, 162–165
unbalanced productivity growth and,
173–177
unions and, 139–140
of unskilled urban workers, 1820–1948,
319–320
of urban and farm labor compared,
71–74, 81, 124–126, 313
of working poor, 182–185
in World War I, 81, 109–110
Walton, G. M., 169
Warden, G. B., 14
Wealth
capital per worker and, 256
share of, held by richest households,
34, 36–37, 43, 44, 48, 52–55, 61, 81,
83, 84, 88, 111–112
total personal, 35, 57–60
Wealth concentration
from Civil War to Great Depression,
46–54
coefficient of variation, 59
in colonial period, 14–21
in first century of independence, 36–46,
281–282
1912–1923, 48–50
time periods in, 33–34
Wealth distribution
age distribution and, 42, 52–53, 57–58,
283
changes in, 136
from Civil War to Great Depression,
46–54
coefficient of variation, 59
in colonial period, see Wealth inequality
in American colonies
in 1890s, 47, 48
human capital, 58–60
measurement of, 34–46
in nineteenth century, 34, 36–46
pensions, 61–62
social security, 60–62
time periods after 1774, 33–34
Wealth inequality, 5–7, 33–63, 281–291
capital formation and, 258

from Civil War to Great Depression,
46–54, 62
in first century of independence, 36–46,
281–282
immigration and, 34, 42
and income inequality, 12, 49–51, 95,
see also Income inequality
international comparisons, 1907–1913,
51–53
leveling in twentieth century, 53–62, see
also Leveling in income equality
measurement of, 34–46
motivation for study of, 34–36
1922–1972, 53–54
in second quarter of twentieth century,
34
sources of, 285–290
time periods, 33–34
Wealth inequality in American colonies, 5,
9–31, 281–283, 295–304
age and wealth, 25–29
average propensities to save, 12–13
data sources, 11–15
decomposition-of-variance approach, 22,
24
fallacy of composition and trending inequality bias, 21–30
growth of towns and cities, 29–30
income inequality and wealth inequality,
12
mercantile wealth, 12, 19
northen colonies, 30–31
personal property, portable, 19
population trends, 22–23
property income and total income, 12
real estate, 12, 13, 19, 21n
southern colonies, 31
trends in wealth inequality, 14–21
Weeks Report, 105
Weiss, G. A., 53, 57, 59, 61
Wells, R., 28n
Whitney, W. G., 196
Williamson, J. G., 21, 22n, 41, 42, 49–51,
58, 70, 71, 72n, 73–75, 77, 79n, 82,
84n, 94n, 100n, 110n, 112n, 117, 124n,
127n, 145–147, 149, 151, 161, 162,
169n, 188, 256n, 259, 260n, 267n, 277,
280n
Williamson, S. H., 223
Wisconsin

income inequality studies, 51n, 77, 80
state income tax, 7
Women
  in labor force, 212–213, 250, 253
  as wage earners, 93
Wood, D. O., 254
Worcester County, Mass., wealth inequality in colonial period, 17, 21
Working poor, *see also* Labor, unskilled
  capital goods and consumption goods in services of, 191–193
  consumption by, 189
  expenditures of, 189–191
  government expenditures and, 188
  low-wage labor, 198–199
  services of, 179, 180
  wages of, 182–185
World Bank, 8, 291
World War I

government expenditures in, 188
income inequality in, 75, 77, 79
labor in, 81, 82, 150, 167
prices and cost of living in, 109–110, 112, 121
wages in, 109–110, 125
wealth distribution in, 33, 49, 53, 62
World War II
  government expenditures in, 188
  income inequality in, 83, 84, 86
  inflation in, 82
Wright, C., 264n, 270n
Wright, C. D., 71n
Wright, G., 43, 44, 74

Z

Zevin, R. B., 138, 162

Institute for Research on Poverty
Monograph Series

Jeffrey G. Williamson and Peter H. Lindert, *American Inequality: A Macroeconomic History.* 1980

Robert H. Haveman and Kevin Hollenbeck, Editors, *Microeconomic Simulation Models for Public Policy Analysis, Volume 1: Distributional Impacts, Volume 2: Sectoral, Regional, and General Equilibrium Models.* 1980

Peter K. Eisinger, *The Politics of Displacement: Racial and Ethnic Transition in Three American Cities.* 1980

Erik Olin Wright, *Class Structure and Income Determination.* 1979

Joel F. Handler, *Social Movements and the Legal System: A Theory of Law Reform and Social Change.* 1979

Duane E. Leigh, *An Analysis of the Determinants of Occupational Upgrading.* 1978

Stanley H. Masters and Irwin Garfinkel, *Estimating the Labor Supply Effects of Income Maintenance Alternatives.* 1978

Irwin Garfinkel and Robert H. Haveman, with the assistance of David Betson, *Earnings Capacity, Poverty, and Inequality.* 1977

Harold W. Watts and Albert Rees, Editors, *The New Jersey Income—Maintenance Experiment, Volume III: Expenditures, Health, and Social Behavior; and the Quality of the Evidence.* 1977

Murray Edelman, *Political Language: Words That Succeed and Policies That Fail.* 1977

Marilyn Moon and Eugene Smolensky, Editors, *Improving Measures of Economic Well-Being.* 1977

Harold W. Watts and Albert Rees, Editors, *The New Jersey Income—Maintenance Experiment, Volume II: Labor-Supply Responses.* 1977

Marilyn Moon, *The Measurement of Economic Welfare: Its Application to the Aged Poor.* 1977

Morgan Reynolds and Eugene Smolensky, *Public Expenditures, Taxes, and the Distribution of Income: The United States, 1950, 1961, 1970.* 1977

Fredrick L. Golladay and Robert H. Haveman, with the assistance of Kevin Hollenbeck, *The Economic Impacts of Tax—Transfer Policy: Regional and Distributional Effects.* 1977

David Kershaw and Jerilyn Fair, *The New Jersey Income-Maintenance Experiment, Volume I: Operations, Surveys, and Administration.* 1976

Peter K. Eisinger, *Patterns of Interracial Politics: Conflict and Cooperation in the City.* 1976

Irene Lurie, Editor, *Integrating Income Maintenance Programs.* 1975

Stanley H. Masters, *Black–White Income Differentials: Empirical Studies and Policy Implications.* 1975

Larry L. Orr, *Income, Employment, and Urban Residential Location.* 1975

Joel F. Handler, *The Coercive Social Worker: British Lessons for American Social Services.* 1973

Glen G. Cain and Harold W. Watts, Editors, *Income Maintenance and Labor Supply: Econometric Studies.* 1973

Charles E. Metcalf, *An Econometric Model of Income Distribution.* 1972

Larry L. Orr, Robinson G. Hollister, and Myron J. Lefcowitz, Editors, with the assistance of Karen Hester, *Income Maintenance: Interdisciplinary Approaches to Research.* 1971

Robert J. Lampman, *Ends and Means of Reducing Income Poverty.* 1971

Joel F. Handler and Ellen Jane Hollingsworth, *"The Deserving Poor": A Study of Welfare Administration.* 1971

Murray Edelman, *Politics as Symbolic Action: Mass Arousal and Quiescence.* 1971

Frederick Williams, Editor, *Language and Poverty: Perspectives on a Theme.* 1970

Vernon L. Allen, Editor, *Psychological Factors in Poverty.* 1970